Breakthrough!

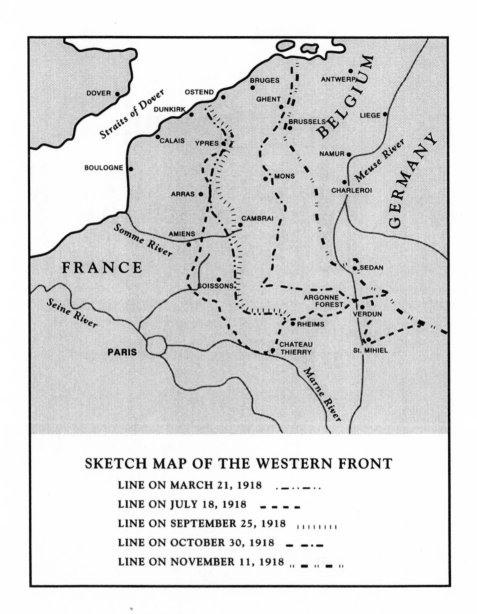

SKETCH MAP OF THE WESTERN FRONT

LINE ON MARCH 21, 1918 . _ .. _ ..

LINE ON JULY 18, 1918 _ _ _ _

LINE ON SEPTEMBER 25, 1918 ׀׀׀׀׀׀׀׀

LINE ON OCTOBER 30, 1918 _ _ .. _

LINE ON NOVEMBER 11, 1918 ׀׀ _ ׀׀ _ ׀׀

Break-through !

Tactics, Technology, and the Search for Victory on the Western Front in World War I

Hubert C. Johnson

PRESIDIO

Published by Presidio Press
505 B San Marin Dr., Suite 300
Novato, CA 94945-1340

Library of Congress Cataloging-in-Publication Data

Johnson, Hubert C.
    Breakthrough! : tactics, technology, and the search for victory on the Western Front in World War I / Hubert C. Johnson.
       p.   cm.
    Includes bibliographical references and index
    ISBN 0-89141-505-X
    1. World War, 1914-1918—Campaigns. 2. Strategy. 3. World War, 1914-1918—Technology. I. Title. II. Title: Tactics technology, and the search for victory on the Western Front In World War I.
    D521.J63   1995
    940.4'2—dc20   93-41188
                                      CIP

Typography and frontispiece map by ProImage

Printed in the United States of America

CONTENTS

LIST OF DIAGRAMS

INTRODUCTION

A VISION OF H.G. WELLS

The celebrated popularizer of science and writer of fantastic novels, H. G. Wells, submitted to *Strand Magazine* a short story that was published in 1903. Addressing himself to war, Wells postulated a fictional confrontation between a primarily urban and industrialized state and one that was rural and agricultural. Perhaps he intended a parable on the coexistence of a mechanized society with one that had yet to experience an industrial revolution. In any event the soldiers in his agricultural society were armed with rifles and other conventional weapons of the day. But their opponents possessed land battleships, hundred-foot-long machines weighing three hundred tons. Bristling with armor plate and possessing portholes through which machine guns protruded, these ponderous machines belched steam and began to crawl slowly over the battlefield. Rifle fire failed to stop their progress, and the soldiers of the backward society were decisively defeated. What was the point?[1] Wells had once again promoted his favorite theme, the triumph of the machine.

Many persons who were later to play important roles in World War I read this story with slight interest, only to recall it later. Winston Churchill stated that Wells had "practically exhausted the possibilities of imagination" in describing an armored vehicle capable of proceeding over uneven ground and over obstacles. E. D. Swinton, one of the fathers of the tanks during the war, remembered reading about the land ironclads but thought them "pure phantasy" at the time.[2]

Wells's vision would never be realized in the sense he intended it, but armored vehicles did finally emerge to play an equivocal role in the First World War. Often assumed, along with aircraft, to be near-magical solutions to the trench-warfare stalemate, tanks really performed in more modest roles in evolving tactics.

Tactics was defined by a French military intellectual as combat. "The objective of combat is to ruin the enemy forces one confronts," wrote J. Colin in 1911. Theories of tactics, then, are inevitably couched as practical means to achieve combat victory. According to an unverified anecdote, the elder Moltke defined strategic planning as campaign planning using chalk and a blackboard. "It is with this that we beat our adversaries every morning, and as for art, here is all we want," he said as he gestured to a series of topographical sketches.[3] Grand strategy of the war, as explored in Churchill's *World Crisis*,[4] for example, considered the subtle interaction of civilian and military decision makers at the highest level of statecraft.

Although senior commanders and their staffs could plan a campaign, the actual carrying out of that campaign had to be coordinated with smaller units. Charles Harrington, chief of staff of Gen. Sir Herbert Plumer's Second Army, remarked that his chief, upon orders from Haig, had to "settle the plan" for the reduction of the Messines defenses by frequent consultations with his subordinate commanders. Plumer and his staff officers visited corps, division, and brigade headquarters daily "and discovered their plans and got their ideas."[5] Through this time-consuming process all commanders came to understand the overall objectives of the projected operation as well as the roles of their units in achieving those objectives.

Tactics in this war quickly became concerned with the conduct of units even smaller, such as brigades, battalions, companies, platoons, and sections of infantry. The peculiar evolution of trench warfare and the frequent, frustrated attempts to end the stalemate entailed numerous patrols and frequent exchanges of fire. James Jack, who ended the war as a brigadier with considerable combat experience, commented in his diary for 24 January 1916 that on "our 'C' Company's front the German trenches are some 200 yards distant, and a report is required by High Command as to how much a ditch midway between the lines would hinder an enemy attack." He had to go forward with as made after weighing a number of difficult, almost imponderable, ctors: How many reserve infantry were available? Could the Royal ying Corps provide close support? Were infantry and artillery trained fficiently to work with the tanks? What would happen if a massive reakthrough occurred? How long could an advance, if initially suc-ssful, be continued?

Tactics, then, was a compromise plan of action, providing for the mployment of military force according to an agreement of the mili-ry professionals, which encompassed many different problems of gistics, interallied cooperation, and interservice cooperation. Everything the war was viewed in terms of its actual as opposed to its pro-cted costs, either in the lives of soldiers or in materiel.

CHEME OF THE WORK

In general terms the war was divided into three main periods: the pen warfare of 1914, the trench war stalemate that lasted from the nd of 1914 until the beginning of 1918, and the open warfare of 1918. ach phase was characterized by the appearance of novel problems, he solutions to which were not readily apparent.

During the first phase the combatants discovered that the prewar actical teachings seemed not to fit existing conditions. How were they lawed and what immediate remedies were applied? To what extent lid logistics cause a breakdown of military action? The pursuit of answers o these problems occupies the first chapters.

The longest period of the war was characterized by the grim stale-nate on the western front. What did existing tactics have to offer those who wished to break through the stalemate? What novel uses were nade of traditional arms like artillery? What new technology was ntroduced and how successful was it? Was the entire period the same or did general tactics evolve to fit it? In the middle part of this ex-amination of tactics much will be said about infantry assault practices and the use of massed artillery. Technology seemed both to reinforce the stalemate and, perversely, to offer, some way out of it.

During the final year substantial changes occurred in the conduct of warfare. Were these changes the result of technological develop-ments such as the tank or aircraft? Or were they due more to a gradual weakening of the German army at the same time as fresh American forces were arriving? Did the Allied powers have superior tactics at

a lance corporal to push a yardstick into the ditch. Jack cla
his chief risk was from a chance bullet or a hostile patrol.

In the early twenties, a German, William Balck, a Frenchm
Lucas, and an Englishman, Graeme C. Wynne,[7] attempted t
rize the development of tactics. Their efforts were importan
essarily circumscribed by their individual perceptions of the wa
they wrote too soon after it ended. Postwar military field ma
staff college curricula drew upon supposed lessons of the G
but increasingly as a means of elucidating postwar battle te
There have been casual mentions in the memoirs of partici
occasional discussions in the official military histories, but
comprehensive way has been written about the developme
tics during World War I. Some extremely valuable works c
with individual combatants have appeared recently but noth
overall nature.[8]

In the literature of the First World War much has been writ
the levels of tactical decision making in larger units such a
and groups of armies but little directly about the lower le\
best sources for the latter are unit histories and war diaries, battl
memoirs, and personal diaries. Despite the care elaborated
for an offensive, if the troops assigned to perform could not at
goals, the plans were failures. A great truth about this war
stated by many: In all armies there existed a great gulf betw
command and platoon, between *Frontsoldat* and *Etappe,* and
officers and other ranks.[9] Within the trench-warfare world t
tinctions often faded to be replaced by a distinction betwe€
and passive soldiers of all ranks. Minor tactics, the humble e
of the staff directives from army headquarters, was the indis
ingredient in warfare. If the opposing frontline soldiers had
to fight one another, no war would have occurred.[10]

In this war, as in others, tactical planning required the c
tion of logistics with the multitude of combat arms. But th
the stalemate lasted, the more everything was geared to its
ance, including technology. To develop tactics in the camp
1918, where a limited return to open warfare occurred, prov
cult. If a decision was made, for example, to use four hundr
in the British offensive at Cambrai in November 1917, that

their disposal? At the end of the war was there a clear, unequivocal tactical doctrine? The intensive examinations of both the great German offensive of March and the Allied offensives of July and August 1918 provide possible answers to some of these questions.

As an exploration in the thought processes of generals and others, the history of tactics becomes a kind of intellectual history. This study is restricted to the development of tactics on the western front partly because of linguistic limitations of the author, but also because the vast nature of the subject prohibited any broader consideration. It is therefore somewhat limited in scope.[11]

I am indebted to the suggestions of my colleague, Ivo N. Lambi, and to those of a number of friends including Charles V. Hopkins and Jack Summers. Don Graves and Bill Rawling of the Department of National Defense, Ottawa, also provided comments. Finally, I would like to thank Dale Wilson and Bob Tate at Presidio Press for their editorial efforts. None of these persons are responsible for any weaknesses or errors.

NOTES

1. H. G. Wells, "The Land Ironclads," *Strand Magazine,* December 1903. See B. H. Liddell Hart, *The Tanks: The History of the Royal Tank Regiment* (London, 1959), 1:14–15, for a graphic excerpt.

2. Winston Churchill, *World Crisis* (London, 1938), 1:514–15. E. D. Swinton, *Eyewitness* (London, 1932).

3. J. Colin, *Les transformations de la guerre* (Paris, 1911), 59–60. The anecdote concerning Moltke is in P. S. Bond and M. J. McDonough, *Technique of Modern Tactics,* (Menasha, Wisconsin, 1916), a manual sold to officers in the U.S. Army during the period of preparedness. Quoted on page 8.

4. Churchill, *The World Crisis* (London, 1923–27). Good general surveys of the war are C. R. M. F. Cruttwell, *A History of the Great War, 1914–1918* (Oxford, 1936) and B. H. Liddell Hart, *The Real War, 1914–1918* (London, 1930). For overall grand strategy Pierre Renouvin, *La crise Européenne et la premiére guerre mondiale* (Paris, 1959) is particularly good. In recent years a number of perceptive studies of British strategy have been published: Tim Travers, *The Killing Ground* (London, 1987) and David French, *British Strategy and War Aims, 1914–1916* (London, 1986) are examples.

5. Charles Harrington, *Plumer of Messines* (London, 1935), 98–99.

6. James Jack, *General Jack's Diary, 1914–1918* (London, 1964), 96–97.

7. William Balck, *Entwicklung der Taktik im Weltkrieg,* (Berlin, 1922). Col. Pascal Marie Henri Lucas, *L'evolution des idées tactiques* (Paris, 1932). Graeme C. Wynne, *If Germany Attacks; the Battle in the West* (Westport, Connecticut, 1976). Wynne, a longtime associate of General Edmonds, editor of the official British history, presents a cautious and conservative interpretation.

8. Michael Geyer, "The German Practice of War, 1914–1945" in Peter Paret, ed., *Makers of Modern Strategy* (Princeton, 1986). Timothy Lupfer, *The Dynamics of Doctrine: the Changes in German Tactical Doctrine during the First World War* (Fort Leavenworth, Kansas, 1981). Bruce I. Gudmundsson, *Storm Troop Tactics: Innovation in the German Army* (New York, 1989). Travers, *Killing Ground* has shrewd

comments on British tactics. Guy Pedroncini, *Pétain, général en chef, 1917–1918* (Paris, 1974) provides an excellent modern French approach. Dale E. Wilson, *Treat 'em Rough: The Birth of American Armor, 1917– 20* (Novato, California, 1989) provides a discussion on tactics that is broader than the title implies.

9. Theodore Bartram, *Der Frontsoldat* (Berlin, 1934), 11–13 was lyrical about the purifying impact of trench war upon character. He represents one extreme position possibly shared by Ernst Jünger, *The Storm of Steel* (London, 1929).

10. Perhaps best known pacifist novel is Erich Maria Remarque, *All Quiet on the Western Front* (reprint, New York, 1975). See 178– 82 for typical passages.

11. Norman Stone, *The Eastern Front, 1914–1917* (London, 1975) has written intelligently about the Russian front, and others will un- doubtedly pick up fascinating hints from the published work of Max Hoffmann, *The War of Lost Opportunities* (London, 1924).

CHAPTER 1
THROUGH A GLASS DARKLY: BEFORE 1914

The objective of peacetime armies is to train for future war. Inevitably, tactics must be studied and developed in the leisure of interwar periods so they can be implemented in battle later. In comparing the evolution of tactics to choreography both similarities and differences become apparent. Patiently, Balanchine worked with ballet troupes in designing complex maneuvers to accompany particular musical scores. When the ballet was presented to the public it was the polished and logical outgrowth of much preliminary work. Similarly the peacetime army prepares patiently for future war with maneuvers, staff studies, revisions of training manuals, drills, exercises of the troops, and consultation with other services or with potential allies. When war occurs, however, the tactical ideas so carefully worked out in peacetime to prepare for this awesome eventuality usually prove to be inadequate. Wartime is not a logical outgrowth of peacetime because a state of war is so fundamentally different from a state of peace. Despite decades of careful work the staffs of the opposing powers in 1914 had not been able to predict the course of combat once the war started.

The generals and their staffs who planned for what became the First World War were not, despite the claims of many critics, incompetent and inhumane butchers. They were neither better nor worse than others in similar jobs in other times. But they were faced with combat conditions quite different in degree, if not in kind, from those expected before 1914.

A pervasive conservatism distinguished the major armies of Europe just prior to the war.[1] Armies in peacetime inevitably acquire a kind of slackness since they have no battles to fight and are constrained by reduced budgets from supporting innovation. Intelligent, imaginative, and energetic officers served in all nations and observed the wars that occurred during the period. Stultifying routine, so characteristic of budget-poor military establishments in peacetime, did not permit them to experiment with ideas they obtained from observing local wars. In France, for example, the colonial army had gained much experience in imperialistic conflicts in Africa and Asia, but its officers had little influence in the separately established army garrisoned in France itself.[2]

Despite such handicaps military theorists did succeed in slowly effecting changes. The primacy of tactics over the other elements of military craft becomes an obsession before 1914. To most acute observers it was perfectly clear by then that the usual tactical mechanics of earlier warfare were no longer viable.

THE OLD WARFARE

Students of warfare knew that the type of warfare associated with Napoleon no longer existed by 1914. The tactical and strategic lessons of that earlier era, so well examined by Jomini and Clausewitz, remained worthy of study. But weaponry had vastly improved, forcing amendments to existing theory.

The volume of firepower delivered on the battlefield had substantially increased, creating much greater hazards for those engaged in combat. Casualties, quite heavy in Napoleonic wars even though the inefficiency of the smoothbore musket, the primary weapon, had limited them, mounted rapidly in mid–nineteenth-century wars. Requiring a dozen movements or more to reload and notoriously inaccurate, the musket was most effective if used in volley firing, where the sheer volume of fire would overcome the weapon's many deficiencies.[3] By the time of the American Civil War, rifled muskets and rifles extended the range and accuracy of small-arms fire to create a much larger and more dangerous "killing zone."

Cavalry had its place as well; it could harass the flanks of the enemy causing him to divert needed troops to those threatened points.[4] The slowness and inefficiency of the infantry left it open to attack.

But if the cavalry was foolish enough to attack frontally a fortified position as in the case of the charge of the Light Brigade in Crimea, its horses and riders provided large and easy targets.

A final characteristic of the old warfare was the insufficiency of its artillery. Smoothbore guns were inaccurate, cumbersome, and too few in number to dominate the battlefield before Napoleon. He placed his greatly increased mass of artillery close to the front and used it in conjunction with infantry attack (the latter by columns).[5] The old warfare was one of physical encounter; the opposing forces could see one another and commanders on horseback could frequently direct changes in the disposition of their forces.

Although the nineteenth century would introduce momentous changes, mostly caused by the spread of the Industrial Revolution, the pace of innovation was slow. Weaponry became more and more sophisticated. The military planners had some difficulty adapting repeating rifles and machine guns to existing tactical schemes. The heavy casualties noticed by observers in the Crimea and the American Civil War, in which obsolescent smoothbore artillery was used, indicated that mass firepower, even of an old-fashioned nature, was destructive. Somewhat later, observers of the Austro-Prussian and Franco-Prussian wars noted that the new rifled artillery produced even greater casualties. Railroads permitted movement of masses of infantry, now armed with rifles, hundreds of miles in a relatively short period. But the lessons of these wars were inconclusive because while weaponry had been improved and logistical improvements achieved, armies still depended most of the time either on horse transport or on plain marching as their chief means of mobility.[6]

How precisely did military professionals view these problems? Illustrative of such men and their opinions was a young cavalry officer, Douglas Haig, who participated in Kitchener's expedition into the Sudan. "Tactical principles seemed to be forgotten!" he reported when his unit was exposed needlessly to Dervish attack. Already noting that in one battle Dervish horsemen had rounded the British flanks, "cutting our line of retreat," Haig reported that the cavalry had only been extricated when a detachment of Maxim machine guns held off the enemy. More and more convinced that coordinated tactics were necessary, Haig noted that an action in which the British tried to use horse artillery Maxims together with cavalry and infantry had been difficult.

The machine guns were too few to halt the storm of Dervishes and the whole unit had to retreat from the high-ground defensive position it had adopted. "I trust for the sake of the British cav. that more tactical knowledge exists in the higher ranks of the *average* regiment than we have displayed in this one." Throughout the Egyptian campaign of 1898, Haig lamented the lack of machine guns.[7]

"Cavalry which can not fight on foot is not up to the requirements of the present day, nor is it worth what it costs the state," Haig claimed in 1892.[8] Colonel G. F. R. Henderson, the leading military theorist in Britain at the turn of the century, determined in regard to the Franco-Prussian War that "the long lines of guns ranged at regular intervals on the bare slopes of Moltke's battle fields, which had rained such ruin on the French columns, were already an anachronism," and that cavalry "was useless either for attack or defense, [and] was a waster both of men and of mobility."[9]

As suggested by Henderson, the role of artillery was as much in dispute by the end of the century as that of cavalry. A lecture delivered by F. B. Elmslie at Aldershot in 1899 summarized the very considerable revolution in weaponry that had occurred during the previous forty years. Quick-firing field guns, the magazine rifle, and the machine gun made "the field of fire . . . intensified in its deadly effect, and its depth is increased owing to the generally increased ranges of modern weapons." The Battle of Omdurman showed "the absolute madness of exposing men to the fire of modern weapons." But artillery could not automatically win battles as Colmar von der Goltz mentioned a few years later. At the Battle of Plevna, he indicated, ordinary rifled field guns were ineffectual against entrenchments.[10] The howitzer, which was capable of shooting a projectile in a high arc, would solve this problem because shells would hit the trenches from above rather than frontally, where the breastworks were strongest.[11] Greater firepower had forced troops into cover during the American Civil War and subsequent wars until the end of the century. Then, theorists posited the howitzer as the main weapon against entrenchments. Haig believed in 1896, however, that "high training" (in infantry skills including marksmanship) had more to do with winning battles than guns themselves.[12]

Henderson summed up the dilemma of infantry by stating that the wars of 1870 and 1877 had shown that "infantry could only attack in open lines; that superiority of fire could only be attained by a close combination at every stage of the attack of infantry and artillery; that reconnaissance was difficult; that the effect of fire against troops in the open was very great, and that cover had assumed a new importance.[13] By the time of the Boer War the old tactics were obsolete, but it was not clear what would take their place.

A QUANTUM JUMP IN FIREPOWER

During the forty years preceding the outbreak of war in 1914, substantial improvements were made in weaponry. The celebrated 75mm field pieces introduced by the French in 1898 inspired similar designs in other armies by 1914. They were examples of the so-called QF or quick-firing type because they used brass cartridge cases and were easier to load than the BL or breech-loading type in British service. In the latter, the propellant was housed in a separate silk bag and loading was slower. Artillery of the smaller calibers was developed in the QF mode during the last two decades of the nineteenth century.[14] By 1900, artillery pieces that were immensely more accurate, of longer range, and quicker firing than their smoothbore ancestors created difficult tactical problems.

Even more of a challenge for military planners was the utilization of the new, clip-fed, breech-loading rifles that became standard in the leading armies by the turn of the century. Advanced rifles, made possible by major improvements in the tool and machine industries, included French Lebel of 1886, the British Lee-Enfield of 1881, the German Mauser of 1889, the Austrian Mannlicher of 1886, and the American Springfield of 1903.[15] All these weapons were in use during World War I either in original or revised configurations.

As an example of the efficiency of such arms, the Lebel was typical. The Lebel rifle of 1886 had precision at six hundred meters, with maximum range on a group target of twelve hundred meters: six times the accuracy and range of a musket from the Napoleonic era.[16] Tubular magazines holding eight cartridges made these rifles even deadlier by permitting a considerable increase in the volume and rate of fire.

Perceptions of trouble appear in the writings of professional military men before 1900, but the Boer War and the Russo-Japanese War really showed the effectiveness of new rifles and field artillery. Count Sternberg, a former German officer who sought service with the Boers, claimed: "The modern rifles, with their immense range and rapidity of fire, and smokeless powder, have completely upset the old principles of tactics . . . in the wars of the past an energetic offensive had led to victory, in the wars of the future it will lead to destruction."[17] Alfred von Schlieffen remarked that quick-firing rifles had rendered suicidal the traditional infantry attack in close order. "A complete change of tactics is necessary" because it was no longer possible, as it had been in the eighteenth century, for two lines to advance against one another nor was it possible to use the Napoleonic deep columns.[18] Observers like Repington also noted that the immense increase in the rate and volume of fire resulted in the unanticipated emptying of ammunition stores noted during the Russo-Japanese War.[19] Rapid fire killed more soldiers than traditional fire in a shorter time, but at the cost of great expenditure of ammunition.

Machine guns increased firepower and destructiveness on the battlefield, according to many commentators. Officers like Haig knew before the Boer War that machine guns were crucially necessary to protect vulnerable units such as cavalry.[20] The French in 1870 and the English in the Sudan in 1898 had massed machine guns in batteries like artillery, but had found them peculiarly vulnerable to enemy artillery attack.[21] The great question by the end of the century was: How should machine guns be deployed in action? Previously, they had been used with inconclusive results, partly because there were few of them.

Again, both the Boer War and the Russo-Japanese War provided illustrations of the use of machine guns, but they did not resolve even a fundamental issue of tactics: How could the machine gun be used advantageously in attack as well as in defense? Friedrich von Bernhardi, cavalry general and rival of Schlieffen in Germany, noted in 1913, "We have adjudged to the attack quite arbitrarily the same force of fire as to the defense, which is superior in this respect."[22] Ample examples of entrenchments protected by machine guns during the Russo-Japanese War might have added emphasis to this warning.

If the professionals were concerned about the tactical employment of rifles and machine guns they were not too worried about the effects of even more recent technology. British Gen. Sir William Robertson attempted to predict the use of exotic devices in a speech given in Glasgow in February 1913. He suggested that the mass armies of the future, signaling, the telegraph, the telephone, balloons, aeroplanes, and so on would improve communication.[23] The field telegraph and telephone and the advent of wireless telegraphy seemed to promise much greater control over large units by commanders.[24] In the few instances in which planners considered communications they tended to view them as adjuncts to offensive action when rapid movement of large units was normal. For defensive action, telegraph service, pigeons, and observation balloons were envisaged, especially during siege operations.[25]

The British army *Field Service Regulations* of 1909 indicated aircraft could also be used to bomb magazines, oil tanks, concealed guns, and the like, but their principal use would be in reconnaissance and in intercepting hostile reconnaissance aircraft. "Aircraft are also capable of offensive action against troops on the ground." Finally, they would be artillery spotters.[26] The Germans developed dirigibles as military vehicles earlier than others and did not express much interest in heavier-than-air craft until 1909. Field Marshal Helmuth von Moltke was anxious to overtake what was conceived to be a French lead in this matter. General Erich von Falkenhayn commented just before the war that he did not anticipate much use for aircraft of any type after the first few weeks of war because no reserves existed to replace those lost.[27] All major armies experimented with aircraft between 1908 and 1914, but the primitive state of technology made it difficult for military planners to do more than vaguely predict the future of aircraft in combat. Certainly in the maneuvers held in England, France, and Germany just before the war few aircraft were used.

Armored trains and motor cars also received cursory attention. Siemens built two armored cars in August 1913 that were armed with machine guns and provided enough protection to withstand "normal infantry fire."[28] Such vehicles were considered experimental. Bicycles, however, were often used for messenger service. Motortrucks could transport munitions and supplies.

Of course, technical limitations in aircraft, automobiles, and trucks were so great that prewar planners might be forgiven for placing so little emphasis on them. It is not possible to be as charitable in the case of machine guns or rapid-fire weaponry of other types because by 1900 these weapons had reached a high state of development. Thus, during the ensuing fifteen years considerable tactical revisions in the official manuals should have been expected. They did not occur for a multitude of reasons.

STAND FAST AND DIG IN

In both the Boer War and the Russo-Japanese War military observers had ample opportunity to note the emergence of strong entrenchments and fortifications. Unfortunately, although siegecraft was practiced, it was viewed by them as a temporary aberration, not a determining condition of warfare.

Boer lines of defense were well organized and strong, prompting observers of the German General Staff to warn that great losses of troops assaulting them could be expected.[29] Friedrich von Bernhardi noted that English artillery had little effect on Boers hidden in trenches and behind other cover. After the barrage lifted, they emerged to fight. General Buller failed, but his successor, Lord Roberts, succeeded in defeating the Boers because he turned their trenches by flanking action.[30]

Haig noted: "An army which is well led cannot readily be out flanked . . . hence to defeat the Boers we must combine a frontal with a flank attack."[31] But the latter had to be a surprise. Another officer told Col. G. F. R. Henderson that "attention should be particularly directed to the training of infantry in shooting from behind cover accurately and rapidly without exposing themselves," during the course of an attack.[32] Turning the Boers out of their trenches required great effort and resulted in considerable casualties.

The Russo-Japanese War was a larger-scale conflict than the Boer War and provided numerous examples of fortifications and entrenchments. The Russian force fought on the defensive while the Japanese fought on the offensive. Foreign military observers tended to accompany the more successful Japanese force.

Charles Repington, the London *Times* correspondent, noted that frontal attacks were exceedingly expensive and only countries utilizing universal conscription could afford the casualties. He maintained that the Russians defended their positions very well, but attacked badly. He did not believe in the virtues of fortifications and placed considerable emphasis on the superior élan of the Japanese "imbued with glorious and invincible optimism,"[33] ready to attack the enemy anywhere with the greatest vigor. "Such a mad jumble of arms and accoutrements mingled with the bodies of those who so lately bore them" testified to the severe casualties. This poignant, if melodramatic, commentary concerned Russian dead,[34] but similar sights of Japanese casualties on other occasions were recorded by another observer, Gen. Ian Hamilton. He noticed that the

Japanese infantry assault lines proceeded by bounds until three hundred and fifty yards from the Russian position. "Here the bugles sounded; the men fixed bayonets and charged in with a loud shout." Hamilton believed this tactic was fundamentally wrong because the troops fired very little during the assault and suffered inordinate losses: "It comes to this, then, that the Japanese expose four of their soldiers to fire at the long range, where one would suffice."[35] Frontal assaults were suicidal during the Russo-Japanese War, yet were used by both sides.

The advantages of cover were appreciated by Hamilton; he believed that if the Russians had built strong fortifications instead of a few trenches, a particular position near the Yalu River would have succeeded in delaying considerably the Japanese advance. It was the *failure* of the Russians to employ proper defense techniques that led to their defeat. The role of the defender is more difficult, Hamilton thought, because the defender must divine "the full intention of his enemy from his preliminary movements" before changing his own troop dispositions[36] in order to mass a powerful force to contain the attack at the decisive point in the line: "a portion of the line of defence, the possession of which enables the defender to hold his ground, but which, once taken by the attacker, forces the defence to abandon the whole position and retreat."[37]

Good entrenchments, according to Hamilton, while helping to provide a powerful defense, do not suffice of themselves. The siege of Port Arthur was conducted against outposts including strong entrenchments and artillery emplacements, yet the Japanese offensive campaign was victorious. The assaults on Port Arthur were particularly noted for the lavish expenditure of Japanese infantry in frontal actions, according to a Russian observer: "A thick, unbroken mass of corpses covered the cold earth like a coverlet." Hamilton noted the effectiveness of the preliminary Japanese artillery barrage from the other side. The gunnery was very methodical, employing high-explosive shells that fell accurately on the Russian gun emplacements and trenches.[38]

Bernhardi, surveying the results of the extensive use of trenches in the Russo-Japanese War, the Boer War, and the earlier Russo-Turkish War at Plevna, believed they merely delayed the final results of campaigns. It was obvious, however, that "in the future, extensive use of spade work will be made with the object of gaining cover against the greater effect of firearms."[39] Schlieffen believed that infantry could no longer use close order in attack, but only loose lines with men spaced one

for each meter. Formerly ten to fifteen men per meter had been collected for an assault, but by the Franco-Prussian War the norm was
ten; in the Russo-Japanese War only three, including reserves, could
be employed per meter.[40] Firepower made the offense extremely hazardous, as all professionals recognized by 1914. Yet both the Boers
and the Russians had relied primarily on defensive strategy and its
accompanying tactics including entrenchments, and they had ultimately
failed. Why should not the military professionals have believed that
offense was still the way to win wars?

PUSH ON, REGARDLESS OF COST

Confronted with the evidently enormous strength of the defense, tacticians before the war had to determine which of several modes of attack would prove likeliest to achieve victory.[41] These options included
frontal attacks, flank attacks, combined frontal and flank attacks, envelopment attacks, and, most striking, the Cannae hypothesis (double
envelopment). All entailed considerable risks against a resolute defender. Nevertheless, an accepted canon was that most battles were
won by aggressive action: the one who was content to defend would
ultimately lose to the one who was prepared to risk an attack. Repington
was a devout supporter of the vigorous attack, claiming that an army
must "pursue a considerable and decisive objective with the utmost
energy and resolution."[42] Mesmerized by this doctrine, prewar tacticians
tried to adapt the theories to the changed specifications of modern weaponry.

Bernhardi expressed the immediate prewar conception of the attack
when he indicated that its success "rests on two things: on the effect
of fire and the force of shock." J. Colin was another advocate of "l'esprit
offensif le plus ardent et le plus résolu," combining heavy firepower
with serious infantry attacks.[43] There was an ominous sound to these
pronouncements because they implied the necessity of heavy casualties, regardless of the mode of attack chosen. In fact, they also implied that there was only one true form of attack, the frontal, and that
flanking or envelopment tactics really entail frontal attacks.

Admittedly, any perception of such a grim reality was subconscious,
and commentators did not fully realize the implications. But observers of both the Boer and the Russo-Japanese wars were quite definite
in describing the difficulties of attack. Count Sternberg noted while
watching Boer action that, as the range of modern rifles increased, the

distance at which troops were deployed had to be increased and the size of units had to be reduced. If men advanced at the run with fixed bayonets, the defense "waits for this moment, for then not a man will escape him," because the attacking forces provide so many easy targets.[44] Colonel Henderson recommended an artillery bombardment against well-constructed entrenchments in order to weaken the defense prior to an infantry attack. Such an attack would still be problematic because it would lack reconnaissance information and could not readily determine the strength of the defense.[45] (In fact, Sternberg noted that on at least one occasion the British suffered because they attacked after the artillery devastated the *wrong* trenches.[46]) Henderson also believed that (1) only the "very loosest skirmishing order" could succeed in breaking through the curtain of fire of the defense, and (2) traditional firing lines at long range cannot defeat one another. Finally, Henderson believed that offensive action should be based upon a strategy of envelopment because simple frontal attacks were suicidal.[47]

Increasingly evident in tactical thought was the belief that the offense must wield superior firepower against the defense in order to prevail. While Henderson felt envelopment was both possible and desirable in the attack, students of the Russo-Japanese War were not so sure.

Schlieffen believed that the defense, operating on interior lines, could quickly reinforce endangered points making it nearly impossible for the attacking force to turn its flank. Despite the attraction of the full-scale envelopment or Cannae, Schlieffen was pessimistic about the chances of achieving it in the face of the inherent strength of the defense.[48] Bernhardi, though often an opponent of Schlieffen, agreed that a "uniform attack on the whole of the enemy's front affords the least prospect of decisive results," but felt that envelopment would require immense numerical superiority. More promising, Bernhardi thought, was a flanking attack that might succeed if pushed before the defense was able to form an effective new front to face it.[49] At this point the debate between Bernhardi and Schlieffen becomes clearer: The first advocated that the defense maintain a reserve to be quickly moved to face a threatened envelopment. Schlieffen was more inclined to limit the size of reserves, arguing that the effective use of most of one's force would be needed. Because the defense was so strong, the attacking force always had a better chance of success if it could use all of its available firepower at the same time in a forceful assault. Goltz noted, however, that while some reserves would have to be maintained for emergencies, "the gradual expenditure of forces is a necessary evil, and not an advantage of the new methods of fighting.[50] Envelopment could be countered if effective reserves were available.

Observers of actual wars were not as optimistic about the success of offensive action. Lord Brooke noted that Japanese General Oku tried to turn the extreme Russian right by using enormous masses of infantry and suffered gruesome casualties as a result.[51] Ian Hamilton noted that sheer numbers of infantrymen, regardless of the élan that might have infused them, could not break a resolute defense during the same war.[52]

Nevertheless, Bernhardi and numerous others (not all French or German) continued to advocate massive infantry attacks, which by sheer force or "shock" would bring victory. Bernhardi recommended successive, loose lines of infantry to enforce this shock: "Yet conquer we must by the shock of the mass."[53]

Once committed to the grand attack, the tacticians tried to reinforce the firepower of the infantry by devising means to use artillery support more effectively. Bernhardi believed artillery must be directed against the front attacked to give the utmost support to the advancing infantry. Although committed to the fashionable shock theory so admired by Ferdinand Foch and others, Bernhardi also believed in training for coordinated infantry-artillery assaults.[54] It is obvious, of course, that such professional theorists were trying to find ways to defeat the very strong defense caused by entrenchments supported by machine guns and artillery.

In the pre–World War I doctrines of offense full recognition was given by shrewd observers such as Schlieffen, Bernhardi, Hamilton, Foch, and Colin to the dangers of trying to attack well-fortified positions. Ample study was made of recent wars, particularly the Boer and the Russo-Japanese wars. Certain assumptions were unconsciously present in their minds, the prime one being that the offense had a good chance of defeating the defense if it could deliver the greater volume of fire. Firepower won battles and decided wars and firepower was an amalgam of rifle, machine-gun, and artillery action. The more riflemen employed in conjunction with other types of soldiers, the more real firepower could be achieved.

WHAT THE TROOPS WERE TAUGHT: THE MANUALS

The various European armies regularly published, or authorized publication of, manuals for training troops in all manner of subjects. Manuals prescribed tactics for small infantry units as well as for artillery batteries and cavalry. In 1914, for example, the British army, through His Majesty's Stationery Office, issued pamphlets of various lengths that dealt with cavalry training, military engineering, and infantry equipment and training. In fact, nearly all such publications were freely available to all purchasers; the military attaches for Imperial Germany regularly made reports on foreign manuals they purchased locally and quite legally. Other armies published similar manuals. Naturally, these publications provided a uniform set of tactical standards for employing regular and reserve troops. Aimed primarily at training inexperienced troops, they did not delve into all aspects of tactics but concentrated on simple notions readily drilled.

A pointed question might well be asked: Why were tactical drills publicized? Usually, the instructions for parade ground drill, ceremonials, and the like were specified in minute detail, but instructions for the infantry company or other similar units in combat were more generally stated. Field commanders were supposed to have discretionary authority to determine minor tactics on the battlefield as seemed necessary, provided certain basic rules were observed.

In the British *Field Service Regulations* as revised early in 1914, engagement with the enemy in combat occurred in two phases: first a "decisive attack" on a weak point using the mass firepower of infantry and artillery, then the "battle" itself. Advance of the infantry would ensue until resistance forced a halt and the construction of trenches. In the inevitable counterattack a "general reserve" would strengthen the defense. Only if the enemy were in disorder or scattered could cavalry be employed. The leit-motif was: "Decisive success in battle can be gained only by a vigorous offensive."[55] In modern warfare all arms had to work together to achieve a common victory: "Infantry depends upon artillery to enable it to obtain superiority of fire and to close with the enemy," and, "the essence of infantry tactics consists of breaking down the enemy's resistance by the weight and direction of its fire and then completing his overthrow by assault."[56]

The German military attache reported to his government in 1912 his conclusions regarding the British army. They were based upon observations of maneuvers and gleanings from other sources supplementing the publicized tactics of the *Field Service Regulations.* He confirmed the general approach of the manual and indicated in addition that the British envisaged that a quarter of the force would attack in the initial phase with the rest divided between a supporting attack force and a general reserve.[57]

In British practice just before 1914, a coordination of the efforts of infantry, artillery, and cavalry was sought, but only the infantry had a really well defined role. In the discussions of that arm emphasis was placed on rifle marksmanship. The *Field Service Manual, 1914, Infantry Battalion (Expeditionary Force),* provided only one machine-gun section of a strength of eighteen men in a battalion of a thousand. The ratio of machine guns to rifles in such a unit was 2 to 828.[58] Given the reports of the Russo-Japanese War by officers like Hamilton, it was odd that the British army did not try harder to strengthen infantry battalions with additional machine guns. When queried about this lack by Liddell Hart in the 1930s, General Edmonds, editor of the British official military history of the war, claimed that he, Haig, and other officers tried from 1908 onward to do this, only to run into budgetary restrictions.[59] The British Expeditionary Force and other armies in 1914 were not well equipped with machine guns even though tactical theory emphasized their contribution to firepower.

The French army had a myriad of manuals covering most of the same topics that concerned the British. Cavalry detachments advanced first in order to locate the enemy. Following them were the infantry advance units accompanied by field artillery. This "preparatory" attack was designed to determine where the front was weakest. Field artillery was then joined by a portion of the rest of the artillery, known as "infantry artillery." The manual continued: "The essential role of the artillery is to push the attacks of the infantry and to destroy all that is opposed to the progress of these attacks." The infantry was the principal arm of service, and it struck the enemy by maneuvering for a strong thrust and then using all its firepower to support this thrust once undertaken. Infantry squads or sections were to advance by "rapid bounds, pushed by the fire of the artillery and by the fire of neighboring units." Cavalry, possessing greatest mobility, was the "arm of surprise par excellence," in its role as the advance arm of the field army. The French manual stressed coordinating the infantry and artillery efforts; it was particularly good on the role of the field artillery in battle.[60] On the other hand, its discussion of cavalry was traditional (although that arm was already controversial in 1914).

A coherent doctrine of attack was included in the French manuals. In an interesting twist, the French prescribed how an artillery barrage would support the vanguard in order to force the enemy to reveal his locations. The main body of the vanguard followed afterward: it also possessed light artillery and special infantry, or "storm" troops, whose mission was to attack in strength on a point of the enemy's front considered weak by the prevanguard reconnaissance units. Such infantry was trained to advance by bounds of 25 to 30 meters in 10 to 12 seconds. This strong attack was designed to force the enemy to commit its reserves to strengthen the threatened sector. While such dispositions were under way the main body of the advancing army was supposed to occupy the places taken by the storm troops of the vanguard. One-third of the entire infantry in the army would then use these positions for the strongest ("decisive") attack and, being the backbone of the army, would maneuver to hit the enemy by surprise at the selected point in the line that seemed weak. If this attack succeeded, all troops in the vanguard and main body would push forward in a massive breakthrough. The main reserves would assist in this all-out effort. All phases of these operations would be accompanied by artillery support; the French stressed infantry-artillery coordination. The artillery would perform two functions during the advance: to weaken the infantry of the enemy so it would be overrun by the vanguard and main force; and to silence, if possible, the artillery of the enemy.[61] Support of the infantry advance, however, always had priority over counterbattery work.

Before 1911, the Prussian army was not noted for tactical innovations; its General Staff was still immersed in analysis of the Franco-Prussian War. Technically there was no German army, but only separate Prussian, Bavarian, Württemberg, and Saxon forces, but the Prussian General Staff shared responsibility for all these forces with the War Ministry. There had been a long-standing debate within the higher ranks of the officer corps over the importance of so-called linear formations. Firing lines (linear) had been used in the Boer and Russo-Japanese wars, but were entrenched; such lines seemed more viable than the Napoleonic deep columns in modern warfare. Yet the French infantry doctrine before 1914 still stressed deep columns behind advanced skirmishers. In the German discussion, officers like Bernhardi stressed linear tactics while others, Schlieffen among them, seemed to stress columnar tactics. The end result by 1911 was an ineffectual standoff where no coherent infantry tactical theory seemed to predominate. Owing to criticism by the famous British military correspondent Repington and negative comments by foreign military attaches, the General Staff by 1914 was finally persuaded to review its maneuver results. Critics had indicated the prevalence of dense infantry formations, machine-like drill, and failure to take into account the new firepower provided by rifles, machine guns, and quick-firing field artillery. The elder Moltke had first emphasized the importance of firepower and after 1905, Schlieffen promoted it, too. By then, senior officers were indeed concerned that defensive firepower made attacks very dangerous. Schlieffen believed troops with high morale and training could still win when on the offensive, even though the odds were weighted so much in favor of the defense. Emperor Wilhelm was not in favor of revising the tactics and helped buttress the conservative leanings of the General Staff. The only change in the German infantry field regulations was to emphasize a strong infantry firing line that advanced between fire by bounds of one hundred meters.[62] There was no effort to modify the requirements of mass assault.

Under the followers of Schlieffen, particularly the younger Moltke, efforts were made to improve and modernize tactics.[63] The result was the formation of machine-gun companies from 1912 to 1914. By the latter date, each infantry regiment was composed of three infantry battalions and one machine-gun company.[64] Tactical manuals for the machine gun were issued in 1913 and 1914, but it is difficult to imagine that German awareness of the importance of this weapon was any greater than that of the French and the English.

It is safe to say that the tactics of the American army were an offshoot of those employed by the major western European armies before the war. The U.S. *Field Service Regulations, 1914,* stressed that "infantry is the principal and most important arm, which is charged with the main work on the field of battle and decides the final issue of combat." Cavalry scouted ahead of skirmishing infantry and the latter was assisted by the field artillery. The American manual emphasized that troops in attack "must understand that the best protection against losses is afforded by an uninterrupted and vigorous advance towards the enemy's position and by the use of such natural cover as the ground offers."[65] The role of machine guns was not any more emphasized in these regulations than in equivalent manuals published by the English, French, or Germans: such weapons were minor elements of artillery.

Surveying the prewar training manuals and field service regulations reveals their authors were aware that infantry attacks were difficult because of the awesome weight of firepower available to the defending enemy. But aside from the technical discussion of siegecraft, these sources inevitably concentrated on attack rather than defense. The roles of all arms of service were therefore considered chiefly within the context of attack. An unsolved problem was how to match the firepower of the entrenched enemy while in the process of advancing or attacking, because troops could not fire while running or walking. When advancing it was necessary to keep an extended order because densely packed formations were easy targets for the defending enemy's machine guns and rifles. But if the assault troop units were separated from one another it became difficult or impossible to concentrate firepower upon the enemy. The advancing infantry was considered to be highly vulnerable whenever it dashed from one firing line to another. Two basic solutions seemed possible: First, the attacking force could be shielded by an artillery barrage that would cause the enemy to take cover; and second, the infantry could run short distances before seeking cover on the ground, minimizing exposure. Vague prescriptions were given for machine-gun deployment during the attack, but the weight of such weapons and of their ammunition meant they could not accompany the first waves of an assault force. Finally, all agreed that perseverance, determination, and the willingness to take losses was needed if any attack were to succeed. No professional military theorist was willing to claim that attacks had become suicidal, as was suggested by I. S. Bloch in an interesting if not very influential book in 1902.[66]

By 1914, cavalry tactical instructions did not urge frontal attacks unsupported by other arms; no one wished to emulate the Light Brigade at Balaclava. No infantry tactical manuals recommended close-order marches on enemy positions. That such actions had been taken in all modern wars, including the Boer and the Russo-Japanese wars, was merely evidence of inferior military leadership and combat performance.

BAD THEATER: SIMULATED COMBAT

All armies attempt to create or to simulate in peacetime some of the conditions of real warfare through periodic maneuvers. Annual maneuvers after 1900 increased in scope as the number of participants rose. The reports of military attaches gave fairly realistic ideas of the conduct of operations. But for reasons that will shortly become apparent, neither those who directed nor those who observed maneuvers could really approximate the reality of actual war. The French maneuvers of 1913 were conducted in Languedoc, between Montauban and Toulouse. Some four army corps, with additional units, made up the equivalent of an army in the field. The two opposing commanders, Generals Pau and Chomer, performed under General Joffre in September. Pau obtained an early advantage for his Blue Force by using airplanes, which discovered that elements of the Red Force were not in the way of a necessary advance. The Red Force was defeated by means of a night march followed by an envelopment. Dirigibles assisted during daylight in perceiving Red movements, while airplanes spotted for Blue artillery. Referees criticized both sides for premature assaults, too dense infantry formations, poorly secured liaisons, inadequate security, and a generally mediocre conduct of operations.[67]

General Joffre had also directed the maneuvers of 1912 in western France and criticized many of the commanders involved for incompetent maneuvers.[68] German observers of these maneuvers were impressed by a massive artillery barrage that accompanied the attack by the vanguard of infantry and cavalry, utilizing the doctrine of penetration at the weakest point of the enemy. Heavy columns of infantry massed behind this vanguard in the Napoleonic manner, ready to exploit a breakthrough. The observers seemed to consider this French operation more favorably than they had viewed the French maneuvers of 1909, which had featured an aborted attack. One French practice the Germans particularly liked was the retention of a strong "maneuver" force behind one flank ready to be pushed into a possible breach in the enemy's line.[69] Curiously, the French were better critics of their own shortcomings than were the Germans; they were beginning to realize the impracticality of Napoleonic columnar attacks.

Of less importance to the German army was the state of the British army. German observers noted in 1912 that cavalry attacks were seldom used in recent exercises since the opinion of a minority of enthusiastic cavalrymen was eclipsed by a majority who rejected such attacks "against the omnipresent machine guns and the overwhelming fire of entrenched units." This change in cavalry tactics was correctly identified by the Germans as resulting from the influence of Lord Roberts, who followed the experiences of the Boer War.[70] General Haig, director general of training at Aldershot in 1912, was responsible for drawing up the maneuvers that year and determined that cavalry would have to play a more important role than specified in the teachings of Roberts. The Aldershot exercises emphasized the involvement of cavalry in coordination with infantry, artillery, and aircraft.[71] The result was unfavorable for Haig since his opponent, General Grierson, used airplanes for reconnaissance and as a result was able to outmaneuver him. A postexercise summation before the king showed Haig even more verbally incompetent than usual.

Nevertheless, Gen. Sir Henry Wilson (as noted for his volubility as Haig was for taciturnity) was struck by the failure of the French cavalry in the 1912 maneuvers to work dismounted as did the English. Eschewing lances, which the French were actually reviving because of their preoccupation with the *arme blanche* ("white arm"), the British army cavalry was trained in marksmanship and resembled mounted infantry.[72]

Writing to his friend Launcelot Kiggell on 20 July 1911, Haig forgot cavalry to opine: "I think that the weak point in our training is the cooperation between the artillery and infantry."[73] Spencer Wilkinson noted in 1900 that when two opposing sides during maneuvers shot blanks at each other, they were congested into "clusters as dense as the old two-deep line, facing each other at three hundred yards' distance." Obviously, the commanders had forgotten "the one thing that reigns supreme on the modern battle field, the bullet."[74] Wilkinson might have made the comment fourteen years later, when artificial firing lines still opposed one another in British maneuvers.

Between 1912 and 1914, the German General Staff was mainly preoccupied with what seemed the fantastic rejuvenation of the Russian army.[75]

As a result, near-last-minute efforts were made to modernize tactics: the German planners were almost reduced to a state of panic by a new respect for Russian power. Finally aware that machine guns were vitally necessary, in 1913 the German army established a school in their use for noncommissioned officers. Maneuvers that year and previously had not emphasized such weapons. Indeed, the comparatively modest military budget prohibited purchases of large numbers of machine guns before 1912. Instead, since 1909, emphasis in the General Staff had been on the improvement of fortresses both in the Rhineland and on the Polish and East Prussian borders. Maneuvers concentrated on defense of these fortresses.[76] General Staff rides were, in fact, instituted because of worry that the Schlieffen plan left the Rhineland exposed to a powerful French thrust through Alsace and Lorraine. The threat of a Russian army, rejuvenated after the Russo-Japanese War, also insured that German military units would be increased in the east.

The most infamous of German maneuvers was that of 1911 in Mecklenburg when 100,000 troops were employed. Aircraft, including dirigibles, were also used for the first time. An interested observer, Col. Charles Repington, the military correspondent for the London *Times,* noted that the Blue Army commanded by Goltz attempted to attack the Red Army by concentrating forces on each flank, denuding its center in the hope of enveloping the latter. Such a course, Repington believed, would have led to disaster in actual battle. The much-vaunted German infantry was slow moving, lethargic, and machinelike and seemed incapable of quick deployment. "No example was noticed of a trench suited to the needs of modern war, or of a parapet which would have kept out modern bullets."[77] Densely massed, the infantry provided many opportunities for devastating artillery fire by the other side.[78] Repington's critique caused great consternation in the German General Staff because other foreign observers seemed to share his negative views to some extent. Recent study has shown that the German army of 1911 was indeed characterized by some of the traits noticed by Repington.[79] At least the new machine-gun companies were included in the exercise.

The peculiar nature of these peacetime maneuvers must be noted. Repington stated that such exercises were not intended to be completely realistic or to echo wartime conditions or plans. But the whole excuse for holding elaborate maneuvers was to give commanders experience in commanding large numbers of troops in mock warfare. No clear lessons emerged from the French, German, and other maneuvers in the years shortly before the war except that aircraft could provide valuable reconnaissance and artillery-spotting information. In no exercise were the troops ever locked in a stalemate in which both sides were entrenched. In fact, trenches were indifferently used and mobility remained possible throughout. Cavalry helped provide reconnaissance from forays behind the lines and was even used for attacking an enemy's flank, rolling it back. Cavalry fought mounted, even as the *arme blanche,* except in the Aldershot exercises, where Lord Roberts had long insisted upon dismounted action.

Truthfully, maneuvers in peacetime were of dubious value because they were dramatic productions in which the casts were coached to follow certain preconceived tactical schemes. Repington might have described all contemporary armies in the same terms as he described the German: "Theory may recognize that great and even fundamental changes are required in tactics and in training to meet the new conditions with success, but all evidence shows that an Army which has not been tried in the fire is constitutionally unable to profit by the experience of others and to adapt itself to the ordeal of modern war."[80]

THE PROBLEM OF DEFENSE

Trained to consider wars that would be won by mobile and offensive armies, the general staffs of the various states would not admit for a second that the writings of I. S. Bloch or of Norman Angell[81] had any practical military significance. Bloch, an amateur military enthusiast and Polish banker, accurately predicted that the next war would be extremely destructive because of the power of the defense. Liddell Hart later believed that Bloch had, in fact, predicted the trench warfare stalemate of 1914–18. Angell, a leading pacifist, claimed war would be suicidal and could not be won by any side because of the technological and economic interdependence of states.

Professional military planners did not take the views of such amateurs seriously. The armies went to war in 1914 equipped with "a twentieth-century delivery system" of railroads and efficient supply services "but a nineteenth-century warhead."[82] Armies moved ten miles a day on foot with horse accompaniment when past the railhead, commanded by generals who thought horse-mounted cavalry could give mobility to their forces where necessary. Reverting to an earlier age, the French cavalry decided to increase the number of lances so all cavalry divisions would be provided with them.[83] The confusion of this force was no greater than that of other mounted forces in other armies in 1914. But on one issue opinion was not divided: wars were won by offensive action; strong defenses, if they hindered success at all, would ultimately yield to a shock attack. After all, the British and the Japanese had won in their wars of aggression in 1901 and 1905.

A gulf existed between the often shrewd comments of European and American observers of the Boer and Russo-Japanese wars and the officially accepted tactical doctrine as exposed in field manuals. Despite the greater strength of the defense resulting from the efficiency of rifle and machine-gun fire, the side that was on the defensive lost. Therefore, such battlefield observation would expose some problems of warfare, but would not necessarily point to the conduct of future wars.

Tactics developed in peacetime are necessarily artificial because they are not worked out step by step in combat. Once the war starts it quickly becomes evident that some tactics are obsolete and must be revised or replaced.

NOTES

1. Sir William Robertson, *From Private to Field Marshal* (London, 1921), 1–33, provides a personal account of life in a prewar army as a common soldier. Douglas Porch, *The March to the Marne; The French Army, 1871–1914* (Cambridge, 1981), 105–33, discusses morale problems shortly before the war. Gwyn Harries-Jenkins, *The Army in Victorian Society* (Toronto, 1977), 133–70, discusses the peacetime world of the British officer corps (but ignores the ordinary soldier). Bernd-Felix Schulte, *Die deutsche Armee 1900–1914* (Düsseldorf, 1977), 258–90, discusses the social crisis in the German officer corps occasioned by the influx of commoners and by the threat of Social Democracy (little on the ordinary soldier).

2. Porch, *March to the Marne,* examines problems of the dual military establishment.

3. B. P. Hughes, *Firepower: Weapons Effectiveness on the Battlefield, 1630–1850* (London, 1974), 164–69, exposed the inefficiency of the smoothbore weapon.

4. David Chandler, *The Campaigns of Napoleon* (New York, 1966), 354–56.

5. Chandler, *Napoleon,* 362–63.

6. Dennis E. Showalter, *Railroads and Rifles* (Hamden, Connecticut, 1975), is an excellent discussion of the Austro-Prussian War of 1866 within the context of weapons development.

7. Haig Papers, National Library of Scotland, Edinburgh, ACC 3155, 6. Letters to Sir Evelyn Wood, 2 September and 26 March 1898.

8. Haig Papers, "Notes on Dismounted Action of Cavalry" of 1892, ACC 3155, 6.

9. G. F. R. Henderson, *The Science of War* (New York, 1905), 414.

10. F. B. Elmslie, "The Possible Effect on Tactics of Recent Improvements in Weapons," Aldershot Military Society (London, 1899), 1–14.

11. Colmar von der Goltz, *The Nation in Arms* (London, 1906), 183.

12. Haig Papers, "Tactics," ACC 3155, 17.

13. Henderson, *Science of War,* 339.

14. Pierre Lorain, *Petite histoire des armes à feu et cinquante ans d'armes françaises, 1866–1916* (Paris, 1975), 34. D. F. Hogg, *Artillery:*

Its Origin, Heyday and Decline (London, 1970), 87–88. H. C. B. Rogers, *A History of Artillery* (Secaucus, New Jersey, 1975), 159.

15. Lorain, *Armes à feu,* 104–21.

16. France, Ministère de la Guerre, Écoles Militaires, *Cours d'artillerie,* Troisième partie, Categorie A-B-C (Paris, 1921), 13. Lorain, *Armes à feu,* 57.

17. Count Adalbert Sternberg, *My Experiences of the Boer War* (New York, 1901), 211.

18. Alfred von Schlieffen, "Der Krieg in der Gegenwart," *Gesammelte Schriften* (Berlin, 1913), 1:11–22.

19. Charles Accourt Repington, *The War in the Far East 1904–1905* (New York, 1905), 405.

20. Haig Papers, ACC 3155, 6.

21. Elmslie, "Weapons," 14–15.

22. Friedrich von Bernhardi, *On War of Today,* tr. Karl von Donat (London, 1913), 2:46.

23. Robertson Papers, Military History Archives, King's College, University of London, I/3, 2. Speech of 4 February 1913.

24. Robertson Papers, I/3, 2.

25. Ministère de la Guerre, *Instruction générale du 30 juillet 1909 sur la guerre de siège* (Paris, 1909), 30, 65.

26. Great Britain, War Office, General Staff, *Field Service Regulations,* Part I, "Operations" (London, 1909 with amendments, 1914), 21, 139. (Hereafter, FSR.)

27. Schulte, *Die deutsche Armee,* 353.

28. Schulte, *Die deutsche Armee,* 335–40.

29. Sternberg, *Boer War,* 110. Schulte, *Die deutsche Armee,* 200.

30. Bernhardi, *War Today,* 2:114–15.

31. Haig Papers, ACC 3155, 38.

32. Quoted in Henderson, *Science of War,* 350–51. Anonymous.

33. Repington, *Far East,* 203–4.

34. Repington, *Far East,* 325, 441–42. The quotation is from Ian Hamilton, *A Staff Officer's Scrapbook* (London, 1907), 2:127.

35. Hamilton, *Scrapbook,* 2:142–43, 144.

36. Hamilton, *Scrapbook,* 2:93–94.

37. Hamilton, *Scrapbook,* 2:94.

38. Hamilton, *Scrapbook,* 2:49, 73, 130–31. E. K. Nojine, *The Truth*

About Port Arthur, tr. & ed. A. B. Lindsay and E. D. Swinton (London, 1908), 70, 200, 208–9, 224. Lord Brooke, *An Eye-Witness in Manchuria* (London, 1905), 103–10.

39. Bernhardi, *War Today,* 2:101.

40. Schlieffen, "Der Krieg," 11–22.

41. Tim Travers, *The Killing Ground* (London, 1987), 62–82, has a discussion of British tactical theories.

42. Repington, *Far East,* 550–51.

43. Bernhardi, *War Today,* 2:47. J. Colin, *Les transformations de la guerre* (Paris, 1911), 289–90.

44. Sternberg, *Boer War,* 211, 214, 217.

45. Henderson, *Science of War,* 419.

46. Sternberg, *Boer War,* 120–21.

47. Henderson, *Science of War,* 419.

48. Schlieffen, "Der Krieg," 11–22.

49. Bernhardi, *War Today,* 2:66.

50. Goltz, *Nation in Arms,* 181.

51. Brooke, *Eye-Witness,* 111.

52. Hamilton, *Scrapbook,* 2:48.

53. Bernhardi, *War Today,* 79–100.

54. Schulte, *Die deutsche Armee,* 208.

55. FSR, 135, 137, 152–55.

56. FSR, 21.

57. Evaluation of German military attaches in Kriegsarchiv München, MKr 990.

58. War Office, General Staff, *Field Service Manual, 1914, Infantry Battalion (Expeditionary Force),* 7, 11, 50.

59. Edmunds also claimed that requests for more hand grenades, light ball pistols, etc., were refused: "Haig who was D.M.T. tried to get similar things; they were turned down by the Finance Branch." Liddell Hart Papers, Military History Archives King's College, University of London, 1/259/73.

60. Ministère de la Guerre, *Règlement sur le service des armées en campagne, France, 1914,* 14–15, 17, 77–79.

61. Evaluation by German military attaches in Kriegsarchiv München, Alter Bestand, Generalstab, Bund 15a. Also MKr 991.

62. Schulte, *Die deutsche Armee,* 15–160, 164–233, 418–534. See

Felddienst-Ordnung (Berlin, 1908). Paragraph 576 did warn of the danger facing advancing firing lines from enemy fire. Also, the appendix of this manual gives illustrations of entrenchments, 11–17.

63. Schulte, *Die deutsche Armee,* 15–160, 164–233, 418–534.

64. Germany, Reichsarchiv, Der Weltkrieg 1914 bis 1918 series, *Kriegsrüstung und Kriegswirtschaft* (Berlin, 1930), 1:155–212.

65. U.S. Army, *Field Service Regulations, 1914,* 72, 74, 79.

66. Ivan S. Bloch, *The Future of War in Its Technical, Economic and Political Relations* (Boston, 1903). The book was well received in pacifist circles, and its interpretations were revived by Liddell Hart in his polemical writings after the war. Norman Angell's *The Great Illusion* (New York, 1910) argued similarly.

67. General Palat, "Les manoeuvres de Languedoc en 1913," *Revue des deux mondes,* vol. 17 (1913), 799–817.

68. Joseph Joffre, *The Memoirs of Marshal Joffre* (London, 1932), 1:33.

69. Kriegsarchiv München, MKr 991 and Alter Bestand, Generalstab, Bund 15a.

70. Kriegsarchiv München, MKr 990.

71. Haig Papers, ACC 3155, 90.

72. John Charteris, *Field Marshal Earl Haig* (London, 1929), 65, recounts an example of Haig's maladroit verbiage: "When called on without warning to present the prizes at an inter-regimental cross-country race, the 'Chief,' to the consternation of his staff, addressed the successful team with the words: 'I congratulate you on your running. You have run well. I hope you will run as well in the presence of the enemy.'" C. E. Callwell, *Field-Marshal Sir Henry Wilson* (New York, 1927), 1:116–17. Military Archives, King's College, University of London, Kiggell Papers, 1:11.

73. Kiggell Papers, 1:11.

74. Spenser Wilkinson, *War and Policy* (London, 1910), 409–10.

75. Norman Stone, *The Eastern Front, 1914–1917* (London, 1975), 37–43. The Germans thought the Russian army possessed 2000 machine guns in infantry units as opposed to 978 in the German army in 1911, and estimated the totals would increase for each army to 4000 and 1686 respectively in 1913. Kriegsarchiv München, MKr 1136 in a memorandum dated 17 April 1913 from the General Staff in Berlin marked *Streng Geheim.*

76. Reichsarchiv, *Kriegsrüstung und Kriegswirtschaft*, 157–71. Kriegsarchiv München, Alter Bestand, Generalstab, Bund 3389.

77. *Times* (London), 19 October 1911, 5.

78. *Times* (London), 28 October 1911, 5–6.

79. Schulte, *Die deutsche Armee,* 48–70.

80. *Times* (London), 28 October 1911, 6.

81. Bloch, *The Future of War,* and Angell, *The Great Illusion.* Although the pacifistic drift of each is similar there is no mention in the index of Angell's book to the earlier book by Bloch.

82. Stone, *Eastern Front,* 50.

83. Kriegsarchiv München, MKr 991 and 992. In 1913, General Sordet, in charge of cavalry tactical planning, also increased the number of cartridges each trooper would carry into action. Finally, each French cavalry brigade was furnished with a machine-gun section in 1911.

CHAPTER 2
WAR IN 1914:
ANTICIPATED AND CHOREOGRAPHED?

A pervasive conservatism distinguished the major armies of Europe just prior to the war. In the usual way, veteran drill sergeants intimidated recruits on the parade grounds and company officers were immersed in a world of petty garrison detail, while regimental commanders worried about maintaining the officers' mess, the stores, the daily reports of manpower strength, the equipment rosters, and almost everything except the intelligent preparation for war.[1] Armies in this long time of peace inevitably became slack because troops had little to do: narrow budgets limited strenuous combat training exercises. Yet the press was full of political debates on the projected conscription of mass armies as international relations continued to deteriorate. Were the regular and reserve forces prepared to fight a major war in 1914?

Each army had a general staff that included as one of its main sections a bureau concerned with war plans. Because planners necessarily worked on theoretical models that could not yet be tested, an air of unreality pervaded their deliberations. Joffre, chief of the French General Staff in 1911, indicated that, while the civilian ministers of the government had the responsibility for finding the means to execute a war plan, "to the generals commanding armies [fell] the business of forming their plan of operations."[2] Quite rightly, he indicated that such plans required close collaboration of military with civil leaders.

Those like Joffre who led the armies of 1914 were ultimately responsible for the tactical dispositions of those armies according to such planning. How capable were the future battlefield commanders?

THE OLD WARRIORS

In May 1919, Eton organized a postwar gathering of its alumni. Giving a keynote speech, General Plumer noted that six thousand Etonians had fought in the war: "We are proud of Eton and our association with it." Most remarkable, however, was the fact that some eighteen generals were present. Besides Lord Plumer, former commander of the Second Army of the BEF, they included Sir Henry Rawlinson, commander of the Fourth Army; Sir Julian Byng, former commander of the Canadian Corps, later of the British army in Egypt; and the Earl of Cavan.[3] The very embodiment of a club, this reunion was more than symbolic, it was a recognition of shared experiences by men who lived according to certain beliefs.

A highly stimulating, if controversial, recent work on the problems of high command, Norman Dixon's *On the Psychology of Military Incompetence,* has attempted to explain the common phenomenon of defective military leadership. During the interwar period a number of writers, including C. S. Forester and J. F. C. Fuller, popularized the notion that the top military commanders of the First World War were bumblers with a penchant for suicidal frontal assaults. Dixon is more sophisticated because he elaborates a theory of interlocking personality traits, which in particular combinations create "ego-weakness and authoritarianism." That, "rather than stupidity," was responsible for the failure of commanders.[4]

Fascinating as such interpretations are, they do not go far enough to explain the behavior of the top commanders of World War I. The personal backgrounds of such men can be illuminated by study of the milieu in which they emerged. While most of the senior commanders of the First World War were at least fifty years of age in 1914, some were considerably older. In fact, Haig was born in 1861, Gough in 1870, Rawlinson in 1864, Ludendorff in 1865, Pétain in 1856, Foch in 1851, Pershing in 1860, and Monash in 1865. Dixon has remarked that they were old enough that they might have lost the mental flexibility of youth. Also important was that most of them were born and raised in rural places by parents whose occupations and social standings were congruent with such backgrounds. Haig, for example, although born in Edinburgh, was raised in Fife. Rawlinson lived in Trent, Somerset. Gough, although born in London, was raised in India, where his father, Sir Charles, was an officer. Foch was raised in Tarbes.[5] Their fathers tended to be middle or upper class: vicars, officers, teachers.

Tim Travers has described the interlocking old-boy system that had such a pervasive influence on the recruitment and promotion of British officers in the small prewar army. "Promotions and removals, personal rivalries, and interventions were all part of a system that displayed a traditional rather than a professional approach to modern war." Undoubtedly, he is right to characterize the British officer corps as a reflection of Edwardian society.[6] Spiers indicated some years ago a similar conclusion for British generals in 1914. Few British officers of the prewar army had important family contacts with the urban and business world.[7] Forty-two percent of English generals in 1914 came from either the peerage or the gentry.[8]

Nevertheless, many such officers were intelligent and flexible in their thinking. In terms of professional education, senior British officers in 1914 frequently shared previous experience as students in the Staff College at Camberley during the 1890s. Haig and William Robertson were both admirers and former students of the famous G. F. R. Henderson. Lord Rawlinson, another future commander in the British Expeditionary Force, was a classmate of Henry Wilson at Camberley in 1892, and came under the same influence.[9] Henderson was truly cognizant, as previously shown, of the latest tactical problems and took pains to describe them in his classes.

In France, the École supérieure de la guerre played a role similar to that of Camberley. After the Franco-Prussian War, especially after 1890, teachers like Colonel Maillard taught future high commanders including Ferdinand Foch, Henri Pétain, and Marie-Eugène Debeney. If, as some critics later maintained, too much emphasis was placed upon the doctrine of the offense at all costs as pushed by Col. François-Jules de Grandmaison, much was also said about the devastating effects of modern firepower. The teachings of this school were summarized intelligently by Colin and Foch before the war.[10] Professionalism did exist and some French officers promoted it.

Social distinctions, well known at the time, differentiated English from Prussian and French officers. Much attention has been paid to the social origins of these officers. Among colonels and generals of 1913 in the Prussian army, for example, some 52 percent were of noble origins while 48 percent were bourgeois. The General Staff was evenly divided between the two groups. Only about 6 percent of the officers of the French colonial army, which produced Gallieni and Mangin, for example, were of noble origin. The proportion of nobles to bourgeois in the army stationed in France was higher, but still small. By the 1880s, the average officer was considered a good match for the daughter of a respectable bourgeois. Even so, it is difficult to make a case for saying that because officers were either bourgeois or noble in origin they were more or less competent. As Porch has shown, such a determination could not be made on the basis of religious preferences either.

More significant may be the breakdown of parental occupations. Demeter indicates the recruitment of officers in the Prussian army in 1913:[11] Only 15.57 percent of new officers came from the families of prominent businessmen. In a recent study Daniel Hughes shows "an overwhelming narrowness [in the range of social origins] of the Prussian officer corps," in contrast to that of Bavaria and Württemberg. Officers were not usually Catholic and never unconverted Jews, but were frequently from landed families. Those from urban and business families were few.[12]

Statistical studies of the social origins of French officers seem to be lacking. The well-studied political role of the army in the stormy crises of the Third Republic, including the Dreyfus Affair and the attempts at democratization of the officer corps afterward, indicates that many younger officers were from lower social strata while a number of senior ones were of a noble background. Bourgeois and lower-class officer graduates of St.-Cyr chose service in the colonies rather than in metropolitan France between 1871 and 1892 because of greater promotion opportunities. In the metropolitan army, fully 21 percent of such graduates had some noble claim while only 6 percent of the colonial graduates were of the same social class. But the colonial army had little impact on the rest of the French army. Professional soldiers, dismayed at the loss of morale and public support for the army, urged reforms after 1905 and some of those reforms involved more modern education for future officers. No evidence has been provided to show, however, that the officer corps had any real connection to the complicated and new industrial sectors of society.[13]

C. Wright Mills has established that small-town notables produced most of the higher officers of the American army. His data, admittedly sparse, indicated that such officers were merely another subgroup of the middle class.[14]

In short, it seems obvious that most officers of all armies were fairly closely connected to a rural or small-town past and had little to do with the great currents of change involved in the Industrial Revolution. The most dynamic sector of the class structure of these states, the entrepreneurial class, did not, apparently, send its sons into officer careers before 1914. Sons of country vicars and small-town teachers did not start their careers with important family connections in an urban, entrepreneurial society. It remains, then, to be seen whether these officers were able to learn to live in a rapidly industrializing world in the immediate period before 1914.

LOGIC AND PREJUDICE IN THE WAR PLANS

Certainly, the most intelligent and imaginative of the various war plans formulated prior to 1914 was the celebrated scheme known under its author's name: the Schlieffen Plan. Schlieffen believed France was a great fortress and could only be taken by a carefully prepared siege. Siege warfare has traditionally been viewed as extremely slow and very expensive in terms of the expenditure of lives and supplies. Those who have invested fortresses pay homage to the great master of the art, Vauban, who suggested that well-built fortifications would only be taken by a methodical advance of parallel trenches that would gradually tighten a hermetically sealed circle around the increasingly helpless and desperate defender. Traditional siegecraft would not suffice to destroy France's army and would simply provide Russia and England ample time to strike at Germany, which was devoting more and more energy and troops to the slow investment of the great fortress. Schlieffen decided—and this decision was a real measure of his genius—that the key to German penetration of French defenses was a powerful and unanticipated thrust using most of the forces available.[15] Russia and England would not have time to react. In the end the Schlieffen Plan was a great gamble that almost succeeded.

It is important to note that although Schlieffen hoped to catch the French forces in the field within a giant envelopment in a Clausewitzian battle of annihilation, he did not place all his hopes on that difficult goal. Such an approach might not work, but something effective, if more modest, might well succeed. Fortress France was to be invaded by a surprise assault through Belgium and along the Channel coast in the direction of Paris, which was the keep of the fortress. The sweep along the coast would have the advantage of separating the besieged from a prospective relief expedition sent by the British, but its main aim was to quickly bypass the best-guarded gates of the gigantic fortress and to penetrate to the inner keep before the defenders had the opportunity to shift their forces from other defensive positions to the point of penetration. As Schlieffen noted, assault forces would move "from position to position, day and night, advancing, digging in, advancing. . . . The attack must never be allowed to come to a standstill as happened in the war in the Far East."

A pronounced weakness was Schlieffen's obsession with taking Paris rather than with the destruction of the French army.

Since speed was essential to success, Schlieffen paid attention to the mundane but difficult problems of logistics. Railroads could be used to transport hundreds of thousands of men quickly, but only within the borders of Germany because he had to assume the Belgian and French governments would destroy marshalling yards and rail lines in the course of the campaign. Preparing his plan before 1905, Schlieffen could not anticipate the rapid development of motor transport and had to assume the massive German force would have to use the roads with horse-drawn equipment. Horses are notoriously difficult to feed in large quantities, and there was a practical limit to the number of them that could be employed before the sheer logistics of their maintenance brought the entire army to a halt a hundred miles or so from the nearest railhead. Most of the troops would have to march in time-honored fashion. They could not all march on the same road at the same time because a modern corps with a full complement of fighting troops would spread over a column of march of twenty-nine kilometers, and it could not come fully into an attack in one day. The advance forces of such a corps would have large numbers of machine guns and heavy artillery so that they could provide a powerful advance thrust (or a strong defense if needed). But Schlieffen knew that this corps would have to keep moving so the enemy would not have a chance to strengthen or stabilize defensive lines if the impetus of the offensive somehow diminished.[16]

Schlieffen feared Russia, as had Bismarck previously, and wished to find some way to incapacitate France before Russia succeeded in launching an offensive on Germany's eastern frontier. The presence of the German army in annual maneuvers and other exercises on the frontier of France and Belgium did not escape the notice of the French *Grand Quartier Général.* Joffre, even before becoming commander in chief of the French army, believed that the French Plan XVI was insufficient because it did not anticipate a German attack through Belgium.[17] Joffre perceived this in 1906, only a year after the first version of the Schlieffen Plan was developed. In 1907, in the preliminary military talks with Russia, General Dubail told the commanders of the tsar's army that the evidence pointed to a massive German assault in the west coming through Lorraine, Luxembourg, and Belgium.[18]

Joffre prepared for possible war with Germany even before he was named commander in chief in 1912. He held frank conversations with the ubiquitous Sir Henry Wilson, who acted as liaison officer with the British army.[19] Joffre determined to strengthen the French left as much as possible, correctly surmising that the German war plan called for a strong offensive through Belgium. Even though he did not know how overwhelming a force was envisaged by the Germans, he still believed Britain should provide as large an army as it could afford in order to help the French counterattack against the German thrust. Joffre tried for a time to urge that the two allies undertake a preemptive strike against the Germans through Belgium. Naturally, the British were shocked by this idea; Joffre could not even obtain a British pledge to defend the neutrality of Belgium if the Germans invaded. His staff then produced a compromise French war plan: Plan XVII.[20] The role of the British army in all of these calculations was minor. Joffre had failed to obtain a commitment from the British.

Aware of the increased tension between Germany and France, the British General Staff began to shift emphasis from imperial commitments and to Europe. General Sir James Grierson suggested in 1904 that a striking force be formed to be used in conjunction with the navy.[21] Sir Henry Wilson was deep in conversation with the French staff in 1911 following the British decision to establish the expeditionary force, but this force would only comprise 6 divisions in contrast to the estimated 85 French and the 110 of the Germans. It was faintly ludicrous for Wilson, according to the recollections of Churchill, to claim that "if the six British divisions were sent to take position on the extreme French left, immediately war was declared, the chances of repulsing the Germans in the first shock of battle were favourable."[22] Wilson was shown French intelligence reports indicating that the Germans had determined to make a strong thrust through Belgium in case of war. He met Joffre for the first time on 28 November 1911, and was shown detailed marching routes in southern Belgium to be used by the British Expeditionary Force in conjunction with the French Fifth Army.[23] But he still could not indicate to Joffre that more than six divisions would be available. Therefore, Joffre had no reason to rely upon the British and could not risk placing more French troops on the left flank because of the dangers of uncovering the easiest invasion route: through Alsace in the direction of Verdun. In a discussion on 21 February 1912, Joffre told the cabinet that a future war would result in either a quick French victory or a long conflict in which the French defended their homeland. Apparently, the contribution of England in either case would be insignificant.[24]

Nevertheless, it is difficult to comprehend Joffre's new plan because it most definitely did not call for the immediate thrust of most French forces into Belgium to avert the German offensive. Instead, three of the five French armies were located on the borders of Alsace and Lorraine between Verdun and Epinal. The Fifth Army, under Gen. Charles-Louis Lanrezac, was the only one positioned on the Belgian border. The remaining Fourth Army remained in the region of St.-Didier and the plan called for its use as a maneuver force either in an assault on Thionville or to shift north to help the Fifth Army when that army invaded Belgium. Neither the Fifth nor the Fourth Army was supposed to advance north until the Germans invaded the Ardennes.[25]

Whether Joffre approved of the extreme position of the offensive at all costs as taught in the École supérieure de la guerre is somewhat vague.[26] He certainly admitted some faith in the doctrine in his memoirs. General Rouquerol wrote many years later that:

> before the war, the word defensive, if it was not eliminated from the military vocabulary, was at least virtually abrogated. Anyone

who pronounced it was disqualified. During manoeuvres or exercises, to obtain the blessings of the commander and his counsellors, it sufficed for him who would promote himself, to say "I attack."[27]

This doctrine, as claimed by many writers later, received official sanction at the highest levels in a meeting of the Superior Council of National Defense on 9 January 1912, when the army renounced "the defensive projects which constitute an acknowledgement of inferiority."[28] Nevertheless, it would be unfair to accept the suggestion that the French officer corps naively believed that frontal attacks on defended positions were the only means for securing victory.

The French war plans prior to Plan XVII were, like the German plans prior to that of Schlieffen, concerned with defense. Indeed, the concept of the great fortress under siege dominated French strategy from the Franco-Prussian War until 1914; general staff planners in both countries became worried about the vulnerability of their frontiers, so considerable money was spent on fortress construction adjacent to Verdun on the French side and in the Rhineland on the German side.

By 1905, the staff studies of the Russo-Japanese War and the Boer War indicated that a defensive posture, while potentially quite strong, did not win either war. The Boers defended their homeland and the Russians defended their Far Eastern possessions; both lost. Defensive strategy lost favor in the thinking of staff officers in all armies. Even so, the existing war plans centered upon the defense of fortresses on the frontier. Suddenly, it was necessary to reorient planning in order to infuse it with what seemed to be an approach to victory: the offense. Simultaneous decisions were made by the German, French, and British general staffs to adopt what seems now to have been foolhardy and adventurous schemes calling for strong offensive action. Imbued with the traditional belief that the best defense is a good offense (a cliché since time immemorial), staff officers produced Plan XVII and Schlieffen produced his scheme. Somewhat cognizant of each other's schemes, each staff tried to amend the basic plans between 1906 and 1914 as information about the other side came in.

But amendments to the newly established war plans, while not changing their basically offensive nature, fatefully weakened their force. Moltke the Younger, worried about the safety of Alsace and Lorraine, could not bring himself to weaken the German forces there as much as Schlieffen urged. As a corollary, he automatically weakened the main drive offensive to the north. Similarly, Joffre, while more and more convinced that the Germans might strike through Belgium, could not denude the main striking force facing Alsace and Lorraine to strengthen his forces on the Belgian border. The chief result of the prewar plans was not, as some have claimed, that they all were offensive schemes, but that they were in essence neither completely offensive nor completely defensive. All bets were hedged.

Therefore, French Plan XVII compromised by placing most available forces on the border of Alsace and Lorraine with orders to undertake a strong offensive into the lost provinces. The younger Moltke, aware of French strength in this region, had no choice but to substantially increase the forces intended to defend Alsace and Lorraine. The crucial area of concentration enclosed Verdun, Alsace, and Lorraine and that portion of the German Rhineland stretching from Frankfurt-on-Main south to Freiburg. Both sides placed great emphasis on this traditional region of conflict.

PLAYING OUT SCHLIEFFEN'S GAMBLE

In the west the first war plans to be translated into action were the German Schlieffen Plan and the French Plan XVII: neither worked as its creators had anticipated. Although the sheer logistics of the plan elaborated by Schlieffen was to prove almost impossible to cope with, the chief weakness of that plan was its reliance on inexperienced reserve troops under inadequate field commanders. The French used many reserves as well, and in common with the Germans they fought without taking cognizance of prewar training dictums that emphasized well-trained infantry. The Belgians were overcome by weight of German numbers more than anything else. Only the British showed the expertise expected of professional fighting troops, perhaps because they alone were a professional army.

Even while the French and German troops were massing at the staging points, there was evidence of approaching trouble. The German troops, moving in accordance with the Schlieffen Plan, did not even use rail transport inside Germany in some cases. Probably because that system was overloaded, a number of artillery trains and military engineers (pioneers) were rescheduled to go on the roads from Munich, for example, on horse or on foot. Contrary to some observers' impressions, the German army did not move with universal efficiency.

A noncommissioned officer of the Westphalian Scout Battalion wrote shortly after the beginning of August that on the evening of the fourth the Belgians threw grenades into their camp: "A fruitless panic broke out."[29] He spent the rest of the night trying without success to restore order. Shortly afterward, Erich Ludendorff emerged as a small-unit commander pro tempore when as a staff officer he attempted to find out why the forward troops had halted near Liège. The German troops began to bunch up in the streets and officers immediately went forward to get them moving. In so doing, a number were killed, including the brigade commander. Ludendorff, trying to rally the soldiers, later recollected: "We were immediately fired at, and men fell right and left."[30] Despite the fire, Ludendorff succeeded in sending an intrepid squad sufficiently forward to evict a strong Belgian machine-gun crew. Afterward, he had constantly to entreat other officers and men to follow him in an advance on the enemy occupying houses bordering the road. Concluding his account, Ludendorff stated significantly: "It was a long time before the situation was clear . . . we had successfully broken through the girdle of forts."[31]

The fortress of Namur was situated in the paths of both the Second and Third German armies and became highly important after the loss of Liège. Commenting on the Liège campaign, which was hard fought by the Belgians, as we have seen, French General Rouquerol would later state: "The experience of the first days of August did not permit the repetition of costly and brutal attacks when the strategic results had been insignificant."[32] This comment aptly summarizes the problems of the opening phase of the Schlieffen Plan. The main difficulty the Belgians had in defending both the networks of forts of Liège and Namur was the effective use of heavy artillery by the Germans. In this case the artillery contingent provided by prewar planning was rapidly supplemented by Austrian 305mm cannon to buttress the less numerous German 420mm pieces.[33] The capture of Liège took ten days and cost many German casualties; artillery knocked down the walls, but machine-gun and rifle fire by the defenders caused the casualties. Several lessons were learned by the combatants of both sides: modern fortifications could be reduced by modern heavy artillery, but their conquest was still a matter for the infantry. Frontal infantry attacks were common in those early days partly because commanders could not rely on inexperienced troops to execute more difficult maneuvers.

By 11 August, the French were advancing into Belgium in efforts to stop the German advance (in accordance with the revised Plan XVII). The marching order was similar to that of the Germans: closely packed infantry plodding down available roads. A French section leader, Lt. Jean Charbonneau, commented: "A column composed entirely of the division was formed . . . corps [sic] effected great detours in order to intercalate in places assigned in the column." Frequent stops were made to straighten out the confusion caused by the hopelessly mixed-up units. On 14 August, Charbonneau's regimental commander ordered a long march of twelve kilometers in order to safeguard the machine guns because "one learned that a regiment of French infantry had lost a quarter of its effectives in three minutes by the fire of German machine guns."[34] In common with German soldiers in their previous advance, the French infantrymen soon experienced fatigue and heat exhaustion: the August weather was hot. Frequent halts were necessary in succeeding days until agitated Belgians informed them of the presence of Germans three kilometers away. Their first contact with the enemy was the sound of fire and the fall of shrapnel when Charbonneau's section was assigned to an assault company: "The 2d company and the machine-gun section gained, as in an exercise . . . , in line of sections of four, the edge of the woods and engaged [the enemy]."[35] Doubtless the opening phase of any war is characterized by some confusion, but that of early August 1914 seems much worse than might be expected.

Those who fought and survived to record their impressions of the dusty and hot August days tended to be highly critical of the leadership of their forces. Pierre Bourget wrote of "The Dinant affair: where an entire regiment was engaged, without immediate support, without liaison between battalions and the artillery, without having the officers made *au courant* of the tactical situation."[36] Lieutenant Charbonneau recalled that food ran out and he had great difficulty in providing each soldier with a bit of bread and an egg. He was proud that his men were able to fight well despite their hunger: "a rude proof of the force, the endurance and the discipline of our soldiers."[37] Much later, Charbonneau would thoughtfully analyze this hectic month. Combat was not the sole difficulty the French army encountered in this war of movement: "Physical fatigue and the long marches executed frequently at night," caused loss of sleep, depressed the soldiers, and predisposed them to an attitude of fatalism and "as a consequence, the inclination to a great indulgence to allow things to happen" without doing anything.[38] The shock of combat between Germans and French and Belgians was recorded by many. Maurice Laurentin's brother was marching in his battalion on 19 August, when "a wave of shot hit maybe fifty men. The Prussians were at 300 meters. . . . They placed themselves in line, man alongside of man." Caught by surprise, the few French survivors in that unit tried to seek shelter, but other sections panicked and retreated.[39] Pétain later recalled that his troops, confronted by a similar volume of fire, instinctively hugged the ground. In these early recollections a grisly air of mystery was sometimes present: soldiers fell when shot by an enemy they could not even see. Attacks led by inexperienced commanders resulted in heavy casualties. Charles de Gaulle was with a unit that was ordered to charge at night with bayonets through an orchard, a fruitless exercise that resulted in many dead and wounded.[40] The sensitive Belgian military physician, Max Deauville, commented ironically that "nothing was more exciting than marching in bright sunlight under a cannonade." His medical team was trying to cycle down a road behind the advance units when it encountered the devastating force of artillery fire. Observing soldiers under the continued bombardment of Dixmude, Deauville thought they looked "like automatons with fixed eyes" on some unknown but dubious vista.[41] A curious phenomenon attracted his attention: a file of Belgian soldiers, impeccably uniformed and precisely spaced from one another, went forward to converge on a point where similar files could be seen to assemble. The soldiers wore képis with bright gold braid; their uniforms were blue. In the opening phase of World War I in the west, only the Germans and the English had clothed their troops in nondescript colors, making them difficult targets at a distance (field gray and khaki respectively). Great numbers of soldiers became casualties because of impractical uniforms and inadequate tactics in August 1914. Such seemingly disparate factors were parts of a greater, antiquated whole. Infantrymen advanced in the open in tight masses with no effort at concealment and no use of available cover. They carried rifles fitted with brightly shining bayonets. Opposing them would be an open firing line: the defenders would kneel in open country spaced a few feet apart, firing their rifles. That was the warfare common in 1870, and thousands would die because of it. The képis with the gold braid and the highly polished cuirasses of the mounted troops were reminders of decades of parade-ground drill and marching bands. Well-groomed horses moved impatiently under the brightly clothed riders as cavalry awaited the orders to advance in scouting expeditions. Horse-drawn field kitchens and other supply wagons gave the impression of pre–Industrial Revolution warfare. August 1914 was not the scene of war envisioned by avant-garde theorists and other professional soldiers; it was more often a scene of slow and poorly coordinated movements of half-trained reserve troops accompanied by horses and mules. The narrow roads of Belgium saw many dusty columns of soldiers, German and French, march during those hot days. After two weeks of campaign both sides were nearing exhaustion. Supplies could not keep up with the movements of troops. Soldiers went hungry and sleepless. Commanders on both sides issued contradictory orders in profusion. The armies of Germany and of France were fatigued even more by the end of August because of continued logistical problems.

Several images from eyewitness accounts illustrate the peculiarities of this month. Belgian villagers went to sleep confident that the war had passed them by but were awakened by shellfire and fled into the woods with a few clothes while their houses collapsed into rubble. Full of aggressive spirit, young Belgian soldiers attacked across a field in which German machine-gun nests were intelligently placed; only one lived long enough to reach the enemy lines. Early reports contain references to corpses falling on one another, intermingled with the wounded. A French night patrol "silently passed in Indian file."[42] A French junior officer commented that he distrusted the competence of some units because "they lunged in assault as if they were still in Morocco, and without knowing what was in front of them." But he had an even more provocative remark: regulations had encouraged rapid bounds by entire units "to the exclusion of any attempts at infiltration." The Germans, likewise inexperienced, seemed to be trying to use small-group infiltration in advances, supported by strong machine-gun batteries. The French offensive *à l'outrance* was a failure according to him and to his colleagues.[43] The destructiveness of artillery and machine-gun fire proved more serious after a month of warfare than anyone had thought it would be. By 1 September 1914, more perceptive officers in all armies were taking stock and coming up with some innovative ideas. Unfortunately, the shape of tactics was not immediately altered because the upper echelons had not yet become convinced of the desirability of change.

During the last few weeks of August, the French armies were pushed out of most of Belgium and suffered severe reverses in Alsace and Lorraine. The German First and Second armies had virtually destroyed the Belgian army and had forced the French Fifth Army under Lanrezac back alongside the newly landed British army at Mons. The tactical debut of the British would come presently, but the week from 23 August to 30 August was a great debacle for the French. No wonder the German High Command was elated and prematurely anticipated victory.[44] The German emperor was persuaded by his eastern front commanders on 25 August to transfer a sizable contingent from the famous Schlieffen right wing to Poland.

Participation of the British army in the war began on 12 August, when the first contingents were shipped across the channel. The plans for their dispatch had been formulated for some time under the guidance of Sir Henry Wilson. But Wilson had envisaged the shipment of only 100,000 men to a war where millions were already engaged. He had no choice because the size of the British Expeditionary Force had been politically determined as long before as 1911. Although some reservists accompanied this force they were definitely overshadowed by the vast majority of career soldiers. Many of these troops and their officers had seen action in India or elsewhere in the empire. The debarkation of these professionals was greeted by joyful crowds. Sir John French, the commanding general, wasted no time in trying to establish marching routes with the French commander in chief, Joffre. Much effort was expended in sending cavalry forward to search for the enemy. In the first few days of action the cavalry division of General Allenby saw no reason to abandon either saber or lance.[45] The anachronistic war continued. Nevertheless, the British first opposed the Germans in force at Mons, a grim industrial town surrounded by slag heaps. General Smith-Dorrien deployed his forces behind a canal in good defensive positions and inflicted great losses on the German attackers: one battalion of Germans lost twenty-five officers and over five hundred men. John Terraine remarked that the "British tactics, schooled by Boer marksmanship, proved distinctly superior to those of the continental armies." Infantry shooting, in his opinion, determined the outcome. Once again, incredulous soldiers noted that the advancing Germans were in "solid, square blocks, standing out sharply against the skyline . . . and you couldn't help hitting them."[46] But if Mons was an impressive demonstration of British infantry tactics, it was also characterized by the absence of the guiding leadership of either the British commander, French, or the German commander, von Kluck. Sir John French soon became convinced that one of his two corps commanders, Smith-Dorrien, was unreliable. Confusion in leadership, well documented and chronicled, led to the follow-up battle to Mons: Le Cateau. Once again subjected to overwhelming masses of German troops the British were forced to retreat. Smith-Dorrien supervised a masterly exit under heavy German artillery bombardments. The sheer mass of German artillery fire came as a rude shock to the British.[47] As August ended, the Belgian army was nearly destroyed, the French and British armies were retreating in great discouragement from Belgium, and the German armies seemed fated to accomplish the great capture of Fortress France envisaged by Schlieffen. Tactically, the month had revealed that mass infantry attacks in close order without any use of cover and without support from the artillery were suicidal and nonproductive. But the lesson was obscured because the sheer weight of numbers on the German side proved adequate to overwhelm the opposition in every case, regardless of good or bad tactics. The "butcher's bill" was heartbreaking on all sides. But the war remained one of movement, and offensive action supported by nearly limitless masses of infantrymen was productive. Who at that point could predict the forthcoming trench warfare stalemate?

HORSES, FOOTPOWER, AND FATIGUE

Liddell Hart claimed with some exaggeration that the First Battle of the Marne ruined the Schlieffen Plan and changed the course of history. Certainly it marked a dramatic turnabout in French fortunes, but the German Fourth and Fifth armies had already suffered a considerable number of casualties, been hampered by overextended supply lines, and encountered stiff resistance from both the French and English. The impetus of the Schlieffen drive was already on the wane at the conclusion of the French retreat on 5 September 1914. A crisis of communication afflicting the commander of the British Expeditionary Force, Sir John French, and his nearest French colleague, General Lanrezac, commander of the Fifth Army, had assisted the Germans up to this point. The preponderance of evidence seems to show that Lanrezac was exceedingly pessimistic and could not push an aggressive policy. On the other hand, Sir John French was in no position to launch unilaterally an overall attack on the greatly superior German forces facing him after the Battle of Le Cateau because of strict orders from Lord Kitchener. His position, however, was by no means strengthened by his own indecisiveness and inability to control his own corps commanders. A confused and equivocal Allied military leadership in Belgium almost insured that a retreat would be ordered before an apparently unstoppable German onslaught. Once the French and English had passed out of most of Belgium, however, it was apparent to the commanders of these forces that drastic action was imperative. Quite simply, if the English did not take a strong defensive stand northeast of Boulogne and Calais, they might be forced into the sea. If the French did not establish a strong defense in northern France they would lose Paris and might see several of their armies enveloped. In other words, the Germans had good reason to be optimistic that the end of the war, and a great victory, was imminent.[48]

The turnaround in Allied fortunes occurred when Joffre worked out a flanking attack with General Gallieni, commander of the garrison at Paris, and Sir John French. By quick action, involving the use of requisitioned automobiles including taxis, Gallieni sent all available troops against the right flank of the advancing Germans. Joffre's staff coordinated extensive railroad movements of troops as well. The BEF cooperated and Joffre convinced Foch and other commanders to hold fast in the center. Suddenly, the German Fifth Army came close to destruction and a precipitous retreat followed. Only when the Germans had retreated to Soissons were they able to stand fast. Subsequent attempts of one side to outflank the other led to the "race to the sea" in the latter part of September and during October. Failure of either to break through led to the entrenchments of November and the beginning of the war of position.[49] This bare recital indicates the chain of events by which the tactics of the war underwent rapid and fundamental change.

From the beginning of their involvement on 22 August, the British used aircraft to great advantage to detect the presence of German forces, because they quickly found cavalry to be ineffectual when it encountered German cavalry guarded by infantry units and machine guns.[50] Despite the surprise caused by aircraft in the opening phases of the war, all armies quickly began to take defensive measures against them. Troops awaiting battle were ordered by their officers to stand or sit in the shadow of trees to hide from enemy aerial observation. In Paris, the crowds were terror-stricken when several German planes dropped bombs in the first air raid. Causing no casualties, these munitions merely blew up the street in front of the two leading bordellos of the city. The first reaction of both military and civilians had been to hide from observation. After September 1914, military operations were conducted under the scrutiny of opposing air forces.[51]

The employment of cavalry in August and September 1914 was characterized by what seem now to be ridiculous anachronisms. Plumed and gorgeously uniformed troops rode many kilometers in fruitless search of the enemy. On 19 August the French Cavalry Corps engaged in full combat with German cavalry and their supporting infantry. Riding in conspicuous costumes with lances, they were easy targets for German riflemen and machine gunners. In contrast to the French, German cavalry held back behind a protective screen of infantry. Marcel Dupont described the initial euphoria: "The charge! That indescribable thing which is the reason for the existence of the trooper; this sublime act." This was soon succeeded by despair when his troop was decimated by hidden machine guns and rifles. The obsolescence of cavalry was underlined by the success of aerial observation in finding enemy positions quickly, even though the pilots and observers were working with primitive equipment and were inexperienced.[52]

Small-unit tactics had to be developed on the spot, under unprecedented conditions. A French company of infantry, for example, tried to find a way around a formidable group of German machine guns that were well placed to command the exit from a village. Soldiers stumbled through underbrush in an effort to flank the enemy and became lost just as many of them reached the limits of a neighboring wood. German machine-gun and rifle fire from that wood caused heavy casualties and the remainder hugged the ground. Only at night were they able to extricate themselves.[53] But the French unit commander had had the right instinct even though his attack failed.

Advancing with the expectation of final victory, the German forces continued to suffer heavy casualties whenever they encountered French troops who hugged the ground. "We saw the Germans deployed . . . in rifle lines as if in maneuver," according to one French observer. On another occasion a French machine-gun and rifle defense had "decimated without pity" the German lines, but the latter had re-formed to push forward again: "It was a massacre without parallel." On still another occasion, Marcel Dupont looked through a telescope to see an advancing line of gray-clad infantry only a hundred meters in front of him. The French were dug in using available shelter, and their officers had kept them from firing until the enemy was quite close. As a result, the Germans suffered heavy casualties.[54]

German accounts of French attacks or counterattacks reveal much the same results. A corporal of the X Corps passed through a field, noting that a considerable force of French had encountered German machine-gun fire shortly before: "Complete firing lines lay on one another, all dead." But a lieutenant of a guard regiment of foot saw little remarkable about a German advance across a field in which the infantry had to be marched in close order to keep a regular front. Another German account mentioned German infantry lying in firing lines awaiting an English attack at Le Cateau. Again, advances were made in bounds from one firing line to the next. German infantry was sent into attacks in close formation as late as the end of August, but some of them were trained to deploy quickly to seek cover. Machine-gun companies sent ahead of infantry suffered heavy casualties because they could be outflanked by the French if unsupported. On the other hand, German machine-gun companies were particularly effective in defending against an infantry attack. English artillery was damaging, too. The English employed trenches and protected artillery emplacements on at least one occasion, making identification of units and estimates of their strength difficult.[55]

When the French and English launched their coordinated counterattack on the Marne on 5 September, the Germans could not oppose it effectively. Some units had marched for three weeks since the fall of the Belgian fortress of Lüttich, averaging about 25 kilometers a day. Short on sleep, food, and probably ammunition, they began to pull back so that by 7 September, units were hopelessly mixed up as the retreat almost degenerated into a panic. At Acy-en-Multien, 6 September, the French had attacked at 5:00 A.M. from positions on heights. Covered by heavy artillery and machine-gun fire, this coordinated attack was successful. The Germans retreated, abandoning equipment as they fell back. At Boissy-Fresnoy, the Germans tried to send dense infantry formations across open fields under grenade and artillery fire from the French, but this old-fashioned counterattack failed. Anachronistically, an officer ordered a general bayonet charge against the French, without artillery or other support. As one diarist noted, the commander, rather than deliver an impassioned speech to the soldiers, should have told them: "Prepare yourselves to die." The retreat was a great defeat for the Germans. Only through effective staff work and the use of reserves were they able to assume a new line in the vicinity of Soissons-Rheims.[56]

From the French point of view, the German retreat was heartening. Marc Bloch noted that he would never forget 10 September 1914, until he became senile. His remembrances were "a disconnected series of images, in truth very vivid, but poorly coordinated" of advance under heavy artillery and machine-gun fire from both sides. The American correspondent Frederick Palmer motored up to the forward positions of the French advance only to be told that the Germans had established rifle and machine-gun positions in covered trenches that enabled them to use a comprehensive zone of fire: "There is no use of an attack in front. We'd be mowed down by machine guns." Palmer recalled that the siege warfare on the Aisne had begun at this instant.[57] The Battle of the Marne was over.

THE CHIMERA OF OPEN WARFARE

By the beginning of October 1914, the period of open warfare was drawing to a close. It had been characterized by heavy casualties, confusion in leadership at all command levels, inexperience of the participants, and overwhelming fatigue. When the opposing forces settled into trenches it was because they had begun to overcome the many weaknesses that characterized warfare at the outbreak of the war. Ironically, the increasing efficiency and competence of the conduct of operations by all ranks on both sides hastened the trench warfare stalemate. Open warfare in 1914 was equivalent to the preliminary sparring of boxers or the first grapplings of wrestlers: neither opponent knew his own prowess or his enemy's. Tactical mobility and fluidity in this period was the result of incompetence; tactical stalemate was the result of newly gained (and mutually offsetting) competence.

The panicky retreat of the French in the last days of August and of the Germans during the Battle of the Marne had resulted in the abandonment of ammunition and even cannon, a sure sign of loss of combat effectiveness. Reports filtered back to the German High Command of the French abandoning not only materiel and vehicles, but also their own wounded. Many rifles and knapsacks were found by the sides of roads. The colorful American journalist, Richard Harding Davis, noted: "The rout of the German army was marked by knapsacks, uniforms, and accoutrements scattered over the fields . . . worn-out horses, bodies of soldiers, abandoned automobiles." Diaries confiscated from enemy bodies and from prisoners confirmed that both French and German soldiers were demoralized by confrontation with heavy rifle and machine-gun fire as well as with artillery bombardments. The pursuers tried, of course, to harass the pursued continuously. During the French retreat, which continued through 4 September, losses west of the Moselle averaged between three hundred and four hundred per day. So precipitous were these two monumental retreats that each was a near rout.[58] It was the last time raw troops of either side would come so close to collapse, since the stabilization of the war would end this period of exhaustion and heavy casualties in fruitless open warfare.

The transfer of large amounts of territory, the taking of immense numbers of prisoners, guns, and other war materiel, and the inflicting of heavy casualties on the enemy would normally constitute a "victory." Certainly, the Germans tended to view their advance until 6 September in such a light. The French likewise considered the Battle of the Marne a great triumph. Paris was saved and the BEF was not forced into the sea; but these accomplishments sum up fairly well the benefits to the Allied side. But all of these advances and retreats were, in fact, mere jockeying for favorable positions. From 20 September on, the opponents found they simply could not continue open warfare because it was too expensive and did not bring about fundamental results.

Of the many critiques of the period of open warfare after it ended the most intelligent French one was that of Gen. Gabriel Rouquerol. He admitted that untried troops and junior officers made tactical errors, but accused the General Headquarters and the senior corps and army commanders of the most crucial mistakes. A certain mentality, engendered by the prewar doctrine of offense, permeated senior commanders and staffs. It was, Rouquerol claimed, responsible for the failure of the French to turn the German flanks during the so-called Battle of the Frontiers. This last struggle followed on the heels of the Battle of the Marne. French troops were heartened by the retreat of the Germans and fought well; they were not responsible for the eventual failure.[59]

Both senior and junior commanders suffered from excessive and naive belief in the offense at all costs, which was the more emotional than rational teaching of Col. François-Jules de Grandmaison before the war. General Estienne, the French tank promoter, supported the views of Rouquerol in an introduction to the latter's work in 1934. The French army failed to achieve success in 1914 because of three weaknesses: devotion to the senseless doctrine of the offensive, inability to see that the war was quickly becoming a siege, and inability to coordinate artillery effectively with other arms.[60]

Although many officers in the German army were deeply disappointed at the outcome of the Battle of the Marne, and some of them would express their criticisms in print later, there was no general soul-searching equivalent to that of the French or the English at the end of 1914. General von Kuhl, for example (chief of staff of the First Army in 1914), believed that "it was not the system which failed us, but the directing personages." By "system" he apparently meant the whole military organization. Nothing was wrong with tactics and with most strategic decisions, but much was wrong with the formulation of grand strategy at the top: the decisions of the emperor, or von Moltke, altered the Schlieffen Plan and made it less likely to succeed. Von Kuhl did admit that the Germans had committed many mistakes during the campaign. "We suffered continually from the defective liaison between General Headquarters and the commands of armies. The telephone sections were much too weak and were not sufficiently equipped with new apparatus."

In truth, lack of contact between higher headquarters and field commanders occurred on both sides during the period of open warfare. Crown Prince William believed that if either side had possessed a military commander with the genius of Napoleon or of Moltke the Elder, the Battle of the Marne would have been decided by such a substantial victory that the war would have ended. The official German military history is circumspect, indicating that the war settled down to a stalemate in territories outside Germany, at least preserving the Fatherland from damage. Max Schwarte believed that the German high command acted too late to try to coordinate the First and Second armies on 5 September, when French General Maunoury's army menaced General von Kluck's flank.[61] Tactical criticism of their own army seems not to have attracted the attention of German military experts at the end of the 1914 Marne and frontiers campaigns.

The chief and most unrealistic error committed by both sides was continuing to emphasize the corridor stretching from Verdun to the Rhine: the traditional route of access to Germany by a French army or to France by a German army. Because neither side could forget the history of this corridor, neither could really gamble profitably on an alternative. The natural conservatism of military planners was undoubtedly an additional inducement to concentrate on the best known cases of invasion rather than to speculate on unknown alternatives.

NOTES

1. See note 1 to chapter 1.
2. Joffre, *Memoirs*, 1:38.
3. Charles Harrington, *Plumer of Messines* (London, 1935), 286–305.
4. Norman Dixon, *On the Psychology of Military Incompetence* (London, 1979), 395. J. F. C. Fuller, *Generalship, Its Diseases and Their Cure* (London, 1933). C. S. Forester, *The General* (London, 1936).
5. Anthony H. Farrar-Hockley, *Goughie* (London, 1975), Frederick Maurice, *The Life of General Lord Rawlinson of Trent* (London, 1928), John Charteris, *Field Marshal Earl Haig* (London, 1929), Geoffrey Serle, *John Monash* (Melbourne, 1982), and Frank E. Vandiver, *Black Jack: The Life and Times of John J. Pershing* (College Station, Texas, 1977), are a few of many general biographies and autobiographies.
6. Travers, *Killing Ground*, 23.
7. Edward M. Spiers, *The Army and Society, 1815–1914* (London, 1980), 8.
8. Karl Demeter, *The German Officer Corps in Society and State, 1650–1945* (London, 1965), 28–29, for the Prussian officers. Porch, *March to the Marne*, 151–52, 165. Spiers, *Army and Society*, 8, for the British officers.
9. Maurice, *Rawlinson*, 25–26. Callwell, *Wilson*, 1:13.
10. After the war the chief critic of Joffre and of the *École* was Jean Perrifeu, who actually served on the staff during the war. See his *Plutarque a menti* (Paris, 1923), 35–46, which accuses Joffre and the *École* of following Bergsonian occultism. An anonymous reply, *Plutarque n'a pas menti* (Paris, n.d.), 93–103, defends those attacked. Colin, *Les transformations*.
11. Demeter, *German Officer Corps*, 54.
12. Daniel J. Hughes, *The King's Finest: A Social and Bureaucratic Profile of Prussia's General Officers, 1871–1914* (New York, 1987), 34, 39–45.
13. David B. Ralston, *The Army of the Republic* (Cambridge, Massachusetts, 1967), 311–15. Porch, *March to the Marne*, 151–54. Richard Challener, *The French Theory of the Nation in Arms* (New York, 1965), 65–70. William Serman, *Les officiers français dans la nation,*

1848–1914 (Paris, 1982), 169, shows that 45.5 percent of the wives of officers were from the middle class, 35 percent from the lower classes.

14. C. Wright Mills, *The Power Elite* (Oxford, 1952).

15. Gerhard Ritter, *The Schlieffen Plan* (London, 1958), 144.

16. Ritter, *Schlieffen Plan,* 59, 144, 146, 180.

17. S. R. Williamson, "Joffre Reshapes French Strategy, 1911–1913," in Paul M. Kennedy, ed., *The War Plans of the Great Powers* (London, 1979), 134.

18. Williamson, "Joffre," 135.

19. Williamson, "Joffre," 135–36.

20. Williamson, "Joffre," 143–45.

21. J. McDermott, "The Revolution in British Military Thinking from the Boer War to the Moroccan Crisis," in Kennedy, *War Plans,* 107–10.

22. Winston S. Churchill, *The World Crisis* (London, 1929), revised ed., 1:39–48. Callwell, *Wilson,* 1:181–85.

23. Callwell, *Wilson,* 1:101–5.

24. Joffre, *Memoirs,* 1:52–53.

25. Williamson, "Joffre," 147–48.

26. Jean Charbonneau, *La Bataille des Frontières et la Bataille de la Marne vues par un chef de section* (Paris, 1928), 48–49.

27. J. G. M. Rouquerol, *Le 3e Corps d'Armée de Charleroi à la Marne* (Paris, 1934), 120–21.

28. J. G. M. Rouquerol, *Charleroi,* 120–21.

29. Wolfgang Foerster, ed., *Wir Kämpfer im Weltkrieg* (Berlin, 1929), 3–4. This compendium includes many excerpts from letters and diaries of German soldiers. See Max Schwarte, *Der Grosse Krieg* (Leipzig, 1921), 108–9, 112–13. On postmobilization movements of the German Sixth Army (Bavarian), see Bayerisches Hauptstaatsarchiv (Bavarian State Archives), AOK, Bd. 30, Orders for 11 and 13 August. (Hereafter, BSA.)

30. Foerster, *Weltkrieg,* 7–10. Some of these soldiers remark on the presence of Ludendorff. Erich Ludendorff, *My War Memories 1914–1918* (London, 1919), 1:32–35.

31. Ludendorff, *Memories,* 1:32–35.

32. J. J. Rouquerol, *Charleroi, Août, 1914* (Paris, 1932), 92–93.

33. J. J. Rouquerol, *Charleroi, Août,* 92–93. German accounts of the Liège and Namur operations are Schwarte, *Krieg,* 1:108–10 (superficial), and Reichsarchiv, *Der Weltkrieg 1914 bis 1918* series, especially

vol. 1, *Die Grenzschlachten im Westen* (Berlin, 1925), 1:119–20. Generals Ludendorff and von Emmich were the first to be decorated by the emperor with the *pour le mérite* for their action in the war.

34. Charbonneau, *Frontières*, 16. Pierre Bourget, *Fantassins de 14 de Pétain au poilu* (Paris, 1964), 93, recounts another march: "The 8th Regiment marched in superb order, . . . preceded by combat patrols, in line of double columns, very open, guided by Colonel Doyen at the head, a switch in his hand."

35. Charbonneau, *Frontières*, 29.

36. Bourget, *Fantassins de 14,* 99.

37. Charbonneau, *Frontières*, 55–56.

38. Charbonneau, *Frontières*, 8–9.

39. Maurice Laurentin, *1914–1918, Carnets d'un Fantassin* (Paris, 1965), 29.

40. Bourget, *Fantassins de 14,* 124–25.

41. Max Deauville, *Jusqu'à l'Yser* (Paris, 1917), 108–9, 122.

42. Deauville, *Yser,* 112. Max Buteau, *Tenir* (Paris, 1918), 124.

43. Charbonneau, *Frontières*, 33–35.

44. Schwarte, *Krieg,* 1:112–14.

45. Anthony H. Farrar-Hockley, *Death of an Army* (London, 1967), does not adequately consider the early weeks of the BEF in France but is of some value for the period following the Battle of the Marne. Tim Carew, *The Vanished Army* (London, 1964), 66–76.

46. Walter Bloem, *The Advance from Mons* (London, 1930), as quoted in Robert B. Asprey, *The First Battle of the Marne* (Philadelphia, 1962), 56. John Terraine, *Mons: The Retreat to Victory* (London, 1960), 91. Terraine does not acknowledge sources.

47. Terraine, *Mons,* 139–56. Edward Spears, *Liaison 1914* (New York, 1968), 126–36, indicates the lack of communications and understanding between Lanrezac and French. French, at this time, thought the French Fifth Army would support his flank, but Lanrezac seemed to have no confidence in the British.

48. B. H. Liddell Hart, *The Real War, 1914–1918* (Toronto, 1930), 82–102, summarizes the battle (which he claims was not a battle). The great Allied retreat from Belgium is described in Asprey, *Marne,* 58–84 and Herman von Kuhl, *The Marne Campaign* (Fort Leavenworth, Kansas, 1936), 35–204 as well as in the official military histories.

49. Of great importance in illuminating the crisis in the Allied high commands occasioned by the retreat to the Marne is Spears, *Liaison 1914.* See also von Kuhl, *Marne Campaign,* 204ff, for a German point of view. Henry Contamine, *La victoire de la Marne* (Paris, 1970), 271, gives a modern appraisal.

50. James E. Edmunds, ed., *Military Operations, France and Belgium, 1914–1918* (London, 1920–1948), 1:47–54. J. G. M. Rouquerol, *Charleroi,* 27–29. J. J. Rouquerol, *Charleroi, Août,* 130–31.

51. Deauville, *Yser,* 7. Wythe Williams, *Dusk of Empire* (New York, 1937), 53–54. Neville Jones, *The Origins of Strategic Bombing* (London, 1973), discusses the start of the British theory and practice of bombing of civilian targets.

52. J. G. M. Rouquerol, *Charleroi,* 105–6. Marcel Dupont, *En campagne (1914–1915)* (Paris, 1921), 67–68, 72–73.

53. Charbonneau, *Frontières,* 47.

54. Marcel Carpentier, *Un cyrard au feu* (Paris, 1964), 35. Victor Boudon, *Mon Lieutenant Charles Peguy* (Paris, 1964), 1–89. Dupont, *Campagne,* 92–93.

55. Foerster, *Weltkrieg,* 36, 48, 49–50, 52–53, 57, 63.

56. Foerster, *Weltkrieg,* 66, 74, 77, 79, 86, 87–88.

57. Marc Bloch, *Souvenirs de guerre* (Paris, 1969), 14–15. Frederick Palmer, *My Year of the Great War* (Toronto, 1915), 63–64. Deauville, *Yser,* 50. Jacques Suffel, ed., *La guerre de 1914–1918* (Paris, 1968), 89–92.

58. Contamine, *Victoire,* 210. Richard Harding Davis, *With the Allies* (New York, 1915), 105–11. Charbonneau, *Frontières,* 53–54. Von Kuhl, *Marne Campaign,* 204, admits that both sides were in perilous retreats and that in the German advance to the Marne, the sudden appearance of a strong French force flanking the German right wing forced the retreat of the latter.

59. J. G. M. Rouquerol, *Charleroi,* 134–36.

60. Estienne was responsible for the development of tanks during the war. J. G. M. Rouquerol, *Charleroi,* viii–x.

61. Von Kuhl, *Marne Campaign,* 31, 282ff. The account of Crown Prince William appears in Anon., ed., *Les deux batailles de la Marne* (Paris, 1928), 55–57. Reichsarchiv, *Weltkrieg,* 4:651ff. Schwarte, *Krieg,* 1:259–60.

CHAPTER 3
L'AUDACE, TOUJOURS L'AUDACE

In the course of maneuvering for advantage against one another after the Battle of the Marne, the Allied and German armies suddenly found themselves locked in stalemate. After November 1914, both sides developed defensive systems which at first they considered to be semipermanent but later realized were almost immutable. Perhaps one combat veteran, Charles Carrington, summed up the beginning of trench warfare best:[1]

> Back in the heroic age of 1914, during the race to the sea, French and German infantry had confronted one another here and had dug themselves in where they happened to be at the end of a skirmish. The first front line followed the string of rifle-pits . . . which men had scrabbled for themselves with their entrenching tools, under fire. Step by step, as labour and expert assistance from the corps of engineers was available, this line of pits was joined into a continuous trench and covered by an apron fence of barbed wire.

THE STALEMATE

Curiously, the beginning of the trench system can be identified with considerable accuracy. One day the tactical situation was still fluid; the next day it was fixed.[2] Private Frank Richards, author of a particularly valuable memoir, mentioned that his unit relieved some French troops near Fromelles on the Belgian border. Two days later the unit retired through that village to dig in: "Little did we think when we were digging those trenches that we were digging our future homes." At first, "we dug those trenches simply for fighting; they were breast-high with the front parapet on ground level and in each bay we stood shoulder to shoulder."[3]

Rudolf Binding described the German reaction to this peculiar change at the end of October 1914: "Everything on the front is rooted to the same spot. . . . The war has got stuck into a gigantic siege on both sides."[4] In his diary, a German pioneer (engineer) soldier dates his awareness of the first trenches to 2 November 1914, when sappers of his unit worked in shifts all night to excavate trenches under enemy fire. All of that month was occupied with improving the trenches. Otto Olde noted in his diary that he was still in a natural ditch on 12 November after two days of fighting. The enemy had dug trenches only a hundred paces away, but the ground in between was littered with both German and English corpses as a result of fruitless assaults.[5]

The war correspondent Frederick Palmer noted that the German advance to and subsequent retreat from the Marne had left signs of open warfare: "One saw the hastily made shelter trenches of a skirmish line; and again, the emplacements of batteries. . . . Here, a rearguard made a determined action which would have had the character of a battle in other days; there, a rearguard was pinched as the French or the English got around it."[6] But eventually the quickly dug firing pits became permanent trenches and posed a new problem for military commanders of all ranks.

The French chose their positions carefully when they decided to end their retreat, and those positions were entrenchments. "Our first trench was the transformation of our last line of riflemen in the war of movement, halted before the German positions."[7] Since many such positions were unfavorable it would have made sense for the French to retreat a slight distance in some areas to positions of advantage. The obsession of the general staff (GHQ) with advance and with offensive action made any thought of retreat dangerous. Another difficulty arose because of mistakes made by junior officers due to their lack of professional training and experience. Although senior commanders had to intervene on rare occasions in the tactical leadership of units on the battlefield, the constant direction of such units necessarily rested on the junior officers.

GENERALS AT A LOSS

Quite early in the war the opposing high commands became aware of the stalemate when they read reports showing a sudden increase in casualties coupled with inconsequential gains of ground. Immediately, staff officers examined recent battles to explain the difficulties. At first they believed that changes in patterns of attack or adjustments in artillery support would suffice to improve the chances for victory. Only later in 1915 would the final horror become clear: there was no reasonable solution.

The Bureau, 3d French General Headquarters, determined on 22 October 1914 in one of the earliest prescriptions for military improvement, that a close liaison between infantry and artillery would decrease "murderous" infantry losses. Quick action, the bureau maintained, would produce victory because of the "incontestable mastery of our own artillery, and the irresistible force of our infantry." Constant communication provided by telephone or signals of various kinds, as well as aircraft observation, could register artillery targets and could relay location descriptions by signals to the ground.[8] Practical suggestions like these stemmed from the offensive preoccupations of Joffre who, on 30 November 1914, ordered that "where an offensive appears possible, our line must be advanced to within 150 yards of the enemy's position."[9] Strengthening artillery support for the infantry and thus carrying constant war to the enemy became objectives of the French army in 1915.

A glaring example of faulty operations was the use of artillery and machine guns in the first two months of the war. In disgust, the iconoclastic French general Rouquerol later described the failings of his own army: the high command blithely assured subordinate commanders that planned operations would be easy if they acted swiftly and with audacity. "Lower commanders, full of an ardor which they communicated to their troops, threw themselves in the direction of the enemy without any preliminary reconnaissance, without artillery support." Most serious was Rouquerol's allegation that artillery was frequently reduced to the role of spectator to suicidal infantry attacks.[10] He and other artillery specialists disagreed with the prewar decision to subordinate the artillery to the infantry. Commanders of artillery at the corps level had been preserved, but their authority was insignificant. Corps commanders often allocated artillery in small lots instead of permitting the corps artillery officer to determine effective utilization of the whole amount as part of an overall tactical plan. Rouquerol pointed out that artillery was finally recognized as important when the war of movement ended and siegecraft began: the artillery officer at army level was reestablished in order to direct the use of assets at that high level. A first step in effective use of artillery had occurred.

Rouquerol was impressed by an attack by the 6th Division on 6 September 1914, which was "a model of an offensive engagement by a division." Artillery was used in mass to effect a heavy bombardment, proving Pétain's contention that "artillery conquers, infantry occupies." Deployed in depth with two battalions out of twelve in the front line, the infantry was accompanied by two companies of sharpshooters. One scouting aircraft effectively signaled the positions of German emplacements, infantry assembly areas, and batteries. Finally, the infantry advanced with prudence. Colonel Estienne, the innovative divisional artillery commander, secured the approval of Pétain for this plan. Two French officers of great future importance, Pétain and Estienne (the father of French tanks) had already provided battlefield success by departing from prewar tactical precepts.[11]

At first, both the Germans and the French were confused about artillery. During the French retreat from Belgium, attacking German infantry units often fought without any artillery support because of the chaos of pursuit. However, the lessons were beginning to be learned: both infantry and artillery were more carefully husbanded in late September than before.[12] The onset of siege warfare became obvious when military units, similarly led and equipped with firepower, could not dislodge each other during the Marne campaign. All too often the artillery had not been used in close support of the infantry in August by either the French or the British.

Neither the French nor the Belgians showed great ability in deploying their artillery pieces in concealed positions. The war correspondent Wythe Williams reported seeing a battery of French 75s wheeled "into plain view, and without the slightest attempt at camouflage." At least Belgian artillery pieces were sometimes covered by hay and separated from one another. The French preoccupation with offensive combat insured a big "butcher's bill."

Foch became convinced at the end of 1914 that victory could not be obtained without greatly increasing artillery and machine guns and munitions for these weapons. He specified to Joffre that "war against fortified positions will more and more be our fate," and such war required "siege artillery" with plenty of ammunition. Besides artillery, siege warfare required military engineering to provide sapping and other specialized functions. Future assaults should be made on the weakest point of the enemy's lines: "A strong attack by our left to start; a strong attack by our right to finish" was his tactical recommendation. In common with Joffre, Foch was prepared to fight aggressively if a lot more artillery support was provided.[13]

The British Expeditionary Force did not react as quickly as the French General Headquarters to the evident tactical crisis of late 1914. Top-ranking officers nearly always remained preoccupied with the survival of the small British contingent during the Battle of Ypres. Sir John French, for example, claimed afterward that the BEF had to be considerably augmented in the supply of "heavy artillery, machine guns, trench artillery, and ammunition." The chances of future British success would most likely increase with the arrival of the Kitchener volunteers and war supplies.[14] French and the War Department probably realized the BEF was lucky to have survived the attack by a much larger military force in the closing days of 1914.[15]

Germans were as aware of the stalemate as the French, and senior commanders began to search for ways out. Falkenhayn noted, however, that the entire German line, east and west, was very thinly held and that no defensive positions in depth had yet been constructed by the end of 1914. Faced with a severe shortage of men and munitions, the German army had to be reorganized to fight a trench war. As a preliminary step, infantry divisions were reduced by one quarter in complement in the expectation that providing them with more artillery and machine guns would make them equivalent to the now numerically superior French units. So desperate was the material shortage, Falkenhayn maintained, that "the failure of one single ammunition train, the breaking of a rail or any other stupid accident, threatened to render whole sections of the front defenseless." He issued a directive on tactics for the new type of warfare in November. Strong trench defenses had to be built to enable a numerically inferior force to hold off the Allies. Each meter of ground would have to be contested by a camouflaged trench system at least two lines deep. Most troops would be concentrated in the first line, together with forward artillery observation posts. Protecting this major line of resistance were machine guns placed to make flank attacks on the enemy. The November directive of Falkenhayn set the tone for German tactical schemes for several years; it was strongly defensive in character and downplayed the possibility of successful attacks. A defensive posture was desirable in view of the inferiority in number of German troops on the western front.[16]

By the end of 1914 a debate raged in the German General Staff over allocating priorities to the eastern and western fronts. Many staff officers believed the opportunities for conducting an offensive were much greater against Russia than against the French and British. Unresolved, that question would surface periodically. In the meantime, Falkenhayn ordered the strengthening of the trench system in the west. Not until February would it be possible for the German General Staff to envision a western offensive, realizing that the Allied powers were also strengthening themselves with men and material.[17]

CHAMPAGNE TO FIRST YPRES

Joffre ordered a full-scale attack in Champagne on 20 December 1914; the size of this effort was noted by the German planners some months later. For this major assault, the first since the stalemate had developed, Joffre ordered 488 medium artillery pieces (75mm), and over 200 heavier artillery pieces to provide a heavy preliminary barrage. Two corps succeeded in taking some trenches before strong German resistance halted them. Degenerating quickly into a battle of attrition, this attack convinced the commander of the Fourth Army, General de Langle, that it was impossible to achieve success, "given the power and depth of the enemy organizations." German postbattle assessments of the Champagne offensive agreed with this conclusion, adding that the French infantry had "moved forward in dense formation, . . . without making use of the system of successive lines of attack."[18]

Nevertheless, the battle was continued by Joffre with attempts to probe other points on the German line. Concentrating on a narrow section of front, the French achieved a narrow breach that immediately became vulnerable to flank attacks. "Insufficient results in spite of anticipated sacrifices" made the French offensive a failure by the end of March. Joffre believed that success would be achieved "when our materiel had been sufficiently accumulated, and when we had perfected our methods of warfare."[19]

The Germans had to determine whether they would launch strong offensives on the eastern or on the western front first. Because Falkenhayn was interested in achieving a success on the western front, he was prepared to listen to subordinates like Gen. Wild von Hohenhorn, who urged an attack on the extreme right facing the Belgian and English fronts. General Krafft von Dellmensingen prepared a memorandum for the command staff of the Sixth Army dated 4 March 1915, advocating a similar attack on the British in the vicinity of Ypres, east of Hohenhorn's site.[20]

Unfortunately, the opportunity suggested by Hohenhorn in December no longer was as attractive in March because in the meantime the British army had doubled in size. Also, the command staff of the Sixth Army did not believe sufficient troops could be obtained quickly because so many units had been sent to the Russian front. Nevertheless, Dellmensingen thought that a two-pronged attack could be made in the vicinity of Arras. Such a battle plan would only succeed if all the heavy artillery available in the west was used. The unprecedented amount of munitions would require a month to collect.

Several other schemes of a similar nature were examined, first by the army staffs of the First and Sixth armies, then by the general staff and by Falkenhayn. General von Kuhl, a stategist of talent, warned that the point of attack on the enemy's line must be carefully chosen so there would be a good chance of causing either the destruction or the envelopment of a large part of the British force. If these desired aims were not achieved, at least the enemy should be prevented from finding another strong and fortified position by being subjected to continuous aggressive pressure. He obviously envisaged a return to open warfare. The Sixth Army field artillery commander suggested a half hour of rapid artillery fire just prior to an infantry attack. This could be supplemented by powerful searchlights to demoralize the enemy. The upshot of all the memoranda considered by the German high command up to the end of March was that limited supplies of ammunition, artillery, and reserves made a major attack dubious. Falkenhayn was not persuaded that the surprise use of poison gas would be important, but many other planners probably hoped it would provide the small margin that might be necessary to obtain a major victory. Preparations were finally complete for the German attack on Ypres in April, in which chlorine gas was used.[21]

Therefore, both the French and the German armies quickly realized that huge amounts of artillery and munitions would be needed to pulverize enemy entrenchments before a subsequent infantry attack could succeed. Ironically, staff studies in both armies by the spring of 1915 indicated that a scarcity of guns and shells made success problematic in any offensives.[22]

Two German postbattle analyses of Champagne stressed remedial actions to counter future formidable French attacks:[23] "Piercing of the line, a purely tactical operation" accomplished by the French, led the Germans to believe that they could do the same with greater success. But the exploitation of the gap—"the development and completion of the piercing of the line"—was far more difficult to manage because, exposed in the salient thus formed, the attacking force would be vulnerable. In essence, this memorandum of the German Third Army headquarters makes a distinction between the mere breaking of the line of the enemy and a subsequent exploitation of that break. The truth of trench warfare, of course, was that the first result was very frequently attained but the second almost never was.

With these observations in mind the German General Staff planned the forthcoming offensive against the British at Ypres. Projected as an attack on a twenty-kilometer front, its objective "should include the capture of the enemy's artillery positions" as a result of a "crushing blow." Each division's front, limited to a maximum of three kilometers, would be not only supported by the usual complement of field gun and howitzer batteries, but augmented by additional field artillery to defend its flanks. Following the artillery barrage the infantry advance would consist of successive waves "which will cross the trenches one after the other and thus give the enemy's front line no time to recover." Attempts of the enemy to bring up reserves would be stopped by artillery fire. German reserves would be thrown against the flanks during the assault to prevent counterattacks. Despite all of these plans, a pessimistic if realistic conclusion had to be faced: "In the most favorable circumstances there will come a moment when the force of the attack will be completely exhausted and the offensive will come to a standstill."[24]

By April 1915, both the French (see Figure 1) and the German general staffs had developed revised tactics designed to achieve a breakthrough in the enemy's defenses. Despite their expressed confidence, planners knew that success would require enormous supplies of ammunition for

FIGURE 1:   ESTABLISHMENT OF THE ATTACK, AFTER THE PLAN OF JOFFRE

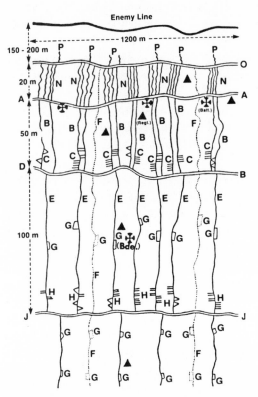

P - Advance trench defenses

O - Departure trenches, 1 meter wide

N - Supply trenches

A - 1st line trenches, 1 meter wide

B. - Communications trenches, 1 meter wide, two for each co.

C - Assembly points for 1st line trenches

D - Liaison trenches, 2 meters wide

E - Communications trenches, 2 meters wide, 1 for each co.

F - Evacuation trenches

G - Equipment storage

H - Assembly points for 2d line trenches

J - Liaison trenches, 2 meters wide

✠ - Command posts for batts., regts., bdes.

▲ - Artillery observation posts

Attack zone on German front:
(about 600 effectives)

The attack consisted of only 1 brigade with 18 companies, (3600 effectives), on a front of 1200 meters wide and 150 meters in depth.

1200 m

150 meters ——————————————————— 6 cos. on firing line:

200 meters — — — — — — — — — — — — 2400 effectives

300 meters ——————————————————— 6 cos. (2 regts.) of 1200 effect.

a greatly augmented artillery force. Many more infantry troops would also be needed. Hand grenades, mortars, and other weapons now needed for siege warfare had to be provided. In early 1915, all powers lacked these resources. The staff planners of the German Third Army stated in one of their memoranda of 15 April 1915 that "in this kind of warfare hand grenades are almost the only weapon which can be used" effectively aside from rifles and machine guns. "An attack over open ground, even for a very short distance (300 metres and less), can be rendered practically impossible by enfilade fire from a single gun or machine gun."[25] Successive waves permitted the first troops to hit the ground to provide rifle cover for the bound forward of the second wave; this tactic offered a slim hope of success for infantry attacks. Both French and German doctrine provided for wave attacks before 1914, but such a tactic was hard to teach to raw troops.

Unfortunately for the planners, the governments of these states were not willing to wait for future action: something had to be accomplished to justify an already huge expenditure of funds on military materiel and manpower. Joffre contemplated how to improve the tactical instructions elaborated in October 1914 because the French campaign in Champagne had not been successful. Sir John French and his subordinates were waiting for massive reinforcements before planning a great campaign. Falkenhayn agreed to the use of poison gas in the forthcoming Ypres offensive because he desperately needed an additional weight to be thrown onto the scales of battle.

THE TROOPS FRUSTRATED

Almost at once trench warfare became an arcane experience for combat troops which higher commanders and staff officers only vaguely comprehended. The longer the troops remained entrenched in virtually immovable positions, the greater was their tendency to convert what had been temporary into something permanent. The elaboration of a trench war society was the result.

This new society emerged because of three factors: the passage of time, the elaboration of trench defensive systems, and the fruitlessness of trench offensive systems. A German company commander described how he first encountered the stalemate by noting that the British had converted their line into a fortification marked by trenches and barbed wire. The Germans had no option except to dig in parallel trenches because all their successive attacks failed.[26] These trenches began as foxholes and were quickly deepened to slightly over six feet in depth. Niches were then carved in the sides to serve as storage caches for munitions and other supplies and to provide shelter from mortar fire. The first-line trench quickly became exceedingly dangerous from constant and direct attacks on it in the form of mortar and howitzer bombardment. Within a short time communications trenches were dug connecting the first line to several parallel lines farther back. By March 1915, a first line punctuated by machine-gun emplacements was connected to as many as six support trenches with the whole preceded by barbed wire. The total defensive system was over a mile deep. Major H. Pasborne of the British 55th Infantry Battalion described the process of trench system construction in mid-1915: At first troops dug narrow fire trenches about four feet deep; two men could do this in two hours. Such fire trenches, deepened and connected together, were supplemented every eight yards by dugouts, recesses, or communication trenches. Six men could hold 24 feet, a platoon 60 yards, a company 240 yards, and three companies of a battalion, 720 yards of the front. Occupying the first line a small number of troops would signal the rear support trenches with red flags in the event of an enemy attack after a bombardment. Already Pasborne, apparently a veteran of trench warfare, had developed successful improvisations to assist in defense construction: "I found it always more satisfactory to make men take their dimensions from their tools" so that the trench would be one pick length wide, for example.[27] Pasborne's ingenious and practical approach was typical of the thinking of the men who inhabited the trenches.

The first trench excavation was automatic and occurred because troops were under fire and needed shelter. Company officers inevitably had charge of preliminary digging and frequently chose sites wisely. When the decision was made by the BEF headquarters to withdraw and establish new lines a serious problem came to light. The old sites were determined by officers on the spot, but the new sites were determined by headquarters without consulting local commanders. One disgruntled British soldier remarked: "The Germans could look right down into it and see our every movement from the dominating Fromelles Ridge. . . . Higher Commands in these days didn't leave their offices to go and look at the ground over which they drew lines on maps."[28] Haig noticed, however, and corrected some of his positions facing the enemy on forward slopes and thus exposed to artillery fire. Local troops had simply dug in using lumber from nearby buildings but without regard to tactical needs. During the first phase of the positional warfare the quality of trench defensive systems differed widely depending upon the ingenuity of troops and of their commanders.[29]

But, again, the spirit of improvisation proved important. Infantry sent in dressed lines against an entrenched foe quickly sought cover as soon as a number of their comrades were hit. "At once the officers and noncommissioned officers began to form ad hoc assault groups" that tried to creep up to enemy trenches.[30] If higher commanders did not always understand the needs of the moment, the fighting troops usually did instinctively.

The society of the trench systems was one that had to transform itself from being essentially mobile and conventional to being essentially static and unorthodox. Within this newly created system the battalion and company officers reigned supreme, assisted by sergeants and corporals. In the Belgian and French systems a battalion commander, a major, was in charge of a sector with constant telephonic communication with the rear. Interpreting the front to the rear echelons and vice versa, he became, in the irreverent words of Max Deauville, the "big chief" of his sector of the front; the four company commanders under him were "little chiefs" who actually were integrated into the life of the trenches and relied on telephones to communicate with the major. The battalion became almost totally concerned with replacing sandbags, building roads and trenches, developing fields of fire for machine-gun emplacements, sending out patrols, protecting advanced guard posts, pushing carts with munitions and supplies, and a host of other maintenance jobs.

Soon, the troops had to huddle like rats to escape bombardment and mortar fire. When moving out on patrol they encountered barbed wire, shell holes, and corpses. Such grisly reminders of war were often found in the immediate vicinity of the rear support trenches, where roads had to be maintained in the face of often severe enemy harassing fire. Trying to find one's trench at dark upon return from either front or rear was often difficult. Since the dark afforded some protection, most excursions from the front trenches forward occurred at night. Movement of supplies from the rear soon took place at night also.[31] The trench society was a society of darkness and clandestine happenings.

Unfortunately, a strong disagreement between conventional and improvisatory military officers soon developed. Sir John French aroused the ire of his soldiers by insisting that church and saluting parades be reinstituted after a hiatus beginning with the outbreak of hostilities. As one officer said, it would have been more practical to use the time for machine-gun training: salute practice was a sure way to lose the war.[32] In both the French and British armies troops were required to "stand to" several times a day. This exercise required the soldier to stand up to view over the trench at stated intervals and caused many needless casualties before it was stopped later in 1915. A kind of macho madness captivated some soldiers who insisted on exposing themselves to fire on roads right behind the trenches: enemy snipers soon stopped that bravado. A French GHQ order tried to control such errors by prohibiting construction of trenches within two hundred yards of a road, but "to observe the order was to increase the risks from snipers and observers in the [enemy held] houses."[33] The excesses of traditional-minded military officers and men consisted of reckless exposure to fire and a concentration on peacetime rituals. Trench war ended such old-fashioned militaria and replaced it with an improvised military society.

New deployments of artillery and other types of units had to be planned quickly because of the unusual circumstances of trench warfare. Field artillery, for example, was brought much closer to the front so that massed firepower could be summoned to help the infantry, a practice considered heresy before 1914.[34] A strange mixture of expedients marked the first months of stalemate.

Charles Carrington summarized the education of the British Expeditionary Force when he remembered that the crammed firing line used in 1914, where "the infantry all in a row won the decisive battle with rifle fire," was succeeded by the defense-in-depth system, in which the first trench line was thinly held but supported at regular intervals by periodic well-sited posts "supporting one another with cross-fire." In theory, as most well-trained officers knew, and as the *Field Service Regulations* of 1914 preached, this defense would permit the collection of a large reserve force farther back to be called forward if the line were attacked or to support or carry out an assault. But many officers and men thought they had to man a firing line "where they could stand up, now and then, to fire five rounds rapid over the parapet where the enemy snipers picked them off from concealed positions."[35] Eventually, these more absurd holdovers from the departed era of open warfare were abandoned.

The trench society had a built-in tendency to adopt what Tony Ashworth called the "live and let live system." A British training manual issued at the end of 1915 denounced the propensity of troops to "lapse into a passive and lethargic attitude." Similar concerns were registered by both the French and German high commands.[36] A trench warfare veteran, Ian Hay, identified this phenomenon with accuracy:[37]

> During these brief hours there exists an informal truce, founded on the principle of live and let live. It would be an easy business to wipe out that working party, over there by the barbed wire, with a machine gun. It would be child's play to shell the road behind the enemy's trenches, crowded as it must be with ration-wagons and water-carts, into a blood-stained wilderness. But so long as each side confines itself to purely defensive and recuperative work, there is little or no interference.

Hay, publishing during the war, was inclined to paint a somewhat rosier picture than the reality, although such periods existed not only on most sections of the front at night, but also in quiet sectors during the day by mutual agreement of combatants on both sides. When a disciplined, competent unit relieved a poor one in a sector, it often found poor trench construction and maintenance because the officers of the previous unit either could not or would not emphasize those duties.

Slovenly maintenance was sometimes accompanied by fear that work parties would be shot even though experienced soldiers knew that the probability of being hit at night was much less than in the daytime. Prudence dictated that patrols be sent out, barbed wire laid, and trench repairs accomplished at night. The live-and-let-live system masked individual incompetence in other ways. Private Frank Richards, a veteran fighter, recounted that one recruit in his unit fired in the air rather than aiming. He was told by his comrades that they "would shoot him dead if he done it again." But such attention to the fear of comrades who endangered everyone by not putting their heads up over the parapet when they fired occurred only where the unit contained many experienced soldiers. The so-called territorial battalions of the British and many reserve units of the French and Germans often were led by superannuated officers and lacked the hard, disciplined cadres of veteran and competent junior officers, NCOs, and soldiers. As a consequence such units lapsed into a kind of perpetual slovenliness. Max Deauville stated that two types of soldiers lived in the trenches: those who panicked at the sound of artillery bombardment, imagining each shell had their number on it, and those who were not bothered by such bombardments. As a military surgeon he thought the skittish ones suffered "psychic" and "physical" symptoms of malaise.[38] Perhaps the trench adaptability of a unit was based on the percentage of unflappable soldiers it contained. But such soldiers depended upon leadership to force them out of a live-and-let-live system, especially if they were inexperienced.

Ernst Jünger wisely remarked: "The security of a position depends on the freshness of its defenders and their fighting spirit, not on the length of the communication trenches and the depth of the firing line."[39] Such a conclusion was most obvious to those in the trenches and least obvious to staff planners at division or higher levels who moved units like interchangeable pawns. At first regular relief of units from front-line duty was not practiced, but trench duty even in quiet sectors was dirty and debasing work, and military efficiency suffered if troops were not rotated regularly. The trench society was a temporary state of living, in which the inhabitants dreamed of relief and once having obtained it knew they would be exposed to the trenches all over again.

Once the decision was made to dig in and the first improvised trenches began to force the formation of a trench society, important tactical questions arose. If the trench system was improved would it provide both a better means of defense and a better means of offense? Improvements in trench construction occurred with some frequency during 1915. But as late as February 1916, Ernst Jünger recounted that the enemy had somehow obtained a good flanking position for its artillery and was raking a section of the German trenches, and that it was impossible to destroy that position by counterbattery fire. The answer was to increase the number of traverses and to heighten them so that the effects of artillery fire were minimized. These constant efforts to strengthen defensive structures also forced units to "sink deep shafts, construct dugouts and concrete posts."[40] In well-tended sectors of the front, concrete blockhouses and deep trenches lined with sandbags were also constructed. Artillery was then protected by placement in ditches.[41] Constant activity soon caused considerable daily casualties where effective local leadership prevailed. The more inactive the sector, the fewer the casualties to either side. Efficiency caused bloodletting.

HOLDING THE TRENCHES

By April 1915, trench systems were providing an effective defense against the most technologically advanced weaponry available. Conventional artillery could cause casualties but could not break defensive systems.

Illustrating the weakness of artillery was the use of shrapnel. Very effective in open warfare against lines of advancing infantry, it was virtually useless against men in trenches. In quantity, however, shrapnel could destroy barbed wire without pitting the ground. Even in the period of open warfare, troops had discovered they could often avoid shrapnel by hugging the ground and seeking shelter in ditches. Unfortunately, while the British army had some shrapnel shells in late 1914, it lacked high-explosive shells as well as the industry to produce enough of them.[42]

Although medium field artillery was of limited utility in trench warfare, all armies possessed plenty of it: the British had 18-pounders, the French 75mm guns, the Germans 77mm guns. Should they be massed close to the front just before an infantry attack? Colonel Samuel Bourguet, an innovative French artillery officer, suggested that such weapons had quickly proved powerless against the German heavy artillery batteries, which were too far back to hit. But placed very close to the French infantry the 75mm guns could and did protect the latter in both defense and offense. Private Richards claimed a bombardment by the Germans did little damage to the British lines because most of the shells fell short. Obviously, the farther removed the artillery was from the planned zone of fire, the more difficult it was to register range and ensure accuracy. In 1915, every effort was made by the combatants to produce high-explosive shells that could be used with more success against trenches than conventional shells. Called "whiz-bangs" by the British because of the characteristic sound they made, they were not effective unless they hit a section of the trenches directly. A frontal hit on the parapet would work only if that defense was inadequate.[43] A nostalgic general told Frederick Palmer that the 18-pounders had been hauled "behind galloping horses" and were "the guns which bring the gleam of affection into the eyes of men who think of pursuits and covering retreats, and the pitched-battle conditions." Medium artillery was of little account in trench warfare.[44]

Heavy artillery, especially heavy howitzers as used by the Germans, produced considerable damage to the defense, but those under fire could sometimes avoid trouble. Rudolf Binding suggested that protection against systematic shelling depended upon staying in place (in the frying pan) rather than going either forward or back (into the fire). Artillery fire, both heavy and light, tended to be predictable in 1915: batteries were infrequently moved and firing sometimes became a routine exercise. Jünger claimed English artillery shelling was so methodical one could sidestep it every time. The Germans had elaborated a rigid system of bombardment by April 1915. Fire would be in bursts: thirty minutes of artillery, twenty minutes of rifle, twenty minutes of artillery, five minutes of quiet, and twenty minutes of artillery. It was hoped that this "fire storm" in which both infantry and artillery participated would weaken the enemy sufficiently that an attack could succeed.[45] Despite the attempts of infantry to figure out when methodical artillery fire would cease, however, high-explosive shell fire from heavy artillery was deadly.

The big guns utterly destroyed trees, underbrush, shallow trenches and emplacements, barbed wire, and any soldiers caught within the field of their explosive impacts. By February 1915, the French discovered they could capture the first line of enemy trenches with infantry after a concerted artillery barrage on that line. But the Germans reacted quickly by bringing up field artillery to the front to give emergency assistance to the defending infantry: the French were thrown back.[46] When the heavier barrage of German howitzers hit the English trenches in November 1914, soldiers fled into the open or to the only fortified positions available: timber and packed earth trenches "constructed by British and French engineers in a connecting chain in rear at Haig's behest."[47] Upon conclusion of the barrage the defenders returned to their now almost-obliterated positions to meet the German infantry attack.

As both sides grew accustomed to artillery its sound was accepted as part of life. German artillery shells, called by the French *marmites,* "destroy the earth, where brilliant circles were furrowed, whistling in the trembling air,"[48] according to Cazin, a self-styled "humanist" at war. Exuding black smoke, these shells were called "Jack Johnsons" by the British in honor of the black prizefighter. They made constant trench repairs necessary and caused many casualties.[49] No one ever saw the guns that launched these projectiles since they fired from behind the lines and were hidden by protective emplacements. To those in the trenches, the heavy artillery shells of the Germans constituted a familiar risk. Because it was always present such a danger became routine and was accepted as an impersonal destructive force that either killed one or missed.

The BEF headquarters produced a position paper dated 2 October 1914, which was widely distributed. Entitled "Notes on Artillery in the Present War," it ordered artillery commanders to cover and camouflage their guns and to change their positions periodically, because the German artillery was "uncanny" in getting a range registration on British guns. Most significant, however, was the claim that "seventy percent of our casualties are said to be due to artillery fire."[50] Regardless of the amount of artillery used in an attack the end result was always the same: failure to achieve a breakthrough. This lesson was not always understood by commanders by April 1915, because many of them saw in heavy artillery, especially, the means to achieve success in the future.

Infantry attacks were conducted by all armies between October 1914 and April 1915 with as much artillery support as could be mustered. In some cases shortage of shells and heavy guns diminished the role of artillery.[51] Any barrages quickly alerted defenders, who realized that if they were of unusual ferocity an infantry assault would surely follow. A German infantry attack on one occasion was stopped at once because the British defenders were warned by the preliminary artillery bombardment to expect it and lined up with rifles on the parapets: "It was impossible to miss." Shelling with high explosives did not inflict many casualties on the defenders, who were well entrenched; and the latter, according to Private Richards, mauled the advancing German infantry. He claimed: "To good, trained, prewar soldiers who kept their nerve, ten men holding a trench could easily stop fifty who were trying to take it, advancing from a distance of four hundred yards."[52] German defenders, on the other hand, threw back French infantry after the latter had captured frontline trenches with heavy casualties on both sides. On another occasion German soldiers waited for the British infantry to advance into range and fired on them, causing a retreat that left 120 British dead. Even if the attackers reached the enemy lines and occupied part of them, it was necessary to repair and reorganize the trench defenses before the inevitable counterattack.

At first, the Germans lacked spades to perform this labor because their commanders believed the preliminary bombardment had destroyed the defenders and delayed any response from their support troops in the rear.[53] Defenders were actually relieved to see the advancing enemy because they "could take it out of the German infantry in payment for what the German guns were doing to them."[54] In the first hundred meters of infantry advance enormous casualties occurred, and officers and NCOs were disproportionately represented in those casualties.[55] The most grim truth about trench warfare was apparent: each foot of ground could only be conquered with great bloodshed and with negligible results.

Finally, defenders were subjected to mortar fire in conjunction with conventional artillery barrages and infantry assaults. Not until 1917 did the English or the French possess trench mortars equivalent to the German *Minenwerfer,* which was in general use by early 1915. With an extreme range of about two hundred yards, the light version of this mortar was well suited against frontline trenches. It fired a projectile about fifteen inches long and eight inches in diameter, which exploded after an interval of ten seconds upon landing on the trench or parapet. Thirty pounds of dynamite insured that the damage was considerable, and the *Minenwerfer* killed and wounded many. One reason for its success was the German practice of firing salvos: an attack on 27 June 1915 saw five *Minenwerfer* sections dispatch 1300 shells. Fortunately, these shells described a leisurely parabola and could be seen approaching by troops, allowing them a little time to flatten themselves on the bottom of the trench. Even hardened troops, however, feared the trench mortar and spent considerable time watching for the approach of their shells. British sentries used whistles to inform others of such a danger. Despite the primitive nature of French and English mortars German troops were just as fearful of them.[56] Jünger remembered that there was "something rending about them and treacherous, and something personally malignant."[57]

Trench mortars and rifle grenades were used more and more frequently by both sides in 1915 and were the most dangerous threats to troops in frontline trenches. Heavy howitzer shelling would come later, but it would be episodic and usually in conjunction with an infantry assault. Mortars and rifle grenades exacted a regular and routine toll of defenders but were not sufficient in themselves to bring about the expected breakthrough in trench warfare. They became tools regularly employed by one side against another in order to keep trench warfare from degenerating into a placid live-and-let-live system, which was anathema to both generals and their civilian ministerial superiors.

Machine-gun emplacements could be quickly set up in shell craters near the trenches by the defenders. Machine guns provided the greatest defense against an attack and efforts were made by the spring of 1915 to increase their number and to prepare emplacements for them. British practice was to keep them back of the front trench part of the time, then to place them individually along the front trench when firing was required. But the British were loath to construct permanent emplacements because their fire would immediately result in efforts by the enemy to identify their locations and shell them.

The French and Germans seem to have preferred strongly built emplacements. (See Figure 2.) Typically, the gun crews would seek shelter when the emplacement was under shelling, but would return as soon as the artillery stopped, just in time to mow down advancing enemy infantry. The Germans had already assigned six machine guns for each company, but the British had only two per battalion. A shortage of spare parts by early 1915 halved British machine-gun strength.[58] Nevertheless, all sides realized the machine gun and the rifle were the powerful defensive weapons of the day. Failure of artillery to destroy machine-gun emplacements was a perplexing problem by April 1915.

One clear lesson emerged from the erection of trench defensive systems: no mode of warfare yet gave any promise of providing a substantial breakthrough. Rudolf Binding complained in his diary at the end of October 1914 that each division had been assigned a sector it was forbidden to alter. "It has to be held without consideration for the character of the ground and the inner strength of our troops, and *is* held to the point of senselessness."[59] Another German combatant, Herbert Sulzbach, commented on the French offensive in Champagne: "It was also our first victory in defense against a force many times our superior in numbers."[60] Trenches were expensive to hold but were virtually impregnable.

OVER THE TOP

Trenches could be used, indeed had to be used, as points of departure for infantry attacks. In that role they were obviously far less useful than in the role of defense. Early in 1915, the 3d Bureau of the French

FIGURE 2: FRENCH TRENCH CONSTRUCTION

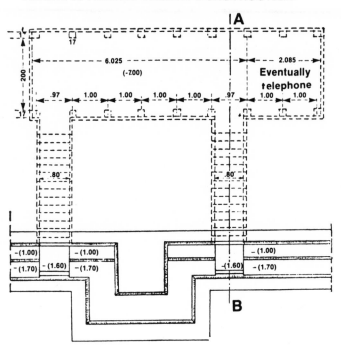

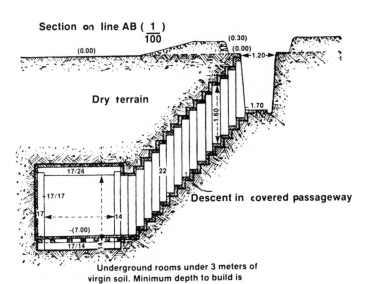

Section on line AB ($\frac{1}{100}$)

Dry terrain

Descent in covered passageway

Underground rooms under 3 meters of
virgin soil. Minimum depth to build is
6 meters.

General Headquarters in prescribing the proper mode of attack ordered careful reconnaissance of the terrain using maps and aerial photos as part of plans of attack. Assault trenches, it determined, had to be dug parallel with the enemy lines at a distance of two hundred meters. Telephone lines had to be laid in triplicate and supplies including sufficient water, food, and ammunition had to be collected. After a methodical and heavy artillery barrage the first wave of infantry followed to be reinforced by successive waves at fifty meters. The first enemy trenches would then be captured and the attack troops would have to consolidate for assaults on lines farther to the enemy rear. The German prescription for attack was similar except that troops were to advance in bounds and to seek cover between bounds. The French advanced in waves of walking riflemen. (See Figure 3.) Rifle fire by the French strove for volume, not for precision marksmanship, unlike the Germans'.[61] The British followed a similar procedure at Neuve-Chapelle on 10 March 1915, according to Charles Carrington. "Instead of advancing by 'fire and movement,' with infantrymen covering one another by rifle fire as they moved in alternate groups, the whole line advanced together, keeping as close as possible to the protective curtain of fire—the barrage."[62] In all cases, the increasing reliance upon the barrage provided by the artillery discouraged rifle fire while advancing. The sole purpose of the infantry advance was to occupy the enemy trenches vacated by shell fire. The distance to be traversed was so small, the degree of exposure of the advancing infantry so high, that it was important to get these troops across no-man's-land as soon as possible, taking advantage of the temporary demoralization of the enemy provided by the barrage.

Unfortunately, this mode of attack really meant that the attacker expected success if he possessed overwhelming artillery support and much greater numbers of infantry than the enemy. Neither condition was fulfilled, except momentarily, by April 1915. A British experience in 1915 was typical: the infantry attack was launched following an artillery barrage and achieved great results at first. Four divisions penetrated the first, second, and third trench lines and broke through to the rear. "Then—from their front and flanks, artillery and machine guns open fire upon them." They were left exposed, far in front of their own lines and without sufficient strength to carry on. With massive artillery support something

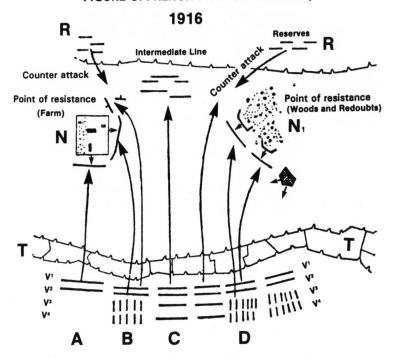

FIGURE 3: FRENCH ATTACK TACTICS,
1916

assault troops attacking in successive waves V^1, V^2, V^3, and V^4

might have been achieved, but shells were in short supply.[63] During 1915 some British officers thought it was possible to break through three lines of defense before great enemy resistance was encountered. More important, the severe infantry casualties suffered in such attacks created a morale crisis in some units of the French and German armies. After one attack was beaten back with heavy losses the remaining troops refused to leave their trenches. The only thing motivating many desperate infantrymen was the fear of being considered cowards if they refused to leave the assault trench when ordered.[64] Regardless of the morale or the skill of soldiers the deadly combination of hostile rifle and machine-gun fire was often too much to bear.

Beginning with his assignment as commanding general, 18th Division, Ivor Maxse took an interest in training troops for trench warfare. He would ultimately become the expert in that subject within the BEF. A typed memorandum dated April 1915, entitled "Cooperation between Artillery and Infantry," outlined the tactical coordination of these two arms. The normal order of battle in France called for grouping a gun brigade (Royal Field Artillery) with a brigade of infantry under the command of an infantry brigadier as Group CO. Artillery officers at that level and lower were to be consulted and to share inspection trips with the commanders. Therefore, the key tactical commander, the battalion commander, had to learn how to work with artillery observers. Maxse had worked on this scheme as early as 1911 and it had been incorporated in the *Infantry Regulations* of 1914.[65] Although similar ideas had developed in the other armies by the start of the war, they had not jelled by 1915. The practical application of a scheme of coordinated infantry-artillery attack entailed the development of aircraft reconnaissance and photography, joint planning of officers from both services, a reliable system of artillery registration using forward observers and aircraft, the supply of massive numbers of guns, and the preparation of a careful plan of attack. Most important, junior officers and soldiers had to be trained in the appropriate tactics. By June 1915, Sir John French was willing to tell the War Office that "however strong the enemy's defenses may be they can be captured if they are sufficiently bombarded and an adequate force of infantry is resolutely employed."[66] This was the same conclusion reached by supreme commanders of all the armies by mid-1915.

THE ROUTINE AGGRESSION SYNDROME

Although commanders enjoined their subordinates always to be prepared to resume open warfare it was obvious that the reality was the stalemate. Periodic attempts ("big pushes") were ordered to try to break the deadlock but the war soon became one of routine aggression. Such actions included frequent patrols, sentry and sniping assignments, wire-laying parties, and artillery spotting. All except the last required the penetration of no-man's-land by small parties. Almost all attempts had to be carried out during darkness. Frequent activity of these types was an indication of how busy the front was in a particular sector. In those sectors characterized by laissez-faire military leadership the level of activity was low; casualties were also low.

Patrolling was dangerous, although Binding facetiously called it a sport equivalent to that of training young dogs. Elsewhere, this German observer more accurately described it as guerrilla warfare where success was sometimes measured by the retrieval of enemy corpses. The intrepid correspondent Frederick Palmer accompanied a patrol and noted that advanced sentries lay in no-man's-land prepared to fire on any German patrol seen. But often rival patrols would try to avoid conflict. Private Richards discovered that the Germans sent out large patrols, which were spread out like a fan. It was dangerous for a smaller British patrol to be caught in the center. Three soldiers, including Richards, went on a patrol one night and found they were in the midst of such an enemy patrol: they moved back quietly and expeditiously.

One great danger was being shot at by friendly troops upon return, and Richards's company had a standing rule not to fire at anything or anyone until a patrol had returned. Failure to institute a similar rule nearly resulted in a disaster for Max Buteau and his French comrades; they had to recite the name of the company commander, the number of the company, and the name of the battalion commander before two trigger-happy sentinels would pass them through. Such patrols looked specifically for gaps in the wire laid by the enemy and tried to map out paths across. Patrol work was frequently routine and each side respected the movements of the other, but unexpected movements in the dark by members of rival patrols could and often did result in an exchange of gunfire.[67] Patrol activity was aggressive, but other forms of routine work were defensive in character.

After shelling, the elaborate systems of barbed wire were heavily damaged and parties had to be sent out to repair and improve them.[68] Sometimes soldiers would decide that a particular kind of wire was no good and pitch the roll in a shell hole. At first the Royal Engineers were ordered to lay such wire in front of the British lines but they used a single, easily breached strand of wire that aroused the immediate contempt of the infantry: "The Old Soldier of the platoon remarked that the British Government must be terribly hard up" to send "engineers up to the front line to stretch one single bloody strand of barbed wire out . . . which a bloody giraffe could rise up and walk under."[69] To experienced troops the state of the barbed wire in a new sector into which they were sent as relief gave a good indication of the quality of the troops preceding them. Private Richards recalled that his unit relieved a territorial battalion that had arrived in France in March and was in the trenches for three months thereafter. The trenches were in poor condition, "in some places being only breast high and the parapet and traverses were crumbling to pieces." Little barbed wire had been laid and stacks of wire and sandbags had not been used. These troops had not improved their trenches or wire protection because when they tried they were shot at at night. Richards expressed the disgust of the regular soldier: "If the Germans had made a raid on them they would have had a beanfest."[70] This case summarizes the routine aggression of trench warfare. Patrol work, wire laying, and trench improvement was done well by well-led, experienced troops and poorly by poorly led, inexperienced troops.

Most troops by early spring 1915 were veterans of several months of trench warfare, but relatively few were survivors of the open warfare of 1914. The quality of training and of leadership within battalions was not high in any army, with the exception of certain units. The influx of hundreds of thousands of raw troops during 1915 would cause enormous problems of training in a style of warfare that was still not well understood by military professionals.

Two basic types of theoretical tactical matrices developed after fall 1914: the most prevalent was siegecraft, which developed out of the trench warfare stalemate. But parallel with siegecraft was open warfare. The reality was siegecraft but the fantasy was still open warfare.

NOTES

1. Charles Carrington, *Soldier from the Wars Returning* (London, 1965), 89–90.

2. Foerster, *Weltkrieg,* 66, 74, 77, 79, 86, 87–88. Bloch, *Souvenirs de guerre,* 14–15.

3. Frank Richards, *Old Soldiers Never Die* (London, 1933), 34–35.

4. Rudolf Binding, *A Fatalist at War* (London, 1929), 20–21.

5. Excerpt printed in Foerster, *Weltkrieg,* 101–3. Rudolf Hoffmann ed., *Der deutsche Soldat Briefe aus dem Weltkrieg Vermächtnis* (Munich, 1937), 69–70.

6. Palmer, *My Year,* 53.

7. J. G. M. Rouquerol, *Charleroi,* 134–36.

8. Archives militaires de Vincennes, 16 N 1965 3e Bureau. (Hereafter, AMV.)

9. Joffre, *Memoirs,* 2:335.

10. J. J. Rouquerol, *Charleroi, Août,* 160–61.

11. J. G. M. Rouquerol, *Charleroi,* 27–29.

12. Williams, *Dusk of Empire,* 59–60. Deauville, *Yser,* 62–65. Bourget, *Fantassins de 14,* 173–76.

13. Ferdinand Foch, *Memoirs pour servir à l'histoire de la guerre* (Paris, 1931), 1:248–52.

14. Sir John French, *1914* (London, 1919), 301–2.

15. Edmonds, *Military Operations,* 1:4–12.

16. Von Falkenhayn, *The German General Staff and Its Decisions, 1914–1916* (New York, 1920), 45–48. BSA, AOK 6, Bd. 328.

17. Reichsarchiv, Der Weltkrieg series, *Die Operatione des Jahres 1915* (Berlin, 1931), 7:6–21.

18. L. Koeltz, *La Guerre de 1914–1918* (Paris, 1966), 208. German Third Army Headquarters, No. 3800 B. "Proposals for the Technical Methods to be adopted in an Attempt to break through a strongly fortified Position, based on the Knowledge acquired from the Errors which appear to have been committed by the French during the Winter Campaign in Champagne." Captured and translated with British army file: [C.D.S. 304], 14 April 1915. Robertson Papers, I/6/2. German Third Army Headquarters, addendum to above, "Experiences gained in the Winter Battle in Champagne from the Point of View of the Organization of the Enemy's Lines of Defence and the Means of Combatting an attempt to pierce our Line." Captured and translated with British army file: [C.D.S. 303], 14 April 1915. Robertson Papers, I/6/1.

19. Koeltz, *1914–1918,* 208–9. Joffre, *Memoirs,* 2:340–41.

20. Reichsarchiv, *Der Weltkrieg,* 7:307.

21. Reichsarchiv, *Der Weltkrieg,* 7:307–23. BSA, AOK 6, Bd. 328.

22. Koeltz, *1914–1918,* 208ff. BSA, AOK 6, Bd. 328.

23. Memorandum no. 3800 B, 2. Robertson Papers, I/6/2.

24. Memorandum no. 3800 B, 2–3. Robertson Papers, I/6/2.

25. Addendum to the Memorandum no. 3800 B, 5. Robertson Papers, I/6/2.

26. Farrar-Hockley, *Death,* 107–8.

27. "Lecture on Trenches," in Maxse Papers, 65/53/5. Military History Archives, King's College, University of London.

28. Anon., *The War the Infantry Knew, 1914–1918: A Chronicle of Service in France and Belgium with the 2d Battalion, His Majesty's 23d Foot, the Royal Welch Fusiliers* (London, 1938), 77–88.

29. Farrar-Hockley, *Death,* 131–32.

30. Farrar-Hockley, *Death,* 90.

31. Max Deauville, *La boue des Flandres* (Paris, 1922), 109–10. Paul Cazin, *L'Humaniste à la guerre* (Paris, 1920), 154. Buteau, *Tenir,* 165–66.

32. Richards, *Old Soldiers,* 27–29.

33. Richards, *Old Soldiers,* 58–59. Ernst Jünger, *The Storm of Steel* (London, 1929), 54–55. Anon., *The War the Infantry Knew,* 77–78.

34. Richards, *Old Soldiers,* 76–77, 92–93. Anon., *The War the Infantry Knew,* 103–4. Carrington, *Soldier Returning,* 83–84. Samuel Bourguet, *L'aube sanglante: de la Boiselle (Octobre 1914) à Tahure (Septembre 1915),* (Paris, 1917), 74–75.

35. Carrington, *Soldier Returning,* 89–91.

36. Tony Ashworth, *Trench Warfare, 1914–1918: The Live and Let Live System* (London, 1980), 43–44.

37. Ian Hay, *The First Hundred Thousand* (London, 1915), 247.

38. Richards, *Old Soldiers,* 37–38, 106–7. Deauville, *Flandres,* 104–5.

39. Jünger, *Storm,* 32.

40. Jünger, *Storm,* 41, 58–59.

41. Foerster, *Weltkrieg,* 104–6.

42. C. R. M. F. Cruttwell, 158–59. Hoffmann, ed., *Soldat,* 62–63. Farrar–Hockley, *A History of the Great War* (Oxford, 1936), *Death,* 126.

43. Bourguet, *L'aube,* 74–75, 129–30. Richards, *Old Soldiers,* 36–37. Jünger, *Storm,* 133.

44. Palmer, *My Year,* 272.

45. Binding, *Fatalist,* 90–91. Jünger, *Storm,* 133. BSA, AOK 6, Bd. 9.

46. Jünger, *Storm,* 20. Herbert Sulzbach, *With the German Guns* (Hamden, Connecticut, 1981), 50–51.

47. Farrar-Hockley, *Death,* 175.

48. Cazin, *L'Humaniste,* 187–88.

49. Cazin, *L'Humaniste,* 122–23. Farrar-Hockley, *Death,* 104. Palmer, *My Year,* 266, 358.

50. Maxse Papers, 65/53/5.

51. Anon., *The War the Infantry Knew,* 91.

52. Richards, *Old Soldiers,* 36–38.

53. Sulzbach, *German Guns,* 50–51. Hoffmann, *Soldat,* 66. Farrar-Hockley, *Death,* 107–8, 175.

54. Palmer, *My Year,* 358.

55. Cazin, *L'Humaniste,* 117–18.

56. Hay, *First Hundred,* 259. Richards, *Old Soldiers,* 110–13. BSA, AOK 6, Bd. 9.

57. Jünger, *Storm,* 40.

58. Hay, *First Hundred,* 278–80. Richards, *Old Soldiers,* 138–39. Cruttwell, *Great War,* 158–59. Jünger, *Storm,* 35. Farrar-Hockley, *Death,* 94. Hermann Cron, *Geschichte des Deutschen Heeres im Weltkrieg, 1914–1918* (Berlin, 1937), 134. Cazin, *L'Humaniste,* 117–18.

59. Binding, *Fatalist,* 20.

60. Sulzbach, *German Guns,* 53–54.

61. AMV, 3e Bureau, "Organisation defensive de 1e et 2e lignes 1915," 16 N 1966. William Balck, *Entwicklung der Taktik im Weltkrieg* (Berlin, 1922), 56–59.

62. Carrington, *Soldier Returning,* 60–61.

63. Hay, *First Hundred,* 236–37, 315–17.

64. Binding, *Fatalist,* 66–67. Cazin, *L'Humaniste,* 222. Jünger, *Storm,* 21. Farrar-Hockley, *Death,* 101–2.

65. Maxse Papers, 65/53/5.

66. Robertson Papers, I/5. A letter dated 23 June 1915 included in the papers of Sir William Robertson, quartermaster general of the BEF at that time.

67. Binding, *Fatalist,* 87, 90–91. Palmer, *My Year,* 306. Richards, *Old Soldiers,* 75. Buteau, *Tenir,* 160–61.

68. Hay, *First Hundred,* 245.

69. Richards, *Old Soldiers,* 44–45.

70. Richards, *Old Soldiers,* 106–7.

CHAPTER 4
ARTILLERY CONQUERS, INFANTRY OCCUPIES: 1915–16

A veteran British officer, James L. Jack, noted on the eve of the Somme offensive in 1916: "Yesterday our intense, ceaseless artillery bombardment of the German positions by pieces of all calibers commenced to pave the way for the approaching assault." The pattern of the preparatory bombardment, developed in 1915 and perfected in 1916, was set. Jack reported that "the air reverberates to the drum of our cannonade, the shells from which we hope are blasting the enemy and his positions into powder." Yet Jack had to admit in the same diary entry, that Germans waiting thirty to forty feet below ground in dugouts survived this massive bombardment.[1] No one else had misgivings; massive artillery bombardments seemed to offer a way out of the trench warfare stalemate.

By the middle of 1915 a crisis in supply had arisen on the western front. Quite simply the consumption of shells and cannon was much greater than either side had anticipated: shortages developed. "Wully" Robertson, newly appointed chief of the BEF General Staff, commented later: "We were still weak in men, practically without heavy artillery, and woefully short of artillery ammunition of all kinds."[2] Unfortunately, the English especially had so few shells that only one round per piece was permitted unless an emergency developed. One disgruntled officer stated: "After the infantry had chafed long at having to endure a strafing without any protection from its guns, permission was given to ask for retaliation."[3] Some months later, by the end of 1915, shell production had been increased substantially, permitting development of a tactic calling for overwhelming barrages of artillery fire. Artillery was to be the bludgeon that would crush the enemy, so the infantry could occupy the foe's ruined and decimated trench system. Once a breakthrough was achieved open warfare might resume and the war would become one of mobility.

Georg Bruchmüller, the most renowned artillery specialist in the German army, recalling this time believed there was confusion in 1915 about the role of field and heavy artillery. Although the latter was associated specifically with traditional siegecraft, it could be readily adapted to trench warfare. Field artillery, on the other hand, had to perform a new role because it was designed for open warfare.[4] Therefore, the mere increase in shell production was no answer. Tacticians had to adapt their artillery to the trench warfare stalemate.

GAS WARFARE IN 1915

Just before the introduction of gas warfare the respective commanders in chief discovered basic flaws in the employment of artillery. The French discovered that a massive bombardment on a very narrow sector did not destroy the emplacements of enemy cannon and machine guns: a follow-up infantry attack was repulsed with heavy losses. At first the artillery was slow to respond to an enemy bombardment and subsequent infantry attack, but battery commanders learned quickly.[5] In the midst of this uncertainty, the first weapon of desperation was employed: gas warfare. It did not deliver all its proponents desired, but did provide a new and grim addition to the arsenal of the artillery. Gas warfare using chlorine gas on a wide scale was initiated by the Germans in April 1915, although both the French and British had also experimented with irritating agents. In January 1915, the front held by XV Corps was chosen for a trial. Anticipating success, the corps commander requested but was unable to get large quantities of ammunition in order to "exploit and consolidate any success that might be gained at the trial."[6] The German army introduced poison gas because along with the mortar and other more orthodox weapons it seemed to offer promise.[7] Research quickly provided mechanisms for storage and release of chlorine gas.

At Ypres in April 1915, the Germans unleashed chlorine gas against two French divisions, causing panic-stricken soldiers to retreat and exposing the British flank. Twenty-five operators released 380 cans on a total front of eight hundred meters. A favorable meteorological report indicated the gas would be blown toward the enemy. Fortunately, the British quickly reinforced this dangerous spot. Absence of follow-up plans by the Germans and their own reluctance to advance into the gas clouds ended the threat. Exultantly, the German report speculated: "This new means of fighting could revolutionize the theater of war in both the East and West, if the enemy does not find a corrective means to it."[8]

Ushering in fruitless combat over the Ypres salient, gas attacks soon became part of trench warfare. A ferocious battle ensued, characterized by Cyril Falls as "one of the most murderous battles of the war." Plumer, new commander of the British Second Army, began this attack on 26 April, preceded by forty minutes of artillery barrage and five minutes of rapid fire from the trenches. Plumer recalled that "our casualties have been very heavy." The 100,000 casualties had been caused mostly by artillery and other conventional means not by gas: the British withstood a strong dose of the latter.[9]

A parallel French effort met with the same unhappy results. The German use of poison gas did not provide a quick key to victory in the face of costly Allied counterattacks.

Not delaying development of poisonous gas, the British were ready to use it at Loos later in 1915. Extensive preparations included digging assembly trenches behind the support line in which ladders were placed. Finally, large gas cylinders labeled "accessory" were hauled to the frontline trench. Briefings of the assault troops included a prediction that the gas would eliminate all German resistance, enabling the leading battalions to "just walk over." Primitive gas masks were issued and everyone except some cynical veteran soldiers went to rest for the night in the midst of euphoria. Launched in the midst of some panic, the attack encountered heavy losses. The gas had been carried by the wind halfway across but at that point was blown back. Troops poised for advance were demoralized by the gas and by accompanying German shelling. The attack failed.[10]

Although added to the arsenal of weapons, gas did not yet greatly influence the conduct of warfare: it was soon accepted as yet another tool of trench warfare.

THOUGHTS ON FIREPOWER: END OF 1915

During the course of 1915, artillery emerged as the foremost arm of warfare. Its evolution occurred in stages. At first, artillery fire tended to be predictable: batteries were infrequently moved and firing sometimes became a routine exercise. Most significant, however, was the British admission that "seventy percent of our casualties are said to be due to artillery fire."[11] So, efficient or not, all the belligerents determined to increase greatly the number of their artillery pieces and the frequency of firing.

The next step was the development of artillery deployment schemes. The BEF position paper of 2 October 1914 ordered artillery commanders to cover and camouflage their guns and to change their positions periodically, because the German artillery was "uncanny" in getting a range registration on guns. Although other armies toyed with similar ideas before the start of the war, they had not been implemented by 1915.[12] Maxse led in the next phase of artillery development: its coordination with infantry.

In 1915, major efforts were expended by both sides to bring an end to the trench warfare stalemate on the western front. All these efforts proved ineffectual. A prevalent attitude of soldiers was expressed in early October 1915: "Loos is not vital, our defeat there is only waste. . . . Gas was the only weapon that gave us a chance. . . . What a plan! And the artillery had a programme that did not fit the infantry movements." Limited success occurred, but "the troops were too few, some were ill chosen and not on the ground when needed"; failure resulted.[13] Such a comment expressed succinctly the dilemma of late 1915. Everyone recognized that massive artillery firepower was needed to support the infantry for an attack that would be wider in scope than the earlier French attempt at Champagne. More artillery, more shells, greater coordination of artillery and infantry, and more careful preparation in general were needed.

From the German side came an appreciation of the technical excellence of British infantry advances in 1915. Walter Bloem and other officers had watched such a movement in admiration from a hill until shelling warned them of exposure. The British Rifle Brigade participated in this particular action and its historian claimed that "had the whole of the British advanced troops acted with the initiative and promptitude of the 11th Brigade, and established themselves swiftly on the high ground beyond the Aisne whilst the enemy was still fatigued and disheartened, the German line would probably have become untenable, and the Chemin des Dames would have fallen in the subsequent attack."[14] But the frustrating truth of 1915 was that such troops were too few, too poorly coordinated with the actions of other arms, especially artillery, and suffered a dearth of ammunition at times. But lessons were being learned.

Foch, writing on 24 January 1916, summed up the dimensions of a broad problem by reflecting on the necessary conditions for a general offensive in the future. A breakthrough limited to thirty or forty kilometers did not give important results, and one had to hit the entire line and "search out at the same time the decisive point to achieve rupture of an important part of the enemy front [100 to 200 kilometers]." Foch enunciated the French doctrine that the infantry was to be used only to occupy and preserve terrain that would be conquered by artillery. "Battle consists of a repetition of operations in which, first, one attacks a position with all the necessary artillery, then one throws enough infantry forward to take that position while the artillery progresses to the following position."

Foch thought that some sixty divisions would be needed to achieve a break 120 kilometers wide, following barrages by 480 pieces of 155mm and 1700 cannon of 75mm. Emphasis was to be placed on the use of heavy, short-range pieces and "trench artillery [mortars]."[15] Foch was one of the first to recognize the need for an enormous quantity of artillery pieces in the offensive. As father of the offensive doctrine in France before the war he succeeded in enunciating the doctrine of artillery bludgeoning.

The results of the French offensives of 1915 were meager but the amount of heavy artillery was staggering:[16]

Table I

Place & Battle	Guns	Preparation	Duration	Width	Gain
Champagne I	100 heavy	some hours	31 days	8 km	2–3 km
Artois I	400 heavy	4 hours	40 days	15 km	4 km
Champagne II	2950 mixed	4 days	12 days	35 km	4 km
Artois II	1960 mixed	4–6 days	17 days	40 km	2–3 km

Some 1500 heavy pieces were used in Champagne II and 660 in Artois II: field artillery of the common 75mm variety supplemented the heavy pieces in the later barrages, with batteries very close to the front line. The results scarcely seem to have justified the effort, especially if casualties are considered.

Symptomatic of Allied thinking was the year-end evaluation of results submitted to the Canadian Corps commander in December 1915. A staff observer commented on the French campaign in Champagne of September: "This great bombardment, extending over many days and requiring vast quantities of ammunition, which entail great labour in transport, apparently seldom enables the attacking troops to overcome, without heavy loss, the enemy works, while it undoubtedly warns the enemy and gives him time to make dispositions to meet the attack."[17]

"Our advance should, in fact, be made in bounds corresponding to the wire-cutting powers of our artillery,"[18] the Canadian commentator continued. Machine-gun emplacements could be destroyed as well. But the French found that heavy artillery had not succeeded in destroying the German emplacements. French and British experience indicated, however, that concentrated field artillery placed close to the front could eliminate German machine guns. "Wherever conditions permit, therefore, the French 75 or the British 18-pr. placed in the frontline trenches, will not only make short work of the hostile wire entanglements, but also of strong points in the front line." Those enemy emplacements behind the lines in support roles would be attacked with similar light artillery which had to be manhandled close enough to do the job. The Canadian 1st Division staff officer completely dismissed the importance of heavy artillery.[19]

Less radical was another Canadian officer's recommendation, which advocated attacks launched with "a more intense and heavier artillery bombardment," the use of larger numbers of infantry, and "more perfect staff arrangements." But he anticipated that the Germans would retaliate with better emplacements and counterbattery work. One difficulty was obvious: one's own troops were usually weakened by heavy casualties and exhausted after a limited attack on the enemy and could not be expected to push on indefinitely. The artillery could only function well close up to the enemy in direct support of "the advances," which "must be short, the objective of each bound being to gain positions from which the artillery can thoroughly bombard." The attack should not be preceded by a barrage, but must be accompanied by it. Grimly, the brigade commander indicated that "we have more troops than the Germans,"[20] and that continued short bounds of infantry supported by artillery close at hand would eventually result in success. If concentrated artillery could not do the job alone, massive infantry assaults in conjunction with it could. The way was opened for the theory of attrition.

The commanding general, Canadian Corps, stated succinctly the major conclusion of 1915: "The extra power conferred on the defence by the most modern weapons and the tax on the resources of the attacker, both in personnel and material, combine to place a distinct limit . . . a point is reached when the effect of the artillery bombardment and the endurance of the troops has spent itself, and it is at this moment that the enemy seizes his opportunity of counterattacking."[21]

This order of 7 October 1915 cautioned subordinate commanders not to place their faith either in a short "hurricane" or in a protracted bombardment. If the objective is limited then a massive bombardment along a wide stretch of front may deceive the enemy as to the precise point of the planned attack. But if the artillery is so dispersed it cannot give adequate support to the attack, it will be of little effect. Sir John French established this interpretation for the BEF on 15 October 1915,[22] and also emphasized the importance of staff work to prevent congestion of troops prior to an attack, training of platoons in the use of grenades, instruction in using gas masks, and better air-artillery liaison.[23] Unfortunately for French, the failure of the Loos campaign would shortly result in his replacement by Haig; French's prescription for victory was insufficient.

By early 1916, the Allies had elaborated a theory of artillery that emphasized the importance of its heavy concentration in offensives. Superior artillery firepower coupled with greater numbers of infantrymen gave rise to hope.

VERDUN: FALKENHAYN'S HOPE

On the German side a complete reassessment of the tactical requirements of war on the western front did not occur until the end of the year. In April 1915, a critical study had been made of the French campaigns in Champagne that resulted in directives to commanders to increase artillery support, broaden attack fronts, destroy the enemy artillery, and achieve the element of surprise. "A plan of attack must be very carefully prepared a long time beforehand."[24] Preoccupation with the Russian front had prevented further assessments until December. The Germans and Austrians pursued a policy of ruthless destruction of Russian resistance in 1915. They also became more and more embroiled in the Balkans as a result of the Allied landings in Salonika and the Dardanelles campaign. But by the end of the year Falkenhayn believed that the focus of war had to shift to the western front. Perhaps he was influenced by the thinking of Schlieffen. The latter had written that in a two-front war, one enemy must be decisively defeated first before the other could be eliminated. Unless an order of priorities was established, the shift of German striking power back and forth between the fronts would ultimately result in the diminution of that power.[25]

Quite frankly, Falkenhayn did not envisage a massive break through the French defenses, but hoped to maul the French army by forcing it to defend Verdun and Belfort with all its resources. Failing to achieve that aim, the French army would suffer such a severe defeat that the government might be forced to sue for peace. With French capitulation, Falkenhayn assumed the English would also quit.[26]

Pétain, writing sometime later, indicated that the French army in garrison in the region of Verdun did not learn of the concentration of enormous quantities of artillery by the Germans, and the subsequent attack came as a complete surprise. The French forces under Herr had already been deployed in depth according to the instructions of the Central Army Group commander, de Langle de Cary. That general was reconciled to see his first lines "smashed by artillery fire in case of attack," but cautioned that "we must not hasten to send up our forces . . . but keep men in reserve for the defense of our other positions."[27] Pétain agreed that this proposal was far superior to the usual determination of commanders at that time not to yield a single inch of ground. But he was otherwise critical of French defensive preparations: the fortresses had not been kept in repair and a well-thought-out defensive scheme had not been set up. The opening phases of the battle, from 21 February on, were disastrous because small units, such as the battalions of chasseurs under Lieutenant Colonel Driant, were isolated and destroyed while the major fort, Douaumont, fell almost accidentally without a fight. Pétain was summoned afterwards to take charge of the defense at the end of February 1916.[28]

The artillery preparation of the Germans had been far greater than on any previous occasion. Some 850 pieces, including 542 howitzers and mortars, were directed against the French positions. Commencing at 8:00 A.M., the bombardment continued until 5:00 P.M. when the first German units began to probe remaining French resistance. Aiming to take enemy positions after the bombardment, specially trained attack infantry (*Stosstruppen*) attempted to get rid of blockhouses and machine-gun nests. Riflemen worked with grenade throwers in this task. The infantry was interspersed in waves between groups of these elite soldiers and was enjoined to use its rifles to supplement their work: "All weapons have to work together." Succeeding days saw the crumbling of French resistance on the second line and the loss of Fort Douaumont. The attack was proving exceedingly costly in French lives but was beginning to take a toll of Germans as well. Joffre agreed to the transfer of numbers of troops to defend Verdun.[29]

From the point of view of the French soldiers in defense, the aim of the Germans was clear: "to exterminate all of us and to occupy our position." To them the attack seemed very methodical because the artillery bombardment of two days' duration was monitored by aircraft that appeared each hour. The reports of such observers were followed by a changed pattern of artillery fire. At the end of this preliminary bombardment "the line of riflemen was so thin, so irregular, the trenches were so reduced, that our principal advantage consisted of the enemy's ignorance of our exact emplacements." The German solution was to try to obliterate the entire French defensive system.[30]

The defenders kept records of the number of shells fired at their fortifications. In a single day, Fort Tavannes suffered fifteen thousand shells while Fort Souville received thirty-eight thousand over two days.[31] Despite the ferocity of this bombardment the French were able gradually to build tunnels and deep trenches. One famous tunnel led to Fort Tavannes from the west side of Verdun and formed the "only entrance for the reserves, for the wounded, for the munitions, and for food." It was especially attacked between February and April 1916.[32]

These concentrated and devastating artillery barrages provoked the French into imitation, illustrating a well-known law of physics: Every action provokes an equal reaction. A directive specified: "The artillery must give the impression to the infantry that it supports it and it must prove to the enemy that it is not dominated." Mortars and field pieces shelled the first lines of trenches as soon as the enemy began a barrage. Heavier artillery hit rear support areas of the enemy and attempted to destroy enemy artillery emplacements.[33] Pétain's artillery subordinates produced another order a day after the previously quoted directive emphasizing that shell fire should not just be defensive or reactive but offensive as well. Each artillery corps had to prepare a daily schedule of bombardments of enemy battery emplacements, materiel depots and parks, and reserve cantonments.[34] Such systematic and intensive programs for artillery bombardments marked a striking and significant increase in shell usage during the war.

The entire vicinity of Verdun was rapidly becoming a crater-strewn wasteland. Telephone cables laid by the French were obliterated in German barrages. Artillery observers, stationed in hazardous posts close to the front, had to use periscopes to check fire results and send couriers to the rear to convey the information obtained. "It is clear that our barrage firings have been impotent in stopping German infantry," the French complained. But the 3d Bureau of Pétain's command recommended that a grid system be used for artillery fire so those points identified as saps or assembly trenches would be systematically bombarded. The key to success lay in greatly increased intensity of fire.[35]

Pétain, concerned about the unanticipated fall of Fort Douaumont on 25 February, ordered that each remaining fort would be supplied for two weeks and that its garrison would be frequently relieved. Most important, however, was his establishment of strong points linking the existing forts to form a chain of "resistance positions." After a bombardment on 6 March, the Germans advanced to meet heavy fire: French units "protected each other's flanks with crossed rifle fire, and kept in close communication with both the artillery and the aviation."[36] A further attack of the Germans launched on 17 March was repulsed primarily by heavy artillery fire. "During the night, systematic fire of great caliber as well as of 75s was executed at intervals, at varying times."[37] Pétain had developed a coordinated plan of defense in which the infantry was entrenched in fortified strong points, linking its firepower with strong artillery barrages on attacking troops.

A French Second Army directive of 19 March emphasized "the necessity for the artillery to operate by *concentration of fire,*" against a particular point such as a blockhouse or a battery. A second type of firing, called the *barrage,* used artillery behind the lines to repel an attack or in support of one's own attack. Finally, some *isolated batteries,* permanently placed, fired on enemy routes and rail lines. All other fire used intelligence furnished by aerial and ground observation. The chief difficulty with this artillery tactical scheme lay in the fallibility of observers and their commanders. Their errors sometimes resulted in shells missing targets. As a solution Pétain required these officers to prepare reports that identified villages, enemy bivouacs, and batteries. Such reports, collated at the army level, enabled systematic and concentrated shelling.[38] Artillery fire was being rationally organized on a large-scale basis.

Shortly after, the 1st Bureau greatly increased the strength of artillery in divisions by adding two batteries of trench artillery to each of them. Equipped with 58mm, 75mm, and 150mm mortars these additional batteries provided greater support for the front as well as greater firepower. Each army also obtained more mortar batteries to supplement divisional artillery.[39] Divisions became oriented to siegecraft because the French high command had abandoned any hope for the return of open warfare.

The old, minor Verdun forts were reinforced by troops from the infantry, artillery, supply, and engineers according to newly recast tables of organization. Officers were drawn from the useless cavalry. Finally, the casements were rebuilt and rearmed with artillery pieces. Many additional turrets were furnished with machine guns as well. Such forts became strong points and aided in flanking attacks on the enemy.[40]

By 18 April, Pétain observed that "reinforced concrete forts resist bombardments very well" because they provided shelter for garrisons during bombardments and enabled troops to emerge afterward to repel attacks. Forts were furnished with fifteen days of rations, telephones, flares, periscopes, pigeons, and wireless equipment. More and more convinced that permanent forts were necessary, the 3d Bureau of Pétain's Second Army noted: "The battle over the last six months has been dominated by concrete and cannon." Of three kinds of construction— masonry blocks of limestone with a thickness of 1.5 meters, limestone blocks with a cover of concrete with a thickness of 2.5 meters, and reinforced concrete—only the third type, suitably thick, could withstand prolonged bombardment by 420mm pieces. Results of tests confirmed the effectiveness of reinforced concrete and protected turrets and casements.[41]

As part of the rethinking of tactical defense problems, the 3d Bureau of the Second Army prescribed holding positions despite any attack. There were to be two main defensive systems. The first line, to be defended at all costs, consisted "of a series of support points connected by a continuous trench preceding listening posts and covered by a network of barbed wire entanglements with a density as great as possible." A support line, the second defensive system two hundred meters behind the line, served as the base for counterattacks. Finally, a "recess line" (reserve) would be constructed a thousand meters back. All artillery units would have observation posts near the first line. The defensive strong points in all lines were to be girded and connected by thirty meters of barbed wire.[42] All in all, the system elaborated by Pétain was the most comprehensive example of defensive siegecraft yet developed in the war. He emphasized that counterattack efforts would not cease until a vacated position was reoccupied.

Incredible as the French defensive preparations were, they were obviously necessary if Verdun was to be held. A French soldier recalled that the enemy bombardment, of two days' duration, was accompanied every hour by an observation plane that verified the destruction and to see if "some still lived." Observation was followed by renewed heavy bombardment. This pattern of assault remained the same during the Germans' entire Verdun offensive. When the rolling barrage of artillery commenced to guard the advancing German infantry, the French defenders crouched low in their trenches. As the enemy infantry approached, the defenders emerged to fight. Rifle, grenade, and machine-gun fire followed. Flamethrowers and small *Minenwerfer*, employed by the Germans against concrete blockhouses, caused some French defenders to panic. But all the efforts of the German infantry to break through the defenses failed. The casualties were heavy on both sides.[43] A correspondent, Wythe Williams, was told it was impossible to maintain trenches in the first line because of the heavy bombardment. Instead, both Germans and French fought from shell holes. Soldiers remained "for hours in the mud and water to their waists." Fort Douaumont had been recaptured by the French, and General Nivelle was amazed that Williams and his party had been able to get through in the face of such lethal barrages.[44]

The German version of the Verdun campaign verifies the French in most respects. The first attack had resulted in estimated French casualties of 63,000, while German losses had amounted to 50,000. Both sides, reinforced between 25 February and 6 March, awaited a second attack on 8 March that was launched on a broad front. The artillery barrage, commencing at 1:00 P.M. on 7 March and continuing for nearly twenty-four hours, consisted of a systematic *Trommelfeuer,* or drum fire, designed to subject the defenders to unending punishment. Storm troops were used in the vanguard to attack Fort Vaux. At the end of this costly assault reinforcements had to be brought up. General von Mudra was then entrusted with responsibility for a new attack intended to capture terrain between 31 March and 6 April. His methodical approach also cost enormous casualties with minuscule results.[45]

Perplexed, Falkenhayn ordered resumption of the original offensive on 31 March. Debating whether to choose the left or right flank of the French defenses, Crown Prince Rupprecht of Bavaria, commander of the Bavarian Sixth Army, chose the eastern (left) on the line running from Fort Thiaumont to Fort Tavannes. This March attack did not succeed.

"Only greater, unified attacks can succeed," wrote General Knobelsdorf on 27 April. He added that this method offered the best chance even though it seemed almost impossible to mass enough artillery on that single point of the line. Falkenhayn was not willing to concentrate all his forces on one point at the risk of leaving other sectors weakened. Reserves would also be depleted dangerously. A less ambitious major attack on 7 May, using thirty batteries of heavy artillery, also failed.[46] Further debate continued afterward among the top commanders.

Shortages of troops and supplies were felt at this time. Shells for 210mm field artillery and the pieces themselves were in short supply. Some divisions, such as the 5th Infantry Division, were not ready because they had been demoralized by losses. Knobelsdorf no longer was willing to take responsibility for the "consumption of men, munitions, and material." At first disagreeing, the crown prince later acquiesced.[47]

Falkenhayn considered either consolidating the existing line from Fleury to Tavannes on high ground, or retreating to the starting position of 21 February. In the end, the French reconquered the Caillette woods and Fort Vaux on 22 May.[48] The Verdun front no longer was the scene of a major offensive and Falkenhayn was disgraced and removed from his post.

German artillery expenditures for the Caillette forest attack on 1 June proved to be very considerable : some 9600 shells of heavy artillery, 8000 of heavy howitzers, and 6000 of light field howitzers were fired during the barrage of thirteen hours. During the actual infantry advance, a further 11,820 shells of these types were expended in a rectangle one thousand meters wide to a depth of five hundred meters. Such firepower dwarfed British expenditure on the Somme slightly later, but was symptomatic of both French and German attacks during the Verdun campaign.

In the course of that campaign the antagonists had ample opportunity to reevaluate their tactics. The French noted that the initial German attack differed from their own practices: The French had usually attacked along the entire front while the Germans had concentrated on the pivot point of the Meuse River. German use of strong points in the front line was the most significant point of departure from French procedures. Also, the Germans preceded their attacks with reconnaissance patrols to check the results of the artillery barrage. Elite troops (storm troops), which were few in number and trained specifically to attack French strong points, then led the mass of infantry. The first wave of infantry included many grenadiers and pioneers with flamethrowers. The intent of both the storm troops and the first line was to seek out and penetrate weak points in the French defensive system through infiltration. Attacks were always on limited fronts so that troops and artillery could be concentrated. Artillery in unprecedented amount was fired, first to destroy as much of the defense as possible in a preliminary barrage, and, second, by *Trommelfeuer,* to provide a staccato bombardment in front of advancing infantry.[49]

Retaliating, the French quickly developed the scheme summarized by Pétain on 30 March 1916. Each sector commander tried to anticipate possible points where the enemy might attack. Defensive systems in depth using infantry and field artillery were then built in these danger areas. Reserves were to be kept nearby for counterattacks to prevent the enemy, if momentarily successful, from holding on to his gains.[50]

The chief lesson learned by both sides at Verdun was that unlimited artillery bombardments followed by heavy infantry assaults were not sufficient to crack permanent fortifications made of reinforced concrete. Once again, defense had triumphed over offense.

THE SOMME: BUREAUCRATIC WARFARE

Both the Germans and the French discovered weaknesses in the theory of saturation bombardment at Verdun. Some months after that campaign opened, Haig ordered preparation of a plan of attack on the Somme based on the same concentrated use of artillery. He and Rawlinson (commander of the Fourth Army) claimed that the infantry would only have to "walk over" to take possession because of the total destruction of the enemy by a preliminary bombardment. The official British history suggested that similar words were spoken by the commander of the German Fifth Army before the assault on Verdun.[51] Did Haig think to review the Verdun campaign before starting his Somme campaign? Caution might have replaced optimism about the effects of artillery fire if he had conducted such a review. A Royal Flying Corps liaison officer with the French forces at Verdun reported in May 1916 that the French artillery had not been able to respond quickly to the German attack in late February because destruction of its communication systems had prevented it from registering on German targets. Of course, repair of telephone lines solved that problem. If enemy batteries could be registered beforehand, the liaison officer suggested, they could be hit when an enemy attack occurred.[52] No evidence exists to indicate that this report, or possibly others not identified, influenced planning in the BEF prior to the Somme offensive.

Haig determined that the Fourth Army would make the major attack with the objective of creating a gap toward Arras. Foch, reviewing this plan, suggested a joint British-French venture in this direction. Haig vetoed this suggestion, claiming needless exposure of his left flank during such an attack. But, given Haig's distrust of Foch, whom he privately characterized as "untrustworthy and a schemer," the decision was no surprise. At the meeting of 31 May with Foch and Joffre, Haig assured the French that he intended to make a separate British attack to force the Germans to take the pressure off Verdun.[53] The inability of the British commander to coordinate his actions with Foch led to serious trouble once the campaign started.

According to the official British history, the theory of the assault prior to the offensive had been stressed in various directives of GHQ down to the division level: "Towards the close of the bombardment, shortly before zero, the artillery would put down an intense barrage on the enemy front trenches." At zero the barrage was to be lifted and laid on the next line of trenches for a set time, then transferred to successive lines of trenches according to a timetable. Infantry would simply creep "under cover of the barrage" to about one hundred yards from the enemy.

As soon as the barrage was lifted from the first trench, the infantry would take over that trench.[54]

The Canadian Corps required reports of recent enemy attacks in early May 1916. These attacks were local, of course, but the response of brigade and division commanders was thoughtful. The German attack on 26 April was preceded by a heavy bombardment registered on some spots in the Canadian front trench line. These firings hit the same places previously bombarded. But, when the attack was launched, the German fire shifted to hit the support and communication trenches. A battalion commander suggested that "in case of future attacks it would be better if men were concentrated in tunnels." They would emerge as soon as fire "lifted to the rear of their position" and would be sent forward immediately "to reinforce the front line, or to counterattack."[55] No doubt similar conclusions were reached by battalion commanders of the German army—indeed of all the armies in the war. But Haig and Rawlinson were too far removed from battalion-level commanders to profit from their advice.

Rawlinson warned Haig in a letter of 19 April that "a very large part of [our] troops to be engaged are new troops with little experience, and amongst whom the standard of discipline, leadership, and tactical training of company commanders, is not what obtained in our troops of a year ago, and amongst whom, therefore, disorganization will appear more quickly." For that reason and others he recommended that the attack be on a limited front with limited objectives and, "Should it be found impossible to capture the enemy's second line in the first attack, and should the troops making the attack fail to gain their objective, I consider that the whole operation may be retarded."

In short, Rawlinson was uneasy and preferred an extended preliminary bombardment to a quick one. No surprise would be obtained anyway, he claimed, and the heavy barrage would "keep the enemy in a constant state of doubt as to when the infantry assault will take place." Such a barrage would also wear down the enemy and demoralize him. Haig agreed to the heavy preliminary barrage but did not limit the operation. Rawlinson noted in his diary, "I still think we would do better to proceed by shorter steps; but I have told D.H. I will carry out his plan with as much enthusiasm as if it were my own."[56]

After five days' bombardment, the attack began on 1 July. Rawlinson, observing the first day's casualties, believed them to be heavy but not excessive. The total for the Fourth Army amounted to 35,600 or 6 percent. But some 100,000 out of the total strength of 511,600 had been used in the attack, so the percentage of casualties in the attacking force was 35 percent. As Frederick Maurice noted, "the attack of 1 July was but the prelude to a long continuous struggle," so the casualties mounted higher and higher with each passing day. Rawlinson initially believed, however, that the German line had been ruptured on a wide front "and, above all, we have already helped the French immensely at Verdun." He was confident that a follow-up attack would breach the second-line defenses on 14 July. That attack had been planned with his subordinate commanders, and reluctantly approved by Haig, and was preceded by a heavy barrage on the wire and the trenches. Rawlinson tried to give the infantry an advantage by ordering a dawn attack at 3:25 A.M. Some objectives were taken and he wrote, "I believe that if I could have persuaded D.H. to let me make the attack forty-eight hours earlier, we might have got the Germans on the run, but it was a big risk for him to take until he was sure our plans were all right."[57]

Successive attacks by the British met with increasing resistance and little success. Casualties were heavy. The German losses were substantial, too. General Gallwitz estimated that between 26 June and 28 August some 1068 out of 1208 field guns had been captured, destroyed, or rendered unserviceable. His heavy cannon had decreased by 371 from 820. The British counterbattery work was quite successful and undoubtedly owed something to the Royal Flying Corps and its observers. A German soldier noted "how the English, with the aid of their airmen, who are often 1,500 ft. above the position, . . . have exactly located every one of our batteries and have so smashed them up with long-distance guns of every caliber that the artillery here has had unusually heavy losses both of men and material." This commentary of 30 August also indicated that dugouts were not necessarily always beneficial: one was hit and a number of soldiers were buried.[58]

The artillery preparation for the series of attacks that occurred after 1 July hardly differed. Field batteries and some heavy artillery were brought forward to assist in the planned assault of 14 July.

A subaltern, Charles Carrington, led an assault in another sector on July 15: "Without preliminary bombardment we crossed a thousand yards of open ground and occupied a knot of trenches in rear of the defenders of Ovillers."[59] He posed this question: Was it better to have a heavy (but accurate) preliminary bombardment, or to make a sudden attack without such bombardment? His attack, without it, was successful while that of 9th York and Lancaster, with preparatory bombardment, on 1 July had been a disaster. Nevertheless, Rawlinson, Haig, and other commanders believed mass artillery fire could cut wire and destroy the enemy in their trenches.

Correspondents noted that, unlike in 1915, the British army was well supplied with artillery in preparation for the Somme offensive of 1916. "Those heavy howitzers, fresh from the foundry, drawn by big Caterpillar-type tractors, were all proceeding in one direction—toward the Somme. . . . Fields were cut by the tracks of guns moving into position; steamrollers were road-making in the midst of long processions of motor trucks." Gibbs noted the enormous quantity of guns and shells.[60]

Indeed, the preparations for the attack reveal a surprising and considerable growth in expertise in the organizational aspects of war. Rawlinson was already developing an ability to plan a set-piece engagement. Palmer remarked about the artillery buildup:[61]

All this preparation, stretching over weeks and months, unemotional and methodical, infinite in detail, prodigious in effort, suggested the work of engineers and contractors and subcontractors in the building of some great bridge or canal, with the workmen all in the same kind of uniform and with managers, superintendents and foremen each having some insignia of rank.

Nevertheless, despite the high hopes of British commanders, such preparations were inadequate to overcome two major obstacles to victory. First, the quality of howitzer shells and some other ammunition was poor, resulting in many duds. The official British history noted: "The amount of damage done to Fricourt by the bombardment had been small on account of the failure of the 9.2-inch shells to explode, the fuzes having come out during flight."[62] Second, the German infantry had sought safety in deep underground dugouts. Because of the English aerial bombardment the Germans began to leave their artillery shell stores some 12 to 15 kilometers behind the line in concrete bunkers. Ammunition was moved in smaller quantities at night to divisional stores close to the battle zone. Once the bombardment was over, the German troops quickly returned to their firing positions and were able to inflict huge losses on the advancing British infantry.[63]

To the right of the British Fourth Army was the Northern French Army commanded by Foch. The attack of that force was conducted with far greater expertise than was manifested by the British. Despite considerable initial success, however, Foch was unable to pierce the German defenses deeply enough to exploit a breakthrough.

The preparatory artillery bombardment by Foch's army began on 24 June, greatly increased in intensity on 26 June, and continued until 1 July; it systematically devastated the first enemy lines. Although many German soldiers were protected because they stayed in underground dugouts, some were entombed by debris. Afterward, reports of prisoners indicated that many were in a state of shock after emerging from their dugouts. One battery of 58mm cannon for every three hundred meters of front and one battery of 240mm cannon for every thousand meters of front provided blanket coverage. Shells were expended at a prodigious rate so that by 1 July there were hardly enough to cover the infantry advance. For the six-day period of fire each 58mm battery fired 800 shells and each 240mm battery fired between 150 and 200.[64]

Prior to this immense attack the French moved a seven-day supply of cannon ammunition by rail using 335 trains with a total of 10,157 cars. The 3d Bureau of the French headquarters noted: "This number explains in itself how difficult it is to resist a modern attack, pushed by an apparent avalanche of munitions which takes fifty days to collect and is used quickly." For the first time the French used very heavy artillery. Pieces of 400mm and large mortars were set up on platforms or railcars and required precise aerial liaison. These cannon, although used during the Somme battle, were frequently inactive since they were a considerable distance behind the lines.[65]

Despite a phenomenal increase in artillery during 1916, and the elimination of shell shortages for the most part, no attack was successful in the long run. Mass artillery bombardment could not in itself bring victory through massive breakthroughs.

POSTMORTEM

During the late fall of 1916 the belligerents began to reevaluate the role of artillery in the war. The results of this study were inconclusive; artillery still seemed to promise the elusive key to victory in the 1917 campaigns.

Staff critiques of the Somme battle by the French centered on the theme of inadequate artillery deployment. It was useless to continue to bombard well-built dugouts and emplacements as "experience in the Champagne, Verdun, and Somme showed." Continuing, the 3d Bureau remarked: "After the taking of the 1st and 2d enemy lines, when we were stopped by enemy structures which were certainly less solid, but imprecise, poorly defended, poorly known because they were all new, certain officers had the theory that it is easier to attack very strong enemy structures which were old, well known, and repaired over a long time, than an unknown structure." Old positions were well studied because of aerial reconnaissance and photography, and were registered for counterbattery fire. The answer seemed to entail making constant aerial reconnaissance reports as the infantry advanced in order to correct the registration of fire in the rear areas. In other words, a much more sophisticated liaison between aerial observation and artillery control was needed.[66]

In observing their British allies, the French were inclined to criticize them for having a "simple and rigid method" of attack in which they "follow an inevitable scenario in accord with a timetable prepared in advance." But both British and French artillery units suffered during the Somme battle when they were moved from secure emplacements forward into exposed sites on open ground. There was little loss of life, but telephonic and supply lines were frequently interrupted by shell fire, isolating such batteries. Some 153 French cannon were destroyed by German counterbattery fire in the Somme.[67]

Revised French artillery instructions published on 16 December 1916 provided a more sophisticated approach to the desired breakthrough. It was no longer possible to believe that the enemy's defensive system could be broken through in a single attack on the first day because of the depth of defenses. Therefore, the attack had to be mounted in phases. The first phase involved an infantry attack preceded and accompanied by artillery bombardment. The infantry could not advance until "protected and pushed by a numerous artillery." It then dug in to anticipate a counterattack by the enemy with field artillery brought forward to protect its new positions. German defenses were in depth so "the conquest of the first objective does not permit the infantry to realize the rupture."

Successive objectives would be taken in phases: "Each phase consists of a preparation by the artillery and is succeeded by artillery fire complementing an attack of infantry." The aim was to conduct each operation with "the maximum of *power* and *rapidity* in order to obtain as much depth as possible." One reconnaissance aircraft was not enough; a number of aircraft would be individually assigned zones of the enemy's artillery sector. More efficient artillery spotting would result. Only the first position of the enemy could be totally destroyed by cannon fire, using mortars or trench artillery over a period of several days. The destruction of enemy support and communication trenches, supply depots, and the like would be accomplished by enfilade fire if possible.[68] The French General Staff was trying to coordinate artillery with infantry and aircraft in a more sophisticated system than existed before.

German responses to the Somme battle included a tactical appreciation prepared by Colonel von der Goltz, commander of the 10th Grenadier Regiment. He believed that the first breach of the German front lines by the English and French had been caused by extraordinarily heavy fire directed by aerial spotters, and by using many heavy artillery pieces. Heavy German casualties and material losses had occurred, and he urged holding on to both first-line trenches and support trenches. But preliminary bombardments caused immense casualties in the first-line trenches. By August 1916, the high command issued directives to evacuate the first trenches in event of an enemy preparatory bombardment. Troops could be held in readiness in support trenches and dugouts and could be rushed back to the first-line trenches upon cessation of the barrage in time to fire on the advancing enemy infantry.[69] In the fading weeks of Falkenhayn's command there was little interest in offensive operations by German staff planners on the western front. Instead, elaborate preparations were under way for the fortification of the Wotan and Siegfried lines.[70]

An air of unreality permeates the reflections of Haig and Rawlinson in their respective diaries in late summer and early fall 1916. Rawlinson noted on 16 August:[71]

With the increase in heavy artillery which is daily coming into the country, with the additions which are being made weekly to our air services, and with practically unlimited amounts of ammunitions which will be available by the end of this year, I feel sure that we shall be able to carry out early next year a successful offensive, not only on the front of one army, but on the front of two, and possibly three.

Haig, worried about Lloyd George's visit to Foch, failed to make a similar appraisal. The new English prime minister asked Foch "why the British, who had gained no more ground than the French, if as much, had suffered such heavy casualties."[72] Foch defended Haig, but the latter knew he was in trouble.

The correspondent Frederick Palmer commented that "it was a commonplace that any time you desired you could take a front of a thousand or two yards simply by concentrating your gunfire, cutting the enemy's barbed wire and tearing the sandbags of his parapet into ribbons, with resulting fearful casualties to him; and possession of the debris."

But such attacks always resulted in counterattacks: "Later, under cover of his own guns, his charge recovered the ruins . . . which left the situation as it was before with both sides a loser of lives."[73] Exaggerated, no doubt, this description seemed to fit the final results of the Verdun and Somme battles, if adapted to much bigger scales. Unprecedented artillery barrages were not the magic solution to the trench warfare stalemate by the end of 1916. Shelford Bidwell, from the point of view of an artillery specialist, believed: "It is a truism that the worse are the infantry in terms of battlecraft and minor tactics the more they lean on the artillery like a crutch."[74] Attempts to make infantry assaults dependent upon artillery bombardments had failed. Infantry could not simply "walk over" or "occupy" the ruins left by massive shell fire.

NOTES

1. James L. Jack, *General Jack's Diary* (London, 1964), 140–42.
2. Robertson, *Field Marshal*, 227.
3. Anon., *The War the Infantry Knew*, 116–17.
4. Georg Bruchmüller, *Die deutsche Artillerie in den Durchbruchschlachten des Weltkrieges* (Berlin, 1921), 1–3. Very valuable are the discussions of firepower in Travers, *Killing Ground*, 62–79, and Shelford Bidwell and Dominick Graham, *Fire-power: British Army Weapons and Theories of War, 1904–1945* (London, 1982).
5. Koeltz, *1914–1918*, 232. Bloem, *Mons*, 180–82.
6. Postwar account provided by the German Reichsarchiv to Edmonds, *Military Operations*, 1:187–91.
7. Schwarte, *Krieg*, 4:485–89, 492–96. BSA, AOK 6, Bd. 333. Ulrich Trumpener, "The Road to Ypres: The Beginnings of Gas Warfare in World War I," *Journal of Modern History* 47 (1975): 460–80, describes the evolution of experimentation and shows that the Germans did not first start research on gases.
8. BSA, AOK 6, Bd. 333.
9. Cruttwell, *Great War*, 155–56. Edmonds, *Military Operations*, 1:257–80. Cyril Falls, *The Great War* (New York, 1959), 111–12. Quoted in Harrington, *Plumer*, 72–73.
10. Anon., *The War the Infantry Knew*, 146, 151–54. Philip Gibbs, *Now It Can Be Told* (New York, 1920), 166–68. BSA, AOK 6, Bd. 9.
11. Maxse Papers, 65/53/5.
12. Robertson Papers, I/5. A letter dated 23 June 1915, included in the papers of Sir William Robertson, quartermaster general of the BEF at that time.
13. Anon., *The War the Infantry Knew*, 161.
14. Bloem, *Mons*, 180–82. The Rifle Brigade history is quoted in a note.
15. "Note du General Foch sur les conditions d'une offensive générale, 24 janvier 1916." 3e Bureau, Somme, 1916. 16 N 1982, AMV.
16. Adapted from J. B. Duroselle, *Histoire de la Grande Guerre* (Paris, 1980), 117.
17. "Some Notes Suggested By . . . the French Operations in Champagne in September 1915." Lt. Col., Gen. Staff, 1st Canadian Division,

17 December 1915. Public Archives of Canada, RG 9 III, folder 85, file 4. (Hereafter, PAC.)

18. PAC, RG 9 III, folder 85, file 4.

19. PAC, RG 9 III, folder 85, file 4.

20. "The Offensive," BG, GOC. 2d Canadian Infantry Brigade, PAC, RG 9 III, folder 85, file 4.

21. PAC, RG 9 III, folder 85, file 4.

22. PAC, RG 9 III, folder 85, file 4.

23. PAC, RG 9 III, folder 85, file 4.

24. "Proposals for the Technical Methods to be adopted in an Attempt to break through a Strongly Fortified Position," translated memoir of the chief of the German General Staff, no. 603, 18 March 1915 (captured document), Robertson Papers, I/6/2.

25. Wolfgang Foerster, *Graf Schlieffen und der Weltkrieg* (Berlin, 1925), 3:24–25.

26. Erich von Falkenhayn, *Die Oberste Heeresleitung* (Berlin, 1920), 183–84.

27. Philippe Henri Pétain, *Verdun,* tr. M. MacVeagh (Toronto, 1930), 49–50, 55–57.

28. Pétain, *Verdun,* 73, 83–87. Koeltz, *1914–1918,* 308–9.

29. Koeltz, *1914–1918,* 305–7. BSA, AOK 6, Bd. 326. See Bruce I. Gudmundsson, *Stormtroop Tactics: Innovation in the German Army, 1914–1918* (New York, 1989), 55–65, for fuller discussion of Verdun.

30. Pierre Chaine, *Les Memoires d'un Rat* (Paris, 1930), 100–101.

31. AMV, 16 N 1981, 3e Bureau, Verdun.

32. Chaine, *Rat,* 95–96.

33. Ministère de la Guerre, *Les Armées françaises dans la Grande Guerre,* IV, annexes, 2:6–7.

34. *Armées françaises,* IV, annexes, 2:38–39.

35. *Armées françaises,* IV, annexes, 2:156–58.

36. Pétain, *Verdun,* 92–105.

37. *Armées françaises,* IV, annexes, 2:503.

38. *Armées françaises,* IV, annexes, 2:562–64.

39. *Armées françaises,* IV, annexes, 2:631–33.

40. *Armées françaises,* IV, annexes, 2:600, 715–25.

41. AMV, 16 N 1981, 3e Bureau, Verdun.

42. *Armées françaises,* IV, annexes, 2:872–73.

43. Chaine, *Rat,* 100–105. BSA, AOK 6, Bd. 326.

44. Williams, *Dusk of Empire,* 79, 85–86.

45. Kriegsministerium, *Der Weltkrieg,* 10:128–36.

46. Kriegsministerium, *Der Weltkrieg,* 10:142–77. Franz Schauwecker, ed., *So war der Krieg: 200 Kampfaufnahmen aus der Front* (Berlin, 1927), 73.

47. Kriegsministerium, *Der Weltkrieg,* 10:142–77. Schauwecker, *Krieg,* 73.

48. Kriegsministerium, *Der Weltkrieg,* 10:142–77. Schauwecker, *Krieg,* 73.

49. *Armées françaises,* IV, annexes, 2:836–40.

50. *Armées françaises,* IV, annexes, 2:836–40.

51. Edmonds, *Military Operations,* 2:229–30.

52. PAC, RG 9 III, vol. 3825.

53. Robert Blake, ed., *The Private Papers of Douglas Haig* (London, 1952), 145–46, 150.

54. Edmonds, *Military Operations,* 2:229–30.

55. PAC RG 9, III, vol. 3859, folder 85, file 3.

56. Maurice, *Rawlinson,* 154–58.

57. Maurice, *Rawlinson,* 163–67.

58. Edmonds, *Military Operations,* 2:229–30. Philipp Witkop, ed., *German Students' War Letters,* tr. A. F. Wedd (New York, 1929), 315.

59. Carrington, *Soldier Returning,* 121. BSA, AOK 6, Bd. 326 also emphasizes coordination of light and heavy artillery during an attack.

60. Gibbs, *Now,* 267. Frederick Palmer, *My Second Year of the War* (Toronto, 1917), 46–47.

61. Palmer, *Second Year,* 46–47.

62. Edmonds, *Military Operations,* 1:356, note 5.

63. Anthony H. Farrar-Hockley, *The Somme* (London, 1964), 116, quotes from M. Gerster, *Die Schwaben an der Ancre* (Heilbronn, 1918). BSA, AOK 6, Bd. 333 and Bd. 326. The Germans were increasingly worried about low-flying British planes which were strafing bivouacs and marching columns. Edmonds, *Military Operations,* 1:356, note 5.

64. AMV, 16 N 1982, 3e Bureau, Somme.

65. AMV, 16 N 1982, 3e Bureau, Somme.

66. AMV, 16 N 1982. 3e Bureau, Somme.

67. AMV, 16 N 1982, 3e Bureau, Somme.

68. AMV, 16 N 1995, 3e Bureau. 47th Division Artillery.

69. Kriegsministerium, *Der Weltkrieg,* 10:383–84.

70. BSA, AOK 6, Bd. 337.

71. Maurice, *Rawlinson,* quotes, 168.

72. Blake, *Haig Papers,* 167.

73. Palmer, *Second Year,* 39–40. Travers, *Killing Ground,* 127–203, gives an excellent analysis of the Somme campaign.

74. Shelford Bidwell, *Gunners at War* (London, 1972), 34–35.

Infantrymen advance on a path just made by a tank through barbed wire entanglements. One man has fallen over the wire. *National Archives*

A French-manned Schneider tank supports doughboys of the 26th Infantry, 1st Division, at Breteuil, 11 May 1918. *National Archives*

Infantry advance at the Battle of Arras, 1917. *Imperial War Museum, London*

Observer Lieutenant J. H. Snyder receives a French 1824 size camera with Berthout color lens, capable of taking photographs from twenty-five thousand feet. *National Archives*

Captain Paul Damm, commanding officer of the 28th French Escadrille, with double Lewis machine guns. *National Archives*

General Franchet d'Esperey inspecting the aircraft of Captain Guynemer at Bonneraison (Marne) on 5 August 1917. © *SIRPA/ECPA France*

Firing a *chauchat.* © *SIRPA/ECPA France*

German grenade launcher. *National Archives*

First Lt. E. P. Brecht explains the Stokes trench mortar to men of the U.S. 108th Infantry Regiment. Aheel, Belgium, August 1918. *National Archives*

Americans using German telephone system at Busigny, October 1918. *National Archives*

Soldiers with armored breastplates man an advanced observation post on the western front. *National Archives*

German storm troopers at Sedan, May 1917. *Imperial War Museum*

German crew mans 77mm gun used in direct-fire mode as an antitank weapon. *National Archives*

French Renault Char FT light tanks near Juvigny on 29 August 1918. The Renault shown here mounts a Hotchkiss 8mm machine gun. *National Archives*

American Caterpillar tractor tests at Vincennes for pulling heavy artillery. © *SIRPA/ECPA France*

Schneider tank. © *SIRPA/ECPA France*

Couty (Somme) train loading platform with Schneider tanks moving off. © *SIRPA/ ECPA France*

British Mark V heavy tank crossing a trench on the way to Cambrai, November 1917. *Imperial War Museum*

Schneider tank interior with commander. ©*SIRPA/ECPA France*

Battery E, 56th Coast Artillery Corps, mans 155mm guns at Charpentry, Meuse, in October 1918. *National Archives*

Armored train with 16-inch cannon on a turntable. Villers-Daucourt, 31 May 1916. © *SIRPA/ECPA France*

Loading a 370mm mortar in the ravine of Baraquette (Somme), 16 September 1916. © *SIRPA/ECPA France*

Fifteen-inch howitzer at Albert, 1 July 1916. *Imperial War Museum*

British and French soldiers, March 1918. *Imperial War Museum*

Engineers bridging a shell crater on the battlefield between Saint-Quentin and Ham, April 1918. *National Archives*

German troops manhandle a heavy long-range cannon into position before Montdidier, April 1918. *National Archives*

Soldiers haul a 210mm field mortar into position on the battleground before Ham during the offensive in the west, March 1918. *National Archives*

German artillery crossing heavily shelled fields, March 1918. *National Archives*

Mont-Cornuillet (Marne). Trenches in Champagne, February 1917. © *SIRPA/ ECPA France*

German troops going through looted clothing in a captured English camp, April 1918. *National Archives*

Royal fusiliers at Arras, April 1917. *Imperial War Museum*

Arrival of American black troops at Sommeilles (Meuse), 22 September 1918. *©SIRPA/ECPA France*

CHAPTER 5
TOOLS AND WEAPONS

T actics seem to lag behind technology. Invention of a new weapon does not automatically suggest how it will be most effective; the machine gun existed in 1914, for example, but how to utilize it was still vaguely defined then. Once the war began, existing weaponry was quickly adapted to actual combat conditions. Technological adaptation was quite evident during the war as innovation followed innovation with dizzying speed. Sometimes frontline troops and sometimes scientific and technical personnel were responsible for bridging the gap between tactical theory and weapons employment.

Sometimes tactics dictated the development of specialized weapons, too. Flamethrowers, mortars, air-cooled machine guns, automatic rifles, and grenades were developed to meet the requirements of trench warfare. Conversely, development of poison gas, tanks, and aircraft forced evolution of new and different tactics.

WHAT WAS TAKEN TO WAR IN 1914

A remarkable efficiency could be discerned in the fall of 1914: mobilization schedules for troop deployment in event of war were rationally established and utilized carefully prepared rail lines, staging depots, and telephonic and telegraphic communication. Mobilization plans, steadily improved since 1873, collected 3,120,000 German troops as well as

860,000 horses at border staging points between 6 August and 17 August. Although part of these forces went to the Russian border, most were assigned to the western campaign. The French paralleled this German effort by mobilizing 2,689,000 during August. Millions of troops were poised on the borders of the small state of Belgum as a result of mobilization.[1]

Norman Stone has described this phenomenon as a twentieth-century delivery system assisting a nineteenth-century striking force.[2] Once the troops had left their debarkation points at the railheads they were forced to march on foot, to mount horses, or to ride in horse-drawn vehicles. Automotive transport was extremely rare. Field artillery, field kitchens, and supply wagons were all towed by horses and mules. Because of the enormous masses of men used in the August and September 1914 campaign in Belgium and northern France, march schedules quickly degenerated into near chaos as the roads were clogged by columns of marching infantry and long trains of supplies and ammunition.[3]

Cavalry was useful for the last time in modern warfare because it was not confined to the roads but could pass rapidly through adjacent fields. In a melee on 13 August, saber-wielding British cavalry surprised a German unit and routed it. Shortly afterward a similar charge using lances worked.[4] Such opportunities for antiquated weapons and an obsolete arm of service quickly evaporated.

The German army took the fortresses of Liège and Namur and forced the retreat of the French and British forces during the last week of August. The great retreat was a study in contrasts. Pursued and pursuers marched accompanied by horse-drawn supply wagons, guarded and preceded by cavalry. Occasionally, rail and motorized road transport would assist, but most artillery and machine guns were still hauled by horses. A more significant sign of changing times was the appearance of aircraft and their use for scouting, reconnaissance, and terroristic bombing.[5]

Portents of future warfare were evident in the frenzied days of war in August and September 1914. As the Germans retreated from the Marne River their supply trains clogged the roads and a hopeless muddle resulted. The retreat of a million troops, mostly on foot, had reached a limit.[6] The German logistical system nearly collapsed under the strain.

Nevertheless, both the French and Germans requisitioned many vehicles at the start of the war. Gallieni used taxis and private automobiles to supplement buses in organized convoys that moved at 12 to 15 kilometers an hour. One road carried fifty to sixty buses, containing fifteen to eighteen hundred men per kilometer (or twenty thousand per hour).[7] Using motorized vehicles on a large scale in war was a superb innovation of the French.

Paradoxically enough, the now-stable front enabled the improvement of existing roads behind the lines on each side and encouraged the heavy use of motor transport to supply the huge garrisons of the trench system. By 1916, about 180,000 metric tons of supplies as well as 300,000 men were transported each month in motortrucks by the French army alone. France had started the war with a greater supply of trucks, significantly more than any other power, and these had capacities of two to three tons and a convoy speed of fifteen kilometers an hour. In the Loretto Heights battle of 3 March 1915, the Bavarian Sixth Army discovered that Foch had used motor transport to move eighty thousand troops from the railheads to the combat zone. The German army soon had a similar force in being. A combination of rail and road logistical support services was quickly established.[8] Naturally, such complex networks did not always function smoothly: typically, they broke down in times of sudden retreats and advances by one side or another. But they were highly effective in trench warfare.

The onset of the war in 1914 showed both sides that the maintenance of armies required unprecedented logistical efforts. Elaborate supply systems came into being once the front became stabilized. When open warfare resumed in 1918 other problems of logistics emerged.

LET'S MAKE DO

Sir John French, commander of the British Expeditionary Force, noted on 5 October 1915 "that the extra power conferred on the defence by the most modern weapons" placed severe limits on offensive actions.[9] Awareness of this grim truth came sooner to the British army because it suffered particular disadvantages. During the Battle of Le Cateau a deficiency in artillery had a serious impact on British operations. Obsolescent 6-inch siege howitzers, quickly brought forward, proved too limited in range. The only artillery pieces the British could use in counterbattery work against the German 210mm howitzers were the four 60-pounders provided to each division. Backwardness of the chemical industry combined with production bottlenecks for ammunition kept the British army in an inferior position to the German army during most of 1915. It is estimated that the Germans could fire ten shells to one British. Even when production of British shells was greatly increased in 1916, their quality was poor. Shells were rationed according to the so-called Mowat Scale at fifteen hundred rounds for each field piece and twelve hundred for each howitzer. That allowance was totally inadequate, but even it could not be met for many months.[10] Consequently, British operations were hampered from the start of the war until the end of 1916.

Modern technology contributed to the prolongation of the trench warfare. Construction of the first and successive defense lines with their communicating trenches followed siege practice. Protecting the first line were separate emplacements for machine guns. The whole front was finally preceded by barbed wire, originally invented by Americans to enclose ranch land in the 1880s. As the front stabilized, earthen trenches were frequently replaced by concrete blockhouses and permanent underground barracks and mess facilities, following French practice at Verdun. The German army acquired expertise in these efforts for the later construction of the Wotan and Siegfried lines. The more permanent the fortifications became, the less disposed were the soldiers inhabiting them to leave them.

Experienced soldiers and officers quickly began to improvise weaponry suitable for trench warfare. Charles Carrington remarked: "There was not even a prototype for a trench mortar, and only a few experimental grenades," and claimed museums were ransacked for Crimean War mortars. A British private noted that "we had bombs made out of jam tins with a fuse attached," and "later we had another kind of bomb called the cricket ball, but these had to be lighted with a match."[11] Obviously, providing weapons suitable for trench warfare was neither automatic nor easy.

By the end of 1915, staff evaluations indicated that while field artillery was effective in destroying enemy artillery emplacements, it was of limited use on trenches because only direct shell hits would cause casualties. Machine guns were cumbersome and heavy and could not easily be carried forward in an assault: they were, however, preeminently successful in defensive positions if their crews were supported by riflemen. Snipers equipped with rifles were effective against carelessly exposed soldiers. Rifles were far more helpful, however, in defense than in offense: the soldier could stay in a firing position and direct fire on advancing troops. In an advance, while walking or running, the soldier was vulnerable to enemy fire and could not retaliate effectively with his own rifle fire.

British improvisations remained dubious. The long-handled Hale stick grenade was not effective when demonstrated on 7 January 1916. "Informing us that the proper action of throwing was that of bowling a cricket ball," a demonstrator bowled it into a ditch where it exploded with a puny force.[12] Lacking mortars, the troops were provided with pipes into which they were supposed to place a projectile with a fuse. These devices were more dangerous to the firer than anyone else. In contrast, the German mortar was highly efficient.

The big brothers of mortars were howitzers, which were specifically designed to lob shells into entrenchments. They were field artillery, however, and could not be brought close enough to the line for continual and routine use. Mortars and grenades of various kinds were required in trench warfare where open-warfare artillery was useless. Certain types of shell ammunition were also ineffective in trench warfare: especially shrapnel, because troops were under cover and not exposed to it.

In 1915, Winston Churchill, First Lord of the Admiralty, ordered the Royal Naval Armoured Car Division to experiment with movable armor. Pushing a portable shield of armor plate on a small tractor base, twelve seamen sweated in trials in May and June 1915 at the Pedrail factory at Fulham. It was not possible to make a sufficiently strong armor plate that was yet "light enough to enable the machine to be pushed by hand."[13]

Finally, improvisations in 1915 included patented suits of armor sold privately to soldiers. Neither these nor portable shields like those used in ancient warfare were any good. A Canadian staff officer summed it up in January 1916: "I do not believe that any system of shields or helmets or any form of portable armour will provide a remedy."[14]

The war would continue to be influenced strongly by the technology of an earlier age. The quartermaster general of the British army, Sir John Cowans, had supervised the provisioning of 800,000 horses to the army by 1917. Under command of a major general, a remount department with a complement of 350 officers and 21,000 soldiers obtained and maintained these animals not only from the British Isles, but also from North America and Argentina, in the face of a serious submarine threat.[15] Symbolic of the attachment to traditional technology is the soldier plodding in the mud alongside a mule-pulled wagon loaded with ammunition. The old and the new operated side by side.

Foot soldiers accompanied by mule- and horse-drawn wagons could not achieve either the mobility or the firepower to wreck the defenses of the enemy and create a real opportunity for battle success. For this reason all governments turned to civilian scientists and engineers to provide technological assistance to military action. Tanks, chemical warfare, and improved aircraft were the results in 1917 and 1918.

THE NEW WEAPONS OF TRENCH WARFARE

During 1915, the belligerent governments began to look for ways and means to find technological innovations in the craft of war. To politicians, the military leadership seemed somewhat discredited because of the arrival of the expensive and unpopular trench warfare. Tremendous waste of the lives of voters could not fail to dismay the political leader. The temptation of Paul Painlevé and of Lloyd George, for example, was to look for a "quick fix" or the easy solution that would end the war. Technology seemed to promise such an attractive solution.

The Chamber of Deputies approved the establishment of a Ministry of Inventions during 1915 under Paul Painlevé. An outgrowth of an earlier Commission of Inventions for the Army and Navy, headed by Joffre in peacetime, this agency sought the advice of leading French scientists and mathematicians. Painlevé immediately began to search out chemists, physicists, electrical engineers, and research medical scientists from the faculties of the *grandes écoles* and institutes. The various technical sections studied ballistics, armament, electricity and wireless telegraphy, medicine, chemical warfare, aviation, and naval technology. Section 7 was devoted to trench warfare. As one politician, Louis Barthou, said, the objective was "to find another, more beautiful, triumph for French science."[16]

H. G. Wells argued that "Modern War is essentially a struggle of materiel and inventions," but that the conservatism of British military leaders blinded them to the need to harness the top scientific talent of the country in order to find inventions that could help win the war. Wells and many French scientists pessimistically believed that the Germans had established a technical superiority in military research by using their inventors.[17]

The end of improvised weaponry appeared in December 1914 when

Winston Churchill formed the Landships Committee in the Admiralty and in the spring of 1915 when the Germans used chlorine gas. The evolution of the tank and of chemical warfare had commenced. From that time on, the scientific and industrial experts of the warring powers were put to work to provide long-term solutions to the trench warfare stalemate. The generals found themselves forced to deal with many strange and brilliant persons who failed to exhibit the conventional behavior expected in peacetime military establishments. The modernization of war had been launched.

By early 1915 the machine gun had proved itself master of the trench warfare battlefield. Each army attempted to increase the number of these weapons, so useful in defense. But it proved difficult to develop revised attack tactics for them. The French and English immediately increased production of Hotchkiss, Browning, and other types of machine guns. On 22 October 1915, the British established a separate Machine Gun Corps.[18]

The Germans organized machine-gun companies and increased the number of machine guns per division from 11 in 1914, to 72 in 1916, and, finally, to 350 in 1918. The heavy Model 08 machine guns had been issued in greater numbers to infantry battalions but by August 1918 the number was reduced to about nine per battalion because of ammunition shortages that increasingly plagued the Germans in the last months of the war. In 1917 a new, light machine gun was introduced, and 42 were issued to each division in the Fourth Army. Training schools in the rear echelons drew future crews from the ranks of the infantry. Independent machine-gun companies were grouped together in units of three. But there was discontent with the effectiveness of independent machine-gun companies and an unsuccessful effort was made to disperse the companies in infantry battalions. The MGS (*Maschinengewehrschützen*) battalions had proven themselves only in defensive action in deep zones just behind the frontline defenses. But better use was made of them when commanders of the machine-gun companies were also made corps and division machine-gun staff officers. As members of the staffs of such units they were in much better positions to plan effective use of their weapons. There were eighty-seven of these units by 1918.[19] Despite a proven record of effectiveness in defense, such companies, British and German, met spirited resistance from conservatives within their high commands.

The Battle of Verdun of 1916 had shown that clusters of machine guns were more effective than isolated ones. A deeply fortified zone of defense had to be protected by numerous machine-gun nests. According to a German directive of December 1917, frequently moving such nests and keeping them separate from regular artillery emplacements made it more difficult for the enemy to identify them and destroy them. Available wood or earth was to be used to make impromptu parapets. Machine guns, especially the new light models, were increasingly used by the Germans in attacks as well. Commanders of such units were reminded that they were not to command fire from their crews without careful coordination with the fire of other troops, especially infantry. No unaimed volley fire was permitted after May 1918.[20] During 1917 and 1918, great efforts were made in the German army to integrate machine-gun action into general fire action involving artillery and infantry. Marksmanship instead of rote firing was also in vogue.

The founder of the Machine Gun Corps in Britain in 1915, Col. G. M. Lindsay, established with the help of Col. Christopher Baker-Carr the Machine Gun School at Wisgues. Instrumental in helping to organize strong machine-gun companies, Lindsay used masses of machine guns and was particularly popular with the Canadian army: "The Canadian Corps, which was always far in advance of the British army in its machine-gun organization and tactics, had already appointed a corps machine gun officer,"[21] according to one officer. Baker-Carr castigated superior officers because they were opposed to "mechanical methods" and favored "hand skill" in warfare. They provided "the wide-spread resistance which I encountered when striving to ensure the recognition of the machine gun as one of the most important weapons of the foot-soldier."[22] The iconoclastic attitudes of the Machine Gun Corps officers frequently made them unpopular with other officers in the divisions to which they were assigned.

E. D. Swinton, afterward to become so closely connected to tank development, knew these officers. At first a favorite with the War Office, Swinton nevertheless began to lose credibility when he told General Whigton that the *Infantry Training Manual of 1914* was obsolete. Finding an appreciative audience in Baker-Carr and Lindsay, Swinton described his idea of a tank in 1915 as "simply a machine that would carry infantry forward, and over enemy trenches."[23] During 1915 these officers were highly instrumental in convincing their superiors to support mass machine-gun companies as well as tank research and development.

Swinton, Baker-Carr, and Lindsay believed machine guns could serve in offensive warfare, but only if they could be carried forward somehow in support of the infantry. To Swinton the answer obviously was to build a vehicle that would, in effect, be a moving machine-gun platform. Another answer, pursued simultaneously by all the powers, was to design and construct light, air-cooled machine guns that could be carried by small crews in direct support of the infantry. The basic issue was the quest for firepower. Infantry supported by machine-gun nests in well-established trench systems was capable of producing a devastating field of fire. In an attack posture, infantry riflemen and machine-gun crews had to advance in spurts, hastily establishing a fire order at each halt. Of course, the attacking force inevitably was subject to the greatest destruction precisely when it was advancing physically across no-man's-land. Already Swinton was beginning to see a possible solution: carry manpower and firepower forward in protected vehicles.

In England, the Ministry of Munitions established the Trench Warfare Department in mid-1915 as a vehicle for experimental work with new weaponry. Experiments with liquid fire, rifle grenades, trench mortars, poison gas, parachute flares, and Stokes guns were undertaken by this naval unit on behalf of the army.[24] The testing grounds at Wembley were a recognition that modern war constantly forced the creation of novel weaponry.

A certain degree of truth lay in the allegation that the German army had been quicker to institute new weapons than either the French or the English. A crash program brought about German use of chlorine gas in spring 1915. Also, trench warfare weapons such as hand grenades, rifle grenades, and improved Model 98 rifles were all issued between December 1914 and March 1915. Gas masks were issued effective 14 December 1915, and steel helmets as of 15 August 1916. Mortars (*Minenwerfer*) developed in three sizes were conceived to be useful against trenches.[25] Progressively, the German army armed itself for trench warfare and deployed modern technology quickly.

More difficult was the procurement of improved artillery under the aegis of an Artillery Testing Commission in Potsdam. Constant testing of the pieces ensured fairly rapid production of new types of howitzers and mortars especially suited to trench warfare. German artillery construction entailed running improvements in established designs during the war. The range of the 77mm cannon, for example, was increased from 7800 meters to 10,700 meters and that of the 105mm howitzer from 7000 meters to 9700 meters. These increases were made possible partly by lengthening the gun barrels.[26]

The German army was plagued by peculiar and nearly constant shortages. At the start of the war industrial capacity was insufficient for the production of either artillery or the standard Model 98 infantry rifle. New factories were built quickly so that, by March 1915, fifteen thousand of these rifles equipped with telescopic sights for use by snipers in the emerging trench warfare had been produced. Supply bottlenecks resulted because of a shortage of priming powder and because of the need to develop a special, hard-jacketed cartridge for sniping. Efforts to remove from service obsolete rifles like the Model 88 failed because it was impossible to build enough Model 98 rifles at any time during the war. In early 1917, the standard Model 98 carbine was in short supply, too. Efforts to use the standard rifle firing special high-powered cartridges against aircraft greatly shortened its life and increased the prevalent shortage. So acute did this problem become by mid-1917 that many rear-echelon troops were equipped with Russian and English small arms. Frontline units had to scavenge no-man's-land and recently fought-over trenches in order to collect abandoned arms of friend and foe alike.[27] At the same time that shortages of conventional weapons and ammunition caused anxiety, the Germans were also busy doing innovative design work for new or improved weapons.[28] Their main difficulty seemed to lie in the domain of production.

French weaponry followed close behind German in terms of innovation. The standard infantry rifle, the Lebel Model 1886, modified in 1893, was equivalent to the German Model 98. Machine guns dated from 1907 and 1914, and were developments of previous designs. Ordinary grenades were introduced in 1915 and were supplemented by tear-gas types in 1916. Rifle grenades appeared in 1916. A 37mm field piece was introduced in 1916 to boost infantry firepower.[29]

By 1916, a variety of mortars such as the French Brandt Model 1916, the British Stokes (3-inch), and the German grenade mortar, Model 1916, were developed especially for defensive combat. These weapons had a range of about four hundred yards and had to be located in the forward trenches. Unpopular with troops, the mortars invited quick retaliation by the other side, resulting in considerable casualties to both armies. Mortars capable of firing projectiles larger than 650 grams, such as the British 6-inch Newton, were good for wire cutting but too heavy for quick transportation forward in an attack.[30] These weapons were all quite similar to one another and although portable were less adaptable to open warfare than to trench warfare.

Production of trench mortars proved to be relatively easy because expensive milling and other machine work was not required. Consisting of a firing pin at the bottom of a tube into which was dropped a projectile, the mortar was light in weight and could be easily taken into the most rudimentary trench positions. Haig noted in 1915 that production of the Stokes mortars did not interfere with regular artillery production.[31]

Efforts were made to develop so-called automatic rifles (submachine guns) that were much lighter and more portable than the existing water-cooled machine guns. The Lewis, Hotchkiss, and Browning versions weighed approximately twenty-four pounds or somewhat more than twice the weight of a rifle and about 60 percent that of a water-cooled machine gun.[32] The Germans were ready to use them early in 1915 in elite storm battalions. In 1915, the French introduced a semiautomatic rifle, the CSRG, which was slightly heavier than a rifle and provided more than twice the magazine capacity. Halfway between a submachine gun and a rifle, it attempted to fill a niche. The Germans knew about it and tried to obtain samples to test.[33] Machine guns designed to be used in offensive combat had to be light yet retain something of the enormous firing capacity of the water-cooled machine gun.

Beginning the war with an efficient stick grenade, the Germans had an advantage over their enemies. But by 1917 the French and English possessed equivalents. British Mills grenades and rifle grenades became reliable and effective weapons; they could be lobbed into trenches and were frequently used by patrols and in assaults.[34]

Flamethrowers, developed and perfected by the Germans, were shown by staff studies to have helped the infantry advance in forty-one cases out of fifty-one in 1915. At that time they accompanied machine guns and the first wave of infantry. Larger flamethrowers were used against concrete blockhouses like the French Fort Douaumont at Verdun. German policy in 1916 and later was to insure that the flamethrowers were always used in conjunction with other weapons, in order to carry on an attack.[35]

A year later Maxse, a leading British infantry tactician, noted that a German prisoner of war had described the new, light trench mortars (*Priestenwerfer*) used by storm troops. But the Germans already had developed attack tactics using flamethrowers and *Minenwerfer* as well. The Germans, unlike their enemies, made real efforts to establish strong infantry storm tactics with these lightweight but powerful weapons.[36] Despite such efforts, the proliferation of large and small mortars greatly added to the destructive power of artillery and increased the strength of the defense more than that of the offense.

CHEMICAL WARFARE

A number of chemical substances had already been used in warfare, including naphtha and bromine. The Prussian War Ministry authorized chemist Fritz Haber to lead a research and development program in October 1914. That program was absorbed into a Chemical Agency (*Chemischen Abteilung*). Easily produced chlorine gas was first dispersed in 1915 at Ypres,[37] prompting the quick development of efficient masks to nullify its effect. Soon more dangerous gases such as phosphor and a mixture of phosgene and tetrachloride were let loose on the Germans by the French in March 1916. A similar attack, on 13 April, was also made on a three-kilometer front. Not attacking on the first occasion, the French advanced in four waves at 4:20 A.M. on the latter date. Despite the potency of this gas no casualties were suffered and the French made no gains. The Germans pioneered development of effective gas masks in early 1916 and educated their troops to use them by showing a training film. Continual testing of used masks, including those of the enemy, enabled the Germans to issue by April 1916 a total of two million masks in successive improved versions.[38]

The German high command also ordered development of more effective gases and of offensive tactics incorporating them. By the middle of April 1916, Type D gas mines designed to be thrown by mortars were issued only to trained pioneer troops who were accompanied by meteorological officers. Everything depended upon wind conditions and the absence of rain. Tactics by August 1916 called for concentrated chemical mortar attacks to precede a normal artillery bombardment in order to demoralize the enemy before the really destructive onslaught occurred.[39]

Abandoning cylinders in favor of gas-filled shells fired by conventional mortars made gas warfare easier. Such shells henceforth formed part of a normal arsenal of artillery. With each improvement in gas-mask protection a further development of gases occurred. As a result gas warfare became a constituent part of artillery practice. But the casualties, once light, became heavier and heavier.

More sophisticated gases, such as mustard gas, caused fear among soldiers because precautionary measures were increasingly ineffectual. Rudolf Binding, a German soldier, stated in his diary of 25 July 1917 that "the English . . . have been plaguing us recently" with a gas that caused lingering death when the lungs of those exposed filled with liquid.[40] Retaliating, the Germans produced shells filled with mustard gas causing increased Allied casualties: total British casualties from the beginning up to July 1917 were 20,000, but they mounted to a total of 160,000 from then until the armistice.[41] Gas warfare became more and more dangerous to all combatants.

At Arras in spring 1917, English phosgene mortar shells caused many German casualties because soldiers neglected precautionary methods despite training efforts. For the first time, massed batteries of mortars became important in gas warfare. The Germans discovered that the new English gas tactics used groups of sixteen to twenty mortars operated by special crews over a range of about a thousand meters. Connected to an electrical firing system in series circuit all could be detonated at the same time. In four minutes, the English could fire three hundred gas bottles of eleven liters each. Copied by the Germans immediately, this system caused a substantial increase in the level of gas warfare for the remainder of the war.[42]

From the middle of 1917 until the end of the war gas shelling either by field artillery or by mortars was a common phase of an attack by any combatant. The German high command decreed that gas was to be used rarely against specific points in the frontline defenses. A still night rather than daytime was better because constantly moving air currents were less common after dark. Gas was also most effective in heavily forested areas where the trees kept the movement of air still or in low-lying terrain like shell holes or trench systems.[43]

Gas shells could also be launched against attacking troops to break up their assaults. German tactics used small mortar gas shells against single batteries or observation posts and medium shells against clusters of machine-gun nests.[44] But gas attacks always depended not only on the vagaries of weather conditions but on the constant upgrading of masks.[45] Chemists and medical specialists in bronchial and lung disorders were regularly consulted about the effect of gases of various types. The development of effective masks required the coordinated efforts of technicians from many specialties.[46]

Although troops accepted gas as yet another danger to their lives, many did not consider it the preeminent one. A number of British soldiers were inclined to discount the importance of gas despite training lectures in rest camps. "The troops were always mildly amused at what they considered the waste of time and money spent in changing and fiddling with gas helmets."[47] Even in 1918 soldiers' attitudes towards gas remained somewhat contemptuous. Some of those exposed told their comrades that their wound stripes were for conventional bullet or shell wounds.[48] Gas warfare yielded ambiguous results partly because most casualties continued to be caused by conventional means.

The most lethal gas was phosgene, a highly toxic respiratory agent, according to experiments conducted by the Germans and Americans. It was one of three extremely lethal gases used by the belligerents, but its effect was lessened because it decomposed in water and, like chlorine, diffused quickly in air. The British also used mustard gas (dichloroethyl sulfide) and lewisite (chlorovinyl dichloroarsine), which were classified by the Germans as Yellow Cross Gases. Each type of gas had certain liabilities: water would dissolve some, some would quickly dissipate in air, and some were highly volatile and tricky to handle.[49] Partly because of these technical difficulties and partly because of the need to use shells to disseminate the gases, their tactical utility was limited. Poisonous gases were an auxiliary to warfare, not a key to victory.

Nevertheless, all armies specifically organized units to conduct gas warfare. German gas battalions after September 1918 included a total of one thousand mortars. These mortars were of both 160mm and 180mm and had ranges up to three thousand meters. For best results in assisting an attack the storm troops were supposed to advance right after the gas bombardment. On one occasion in October, some 776 gas shells failed to stop an Allied attack. Even by this time most poisonous gases could be delayed in effect or even rendered useless by effective head masks.[50] By the close of the war the results remained dubious.

MECHANIZATION

Between 1903 and 1914, the emergence of practical airplane designs, mass-produced internal combustion engines fueled by either gasoline or diesel, and reliable automobiles, trucks, and motorcycles created a mechanized revolution. These developments were largely ignored by the major armies because they did not seem to have an immediate military application.

Agricultural tractors originally had been steam powered and had relied upon large, cleated wheels for traction. In 1901, Benjamin Holt of Stockton, California, designed the first Caterpillar-type, treaded steam-powered tractor. In 1908, gasoline-powered tractors, including a Holt, began to be available to farmers.[51] Although an Australian named de Mole submitted a design to the British War Office in 1911 describing an armored fighting tractor that adapted agricultural designs, it was ignored.[52]

Operating on a pinched peacetime budget, with little or nothing as a research budget, the British army relied upon horses. The King's Regulations for the army published in 1912 specified training and supervision of farriers, blacksmiths, wheelers, shoemakers, tailors, and orderlies.[53] The few staff cars, motorcycles, trucks, and bicycles in the table of organization were anomalies. Despite renewed emphasis on science in warfare in the General Staff College and elsewhere in the service, the great mass of officers remained hidebound in their approach to technology in war. Few of them, except in the engineering service, seem to have had any understanding of modern technology. It is only fair to add that the same conservatism existed in other major armies of the world.[54]

During December 1914, First Lord of the Admiralty Winston Churchill received a letter from retired Admiral Bacon "stating that he had designed a 15-inch howitzer that could be transported by road." Intrigued by this proposed tracked vehicle, Churchill sent it to the master general of ordnance at the War Office. The device was eventually built. Bacon's next armored vehicle was designed to cross trenches, but a prototype was rejected by the War Office in May 1915 because it could not descend a four-foot bank or go through three feet of water. Churchill maintained the Admiralty had taken the lead in this first unsuccessful design.[55]

A second possibility opened up when Col. E. D. Swinton, well respected in the army for his tactical writings following the Boer War, was reminded by Hugh F. Marriott, a civil engineer, that the Holt machine was used on the Antwerp docks to transport heavy goods.[56] The director of artillery and transport in the War Office did not follow up this suggestion, and Swinton found a more sympathetic listener in the secretary of the Committee of Imperial Defence, Maurice Hankey. Swinton suggested to Hankey that the Holt tractor could be converted into a trench-crossing device that would break the stalemate that already seemed apparent by October 1914.[57] Working independently of Churchill, Swinton and Hankey persuaded the War Office to study this proposal. A Holt tractor failed to cross a trench through mud, and the War Office abandoned any interest in it by March 1915. Nevertheless, Hankey's memorandum of 18 December 1914 contained the first practical suggestion for a tank. The machine would have been propelled by bulletproof rollers fitted with Caterpillar-type treads and would have mounted a machine gun. "The object of this device would be to roll down the barbed wire . . . to give some cover to men creeping up behind, and to support the advance with machine-gun fire."[58]

Disgusted with the lack of interest by the War Office, Churchill determined to use the resources of the navy in pushing for the development of a fighting vehicle. Swinton and Hankey agreed later that if Churchill had not persisted any tank design would probably have languished from inattention. Churchill called up the resources of the Royal Naval Air Service, the Royal Naval Armoured Car Service, and the Royal Naval Construction Department. Expert in naval matters, specialists in these agencies were called upon to work on a project that was totally foreign to their experience.

On 15 February 1915, the Landships Committee of the Admiralty was formed under the director of naval construction, Sir Eustace D'Eyncourt, to consider a design submitted by Major Hetherington, an officer from the naval air service. This scheme promoted construction of huge vehicles with large-diameter wheels (the pedrail concept), mounting 12-inch naval guns, heavily armored, and forty feet long. Strikingly reminiscent of H. G. Wells's land ironclads, these "landships" were "designed to transport a trench-taking storming party of fifty men with machine guns and ammunition."[59] This project was abandoned as impractical in June 1915.

Although at the end of August 1915 the R. N. Armoured Car service was disbanded, one squadron was retained because it was doing all the tank trials previously done by the Trench Warfare Department of the Ministry of Munitions. Squadron 20 continued to test "land battleships" and was, in fact, disguised as a unit of the Royal Naval Air Service until that organization was absorbed into the Royal Air Force.

The Landships Committee began to apply rational engineering criteria into its design. "Experiments have determined certain definite ratios between the length and height of the landships and the width and height of trench and parapet to be crossed."[60] After studying two experimental machines, the committee determined by late summer 1915 that the desired height of a practical machine should be seven feet, six inches, its length twenty-six feet, its width nine feet, and its total weight without guns and ammunition twenty-two tons. These figures emerged after conferences between the Landships Committee of the Admiralty and a committee of the War Department. Serious work was undertaken late in 1915 on two Caterpillar-type treaded experimental machines known as "Mother" and "Little Willie."[61]

Before Churchill resigned from the Admiralty, as a result of the Dardanelles crisis in May 1915, he persuaded D'Eyncourt and Gen. Sir George Scott-Moncrieff to head a joint Admiralty–War Office committee to develop future designs. Swinton had finally persuaded his superiors to consider military applications of the Holt tractor a few months earlier. This particularly crucial step involved the transfer of men from the Naval Air Service to the testing grounds. As a consequence, Admiralty personnel continued to play very important roles in the evolution of the first tank and, indeed, in future tank design.[62]

Navy influences were strikingly important in the development of the prototype Mark I heavy tank as it emerged in 1916. A lozenge-shaped object with high sides reminiscent of a landing craft or similar amphibious vessel, this tank carried naval 6-pounder cannon mounted in sponsons on the sides, suggestive of the secondary armament of capital ships of the day. Its construction, however, was undertaken by William Foster of Lincoln, a firm that usually built agricultural implements and other heavy machinery. Few or no automotive experts were involved in its design.[63] On 29 June 1915, General Scott-Moncrieff uneasily noted that the design calculations "were more analogous to a battleship than an ordinary land transport vehicle."[64] The earlier land battleship had been abandoned because of its unwieldy size: one of Hetherington's devices would have weighed 300 tons. This design hit a dead end when measurements of railroad cars and roads in France indicated vehicles of this size could not be transported.[65] Thus, the important change of direction came in June 1915 when the Admiralty had to share its work with the War Office. But the Admiralty's sea-faring designs left an impact. The first British tanks, designated Mark I, were the fruits of the design teams of 1915. In appearance they betrayed their peculiar naval origin.

The future commander of the Tank Corps, Hugh Elles, summarizing prospective tactics before tanks were actually built, claimed that the first machines were designed to cross open territory relatively free of shell holes and were not durably made. At Loos, some three-quarters of a million shells were fired in three weeks, but "the actual shell consumption in the opening week of the Somme was nine times as great, at the third Ypres twelve times as great." Elles correctly indicated that early battles, such as Loos, did not yet show the effects of heavy artillery bombardment. "No one could have visualized ground such as the Somme in September 1916 after rain." Tanks designed in 1915 to cross only moderately shell-pocked terrain were not suitable for combat later, when massive bombardments completely roughened the soil.[66]

FRENCH MECHANIZED INNOVATIONS

Toward the end of 1914, when the front stabilized, a number of persons in France suggested mechanical devices to overcome the strong defensive system of trench fortifications. A Lieutenant De Poix designed a machine for breaking barbed wire and crossing trenches, and the firm of Schneider sent two engineers to study his plans. Schneider's technicians happened to see several American Holt agricultural tractors at work at Aldershot and ordered two from the United States. During 1915, Schneider and Creusot built machines using Caterpillar-type traction.[67]

A deputy of the Chamber of Deputies, Jules-Louis Breton, saw demonstrations of the Schneider machine and contacted General Headquarters.

At trials held in December 1915, the military experts remained dubious about the combat possibilities of the machine because even if it survived artillery fire in its advance it would not be able to cross a trench more than a few meters wide. At this time, an artillery officer, Col. Jean Estienne, independently noticed Holt tractors and, like Swinton, saw how they might be useful. Estienne approached General Headquarters and obtained authorization to take charge of experimental work for the army. He met Breton and the two evidently were able to obtain a contract for four hundred machines for Schneider on 25 February 1916.[68]

After the war a quarrel arose between Estienne and Breton when the latter published an article claiming he invented the French tank in 1915. Just as it happened in England, the notion of a tractor fitted with armor and guns breaking through the trench war defensive systems also occurred to a number of French military and civilian persons at the same time, so sole credit for the design cannot be ascribed to any one of them. Thomas Kuhn has argued that the development of new paradigms in the history of science produces such a phenomenon of multiple innovations.[69]

Unfortunately, jealous opponents of Estienne in the Automobile Service of the army and in the government succeeded in obtaining a parallel contract for four hundred tanks for St.-Chamond in April 1916. Estienne claimed he had not been consulted before the contract was let, nor had the Caterpillar company been approached.[70] When design efforts were divided between the two projects and basic problems involving the belted metal tread systems were not satisfactorily resolved, both the Schneider and the St.-Chamond tanks were seriously flawed and obviously inferior to the British Mark I.[71] Although this discouraging result was not apparent until 1917, Estienne, entrusted with tank design by Joffre in early 1916, already had reservations about these heavy tanks.

On 27 November 1916, Estienne wrote to Joffre recommending the development of light tanks of four tons weight as preferable to the cumbersome and troublesome heavy tanks. From this demarche emerged the Renault light tanks, of which four thousand were constructed before the armistice. A chance conversation with the head of France's largest automobile company, Renault, led Estienne to make this highly important recommendation. Renault produced these light tanks using automobile assembly techniques and they were successful in the 1918 campaigns.[72]

In summary, the British produced a workable, if flawed, heavy-tank design of thirty tons, which they christened the Mark I. Taking advantage of lessons learned in combat in 1916 and 1917, they also produced a medium tank of quality, the Whippet, in small numbers in 1918. In contrast, the French had little success with heavy tanks, but achieved good results with light tanks. By the armistice Estienne had obtained some British Mark V tanks to replace his own heavies. The Americans used Renault light tanks because they could get no heavy tanks from the British and their own production was lagging. As a consequence, by the latter part of 1918, production of these various types of tanks was considerable and, if the war had continued until 1919, many more tanks would have been present in battle.[73]

AIRCRAFT PRODUCTION

Unlike tanks, aircraft proved increasingly important in the tactics of both offense and defense. Given continuous attention and financing by the high commands of all powers until the armistice, military aircraft production was not hampered by periodic stoppages as was the case with tanks. Even early in the war the relatively few scouting planes available quickly proved to be efficient replacements for obsolete cavalry. Subsequent combat experience revealed great advantages of using aircraft in artillery spotting. Because of their versatility and obvious uses in trench warfare, aircraft were built in numbers during the war.

As soon as the value of aircraft was demonstrated, all of the countries in the war tried to expand production. In 1914, the RFC and the Royal Navy Air Service had a total of 272 aircraft, but a substantial increase in manufacturing occurred thereafter. In the British Isles in the first ten months of 1917, some 14,000 airplanes were made; in 1918, up to October, 25,685 were manufactured. The monthly production rate by the end of the war had reached 3500.[74]

French production was remarkable as well. A total of 541 aircraft were produced between the end of July and the end of December 1914. Production in 1915 was 4489, in 1916 it was 7549, in 1917 it was 14,915, and in 1918, 24,652. The cost increased from 15,000 francs per unit at the start to 30,000 at the end, not counting engines. Engines cost over 100,000 francs each by 1918. The Inspectorate of Construction was a bureaucratic brake on new designs. In France, as in England, production of spare parts for existing aircraft had to be pursued at the same time as new designs were developed. The inspectors of construction were not always trained persons and they acted rigidly in allocating priorities. Colonel Guiffard recommended the abolition of the inspectorate and its replacement by a number of autonomous units attached directly to him: for aircraft, engines, arms, and aviation instruments. Reduction in the number of types of aircraft and their engines also led to increased production.[75] The productive records of both France and England were astonishing. They individually built more aircraft than the Germans and together, by the middle of 1917, were in a position to dominate the skies by numbers alone.

Comparative figures from Germany are disputable, but approximately 694 airplanes were delivered in the last months of 1914, 2950 in 1915, 7112 in 1916, 13,977 in 1917, and 17,000 in 1918. The weakest aspect of German production was engines. Until the end of 1916, German engine production kept pace with French and exceeded English, but it fell behind afterward. A near-monopoly by Daimler along with unfortunate decisions by inspectors combined to insure weakness in engine production until the end of the war. John Morrow in *German Airpower in World War I* concludes: "German aviation mobilization in 1917 and 1918 was plagued by administrative confusion and inefficiency, the breakdown of transportation, and shortages of raw materials and labor." Bumbling attempts by the army to dictate to industry contributed.[76]

Technical and engineering leadership also was developed by the Allies in the aircraft industry. Lord Weir mentioned in a postwar lecture that some eighteen months elapsed between the inception of an aircraft design and its completion and "during most of this period no useful practical experience can be obtained." Only actual service could provide the data for revised versions. "By the time bulk experience of its behavior is available, it is necessary to supersede it by another more advanced type." He also said, "Less than half the time needed for the development and trial of an aeroplane design was devoted to engine design."[77] An especially spectacular evolution in engine design took place in 1917. In France, for example, fighter engines were increased in horsepower from about 85 in later 1914 to nearly 400 by the end of 1918. The German aircraft engine industry could not keep pace because its design parameters were determined bureaucratically. Early, the German inspectorate limited aircraft engine production to 150 horsepower in order to keep from interfering with existing production. A further mistake was made when the inspectorate rejected the Benz 240-horsepower engine and ordered work on 500–600-horsepower engines that were never produced. English, French, and American engines in 1918 approached 300 and 400 horsepower, so the Germans never caught up in the horsepower race.[78]

Despite production problems, the German air force was a formidable opponent to the Allied air services. Nevertheless, the expertise of German aviators could not compensate for lagging development of innovative technology. When the German aircraft industry ceased to be competitive, the air war was lost. The rapid technical evolution of aircraft had made it possible for the Germans to seize command of the airspace over Verdun earlier in 1916 and over the Somme by the closing months of the same year. More important, the Germans seem to have settled on a succession of aircraft designs that were each temporarily the best available. For example, the Fokker single-wing fighter was superior to anything it fought up to the summer of 1916. It was then rendered obsolete by new British and French designs. Oswald Boelcke, an ace, was killed in such an aircraft in the fall. Baron Manfred von Richthofen flew in the Albatros, which was a very formidable aircraft during much of 1917. Further Allied design improvements rendered that plane obsolete by the beginning of 1918. Richthofen then flew a Fokker three-wing fighter until his death in April 1918. But German design success lagged in the last year of the war.[79]

Greatly transformed by the tremendous increase in production of arms, military equipment, ammunition, and aircraft, the civilian economy was permanently changed. It can truly be said of France that she entered the First World War almost as a preindustrial power and emerged as a world-class leader in technology. The full story of the industrialization of France is not yet known. As an example of burgeoning growth, the French quantitatively dominated the manufacture of aircraft engines throughout the war. Monthly production rose from 25 in 1914 to 4490 in July 1918. Some 92,386 of all types were manufactured in total.[80] Production of this nature was not possible in Germany. The British lacked technical expertise in engine design for reasons still not determined and relied heavily upon French engines.

Aircraft technology was a strange mixture of the old and the new. Great employment opportunities arose for cabinetmakers, carpenters, painters, and workers in cloth-making trades. Thousands of women were employed in England and France in sewing linen or other cloths to wooden fuselages, wings, and tail assemblies prepared by cabinetmakers and carpenters. These traditional technologies paralleled new technologies in developing aircraft prototypes and production models. Mechanics, tool and die workers, machinists of many different types, electricians, and others had to be retrained from existing jobs in the automobile or other mechanized industries. New technicians employed in the making of radio equipment had to be trained fresh because there had been no viable industry of that type before the war. The aircraft of the war epitomized, in their bizarre mixture of sophisticated technology and old-fashioned handiwork, the ambiguities of the war itself.

TECHNOLOGY, MANPOWER, AND STRATEGY

Because of the wastage of trench warfare the allocation of men and material could only be resolved by a grand strategy for the conduct of the war. A pool of trained technicians existed in factories, but it was constantly under pressure from military conscription officials because of the incessant need for infantrymen to replace the heavy losses on the western front. But after the middle of 1916, certain political leaders such as the new prime minister, Lloyd George, and the French and German governments, placed limits on conscription. The public was becoming restless and disillusioned with the progress of the war and was beginning to view the trenches as charnel houses in which unlimited numbers of soldiers were killed because of the incompetence of military leaders.

Also dangerous, and increasingly a problem in late 1917, was the growing shortage of skilled workers in the factories. A report to Albert Stern, the British director of tank production, indicated that in order to produce forty Mark IV tanks per week industry needed 1650 skilled, 300 semiskilled, and 200 unskilled workers. The skilled included millwrights, machine hands, and fitters. None of these could be removed by the army through conscription into the forces without a decrease in tank production. Between 7 February and 30 May 1917, Mark IV tanks were, in fact, produced at the rate of twenty per week partly because Haig agreed with Stern to release 380 skilled workers from the army.

But as 1918 arrived, industrial exemptions proved harder and harder to obtain. Attempts to conscript skilled workers caused strikes and slowdowns and otherwise adversely affected production.[81]

A political problem of the greatest magnitude existed: What would be the disposition of the available manpower? A number of writers have devoted their attention to this difficulty.[82] Although women were hired to perform many assembly and even some semiskilled jobs in munitions and aircraft factories, they could not totally make up the loss of men in industry. As a consequence, the British high command especially had to consider ways and means to stretch their manpower and still keep a viable combat role.

Haig opposed the imposition of a general reserve and the dispatch of troops to the Italian theater in 1917 and 1918 because of the manpower crisis. Lloyd George also pressed General Pershing, the American commander, to assign large numbers of American troops to fight in British units. This pressure was exerted to a lesser degree by the French. Pershing convinced Secretary of War Newton Baker and President Woodrow Wilson that American troops had to fight in their own units and in a separate American army, and should not be used as cannon fodder by the Allies.[83] Arguments between Pershing, Foch, and Haig over this issue raged up to the middle of 1918.

Noting the manpower shortage, some exponents of tanks, like J. F. C. Fuller, argued that these vehicles should be produced in large numbers because they were labor-saving devices. A single tank was worth more on the battlefield than a large number of infantrymen. What better way to make ends meet than to utilize mechanization in war? Fuller suggested. The saving of human labor by the use of machines would have as pervasive an impact on the battlefield as on the civilian economy of the Industrial Revolution. Fuller argued in July 1918 for the abolition of cavalry divisions and their replacement by tank divisions, claiming: "If half of [the] horses in Cavalry Division could be replaced by petrol-driven tractors . . . over 250,000 tons of shipping would be saved yearly." A field artillery brigade relying solely on horses needed 723 animals, of which 560 were used for transport. Some four tons of forage per day was needed by this unit alone. If twenty-four tanks were used instead, six per battery, three for ammunition, and three for guns, the total petrol needed would weigh the equivalent of the forage needed to feed five hundred horses, assuming average use of transport of forty miles per day. It was cheaper to use mechanization than horses, and one gained elsewhere: motorized vehicles could move an army much faster than horse-drawn vehicles: "Success in war depends on mobility."[84]

Shortage of labor and shifting production priorities resulted in a shortage of tanks and weaponry. When the War Office fiddled with priorities a decrease in tank production occurred at one juncture. Haig also reduced their priority in March 1917 when he placed aircraft first, and railway and road mechanized transport second, with tanks third. The immediate impact of this decision was the War Office directive to Kitson's Works ordering them to manufacture both tanks and locomotives, but with priority to the latter. Stern observed: "It is useless to hope for enthusiastic work in the shop, when the manufacturing staff do not know from day to day if they are to make tanks, or if they are to make locomotives, or if they are to try half and half." Fortunately, he convinced the military authorities to permit the completion of the tank order before starting the locomotive order.[85]

The German war effort was plagued by shortages of both manpower and material. As indicated previously, a systematic policy of scavenging the battlefields resulted because of the shortage of the standard Model 98 infantry rifle. In August 1918 collection parties were taking not only weapons but ammunition, steel helmets, and water flasks from battle sites. Rifles found in the mud were carefully cleaned and oiled and repaired when necessary throughout the war. The Germans also used French laborers and Russian prisoners of war to build fortifications because the pioneer companies were not equipped to do large-scale military engineering projects. Efforts were made to scour the streets of major German cities to find unemployed persons with some skills as ironmongers, masons, concrete workers, shoemakers, and so on to be enrolled in special engineer companies as early as 1915. Despite such efforts to free troops for combat, the German forces steadily developed a large and complicated rear-echelon or service component, which utilized great numbers of soldiers as grooms, motor vehicle drivers, weapons repairmen, medical services aides, veterinary technicians, and so on.[86] Because of its need to conduct a two-front war, the German army had to be frugal with its supply of men and weapons.

Finally, the evolution of military tactics was directly influenced by the availability of troops, their nature, equipment, and training. Large amounts of artillery ammunition and of numbers of infantrymen in early 1916 permitted the German attack on Verdun and the English offensive on the Somme. By contrast, the shortage of manpower and the availability of tanks encouraged Haig to adopt the innovative plan for the attack on Cambrai in November 1917. The presence of a large number of eastern front soldiers on the western front in early 1918 permitted Ludendorff to stage the general offensive of 21 March. Foch was in an admirable position in July 1918 to allocate specific jobs to his Allied subordinates because of the large American army then present in France and because of the availability of large numbers of weapons, including French and English tanks. Out of these strategic decisions arose, of course, the revisions in tactics.

THE LIMITATIONS OF TECHNOLOGY

The story of the development of new weapons and the improvement of existing ones during the period from 1914 to 1918 reveals many curiosities and many contradictions. The easiest weapons to develop and produce were mortars of all sizes because they required no high technology and could be manufactured by firms not manned by specialist trades or dependent upon expensive tool and die machinery. The most difficult were tanks, which were truly innovative, but which directly impinged upon the routine conduct of the war because they required myriads of engineering technicians and artisans as well as machinery that ordinarily could be used for the manufacture of road and rail transport vehicles. Trucks, railroad cars, and locomotives were always needed to keep the huge trench warfare armies supplied; they were preeminently suited for stationary warfare. But tanks seemed to promise a means to restore open warfare.

In the end, the production of weapons reflected the divergence of aim of the military commanders and their staffs. Existing technology proved to be the foundation for the wartime development, first of siegecraft technology, then of open-warfare technology. Pershing was right in maintaining in 1917 that the Allied powers had to make a conscious decision to endorse open warfare and end their dependence upon siegecraft. Without continued and conscious endorsement of the tactics of open warfare it was impossible to provide the weapons needed for that warfare.

The introduction of poison gas proved disappointing because it did not provide the immediate results anticipated by some. But the introduction of every new weapon in the war met the same fate. Before such innovations could be used successfully they had to be tried, and the best trials were battles. But trials showed the enemy the secret and enabled him to start planning to counteract. This dismal pattern was repeated with tanks later in the war.

The development of tactics may well entail the invention of a new type of weapon. But such a weapon could not emerge until certain preconditions were met. It was possible, but expensive, to rifle musket bores in the eighteenth century, but the armies of that era were equipped with smoothbore muskets because they could be cheaply built in large quantities without the specialized work of gunsmiths. In the nineteenth century, the invention of steam-powered milling machines and lathes made it possible to decrease the unit cost of rifles to the point where such weapons could be mass produced.[87] Therefore, the theoretical design of a weapon can never be elaborated until there exists a technological support for its evolution as well as a long-standing commitment of research funds. Tactics, then, must use those tools that already exist and can only suggest in theory a possible future application of an innovation.

NOTES

1. Reichsarchiv, *Der Weltkrieg*, 1:82, 137–58.
2. Stone, *Eastern Front*, 50.
3. Charbonneau, *Frontières*, 8–9.
4. Farrar-Hockley, *Death*. Carew, *Vanished Army*, 66–76.
5. Edmonds, *Military Operations*, 1:47–54. J. G. M. Rouquerol, *Charleroi*, 27–29. J. J. Rouquerol, *Charleroi, Août*, 130–31.
6. Foerster, *Weltkrieg*, 66, 74, 77, 79, 86, 87–88. Bloch, *Souvenirs de guerre*, 14–15.
7. Georges Blanchon, "La guerre nouvelle," *Revue des deux mondes*, 1 Jan. 1916, 82–119; 15 Jan. 1916, 326–64.
8. Blanchon, "Guerre nouvelle." BSA, AOK 6, Bd. 9a.
9. PAC, Ottawa, RG 9 III, vol. 3858, folder 85, file 4.
10. Bidwell and Graham, *Fire-Power*, 68–69, 96.
11. Carrington, *Soldier*, 83–84. Richards, *Old Soldiers*, 92–93. Arthur Guy Empey, *Over the Top* (New York, 1917), 287, stated: "Tommy does not use it to play cricket with."
12. Anon., *The War the Infantry Knew*, 105.
13. Public Records Office, London, MUN 5/391, 2–3. (Hereafter, PRO.)
14. PAC, Ottawa, RG 9 III, 3858, folder 85, file 4.
15. Desmond Chapman-Huston and Owen Rutter, *General Sir John Cowans* (London, 1924), 2:92–93.
16. Charles Nordmann, "Le ministère des inventions," *Revue des deux mondes*, 1 Feb. 1916, 687–97.
17. Charles Nordmann, "Science et guerre," *Revue des deux mondes*, 1 Dec. 1915, 698–708.
18. John Ellis, *Social History of the Machine Gun* (New York, 1975), 113.
19. Ellis, *Machine Gun*, 115–16. BSA, AOK 6, Bd. 350.
20. BSA, AOK 6, Bd. 326, Bd. 350.
21. Liddell Hart Papers, 9/28/59, letters from Lindsay, 19 December 1948 and 1 November 1947.
22. Ellis, *Machine Gun*, 118.
23. Liddell Hart Papers, 9/28/59, letters from Lindsay.
24. PRO, MUN, 5/391, 7–8.

25. Cron, *Weltkriege,* 117–18.

26. Wilhelm F. Seesselberg, *Der Stellungskrieg* (Berlin, 1926), 259.

27. BSA, AOK 6, Bd. 107, Bd. 115.

28. BSA, AOK 6, Bd. 107, Bd. 115. Production difficulties are described by Gerald Feldmann, *Army, Industry, and Labor in Germany, 1914–1918* (Princeton, 1966), 493–95.

29. France, Grand Quartier Général, 3e Bureau, *Manuel du chef de section d'infanterie,* 1917 ed., 117–46.

30. Ministère de la Guerre, Écoles Militaires, *Cours d'artillerie,* 3e partie, Cat. A-B-C, 1921, 111–20. Bidwell and Graham, *Fire-Power,* 124–25.

31. Haig Papers, ACC 3155, 96.

32. *Cours d'artillerie,* 72–89.

33. *Cours d'artillerie,* 85–86. BSA, AOK 6, Bd. 107.

34. Bidwell and Graham, *Fire-Power,* 125.

35. BSA, AOK 6, Bd. 9a, Bd. 326.

36. Maxse Papers, 69/53/6. Seesselberg, *Stellungskrieg,* 69.

37. L. F. Haber, *The Poisonous Cloud* (Oxford, 1986), provides a modern interpretation of poison gas use in this war. See 2–3 on Fritz Haber, and 22–35 on the first Battle of Ypres.

38. BSA, AOK 6, Bd. 333.

39. BSA, AOK 6, Bd. 328, Bd. 333.

40. Binding, *Fatalist,* 175–76.

41. A. F. Barnes, *The Story of the 2/5 Battalion Gloucestershire Regiment 1914–1918* (Gloucester, 1930), 99. Frederic J. Brown, *Chemical Warfare* (Princeton, 1968), 1–12.

42. BSA, AOK 6, Bd. 326, Bd. 333. Haber, *Poisonous Cloud,* 180ff, for a description of the British gas effort.

43. BSA, AOK 6, Bd. 326, Bd. 344.

44. BSA, AOK 6, Bd. 326, Bd. 344.

45. Barnes, *Gloucestershire Regiment,* 130.

46. BSA, AOK 6, Bd. 344, Bd. 333.

47. Barnes, *Gloucestershire Regiment,* 130.

48. Leonard H. Nason, *Chevrons* (New York, 1926), 254.

49. Mario Sartori, *The War Gases* (London, 1940), 4–28.

50. BSA, AOK 6, Bd. 344. Haber, *Poisonous Cloud,* 176–86.

51. Roy B. Gray, *The Agricultural Tractor, 1855–1950* (St. Joseph, Michigan, 1975), 85.

52. B. H. Liddell Hart, *The Tanks* (London, 1959), 1:16.

53. *The King's Regulations and Orders for the Army* (London, 1914) with amendments up to August 1, 1914, 1193–1265.

54. Jay Luvaas, *The Education of an Army* (London, 1964), remains a key discussion. Colin, *Les transformations,* and similar important prewar works by French, English, and German theorists seem to have ignored contemporary technological developments.

55. Churchill, *World Crisis,* 4:508–9. Liddell Hart, *Tanks,* 1:32ff.

56. E. D. Swinton, *Eyewitness* (London, 1932), 31–32.

57. Stephen Roskill, *Hankey, Man of Secrets* (London, 1970), 1:81.

58. Churchill, *World Crisis,* 1:512–13. Roskill, *Hankey,* 1:148.

59. Liddell Hart, *Tanks,* 1:32. PRO, MUN, 4, 4979. Churchill, *World Crisis,* 1:513. Liddell Hart, *Tanks,* 1:29.

60. PRO, MUN, 5/391, 2–25.

61. PRO, MUN, 4, 4979, "Tank History, 1915."

62. Swinton, *Eyewitness,* 139–81.

63. Churchill, *World Crisis,* 1:516. Albert G. Stern, *Tanks, 1914–1918: The Log Book of a Pioneer* (London, 1919), 38–48.

64. Stern, *Log Book,* 54–88.

65. Liddell Hart Library, King's College, University of London, Stern Papers, I/C/1, 20.

66. Hugh Elles, "Some Notes on Tank Development During the War," *The Army Quarterly,* July 1921, 2:267–81.

67. AMV, "Historique de l'Artillerie d'Assaut" in 16 N 2121.

68. AMV, 16 N 2121.

69. AMV, 16 N 2121. Thomas Kuhn, *The Structure of Scientific Revolutions* (Chicago, 1962).

70. Estienne, "Note resumant la question du materiel de l'artillerie d'assaut," 28 November 1916, 16 N 2121, was very critical of the St.-Chamond tank design and tests.

71. The technical descriptions of the St.-Chamond, Schneider, and Renault tanks are in AMV, 16 N 2131, and bear out the major weaknesses of the heavy-tank designs especially.

72. AMV, 16 N 2121.

73. Stern, *Log Book,* discussed tank supply matters of the Allies with inside knowledge.

74. George A. B. Dewar, *The Great Munition Feat* (London, 1921), 187–88, 205. Lee Kennett, *The First Air War* (New York, 1991), 93ff.

75. Maurice de Brunoff (ed.), *L'aéronautique pendant la guerre mondiale* (Paris, 1920), 391–94.

76. John H. Morrow, Jr., *German Air Power in World War I* (Lincoln, Nebraska, 1982) 189–90, 202. Feldman, *Industry and Labor*, 371ff.

77. Dewar, *Great Munition*, 187–88, 205.

78. De Brunoff (ed.), *L'aéronautique*, 145–46.

79. Manfred von Richthofen, *Der rote Kampfflieger* (Berlin, 1917), 65, 77–78.

80. De Brunoff (ed.), *L'aéronautique*, 398.

81. PRO, MUN, 4, 2791; MUN 5, 391.

82. See, for example, Feldman, *Army, Industry, and Labor*, 362–402 describing the fall of Groener, who tried to reconcile conflicting objectives. Frank P. Chambers, *The War behind the War, 1814–1918* (London, 1939). Arthur Fontaine, *L'industrie française pendant la guerre* (Paris, 1926), described the hard choices between industrial and military demands for manpower in France.

83. John J. Pershing, *My Experiences in the World War* (New York, 1931), 2:20–38.

84. PRO, MUN, 4, 4979.

85. PRO, MUN, 5, 391. Production of tanks gradually accelerated so that, by 28 July 1918, the Ministry of Munitions estimated 900 Mark Vs and 2440 Mark VIIIs could be produced in 1919. PRO, MUN, 4, 4979.

86. BSA, AOK 6, Bd. 107, Bd. 115, Bd. 328, Bd. 350.

87. Pioneering work in the history of military technology includes William H. McNeill, *The Pursuit of Power* (Chicago, 1982), 232–41, and Martin Van Creveld, *Technology and War* (New York, 1989).

CHAPTER 6
CAVALRY OF THE SKIES

Almost at the start of the war aircraft proved useful in reconnaissance and by 1915 were increasingly employed for for artillery registration or "spotting." But in other functions, such as bombing or strafing to support an infantry attack, they disappointed military planners. Air power possessed a potential for application in war, as many guessed at the time. William Mitchell, American air power advocate, would boast: "Air power, therefore, conquers the opposing state in war by paralyzing its nerve centers" while "the army occupies the ground so conquered."[1] Technological limitations prevented the fruition of tactical innovations, nevertheless, and Mitchell's claims could not be verified during the war.

In 1914, the Royal Flying Corps and the Luftwaffe existed in mere embryonic forms and most of their development occurred after the war started. Maurice Baring described the ad hoc and small-scale activities of the infant RFC in the first six months of the war under General Henderson. Brigadier Gen. Hugh Trenchard, later commander of the Royal Flying Corps, had been left at Farnborough in charge of the Administrative Wing of the RFC and Baring recalled that "he afterwards told me that all the nucleus consisted of was one clerk and one typewriter, a confidential box with a pair of boots in it, and a lot of unpaid bills incurred by various officers of the Flying Corps, during the rush to the front."[2] The number of aircraft was few and the place of the RFC was modest indeed within the total context of the British army.

German Gen. Ernst Hoeppner, later in charge of the inspectorate of the Luftwaffe, mentioned that the occasional use of dirigibles and aircraft in maneuvers before the war had not resulted in rapid expansion of the air arm by the 1912 *quinquennat* (budget for 1912 to 1916). Lack of infantry officers, lower soldier complements, and budgetary cutbacks combined to keep the Luftwaffe small and experimental. Only in 1913 was there a supplementary increase because the military lobby finally succeeded in outflanking the naval lobby in apportioning the defense budget. Some five "flying battalions" emerged. The General Staff hoped that "this simple arrangement had already brought the flying troops into a close relation with the Ground Troops Command (*Truppenführung*) before the war."[3] But the arrangement was pro forma and the Luftwaffe was even less prepared to fight a war by 1914 than the RFC.

The civilian support systems for the air arms of England and Germany were even less developed than the military structures by the outbreak of war. In neither country had great industrial interests been involved in the design and construction of aircraft. In neither country was there in place a governmental procurement system for aircraft and their mechanical components. But at least it was possible to envisage the future development of both civil and military tactical support systems by August 1914. Baring indicated, however, that at a time when Kitchener was planning fifty squadrons for the RFC, it "seemed the most wild of dreams."[4]

F. W. Lanchester, an engineer on the British Advisory Committee for Aeronautics, wrote an analysis of air power in November 1914 in which he anticipated its future value. "The aeroplane has, in the present war," he claimed, "been able to give information of the positions and movements of the enemy such as would have been otherwise unobtainable," and has made it possible to attack some places not reached otherwise. Therefore it was true to say "it has invented or originated new duties not overlapping those of the older Arms—it has not replaced cavalry in any measurable degree, neither has aeroplane bombardment been found effective as a substitute for gun-fire."[5] The effectiveness of aircraft was doubtful at this early point, but Lanchester did identify, partly correctly, the mixture of advantages and disadvantages which his "fourth arm" possessed.

FLY OVER AND LOOK DOWN

Substantial limitations of aircraft design and construction during the war affected their tactical applications. Lack of effective speed for many aircraft (slightly more than a hundred miles per hour) combined with wooden-frame and fabric-cover construction made flyovers at low altitude hazardous. Deficient communication systems meant that artillery spotting, reconnaissance, and ground support work did not always function smoothly. Low-flying aircraft were vulnerable to attack from above as well. Pilots of the First World War did not like flying of this type; many victims of the aces were hapless pilots and observers in slow-moving, low-altitude artillery-spotting aircraft. Until speed was increased and construction strengthened, aircraft had real limits in assisting ground forces.

Bombing in the period up to the end of 1915 was largely ineffectual. The German air force attack on St.-Omer on 28 July 1915, accompanied by a threat to destroy the whole town in several raids, was a farce. French and British aircraft, between 1 April and 18 June 1915, dropped some 4062 bombs with equal lack of success. Attempts to hinder German movements by bombing railway junctions and stations produced minor damage. The Royal Flying Corps in July 1915 concluded pessimistically that "it may be as well to eliminate bomb dropping altogether," and to confine aircraft to "reconnaissance, observation for artillery, and fighting in the air, in which they have proved their value and for which the Allies cannot have too many aeroplanes."[6] General Trenchard, commander of the RFC since late 1915, was convinced by November 1916 that bombing was "entirely secondary and comparatively unimportant."[7]

Although the Luftwaffe used dirigibles in what later became known as "strategic bombing," their use became too dangerous over the front lines. However, zeppelins had an average bomb load of 3000 kilos and were used in raids on London and Paris by the end of January 1916. Such bomb loads were far in excess of the capabilities of heavier-than-air aircraft. The British Handley Page 0/400, a two-engine biplane, could haul about six hundred kilos, for example.[8] Only in 1918 would bombing by heavier-than-air planes prove to be of some value.

All of the air forces began the war with one obvious role: reconnaissance. In the first phase of open warfare, aircraft quickly showed the ability to find enemy forces and report them, although bad weather and inexperience sometimes greatly limited these efforts. The scouting function, traditionally that of the cavalry, became an aerial preserve. Although Lanchester had believed that "there will still remain country in which cavalry can be advantageously employed," this view proved overly sanguine.[9] Once the period of open warfare was over, however, reconnaissance duties changed. The general position of the enemy was fixed in trench warfare, but the specific locations of enemy force components changed frequently. Artillery batteries were moved, augmented, or diminished in number, while infantry was transferred in and out of rear areas and support or frontline trenches. Railroad and road traffic, if observed, could enable an opponent to anticipate possible surprise attacks.

Aerial photographs helped plan artillery barrages and infantry attacks. In the Somme offensive of 1916, the British used fighters in formation to protect reconnaissance planes over the German front lines following French practice at Verdun. Slow-moving, two-seater planes flying close to the ground could photograph with some degree of safety because fighters provided a cover above. Such aircraft still remained exposed to fire from the ground; radio antennas were frequently shot away and fuselages riddled with shot. Photographs contributed to the success of the British attack of 14 July because they identified enemy positions. Unfortunately, the battle was spoiled later because reconnaissance reports of feeble enemy strength in front of the advance were not believed.[10]

Successful aerial reconnaissance was based upon aerial superiority. General Rawlinson noted on 23 May 1916 that since the RFC had chased the Fokker monoplanes from the skies, "we have successfully photographed the whole of the enemy's trenches in front of the Fourth Army."[11] By the end of 1917, each side equipped its planes with cameras with the specially long focal-length lenses needed for high-contrast photography in order to form an accurate picture of the enemy lines.

Artillery spotting, which had become important in 1915, was organized into a sophisticated activity in 1916. Specially designed single-seat fighters built to defend observer aircraft no longer engaged one another in individual combat but in mass formations. The conflict of fighter aircraft was soon seen as necessary to take command of the air. Only through control of the airspace could artillery spotting as well as photographic reconnaissance be done on a continuing and reliable basis.

The use of artillery observation aircraft, more and more widespread during 1915, paralleled the growth of artillery units themselves. By November, the RFC war diary entries showed that while bombing results were uniformly meager, artillery spotting often produced information that enabled batteries to accurately register their shooting.[12] Nevertheless, air observation in 1915 remained episodic and opportunistic.

During 1916, a gradual improvement in aerial observation occurred. On 12 February 1916, for example, the RFC used a "pre-arranged programme, which had been worked out in detail with both Heavy Artillery and Corps Artillery and army Headquarters." Three planes were sent up, of which two protected the one that registered hostile batteries. Six enemy trench targets were reported by wireless. A subsequent foray was also successful. A German attack had been "nipped in the bud" because of this system. On 2 March 1916, some fifty-one German batteries were registered, and the commander of the V Corps enthusiastically complimented the "aeroplane observers" who "have been indefatigable." The Fourth Army reported similar success in May using dropped messages and sketches as well as wireless.[13]

The success of the Royal Flying Corps did not continue unchallenged. Trenchard had already noted the problem of finding adequate pilots and observers in December 1915. Each of the pilots from England had only twenty-five flying hours, but had never flown the BE-2C, the standard observer aircraft in France. Trenchard did not want to train the pilots in France because they would damage or destroy valuable aircraft while learning. But he needed a constant and growing supply of aircrews that could "combat the German machines which are getting very active and numerous."[14] A serious problem of the war continued to be the provisioning of such replacements.

British control of the air continued during 1916. Successful artillery shoots were recorded for 16 March and April, showing that co-ordination of observers and artillery fire was improving. On the latter occasion: "No. 4 Squadron working with 8-inch howitzers obtained a direct hit on a gun emplacement completely destroying it." But poor weather could reduce the effectiveness of air observation to nil.[15]

Trenchard, more and more convinced that aerial observation had to be improved, urged on 1 June 1916 that aircrews be given more training in the cooperation of artillery and air. A debate raged in General

Headquarters over the responsibility for aerial observers, caused by the demand by the Royal Artillery that air artillery observers be subject to control by the artillery units. Trenchard prevented this jurisdictional assault, but believed, nevertheless, that both flying and artillery personnel should be trained in better methods of cooperation. "Artillery personnel are not trained in the use of wireless," or even in basic coordination with air observers. As a result of Trenchard's efforts the air-artillery course at Lydd was expanded, using veteran combat aircrews. It is astonishing that the artillery service would not have tried on its own initiative to improve cooperation.[16] Sometimes guilty of error, Trenchard and the RFC at least were not bound by the natural conservatism of an older service. The Royal Artillery had its accustomed rules and procedures.

The quarrel over who ruled the air observers bedeviled Trenchard during the Somme campaign when Rawlinson, commanding general of Fourth Army, and Horne, commanding general of First Army, urged Haig to give control to the artillery. Haig's artillery commander, fortunately, supported Trenchard's view that the observer craft were to remain under RFC control, and the threat disappeared by November 1916. Trenchard noted that the Somme offensive perfected cooperation with artillery "and that from the end of the battle onwards, improvements were only in detail."[17]

Air-artillery cooperation depended upon wireless communication. Efforts to use other means such as light signals in January 1916 had not proved too successful. In May 1916, Trenchard issued new regulations requiring wireless training not only for artillery observation pilots but also for those who bombed trench and support positions. In late 1916, a manual entitled *Cooperation of Aircraft with Artillery* established a new ranging system based upon zones. Each zone corresponded to a square identified by a letter on a 1:40,000-scale map. Wireless communication using signals corresponding to the zones proved far superior to the cumbersome method of laying ground sheets with coded messages. The latter drew enemy fire, as did any visual or audio signal. By the spring of 1917, it was possible to have one wireless observer for every thousand yards of front.[18]

Also used in the Somme campaign of 1916 was a clock code. The aerial observer identified an hour on an imaginary clock face in his wireless report. If the signal "H.H.HE. 10" was sent, for example, it meant the range was to be lengthened in the direction of ten o'clock. The RFC pioneered in developing effective artillery-air cooperation.[19]

But with the development of a strong German fighter force in the summer of 1916, the RFC lost control of the air, exposing the infantry to enemy harassment. Capture of German airmen revealed that each corps and army had been provided with a squadron of at least six machines for reconnaissance and artillery spotting. More formidable was the sudden appearance of *Kämpfgeschwader*, or wireless-equipped combat squadrons with which the high command hoped to seize control of the air. Ground commanders complained that these German aircraft bothered air observers, jammed signals, and made counterbattery fire difficult. The RFC replied that "fighting patrols of scouts," which engaged enemy aircraft in combat, were the only effective solution, not the dispersal of aircraft to guard observers.[20]

As a result of problems like these, Trenchard determined to establish a new policy, declaring on 23 August 1917 that the airplane was not a defensive machine and that the "battle in the air can only be won by taking the offensive and persevering in it." In common with Haig, he emphasized maintaining an offensive posture in the air as on the ground. The French, during the battle of Verdun, had encountered disaster when they had not followed this policy. During the Somme battle the Germans had discovered the value of the offensive and found that to "win the battle on the ground they must first win the battle in the air." The Germans had then reorganized the Luftwaffe, Trenchard claimed, and increased the production of machines using a "rigid system of standardization in types and material."[21]

Trenchard described other significant changes that had occurred in the aerial war after the Battle of the Somme. The Germans, between October 1916 and August 1917, had not gone over completely to the offensive, but had preferred to stay in strength on their own side, receiving the offensive thrusts of the British. The altitude of aerial fighting had increased from seventeen thousand to twenty thousand feet, although some battles occurred at twelve thousand feet. Formations of aircraft had taken the place of individual flights.[22] As a result, the aftermath of the Somme had evolved into a protracted struggle for control of the skies. The working-out of tactics to gain supremacy came above all else: artillery spotting and reconnaissance could only be done successfully if the fighters achieved overall control.

Developing a concept of aerial supremacy similar to that of the British by October 1916, the French created combat flying formations: Gabriel Voisin, French aircraft manufacturer, claimed, "Experience has shown that it is necessary . . . to assign in active sectors squadrons particularly trained in aerial combat." But there were disclaimers: constant protection had to be given to observation flights, which were vital. Supremacy in the air meant that the fighter aircraft would eliminate the threat of enemy aircraft interference in aerial observation. Yet the French were hard pressed in August 1917 and lost control of the air in some sectors, exposing their infantry to considerable aerial attack. An appropriate aphorism summed it up: "The rifleman, master of the ground, needed to believe that our aviators are masters of the air."[23] The struggle for control of the air continued.

German ideas evolved applying experience gained at Verdun. The high command created "infantry pilots" who were supposed to maintain a liaison with the infantry in order to fathom the nature and depth of enemy artillery firing. Manfred von Richthofen remarked, "If I had not been a combat pilot, I believe I would have attempted infantry flying" and believed that such pilots helped "our hardest fighting troops." During the Arras battle of 1917, Richthofen had helped provide fighter protection for these low-flying infantry liaison planes.[24]

Another category of pilot, the combat pilot, was successfully advocated by the first German ace at Verdun, Oswald Boelcke. Unlike his famous predecessor, Max Immelmann, Boelcke was renowned less for his individual tactics in combat than for his pioneering of squadron formation flying. By October 1915, Boelcke was already achieving fame, and he became an object of emulation to Manfred von Richthofen. Boelcke's fighter squadron achieved great success in the destruction of enemy aircraft even before it was transferred to the Somme. The coordinated attacks of these spectacular pilots (including Richthofen) actually cancelled English air control for a period.[25] Therefore, Trenchard was right to identify the Battle of the Somme of the summer of 1916 as a turning point in the air war.

In the new era of air warfare large formations battled one another solely to achieve aerial supremacy. In theory, reconnaissance and artillery observation planes were helpless unless enemy fighter aircraft were eliminated. In reality, such aircraft frequently eluded pursuit and destruction even if the other side possessed a momentary superiority of aircraft. It was true, however, as Rawlinson remarked during the Somme battle, that improved British aircraft and better-trained pilots did keep German fighters away while photography was going on.[26]

Although it was long believed that the Germans had pioneered formation flying, Trenchard pushed for this innovation early in 1916, even before Boelcke popularized it. By mid-January of that year, determining that reconnaissance work should be done by groups rather than by single planes, he created formations of four aircraft. The French had the same idea at the same time. By June, air superiority was achieved because of better Allied tactics, aircraft, and the fact that the RFC in particular had more than 50 percent of its strength in fighter aircraft. These swarms of fighters escorted the reconnaissance and artillery-spotting aircraft behind the enemy lines.[27]

The Verdun and Somme engagements of 1916 were disastrous for the Germans because their prime fighter, the Fokker *Eindecker* (single wing), was obsolete and because they did not produce nearly as many aircraft as their enemies. Only in 1917 would they have substantial numbers of new aircraft that would serve effectively in group or formation flying to combat the Allied planes.[28] In fact, the Somme battle had evoked a real crisis in the administration of the Luftwaffe: concerned about failures in the air, the high command reorganized the squadrons and expanded the training program for pilots.

So rapidly did the fortunes of the air war change that by early 1917, the RFC was at a decided disadvantage. Only 12 out of 39 squadrons were suitable for escort work, offensive patrols, and combat. Only five squadrons were equipped with the latest fighter aircraft: Sopwith Pups and Nieuport 17s. These—and later others such as the Bristol F2A two-seater, the Sopwith Camel, and the SE 5—could meet the German fighter formations (*Jastas*) on near-equal terms. But the formidable fighting formation of the Germans, which Richthofen perfected, enabled them to send up far more planes at a particular time and place than could the English.[29] The German command and communication network was probably also superior to that of the British.

Trenchard remarked in 1917: "Fighting not only extended upwards, but downwards; low-flying machines cooperated with infantry and attacked men, guns, trenches, transport, and hostile aerodromes, flying at a very low height."[30] But the salient fact about the air war of 1917 was that it had become a gigantic struggle for control of the air. Because neither side was able permanently to grasp this control, the work of artillery observation and infantry support became much more hazardous and less effective.

TO STRAFE THE ENEMY

Arras, the name given by the British to a series of battles in April and May 1917, relied heavily on air support. Haig planned the battle with the capture of Vimy Ridge in mind, because of its commanding position in the vicinity of Amiens. The attack was coordinated, first with Joffre and, after his fall from power, with General Nivelle. Arras saw the start of effective air support of infantry advances.[31]

The British attack at Arras was set for April 1917 and was planned to support French attacks. Tanks were employed to facilitate a number of short infantry advances, under cover of a "creeping" barrage of shrapnel. A preliminary barrage, also considered necessary, provided a "pillow" bombardment of the entire enemy trench system for 96 hours commencing 4 April 1917.[32]

Although aircraft had a major role in the enterprise, unexpected bad weather caused a hitch. The opening of the Somme battle the previous year had been plagued by similar troubles. Planned artillery firings had to be abandoned or proved ineffectual. Nevertheless, the appearance of large formations of enemy aircraft caused little interference with artillery spotting. The careful planning of wireless communication paid off: receivers on the ground near batteries were tuned in to the frequencies used even before the aircraft transmitted. This method provided quick coordination of artillery fire on a target and gave good results despite the doubts of the RFC. Observers could range as many as six batteries on a hostile battery site during a two-hour period, providing exact locations marked on detailed maps.[33] New techniques for artillery-aircraft cooperation were successful.

In spring 1917, the English began a policy of strafing enemy trenches, supply dumps, railroad lines, and marshalling yards. Although these flights were dangerous to the pilots because they had to fly low in the thick of ground fire, Sholto Douglas, an experienced pilot, later claimed the flights proved successful.[34] Increasingly concerned about this problem, the German high command in August 1917 issued a directive denying the efficacy of using flak and combat aircraft and ordering concentrated machine-gun and rifle fire on strafing aircraft. Single sharpshooting was useless; a heavy curtain of fire was needed. Inaugurating a complicated defensive policy that lasted until the end of the war, the Luftwaffe built up an antiaircraft flak organization as well as special rangefinders for machine guns on the ground. The sheer volume and detail of successive edicts indicates clearly the obsession the Germans had with stopping low-flying aircraft. Above one thousand meters, enemy aircraft were fought by the effective fighter squadrons based in airdromes close to the front. Below that altitude ground attack had to be the preeminent means of combat. By the end of 1917, Ludendorff ordered the training of machine-gun crews. He emphasized exercises like a one-hour flyover of planes over a division front so crews could aim at Very flares set off at various altitudes. Machine-gun emplacements containing column mounts for the guns enabled one man to aim and fire. Finally, troops were taught to lead the target. This led, naturally, to special gun sights for antiaircraft use in early 1918. With the increase in enemy aircraft attacks on ground troops in the last year of the war, the German army devoted itself more and more to antiaircraft defense.[35]

Effective use of aircraft using wireless to range trench systems and rear areas enabled British pilots to machine-gun troops and to direct artillery attacks. During the actual infantry attacks, however, observer planes used klaxon horns rather than wireless to communicate with the troops. Flares were attempted, but the infantry frequently neglected to ignite them to mark their advance.[36] On the occasion of an attack on 3 May, some fifty-seven hostile batteries in the Third Army area were registered by aerial observation, and some forty-two shoots on emplacements were successful. The new techniques for artillery counterbattery work proved more successful than for infantry-air coordination.

Not remaining idle in the face of Allied advances, the Luftwaffe was defensively reorganized. Enemy aerial activity was monitored on the ground by special air protection officers (*Luftschützoffiziere*), whose reports determined whether air group headquarters sent up formations of interceptors. Soon, rival formations fought for control of the airspace over the entire front lines. "Fighters fought fighters, while those doing artillery work engaged enemy two-seaters employed on a similar mission," according to Hilmer von Bülow. Hard pressed, the English fought until May, when Richthofen went on leave and the German aerial campaign ceased.[37] The pressure on German resources was great: a German commentator noted that the English held fast to their goals in the Arras attack. "They always threw new masses of infantry and batteries in the battle zone. The attack strength in the air became stronger and stronger . . . some eighty formations with about seven hundred aircraft were reached." By the middle of July the English had a substantial numerical superiority of aircraft on the front.[38] Once again, struggle over artillery observation had led to massive air battles. But significantly, some of the mass struggle for control of the air by July 1917 was the result of fear on both sides that infantry contact work might really develop into a formidable assist to ground attacks.

The new tactics of the RFC by mid-1917 emphasized reconnaissance, photography, and bombing. But increased escort fighter protection for all aircraft had recently been added as an important duty. The English scout patrols of Nieuports were supposed to drive off enemy artillery spotter planes and to protect their own spotters. Trenchard did not adopt the large fighter formations of the Germans at this time because he thought they lost flexibility in action and encouraged aerial fights of a "confused and disjointed nature which seldom ended really decisively for either side."[39]

French tactical concepts emphasized the need to obtain "absolute freedom of the air." Attacking ground targets as a priority, combat aircraft designated as "infantry aircraft" followed the advance of infantry and used signals to inform them of the enemy's dispositions. Using "flexible zones" similar to the English ones, the French allocated four artillery spotter aircraft to the entire front of the corps artillery (two for each division). The Germans remarked that the French definition of the duties of the infantry pilot identified the situation accurately by August 1917, because aircraft on both sides now "fly over at low altitudes using machine-gun fire to halt and turn back the enemy."[40] Air power was slowly being harnessed to ground power.

NEW COMBAT ROLES

By July 1917, air power was definitely considered important in warfare, but the definition of its tactical role remained contentious. Overriding everything was the need to determine how much it or any other weapons system contributed to ending the trench warfare stalemate. On Monday, 16 July, Haig noted that at dinner Pétain had argued with Trenchard, advancing the French concept "of close protection of artillery machines," as opposed to the RFC preference for "distant attacks to draw off his machines. Trenchard had the best of the argument."[41] But the policy of the RFC to engage in aggressive forays behind enemy lines had proved immensely costly and had led to the great aerial formation combats that vitiated the ground-support role of air power during 1917. A solution had to be found to the near stalemate in the sky that existed in mid-1917.

NOTES

1. William Mitchell, *Memoirs of World War I* (Westport, Connecticut, 1975), 4–5. Originally written in 1926. Kennett, *First Air War,* is an excellent overall study of airpower in this war.

2. Maurice Baring, *Flying Corps Headquarters, 1914–1918* (London, 1930), 45.

3. Ernst Hoeppner, *Deutschlands Krieg in der Luft* (Leipzig, 1921), 2–3.

4. Baring, *Flying Corps,* 45.

5. Frederick W. Lanchester, *Aircraft in Warfare: The Dawn of the Fourth Arm* (London, 1916), 125–27.

6. Baring, *Flying Corps,* 101–2. S. F. Wise, *Canadian Airmen and the First World War* (Toronto, 1980), 354. Document of July 1915, quoted by Jones, *Strategic Bombing,* 64–65.

7. Haig Papers, Haig to Secretary of the War Office, 1 November 1916.

8. Reichsarchiv, *Weltkrieg Beilage,* 3:396–402. Jones, *Strategic Bombing,* 122.

9. Lanchester, *Aircraft in Warfare,* 37.

10. Wise, *Canadian Airmen,* 372–75.

11. PRO, AIR, 1, 131, 15/40/223.

12. PRO, AIR, 1184. RFC War Diary.

13. PRO, AIR, 1184. RFC War Diary. Montgomery-Massingberd Papers, 47.

14. PRO, AIR, 1, 131, 15/40/218.

15. PRO, AIR, 1, 1184. RFC War Diary.

16. PRO, AIR, 1, 131, 15/40/224.

17. PRO, AIR, 1, 676, 11–14.

18. PRO, AIR, 1, 676, 14–26. AIR, 1, 131, 15/40/218. Haig Papers, ACC 3155 96.

19. PRO, AIR, 1, 676, 26.

20. PRO, AIR, 1, 1512/204/58/25 3d Brigade, RAF, Third Army, WO 157, 5. Summary of intelligence information.

21. PRO, AIR, 1, 718/2919 Trenchard.

22. PRO, AIR, 1, 718/2919 Trenchard.

23. André P. Voisin, *La doctrine de l'aviation française de combat* (Paris, 1932), 18–20. AMV, 16 N 1994, 16th Army Attack Report.

24. Richthofen, *Kampfflieger,* 180.

25. Richthofen, *Kampfflieger,* 65–66. Cron, *Geschichte,* 205–6.

26. PRO, AIR, 1, 131, 15/40/223.

27. Wise, *Canadian Airmen,* 362–69.

28. Hoeppner, *Deutschlands Krieg,* 85–89.

29. Wise, *Canadian Airmen,* 395–417. Richthofen, *Kampfflieger,* 144–46.

30. PRO, AIR, 1, 718/2913 Trenchard.

31. Cruttwell, *Great War,* 404–8. Edmonds, *Military Operations,* 1:60ff.

32. PRO, AIR, 1, 676.

33. PRO, AIR, 1, 676.

34. Sholto Douglas, *Years of Combat* (London, 1963), 193–94.

35. BSA, AOK 6, Bd. 350.

36. PRO, AIR, 1, 676, 66 for quote.

37. PRO, AIR, 1, 676.

38. Hilmer von Bülow, *Geschichte der Luftwaffe* (Frankfurt am Main, 1934), 92.

39. PRO, RFC, conclusions in AIR, 1, 676.

40. AMV, 16 N 1988, 3e Bureau. "Note sur le fonctionment de l'aviation," BSA, AOK 6, Bd. 350.

41. Blake, *Haig Papers,* 245.

CHAPTER 7
WELLS'S DREAM FULFILLED

P rior to 1914 the tactics of mobility depended on foot power
and horsepower, but only peripherally on rail power. In the
ensuing stalemate the development of artillery, aircraft,
motorized transport, and especially tanks brought about a
revolution in mobility.

Horse-mounted cavalry had once acted as a reconnaissance force,
as a mobile striking force, as a powerful force assisting infantry, even
as a protector of artillery. After the introduction of rifled weapons in
the nineteenth century, cavalry's future became problematic, but the
cavalry itself remained because it was the only arm promising mobility on the battlefield. Increasingly, since Napoleonic times, great struggles
of massive infantry units supported by artillery fastened combat to rather
constrained locations. Cavalry traditionally provided one means for
breaking such deadlocks and thus returning the battle to fluidity. Therefore,
despite cavalry's serious limitations by 1914, no one was prepared to
abandon it. The end of open warfare, however, quickly showed that
mobility had ended; how could it be brought back?

The proponents of early tank designs always believed they had found
one of the keys to renewed mobility. Since many were not professional
military officers, the War Office assumed that their tactical recommendations were the dreams of enthusiastic if ignorant amateurs. Thus,
the tactical doctrine for tanks had to be formulated, presented to higher

authority, adapted to fit the needs of other units of the service, and tried in action by a few military professionals. The evolution of these tactics required long periods of committee deliberations within the army. In France, Estienne had to fight hard to establish a tank program under similar handicaps. Considering the radical nature of tanks it is truly remarkable that eventually they did play very important roles in combat during World War I. Only sheer desperation on the part of such commanders as Joffre, Pétain, and Haig, who were seeking a solution to the trench warfare impasse, permitted development of this untried expedient.

HOW DO YOU USE TANKS?

Early tanks were designed to be armored vehicles that would break through a heavy infantry defense system without incurring severe casualties. Therefore, the tactical ideas that influenced early armor design were from the beginning offensive rather than defensive. In 1917, it was possible to envisage a return to open warfare using tanks. The second phase of tactical evolution then occurred: breakthrough followed by exploitation.

Amateur enthusiasts included literary figures and social commentators and reformers before the war. In 1855, James Cowen hoped to produce a "locomotive land battery" that would be fitted with scythes to "mow down infantry." H. G. Wells envisaged "land ironclads" that would destroy enemy defenses and render infantry impotent.[1] A mining engineer, Hugh F. Marriott, thought the Holt tractor could be adapted to military purposes. Although these men lacked military qualifications, they did obtain some prewar notice from the service professionals. E. D. Swinton, widely known in the prewar army for his minor tactics doctrines, was an intellectual as well as a professional military officer. Maintaining a friendship for many years with Marriott, he was receptive to the Holt tractor suggestion in July 1914. Marriott's ideas were sent to the Committee on Imperial Defense and came to the attention of Maurice Hankey, its secretary. The War Office did nothing, however.

Swinton was sent by Lord Kitchener to France after the war broke out as the official journalist, or "eyewitness." As early as 21 September 1914, he reported that battles of position like those found in the Russo-Japanese War had succeeded battles of motion. In October, back in London, he suggested to Hankey that the Holt tractor could be used as a siege engine to break through trenches and perform as a "machine-gun eater."[2] Influenced by Swinton, Hankey prepared a memorandum, dated 28 December 1914, advocating a large vehicle that could "roll down the barbed wire by sheer weight, to give some cover to men creeping up behind, and to support the advance with machine-gun fire."[3] The question was brought to the highest circles.

Illustrative of the difficulty that Swinton and Hankey faced was the comment of the latter: "Swinton did not have much luck at G.H.Q. Nor did I at first . . . Asquith was most appreciative and promised full support—if I could get W.[ar] O.[ffice] to play." Kitchener, however, believed that "the armoured [C]aterpillars would be shot up by guns."[4] Now proselytizing with vigor, Swinton told his friend General Lindsay, future commander of the Machine Gun Corps, that the design would be "simply of a machine that would carry infantry forward, and over enemy trenches."[5] In the end, the War Office, under the direction of the master of ordnance, General von Donop, decided to table the entire idea after an inconclusive test of tractors on 2 February 1915.[6]

Swinton later complained that "it is extraordinary that the Army in the Field and the War Office should have allowed nearly three months of trench warfare to progress without addressing their minds to its special problem." He believed, certainly, that six months after the first Ypres battle of 1914, "we ought to have realized that our established methods were useless in warfare of such a nature." The slaughter of infantry was the glaring reason for this conclusion.[7]

Not hearing of any progress, Swinton wrote a memorandum to General French, which the latter sent to the War Office on 22 June 1915. Since machine guns prevented breakthroughs with traditional infantry attacks, more firepower was necessary. Either high-explosive shells could "blast a way" or "some other means of destroying these weapons or at least of meeting them on equal terms" could be developed. Although the first was not yet possible, the second was if one used "armoured machine gun destroyers." If made in secret and used in a surprise action, some fifty of these machines, one hundred yards apart, could cover a front of five thousand yards. "The machines being in position ready, the wire entanglements in front of the hostile trenches will be bombarded and cut early in the night before the assault is intended to take place." At dawn they would leave their pits and advance directly on the German lines, aiming for known machine-gun nests.

The infantry would advance with them in comparative safety because enemy fire would be directed on the machines. For defensive purposes, the machines could be brought forward to act as mobile strong points in case of enemy attack.[8] Swinton's memorandum was the first attempt to develop a tactics for tanks, even before they existed.

Trials of the prototypes, Little and Big Willie, in January and February 1916 in the presence of Lord Kitchener, cabinet ministers Arthur Balfour and David Lloyd George, and chief of the Imperial General Staff William Robertson did not convince everyone. Despite the misgivings of Lord Kitchener, Robertson claimed to have persuaded him to approve the immediate order of a hundred machines. Not knowing this, if indeed it was true, Swinton prepared another tactical scheme by the end of February, suggesting that "tanks should accompany the infantry in its advance" and "should not be used in driblets" but be kept secret until large numbers were ready for a surprise assault. Concentrated behind the front until attack time, some of the tanks were to use radio receivers, some were to rely on visual signals, while others used field telephones. Afterward, Swinton claimed that he had laid out the scheme subsequently used at the Battle of Cambrai in November 1917.[9] This was a pardonable exaggeration.

Swinton argued at this point that "the tanks cannot win battles by themselves" but had to accompany "the infantry to sweep across obstacles which shell fire misses." Cautiously, he recommended silencing enemy batteries "by dropping bombs on them from the air," since they constituted the greatest danger to the machines. After a normal preliminary attack, which would not arouse suspicion (he argued in an unfortunate lapse), the attack should occur on a five-mile front with one hundred tanks. One very important point was successfully made by Swinton: tanks should *precede,* not *follow,* infantry. He emphasized that a coordinated advance would help both tanks and infantry: one without the other would be disastrous. Following close on the tanks would be successive waves of infantry. The tanks would halt at the front line only until the infantry caught up and would then move on to hit the next trench-line defense. Swinton emphasized concentration of firepower: the tanks, with infantry, would "burst right through the enemy's defensive zone in one great rush" rather than making ponderous step-by-step progress.[10]

The suggestions of Swinton resulted in the War Office appointing him lieutenant colonel in command of the "Motor Machine Gun Service" on 28 March 1916. Concerned with production initially, Swinton took Lt. Albert Stern and W. G. Wilson as his chief assistants. He told Haig he would have no tanks as early as June 1 but the entire one hundred ready for August. Haig, earlier anxious to have about twenty tanks for a tactical exercise, met with Swinton on 14 April and recounted: "I gave him a trench map as a guide and impressed on him the necessity for thinking over the system of leadership and control of a group of 'tanks' with a view to maneuvering . . . during an action."[11] Haig's enthusiasm, not shared by the War Office, made development of the tank a reality.

Production difficulties postponed completion of the first batch of tanks until September. Haig probably persuaded the War Office to increase the preliminary order to two hundred and fifty. To Stern and Swinton the newfound pressure from Haig threatened to bring the tank into disrepute. Both thought it was wrong to introduce it "before experience had shown to what extent the Tank, as then designed, could be of use in the field." Despite these protests, Stern found out from the minister of munitions, Lloyd George, the CIGS, Robertson, and Swinton that a small number of machines were to be used in action in September.[12] To the enthusiastic supporters of tanks it must have seemed ironic that the military authorities, after first ignoring the machines, finally and without taking expert advice decided to throw them into action.

Hoping for success, Haig took Joffre to see a demonstration of eleven tanks accompanied by two battalions of infantry on 3 September. Joffre was impressed and "ran about on his little feet till he poured with perspiration." But Haig was determined that the tanks would be well used in their debut. He talked to Rawlinson, commander of the Fourth Army, who was in charge of the attack in which the machines were to be used, urging "advancing quickly so as to take full advantage of the surprise."[13] The attack, on Flers, was planned as a local action for 15 September.

A crew-training program started in February 1916, when Swinton produced his *Notes on the Employment of Tanks* and selected a number of officer cadets with engineering experience. They believed they would serve in armored cars. No tanks were available for months, so the personnel were trained in the use of the armament of the vehicles. Finally, a course was laid out for the actual training in tanks in early June. So hurried was the training that "there was no time for everything." One tank officer stated that "the Tanks did not arrive till the last minute, and I and my crew did not have a Tank of our own the whole time we were in England."[14]

A typical military foul-up occurred the day before the battle of Flers was to start (14 September), when verbal orders were substituted for written instructions, causing confusion. About fifty tanks were moved up in pitch-black darkness and many broke down in the mud and in shell holes. "Most of the men had never heard guns before."[15] When the attack was launched the next morning some tanks led and some followed the infantry: no effective training with infantry had occurred.

Rawlinson reported late on 15 September that "certainly some of the Tanks have done marvels! and have enabled our attack to progress at a surprisingly fast pace." General Byng reported that the commander of the German 211th Regiment, when a tank lay across the trench and fired into the troops on either side, surrendered with the remark: "This is not war, it is butchery." Nevertheless, out of forty-nine machines that started, only thirty-two reached the starting point for the attack. Subsequently, five more were ditched and nine broke down.[16] The Mark I proved to be mechanically unreliable.

Paradoxically, while everyone was impressed by reports of the individual tank actions at Flers, few could agree on whether the tanks would prove to be superb weapons or not. The small scale and ambiguous results of the operation prevented the speedy evolution of better tactics. Only future experience in action would assist that theoretical development.

FROM FLERS TO MESSINES

After Flers the tanks continued to be tested in small combat episodes. Some of the pioneers, particularly Swinton, professed to believe that the Battle of Cambrai in November 1917 simply followed the lines of the September 1916 battles.[17] In fact, only in barest outlines did it do so. Tremendous progress had been made in tank tactics in the previous year. Swinton was replaced by Hugh Elles as the field commander of tanks when the Tank Corps was established; Swinton lost touch quickly.

Prior to his assignment, Col. Hugh Elles, Royal Engineers, had little contact with tanks. Haig had sent him to check on the progress of tank design soon after he assumed command of the BEF in January 1916. Elles was nominated by Swinton to be the Tank Corps commander because of his acceptability to headquarters in France. Despite the political nature of his appointment, Elles competently supervised a crew-training program and the organization of the Tank Corps. Three brigades of three battalions each, together with a massive support structure, including a central workshop, composed the corps.[18]

Were the tanks prematurely employed at Flers? G. le Q. Martel, the brigade major under Elles in the new Tank Corps, summarized quite clearly the debate on this issue. Those who supported the use of tanks at that time believed they were justified because, first, "the correct mechanical design of tanks and their proper tactical employment" required combat experience. Also, no commander would have staked an offensive on the theoretical capabilities of an untested machine. Finally, the Ministry of Munitions would not have devoted scarce resources to manufacture such machines.[19] J. F. C. Fuller, who was appointed to the Tank Corps shortly as General Staff Officer One, later told Liddell Hart: "The use of tanks on 15 September 1916 was not a mistake. Serious mechanical defects manifested. No peace test can equal a war test."[20] Haig noted the action at Flers and asked the War Office to send as many machines as possible but at the same time to improve their armor.[21] Obviously, the use of tanks at Flers could be justified.

Despite the evidence for this belief, many others refused to accept it. Lloyd George, Churchill, Stern, Martel, and Swinton objected to the introduction of tanks in battle in September 1916. As minister of munitions, Lloyd George talked to Churchill, who then beseeched the prime minister, David Lord Asquith to stop the action. Failing, Churchill believed that "a secret of war which well used would have procured a world-shaking victory in 1917 had been recklessly revealed to the enemy."[22] Martel commented that the Mark I tank differed little from its successor, the Mark IV of 1917, except that the latter had better armor and strengthened track rollers. Swinton had been wrong, despite Martel's apology, for using unarmored machines because he "counted on a sufficient degree of surprise to ensure that the enemy was not prepared with unlimited supplies of armour-piercing ammunition." The handling of the Mark I tanks according to Martel was better than that of the Mark IVs because they were lighter than the latter. But precisely the opposite view was taken by A. Williams-Ellis, the official historian of the Tank Corps.[23] In any event, the attack at Flers was followed by other small-scale attacks later in the month.

The modest attack at Flers had revealed major problems. Because of the absence of tactical theory and training beforehand, the movement of tanks had been haphazard. The pitifully few tanks available were dispersed among a number of divisions instead of being concentrated for maximum effect. It is possible that a major breakthrough might have resulted if a much larger force of tanks had been employed, as recommended by Swinton and Stern. But the Ministry of Munitions could not provide four hundred or more tanks earlier than January 1917.

Moreover, the tactics had not really been worked out. Detailed staff work involving coordination of tanks with infantry, as well as the training of accompanying infantry and tank crews, had not been done. In fact, the cancelling of previous written orders only hours beforehand and the substitution of vague verbal orders indicate clearly that Swinton did not have a real grasp of the use of tanks in an attack. How could he or anyone else have understood everything? Fuller was right to claim that battle experience was absolutely necessary.

More serious was the lack of confidence in tanks of the chief field commander, Rawlinson, manifested in his comments afterward that the tanks had "rendered very valuable service" but had failed to live up to the exaggerated claims of their proponents. Inexperience of the crews, low speed, poor terrain, and inadequate engine power prevented the machines from being "of much value to an infantry assault." But if these problems could be overcome the tanks would achieve their potential.[24] Swinton misinterpreted Rawlinson's critique by claiming that he denied the importance of tanks.[25] More important was Haig's enthusiasm. Haig even suggested to Admiral Bacon on 18 September "that he should carry out experiments with special flat-bottomed boats for running ashore and landing a line of Tanks on the beach."[26] This was a remarkable, if stillborn, suggestion to land on the Belgian coast.

As battle experience with tanks was studied it was clear that they were more vulnerable than their promoters realized. Rawlinson unreasonably expected them to go fast over very rough ground; terrain too broken by shell holes or too muddy could not be traversed by them. Tanks, Haig thought, should be moved at night to concealed launching points and should not move across open fields in daylight because they might be "knocked out by a direct hit by enemy's guns." General Gough agreed to send his tanks across during the early morning mist.[27] In the attack of 25 September, the tanks were accompanied not only by infantry but by aircraft as well.[28] Haig went to considerable trouble to persuade both Rawlinson and Gough to use tanks in different situations.

Haig produced a substantial memorandum entitled "Note of Use of Tanks" dated 16 October 1916, in which he claimed tanks were "entirely accessory" to the "advance of infantry in close cooperation with artillery." When they had reached the enemy lines slightly in advance of the infantry they had accomplished some startling successes: they demoralized the enemy, diverted machine-gun fire, and did great damage to personnel in trenches. Haig believed they would be able to eliminate enemy strong points that were holding up the infantry. He thought tanks should move about fifty yards ahead of the infantry, but separating the two forces created problems with creeping artillery barrages. Lanes could be left unshelled for tank movement forward. Crews had to keep their tanks in motion to make enemy fire more difficult. Tanks could be guided forward at night by the use of tapes on the ground. Finally, very careful orders with maps must be provided to the tank commanders prior to the attack.[29] Clear sighted and intelligent, Haig's memorandum was based upon study of the battle results and constituted a benchmark in tactical development.

In contrast, a long memorandum entitled "The Tank Army," prepared by G. Martel, brigade major of the newly constituted Tank Corps, envisaged a totally mobile army. J. F. C. Fuller no doubt was influenced by this memorandum, dated November 1916. Squadrons of fast (20 miles per hour) tanks accompanied by sappers and signalmen (also mobile in tanks) as well as mobile workshops and medical facilities would constitute the mechanized corps.[30] It was an immense extrapolation from meager evidence and of little immediate use.

The ebullient Stern, who never feared to speak about matters he might not have the professional military background to comprehend, advocated that tanks be used independently of infantry as a mobile force that would rapidly cross land not previously damaged in bombardment. Light tanks, he thought, could act as cavalry in reconnaissance roles. The British General Staff representatives argued that tanks were not yet reliable enough mechanically to be independent of infantry. They also were not fast enough, and it was premature to expect them to act the role of the cavalry.[31] In fairness to Stern, ideas of a so-called tank army had been floating around the Tank Corps as early as November 1916, and he did not invent them. What was lacking in the entire discussion was realization of the need for interdependent employment of tanks with other arms. Until April 1917, when the Battle of Arras began, great efforts were made by Stern to increase production. Stern had heard that Haig "was quite enthusiastic . . . I fancy you will have received a demand for another 1,000 by this time."[32] Starting with the initial order for this amount in October 1916, Stern issued a number of contracts to manufacturers for various components. He was astonished to hear that the Army Council had cancelled the order on 10 October. Minister of Munitions Lloyd George was able to persuade CIGS Robertson to rescind this order when Stern protested.[33] But he warned Colonel Elles, commander of the Tank Corps, on 25 January 1917 that delays in production and shipments could still prevent the buildup of large quantities of tanks for some time.[34]

Unimpressed by the combat record of tanks in various small engagements, the War Office told the Ministry of Munitions in June 1917 that it placed them in third priority behind aircraft and mechanical transport vehicles for both railroad and road use. Haig had earlier, in February, refused to increase the order from one thousand Mark IV tanks and had placed aircraft engines and light railroad engines in superior priorities.[35] The proponents of tanks had to produce something major, and Colonel Elles and his new chief of staff, J. F. C. Fuller, were busy organizing the Tank Corps with that in mind.

ESTIENNE'S MOBILE GUNS

French interest in tanks owed much to Colonel Estienne, who played a role in the French army similar to that of Swinton in the British. As commander of the 6th Divisional Artillery, he sent a letter to Joffre on 1 December 1915 in which he advocated the construction of a Caterpillar-type treaded vehicle similar to the Holt tractors. He had observed the latter servicing British artillery. General Headquarters took notice and after interviews and consultation with the Schneider firm, orders were let for the first batch of four hundred tanks. Not directly involved with tanks again until September 1916, Estienne then organized and commanded the "Artillerie d'Assaut."[36] The French tank program thus began later than the British and did not benefit as much from the force of novelty, since the British had actually used their machines in September 1916.

Estienne's first general order of 1 January 1917 stated that attacks should be made in early morning and in fog, if possible. Tanks would be given objectives to reach and would not wait for infantry, but proceed directly. Recognizing that infantry had to work in mutual support of the tanks, Estienne tried to develop a tactics of coordination. If a tank in front was forced to stop, the rest of the machines would search for ways around it so that "a fixed range point [would] not be offered to the enemy artillery." Best results, he determined, were achieved without a preliminary artillery bombardment, and tanks had to keep from bunching up under fire.

Capable of two kilometers per hour for six hours to a total of ten to twelve kilometers, the French tanks were followed by treaded carriers with supplies and fuel. This important innovation of Estienne's, not yet realized by the British Tank Corps, enabled a continual advance if a breakthrough was achieved. He also insisted that a complete plan of attack be explained not only to the tank crews, but to the infantry, artillery, and air forces. Assigned to divisions, not corps, as in British practice, tank units had to work closely with other units.[37] The broad outlines of tactical theory were being worked out.

Needing battle experience for the yet-untested tanks and their crews, Estienne persuaded the 3d Bureau of GHQ to include them in planning for the general offensive commanded by Gen. Robert Nivelle in the spring of 1917. The debut of the *chars,* as Estienne preferred to call the French tanks, was scheduled for the region of Bethany on the ridge of Berru. General Micheler, army commander in charge, believed the position could be taken by conventional means, but was not averse to the "cooperation of *chars d'assaut.*" Nearly two hundred tanks in ten groups accompanied two divisions of infantry. The objective was the canal behind the lines because the bridges there were not strong enough to handle tanks. The planners envisaged the tanks to be not only "guides for the infantry but also as accompanying artillery."[38]

The attack sector was divided into three zones with the tanks concentrated in the major zone. Obviously, the French hoped the main attack would be masked to some extent by secondary attacks in the other zones and that the enemy would be surprised. Tanks would move fast to "destroy or reduce local resistance of elements of the enemy." In the course of the advance all depots were to be seized and convoys of supplies captured or destroyed to prevent the enemy from obtaining food and munitions "and to assure ourselves of the same."[39]

Nivelle decreed that "Tanks will be employed exclusively on J Day in the region north of Aisne in combination with 32d and 5th Corps Artillery." If successful, Nivelle stipulated that they could be used later in the day south of Aisne. But Micheler had to modify his plans because of the unanticipated German withdrawal. In the ensuing confusion, orders were changed to emphasize a methodical, traditional advance of the infantry supported by artillery. Reconnaissance of the area in the vicinity of Reims indicated that "an attack executed by surprise with *chars d'assaut* has very small chance of success because of the nature of the terrain, the number and importance of French and German works to cross, and the fire of batteries."[40] But little was really changed in the proposed employment of tanks.

After the Battle of Juvencourt, Estienne described the work of the *chars* to his English colleagues. A group of eighty-two tanks and another group of fifty-two had great difficulty in getting to the starting point. "They expected that they would only be needed to take the 3d and 4th lines, but had to take the first and second lines." The night march was difficult because of snow, and the tanks could not cross the first trenches until the infantry filled up some sections. Afterward, a strong German barrage kept the infantry from continuing. The tanks were defective because they were peculiarly vulnerable to high-explosive shells: a number were set on fire because of shots on the underprotected lower part of the machines. Many of the crews were burned alive when they could not get out. Twenty-three tanks out of fifty-three in one group were knocked out by the German artillery before they came into action. Out of eighty-two in the other group, some thirty-nine were lost. To Stern and his associates, the French "seemed highly dissatisfied with the [their] Tank."[41] What had obviously been underestimated by Estienne was the devastating effect of high-explosive shells on tanks. The same problem afflicted the English. The single most damaging opponent of tanks was enemy artillery.

In interviews with Stern, the British General Staff, and representatives of the Ministry of Munitions, Estienne indicated his tactical concepts as early as 4 March 1917. Tanks would assist when "the infantry advance is checked by the enemy's strong points . . . which have not been subjected to sufficient artillery bombardment." Unlike the British, Estienne as an artillery man conceived of tanks as a sort of artillery substitute: "The Tank should be regarded as portable artillery."[42] By mid-1917 the supporters of tanks in both Britain and France had to concede that German artillery was a very effective antidote to the tank threat. How could this problem be solved?

GETTING PLANS ADAPTED TO REALITY

Estienne, in common with Swinton, possessed a flexible mind and was prepared to admit that in the future, "we must provide for the use of Tanks as the result of a successful attack or in open warfare." After the infantry had taken the trenches crossed by the tanks, the latter were to prepare to attack the next trench line. Both the English and French military men agreed that tanks should approach battle in column order but deploy when obstacles were found.[43] Estienne had worked hard to develop a winning tank tactics, and his ideas were similar to those of the English in March 1917.

Stern, pursuing his idea of an independent mobile force, asked Estienne if the tanks should be regarded as cavalry "immune from wire and machine-gun fire." Estienne replied that this was premature because "tanks unsupported by infantry would be at the mercy of the enemy's batteries."[44] By March 1917 he had decided that tanks should start several kilometers behind the infantry in an advance but deploy in support of it when close to the enemy.[45]

Tanks were vulnerable but obviously useful. Gradually staff studies and postbattle analyses suggested that they had to be employed as part of a coordinated assault involving artillery, infantry, and air power. Moving in this direction Pétain, on 4 July 1917, stipulated that each corps and division would henceforth have motorized traction artillery, which included 105mm and 155mm Schneider cannon. Each corps was to have a combat group consisting of eight squadrons of aircraft. Reconnaissance and new close-combat squadrons would provide "absolute mastery of the air." The *poilu* (French soldier) had to be protected by air as by massive artillery fire on land.[46]

Estienne, aware of this order, determined to emphasize the need for an intimate liaison of the tanks with the infantry. In May a small success was obtained when infantry and tanks attacked in tandem at an assigned time. Afterward he tried to convince leading generals of the value of tanks. General F. F. G. Passaga, a leading defender of Verdun, did not believe the tanks could be used to breach second trench lines but could be used as machine-gun posts in the field commanding enemy strong points. General Pierre-Emile Berdoulat, I Corps commander, disagreed, having noticed tanks going over enemy trenches on 5 May. General Antoine-Philippe Boissoudy, V Corps commander, tended to be as pessimistic as Passaga, the 133d Division commander. Nevertheless, all three emphasized that the tanks needed the protection of aviation and of artillery. Even more important was their conclusion: "An intimate liaison with attack troops cannot be realized until the tanks have executed numerous previous maneuvers with these troops." This conclusion led directly to the concept of training an elite formation of infantry to accompany the tanks.[47] Gradually, French planners were integrating tanks into combat formations.

General Marie-Eugène Debeney, Commander, Armies of the North, warned, however, that a "detachment of elite troops accompanying tanks will not be too useful unless [it is] well trained." On 5 May, detachments of the 17th Battalion of chasseurs successfully attacked with tanks after having worked with them for three months. The cavalry expressed the greatest interest in this lesson, hoping that after the tanks achieved a breakthrough, mounted troops could hunt down fugitives and generally demoralize the enemy.[48] Cavalry might after all find a role in war.

On 7 August 1917, Estienne summarized tactical concepts to Major Parker of the U.S. Army. After a sudden artillery preparation in quiet sectors or a methodical preparation of artillery to aid the infantry in its advance up to the first position, the tanks would advance with their accompanying infantry.[49] He emphasized that the commander of the infantry would have absolute control over the tanks in order to achieve perfect coordination. Estienne hoped to provide each regiment with a company composed of fifteen of the new Renault light tanks. The unsuccessful Schneider and St.-Chamond machines would be withdrawn from service.

Pétain ordered on 22 August: "The advance of the tanks must be protected by pursuit airplanes specially designed to destroy enemy aircraft and to inform our artillery of the enemy batteries which remain active."[50] Further protection of the tanks from their worst enemy, artillery, could come from the use of smoke screens during the advance. The framework of French tactics was now quite clear. A multitude of small two-man tanks would accompany infantry in attacks under strong artillery and air protection.

British tactical thinking differed and emerged in 1917 as a result of the experience of the new Tank Corps. The document that formed the basis of the tactical thinking of the Tank Corps was Martel's "Tank Army" of 1916. Martel later evaluated brigade officers, claiming that Col. Theodore Uzielli, Tank Corps staff officer, got cooperation from General Headquarters while Lt. Col. F. Searle, Tank Corps engineer, offended many high-ranking officers because of his "common" manner. Another officer, Col. Christopher Baker-Carr, commander of 1st Tank Battalion, unfortunately persuaded Elles to substitute Lewis machine guns for the Hotchkiss: a retrograde step that caused considerable trouble. All were competent combat commanders. Fuller became the most enthusiastic of the top officers of the corps. Brigadier Elles himself was not a rigid disciplinarian and trusted Fuller, his deputy, and the brigade commanders to use initiative. Martel commented that "the Army was still rather feudal" because many of these men had not previously been recognized for their abilities.[51]

The greatest test of tanks in the first part of 1917 was the immense Battle of Messines. Engineered by wily General Lord Plumer and his able chief of staff, Col. Charles Harrington of the Second Army, Messines was a set piece of siegecraft. Plumer refused to allow the infantry to advance without prior destruction of 280 miles of barbed wire. But the keystone of this unique battle was the surprise detonation of nineteen mines containing 957,000 pounds of explosive on 7 June 1917. After the explosion, which caused the near-obliteration of the Messines Ridge, the infantry and accompanying tanks waited a predetermined number of minutes to allow the dust to settle before advancing.[52]

The tanks of the 1st Battalion advanced and passed the devastated ridge. "They saw the enemy in full retreat and followed them up as fast as possible." Some tanks, observing enemy artillery-spotting balloons, sent pigeon messages to the RFC to get them shot down. Four of six tanks that reached the final position were able to beat back a German counterattack.[53] Playing a modest supporting role to the infantry advance the tanks of this battalion had nevertheless done well.

Also successful were the tanks of the 2d Tank Battalion, which debouched from woods over shell-riddled ground. As planned, aircraft flew over at the moment of attack, and their noise, together with machine-gun-barrages, successfully masked the tank advance. Of ten tanks used, four reached the Messines ridge only to find that the infantry had already taken it. Two tanks cooperated with each other and with infantry in taking machine-gun nests. Nineteen out of a total of thirty-six fighting Mark IV tanks and four of six supply tanks returned to their rally points. The armor of the new Mark IV tanks resisted German armor-piercing K ammunition and enabled more of these machines to survive combat.[54]

The future of tanks nevertheless seemed ambiguous by August 1917. Lieutenant Gen. Sir Launcelot Kiggell, Haig's chief of staff, tried to reassure Gen. Hugh Gough, Commander, Fifth Army, on 7 August: "They certainly are unreliable still, and easily done in by artillery fire" and their value was undetermined, but "at the same time they . . . have by reports done very valuable work under suitable conditions and very many of the failures seem to be due to trying to use them under unsuitable conditions." They could silence machine-gun nests, cut wire, and work with cavalry when they developed greater speed. Examples of tanks helping infantry overcome resistance were common. "I showed your letter to the Chief, who is convinced they will be valuable within their limitations."[55] As Kiggell and Haig now recognized, tanks had to be used over the right terrain at the right time in connection with carefully planned attacks.

Unfortunately, tanks were still misused, usually because they were put into action in small numbers. During June and July 1917, the 1st Tank Battalion commander charged that they were employed in "a series of wasteful actions which occasioned a loss of most of the remaining tanks and of many irreplaceable officers and men." Tanks took nine and a half hours to cover one and a quarter miles of the approach march on 27 August, only to discover that the infantry did not know they were coming. The crews were "dead beat," and the unit commander was killed by a shell blast shortly afterward.[56]

Complete tank tactics for large-scale actions had not been worked out although much-needed battle testing of crews and equipment had provided invaluable information for the future.

NOTES

1. *History of the Ministry of Munitions* (London, 1919), vol. XII, part III, Chapter I, as found in King's College, University of London, Liddell Hart Library, 9/28/59, 1–2.

2. Swinton, *Eyewitness,* 1–81. *History of Munitions,* 3.

3. Roskill, *Hankey,* 1:147–48. See also *History of Munitions,* appendix I.

4. Roskill, *Hankey,* 1:147–48.

5. Interview of Liddell Hart with Lindsay, 1 November 1947, in Liddell Hart Papers, 9/28/59.

6. *History of Munitions,* 15–16.

7. Swinton, *Eyewitness,* 103–15.

8. *History of Munitions,* 45–47. Swinton, *Eyewitness,* 148–49.

9. Robertson, *Field Marshal,* 268. Swinton, *Eyewitness,* 189–205.

10. PRO, MUN, 4, 4979 (Tank History, 1916).

11. PRO, MUN, 4, 4979. Blake (ed.), *Haig Papers,* 138.

12. PRO, MUN, 5, 291 (Tank Supply Committee).

13. Haig Papers, ACC 3155, 108, 3 and 12.

14. Clough Williams-Ellis and A. Williams-Ellis, *The Tank Corps* (London, 1920), 16–20.

15. Williams-Ellis, *Tank Corps,* 26–29.

16. Haig Papers, ACC 3155, 108, 17. PRO, MUN, 5, 391 (Tank Supply Committee).

17. Swinton, *Eyewitness,* 289.

18. Swinton, *Eyewitness,* 189, 288. Williams-Ellis, *Tank Corps,* 41–42.

19. G. le Q. Martel, *In the Wake of the Tank* (London, 1931), 10.

20. Liddell Hart Papers, letter of J. F. C. Fuller, 22 September 1916: 1/302/100. Also letter of J. F. C. Fuller of 1 October 1916: 1/302/101. See Anthony J. Trythall, *Boney Fuller: Soldier, Strategist, and Writer 1878–1966* (New Brunswick, New Jersey, 1977).

21. Haig Papers, ACC 3155, 108, 80ff.

22. Churchill, *World Crisis,* 2:1082–83.

23. Martel, *Wake,* 10–11. Williams-Ellis, *Tank Corps,* 24–40.

24. Maurice, *Rawlinson,* 170–71.

25. Swinton, *Eyewitness,* 289–90.

26. Haig Papers, ACC 3155, 108.

27. Haig Papers, ACC 3155, 108.

28. PRO, MUN, 5, 391, 17.

29. Haig Papers, ACC 3155, 108. The memo was signed "Lt. Gen. Chief of Gen. Staff. adv. GHQ" so it was the work of Kiggell with Haig directing, no doubt.

30. Martel, *Wake,* 14–16.

31. PRO, MUN, 4, 2791. Stern Papers, I/C/3.

32. Stern Papers, I/C/2. Letter from Heseltine dated 18 November 1916.

33. Stern, *Log Books,* 107–8.

34. PRO, MUN, 4, 2791.

35. PRO, MUN, 4, 2791.

36. Stern, *Log Books,* appendix V gives a convenient summary of these early developments, 277–79.

37. AMV, 16 N 2142.

38. AMV, 16 N 1988.

39. AMV, 16 N 1988.

40. AMV, 16 N 1988.

41. Stern Papers, I/C/3.

42. Stern Papers, I/C/3.

43. Stern Papers, I/C/3.

44. Stern Papers, I/C/3.

45. Stern Papers, I/C/3.

46. AMV, 16 N 2142.

47. AMV, 16 N 2142.

48. AMV, 16 N 2142.

49. AMV, 16 N 2142.

50. AMV, 16 N 2142.

51. Liddell Hart Papers, 9/28/59. When the corps was established in September 1916, Swinton was not named commanding officer despite the obvious importance of his work with tanks. He believed General R. H. K. Butler had been responsible for this step. Butler and General Wigram were lukewarm about tanks but wanted someone with recent experience in France. Haig apparently agreed and chose Elles.

52. Harrington, *Plumer,* 87–96.

53. Military History Archives, King's College, University of London, Fuller Papers, TCWH 1, vols. 1–3.

54. Fuller Papers, TCWH 1, vols. 1–3. Ralph E. Jones et al., *The Fighting Tanks, 1916–1918* (Washington, D.C., 1933), 16–18.

55. Kiggell Papers, v/114.

56. Fuller Papers, TGWH 1, vols. 1–3.

CHAPTER 8
OVER THE TOP: 1917

R aymond Poincaré, president of France, noted in his diary for 6 November 1916: "There is, everywhere, in the Parisian population and in the Chambers, a wave of illness. The 'defeatists' win more ground every day . . . suspect miasmas float in the air."[1] The confidence of heads of governments was at its lowest at this grim point in the war. Poincaré expressed what others felt: pessimism.

In mid-1917 Henri Pétain, successor to the disgraced Nivelle, reflected a new awareness of public opinion on the part of the generals. He listened to Poincaré. In Germany, Hindenburg and Ludendorff, given absolute authority by a desperate emperor and Reichstag, searched for ways to end the war victoriously with new ardor, pushed by a sense of urgency. Lloyd George, lacking confidence in Haig or Robertson, subjected both to continual scrutiny and began to deprive the BEF of troop reinforcements. For the first time since the war began even the most conservative military commanders were willing to listen to new tactical ideas because they might prove to be keys to future battle success—a success the commanders badly needed to maintain their credibility.

IVOR MAXSE: MASTER TACTICIAN
Most imaginative of the British tacticians was Ivor Maxse, who had studied small-unit infantry tactics as early as 1911. Not particularly

divergent from accepted doctrines at that time, his view was summed up: "Victory depends chiefly on the heroic qualities of infantry—the determination to keep on fighting wins."[2] In a lecture that year he thought troops should be massed "opposite one point" in "a great wedge." Effective use of firepower could only be the result of careful training in which all troops acted in a coordinated way.[3] Maxse emphasized, then, the prevalent doctrine of the offensive and did not envisage a trench war stalemate.

In "Notes on Company Training" in 1911, in reference to the Russo-Japanese War, Maxse stressed the importance of cover, placing skirmishers in front, and concentration of firepower in the infantry assault. As a brigadier in 1911, he complained: "In the British Army we have usually neglected cooperative fire tactics and performed a mere attack drill." Each soldier must be trained to use his imagination in looking for cover: "The ground and its study dictates all tactics." Each company commander would train his troops in his own way, but training had to concentrate on teamwork. Finally Maxse summarized his tactics: "We cannot win battles by means of overwhelming numbers. We can only win by quality and training."[4] He underscored the importance of training the individual soldier in marksmanship and in military topography. Every officer was to be part teacher as well as unit commander and was responsible for developing a smoothly working unit in which all soldiers cooperated with one another in a common effort.

In June 1914, Maj. Gen. Sir John Capper, the inspector of infantry, paid a formal visit to Maxse's brigade and criticized only the use of machine guns. Otherwise, he was very impressed with the mock attack Maxse staged. "The brigadier works by means of a system of bounds and restrictive orders advancing troops to make good a certain line." Meanwhile, Maxse brought up the main body near the line as soon as it was made good. Cavalry was used as flank security. "The system of command and handling of troops in this brigade is most excellent. Command is decided and thoroughly suitable. Everything is done with direct reference to training for war."[5]

In 1916 Maxse, an accomplished divisional commander under General Rawlinson, reviewed the Somme battle then in progress. Troops needed more training in open country fighting and in the use of Lewis machine guns and mortars. Battalion and company commanders were not checking the ground carefully enough before sending troops out over it. "The casualties were mostly inflicted in the open by barrage fire and machine guns." Far too much time was spent by infantry in digging and other engineer work. Maxse urged the establishment of a separate engineer battalion to do these jobs so the infantry could be trained for combat. "No rest and no training" kept the infantry from attaining combat readiness. He felt that only the best officers and men should be placed in machine-gun companies. "I rather feel we are trying to do every attack by barrage. . . . I feel certain the Boche always knows by our barrage when we are going to attack and where [we are]." Attacks should not be preceded by barrages but accompanied by them. Barrages should then be used "to stop reinforcements being sent to the point attacked."[6]

Liddell Hart later recollected that Maxse had been commander of the 18th Division on 1 July 1916, the first day of the Somme: "Almost along our whole line our troops were driven back to their trenches with appalling loss, but alone Maxse's division [penetrated] deeply into the German positions and put out of action a proportion of the enemy greater than its losses." He retained the highest admiration for Maxse, writing in an obituary of the latter in 1958, "Infantry, losing initiative, had declined to the level of mere barrage followers—until Maxse was given a wider chance to initiate a tactical renaissance."[7]

Plumer, commander of Second Army, asked Maxse on 30 September 1916 to describe his successful methods of attack and of "training and careful organization of the smaller units of formations." In a study of the Somme campaign Maxse eventually did develop a comprehensive attack scheme, summarizing it in November to the Fourth Army: "Each infantry unit should have but *one* order for every attack, namely 'go straight to your objective and stay there!'" He did not approve of the prevalent practice of leapfrogging, which consisted of one wave of infantry bypassing another as part of an attack. The original troops should first try to obtain their objective and "if fresh troops are wanted, order a relief at night and continue the fight." He wrote that specially detailed troops should be assigned to mop up enemy machine-gun nests and other strong points. "This division in its seven attacks has *always* put a 'Y' Battalion to mop-up—and we have never once been shot in the back." If the assaulting battalions were held up by such nests, they should "work round the flanks of the obstruction, barraging it at the same time with all weapons available."[8]

Maxse immodestly asserted that the 18th Division had successfully attacked seven times, attributing this to careful training "especially in attack formations." Convinced that intensive drill in attack procedures was necessary at the platoon level, he was one of very few generals in any army who had an interest in the primitive but essential tactics of the small infantry unit.[9]

The actual assault formation was worked out in detail by Maxse in the same month (November 1916). It was later diagrammed (see Figure 4).[10] Impressed, Gough distributed copies of the scheme to units of the Fifth Army. The first wave of attack was composed of sections 6 and 5 of the 2d Platoon and 2 and 1 of 1st Platoon. They were quickly followed by sections 8, 7, 4, and 3 of the respective platoons. The third wave provided immediate support, incorporating the remaining sections and cleanup parties accompanied by a Lewis machine-gun company.[11] Regulating the movements of sections, adhering to specified sectors of front, and confining itself to an exacting timetable, the plan was overly prescriptive and rigid.

Maxse believed that the "elementary lessons" of the Somme consisted of recognizing that assault troops needed men who were specially trained to act as members of teams of: trench clearers, moppers up, consolidators (who improve and repair captured trenches), carriers (of stores and ammunition), communication openers (who dig connecting trenches from the rear), signalers (who with flags, flares, and so on signal progress to ground observers in the rear and to aircraft), coverers (who by fire protect the previous six teams), and exploiters (who bomb the enemy's lines of retreat). Success could be achieved only with a quick advance under cover of artillery after wire had been cut in secret.[12]

Perhaps unaware of the fashionableness of his theory, Maxse was working in parallel with Frederick Winslow Taylor.[13] This American industrial management expert argued that each worker had a strictly limited but well-defined task he was supposed to accomplish within time and space parameters as part of an overall production plan. In accomplishing any great task, such as assembly-line production of a commodity or a successful attack in war (to use the analogy suggested by Maxse), each person participating had to have a well-defined role. The manager (commanding officer) had to orchestrate the efforts of all the participants in the common enterprise. The description of an

FIGURE 4: INFANTRY ATTACK SCHEME OF IVOR MAXSE
NOVEMBER, 1916

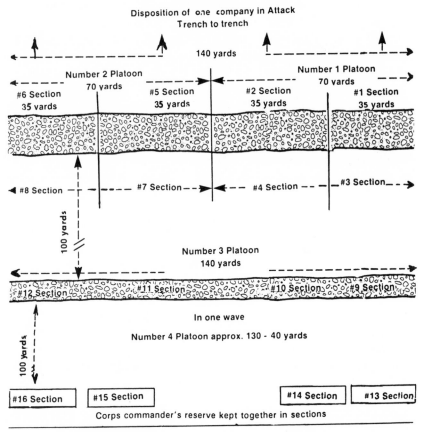

Disposition of one company in Attack
Trench to trench

140 yards

Number 2 Platoon
70 yards

Number 1 Platoon
70 yards

#6 Section
35 yards

#5 Section
35 yards

#2 Section
35 yards

#1 Section
35 yards

◄ #8 Section — #7 Section → ◄ #4 Section — #3 Section →

100 yards

Number 3 Platoon
140 yards

#12 Section   #11 Section   #10 Section #9 Section

In one wave
Number 4 Platoon approx. 130 - 40 yards

100 yards

#16 Section   #15 Section   #14 Section   #13 Section

Corps commander's reserve kept together in sections

1st wave: 1 and 2 sections
2d wave: 3 and 4 sections

Dugout cleanup parties of 4 battalions to be
formed up with 3d wave and advance close
behind Lewis gun company.

Rear forms up
trench for company
reserve

Front forms up trench for 2 waves

infantry attack as requiring the coordinated efforts of specially trained cadres of troops performing different roles was an important breakthrough in tactical theory. Therefore the vision that Maxse possessed, despite its pedantic and drill-sergeant appearance, was innovative. Still missing, however, was any true application of mechanization.

By February 1917, Maxse had been promoted to command a corps in the Fifth Army under Gough. The brigadier commanding the Senior Officer School of the BEF wrote that his 18th Division had taught the British army the importance of training. He suggested that Maxse's divisional school should be a prototype for the entire army. A director of military training would be needed in such an eventuality.[14] Naturally such praise encouraged Maxse.

The following May, in a lecture to company officers at the Corps School, Maxse urged constant training in marksmanship and in mock attacks. "If you have not got a range, make the men snap at any target you can see—a tree or a bucket or the Corps Commander's car . . . do it for three quarters of an hour, or half or quarter . . . do it *daily*."[15]

Maxse developed his tactical ideas further in a report on the third Battle of Ypres. That battle constituted a limited success for the corps because of "superior artillery and thorough organization before attack." On zero day the machine guns opened a protective barrage through which sixteen tanks led the assault of one division and eight tanks that of the other. It showed "that rapid organization, making skillful use of new methods and new arms, may restore to Commanders a weapon which the modern warfare of masses was supposed to have neutralized—namely, the element of surprise." The new arms Maxse referred to were the tanks and aircraft. The tanks foundered in the mud, and the RFC was hampered by poor weather conditions, but Maxse discerned their value nonetheless.[16] In a battle where each side was roughly equal to the other, this attack was a success, contradicting the military assumption that to prevail the attacking force should have two or three times the manpower of the defense.

Reflecting on this experience to his army commander, Gough, Maxse stressed preparatory training, which coordinated machine guns, artillery, and infantry in the attack. "During the attack, massed machine guns covered the advance of the Infantry to each objective by searching the ground about 400 yards in front of the Artillery barrage." Enemy reinforcements for "the counterattack, such as main roads or railways" were subjected to continual artillery and machine-gun barrages. Special units followed the regular infantry waves for the express purpose of reducing enemy strong points. Use of cavalry, however, was diplomatically characterized as flawed because it suffered great casualties while mounted.[17]

According to Maxse, the Germans had developed more sophisticated defenses in depth: the forward zone of shell holes was supported by strong points that did not show up in aerial observation. The main line of resistance consisted of trenches on the reverse slope. Since they were hidden from ground view, they were used to stage counterattacks. Reserve troops were also concealed from air observation and protected in many cases by concrete, shell-proof dugouts. Near St.-Julien, the minimum depth of such a fortified area was about two thousand yards.[18] Clever use of camouflage and of well-constructed fortifications made the German lines exceedingly difficult to penetrate.

Reacting quickly to this threat, Maxse suggested innovative use of the new arms. Tanks and low-flying aircraft had to be used to better advantage. "A more elastic infantry formation [was needed] for the attack, built up of platoons working in depth" rather than the usual waves of battalions. Motorized vehicles should accompany the infantry to carry supplies and ammunition, lightening the soldiers' loads. Aiding the infantry would be the seizure of temporary command of the air "in front of our offensive with sufficient aeroplanes to attack strong points, nests of machine guns, infantry advancing or massing for counterattack, and the personnel of [the] enemy's batteries."[19]

Finally, in this astonishing document, Maxse suggested three conditions for effective use of tanks. First, aircraft must be supplied in enough numbers to destroy antitank guns and forward batteries. Then, friendly artillery should not make no-man's-land impassable during the preliminary bombardment. Third, a smoke barrage should be laid to blind the enemy's observation posts. Once such conditions were met, "tanks should be used in sufficient numbers to neutralize strong points, nests of machine guns and generally to facilitate the task of the infantry." They had to be given definite objectives and certain infantry units had to be assigned "to cooperate in attacking each tank objective but not necessarily to accompany the tanks." Tank formations had to consist of several echelons according to the depth of the objective. "The infantry formation (already practiced) aims at stalking the tank objective under a barrage and assaulting it simultaneously with the tank." At that time, the use of delayed action fuses in artillery shells resulted in destroying the ground over which an advance was to be made to such an extent as to hinder movement either by "Infantry or Artillery, and to render Tanks immobile in wet weather."[20] Maxse concentrated on use of artillery as a key to battle success.

If less powerful shells were used by the artillery (except on strong points and the enemy batteries), the ground would not be broken as much and would provide "good going" for the infantry, a better terrain for tanks, and improved mobility of infantry and artillery. Although destruction of the enemy defensive system would not be as complete as previously, the assault could proceed under more favorable conditions.[21] By choosing mobility over demolition Maxse was solving a difficult problem with a risky but logical answer.

Formations of infantry in the attack, by current practice conducted in "waves" or lines, was to be organized in groups, or "worms," which proceeded across the battlefield seeking cover on the way. "Each section of infantry should be a self-contained fighting unit including riflemen, rifle grenadiers, and a few bombers." Although the first infantry, following a creeping barrage, would have to be in wave formation carefully drilled to avoid that barrage, successive advances would be by worms. Each leading platoon had to attack a particular farm, hedge, or area of ground in a narrow front close to the barrage. The wave formation was now impractical because it did not provide the "power of maneuver" for supporting troops. Marksmanship had "to be restored to its proper place in the minds of all infantry officers trained in England."[22]

By October 1917, Maxse still believed that artillery won terrain and consequently battles, but he also recognized the potential value of tanks, which were "a decisive factor in our success on the left flank" at the Battle of Poelkapelle. But the infantry success was more important as one of his division commanders suggested. The new, flexible tactics enabled some soldiers to maintain fire on the enemy's front "upon meeting with a point of resistance," while "the remainder work around its flanks and *behind* it."[23] All in all, despite contradictions, Maxse's thoughts were slowly beginning to form a cohesive theory of tactics centered on the attack.

Again he emphasized the use of "mechanical carriers" or motorized vehicles to carry loads and to free the infantry so it could be more mobile. "Manpower will be the deciding issue in this war, either this year or next," he claimed, and "the only alternative to manpower is mechanical power. The Tank, if used in the battle with discretion, is capable of economizing manpower and minimizing casualties."[24]

Neglected certainly by General Gough and to some extent by Maxse was the formulation of a defensive tactical scheme prior to November 1917. Part of the reason for this strange neglect lay in the traditional and received military wisdom of the British army, which in common with that of other contemporary armies emphasized attack rather than defense. One would assume that since trench warfare was the ultimate in siege warfare and a horrendous example of defensive tactics employed on a large scale, tacticians would concentrate on these tactics. But the obvious answer to the trench warfare stalemate was to break that stalemate through aggressive action: the breakthrough attack. The German army paid more attention to defensive works and the adaptation of tactics to siege warfare than either the British or the French. After the Verdun battle the French took a possibly exaggerated turnabout to emphasize field fortifications and in-depth defenses. In a rare moment, Maxse said: "Infantry in defense should not be in crowded trenches,"[25] but his tactics emphasized the attack.

ARRAS, VIMY, AND MESSINES

The battles of 1917 that provided the lessons on tactics to Maxse included the March campaign at Arras, the Canadian Corps' capture of Vimy Ridge, and the monumental Battle of Messines by Plumer and his Second Army. Conducted with an expertise unknown previously in the BEF, these battles entailed careful coordination of the efforts of the infantry with artillery, tanks, and aircraft. It would be a mistake to think Maxse was the only officer with innovative ideas in the BEF. In the Arras campaign he lacked influence, having his hands full as a corps commander in the Fifth Army in a supporting role.

Another tactician was Maj. Gen. Archibald Montgomery, the chief staff officer of Rawlinson's Fourth Army, who corresponded with Maxse and visited French units. In January 1917, Montgomery visited the French training school at Chalons and interviewed officers who were veterans of the Somme and Verdun campaigns. He returned to urge adoption of the French practice of continual drill in attack formations. Lieutenant General Sir Frederick Cavan, seconded to the Italian army, agreed, claiming: "No division in the Army has probably more than 10 per cent of Officers and N.C.O.s who can, by any stretch of imagination, be called fully trained." The prewar infantry training manual forbade "fixed and unvarying system of battle formations," but Cavan and Montgomery now believed in them. Both urged Gen. Sir Richard Butler, deputy chief of staff, BEF, to start attack formation training: "Principles were all very well before the war when you had a lot of experienced officers who could be relied upon to use their own intelligence," but the new junior officers lacked this competence.[26]

Rawlinson wrote to Haig urging the same thing in January because he thought the British had consistently underrated the morale of the Germans and expected "a general collapse in his defense." This unfounded belief had resulted in many fruitless general attacks accompanied by high casualties. Rawlinson emphasized that attacks could at the most only break the "crust" of the enemy defenses. In a war of attrition attacks had to be confined to limited objectives, consisting of a "succession of carefully worked out hammer blows on the enemy." A limit of infantry advances to two thousand or twenty-five hundred yards rather than three to four thousand yards might work better.[27] Artillery could then cover the attack more effectively.

Indeed, 1917 was to be the year of the carefully calculated limited attack, although that year began with the ill-fated Nivelle offensive. Negotiations between Nivelle and Haig resulted in the latter's promise to launch a major offensive to support the French effort. Haig instructed his army commanders to plan what came to be called the Battle of Arras, which started on 9 April 1917.[28] Nevertheless, he did not desire to prolong this campaign once certain limited objectives were taken.

General Lord Allenby, Third Army commander, entrusted preparations for the seizure of Vimy Ridge to the Canadian Corps commander, Gen. Sir Julian Byng, even before Haig concluded the Calais Agreement with Nivelle. The attempt to seize Vimy Ridge, regarded by Haig as absolutely necessary, started with a week's heavy bombardment in which the new 106 fuse was used on shells to maximum effect.[29] Crown Prince Rupprecht commented that this bombardment, also characterized by heavy gas shell usage, imposed severe strains on the German defenders. Four Canadian divisions, held back for the first attack wave, sortied from underground bunkers, passed through the original attacking troops, and continued without interruption using the maneuver known as leapfrogging. This attack on 9 April garnered some two hundred guns and thirteen thousand prisoners as well as the ridge. But no one knew how to exploit this opportunity. Instead, the Canadian Corps dug in, used counterbattery shelling, and solicited improved aircraft protection.[30]

The RFC, according to many in the Canadian Corps, failed to prevent German aircraft from flying with impunity. Since February, poor antiaircraft defense against planes flying low had been a nagging problem for the corps. No airplane as low as two thousand feet could, as a rule, be engaged because antiaircraft guns could not be depressed sufficiently. Few noticed that the Germans, not the English or Canadians, were beginning to develop a tactical role for aircraft in ground support. Vimy, nevertheless, was a significant Canadian contribution to the war. Its possession served to protect Arras and Amiens in stopping the great German offensive of March 1918.[31]

Another localized and striking success, the conquest of the Messines Ridge by the Second Army under Plumer, was characterized by Liddell Hart as a rare and superb example of siegecraft in a war in which few generals thought in terms of military engineering.[32] Mining and sapping had always been used in attempts to reduce a fortress methodically. The elaborate planning and execution were the responsibility of Plumer and Charles Harrington, his chief of staff. Plumer, omitting no details, made great efforts to visit units down to the brigade level very frequently. Discussing the impending attack on Messines with these responsible subordinate commanders, he made sure each understood his role. The overall plan was modified after consultation with them. Plumer had the ability to get enthusiastic work from his own staff; their loyalty to him was obvious. At the same time he delegated responsibility once his subordinates understood his precepts of trust, training, and thoroughness. Trust was established when all commanders and their staffs undertook to work in harmony in carrying out the plan. Training consisted of instructing platoon leaders and other junior officers by using a giant model of the Messines German defensive system. Junior liaison officers worked constantly to maintain coordinated efforts of the units. Thoroughness marked the methodical approach of Plumer to all problems.[33] Since he did not possess a flashy personality and looked like a kindly, easy-going grandfather, Plumer was not highly esteemed by many of his contemporaries. Haig, although he had had doubts about him earlier, stood by him and gave Plumer every support for the Messines operation.[34]

The Messines plan was an exercise in coordination of arms. First, a number of companies (mostly Welsh miners) had been tunneling and placing explosives under the German lines for over a year. Massive amounts of artillery, including ammunition, had also been stored. Plumer wished to obliterate enemy defensive posts and provide cover for the infantry advance after the gigantic explosion in the tunnels was set off. Machine-gun crews were trained to work with advancing infantry to assist in providing this cover. Before the attack Plumer made sure that wire had been cut and that substantial damage was done to the enemy defenses by artillery. He obtained daily progress reports from his corps commanders on these issues. Hoping for an early dawn attack, Plumer ordered experiments to determine the earliest light sufficient for the infantry to discern shell holes, wire, and so on. On 7 June at 3:10 A.M. the attack began. Nineteen mines in the tunnels, filled with 957,000 pounds of explosives, set off probably the largest explosion until the atomic era. The effect was devastating: many Germans were killed by shock in concrete bunkers. Again according to plan the infantry assault and the enormous artillery bombardment followed the detonation of the stock of explosives.[35] The RFC provided first-class artillery spotting and reconnaissance information. Some fifty-four tanks participated but were not really necessary because of the outstanding infantry success. All objectives were reached at the end of the day: Messines was British.

Haig, anxious to exploit what might become a breakthrough, asked first Plumer, then Gough if they would like to pursue this possibility. Both declined, aware that the Germans, very effective in counterattacks, would quickly move artillery forward and would also strengthen their new defensive lines. Several strong, if unsuccessful, counterattacks did materialize, in fact.[36]

Plumer's well-engineered Messines operation and the Canadian attack on Vimy Ridge were successful because they were accomplished with a great deal of manpower and artillery in a limited time and space framework. Surprise was also an important element in their success.[37] But Haig certainly did not believe that such operations would bring victory. Each battle had provided a tantalizing opportunity for exploiting a breakthrough, but no one knew yet how to do that. Only Haig had any hopes that the obsolete cavalry might be effective in this role.

NIVELLE'S MISFORTUNES

France reached a crisis as a result of the bloodletting of Verdun in 1916 and the Nivelle offensive; by May 1917, the failure of the latter ushered in widespread mutinies and a political peace movement. Haig ceased to have much confidence in French arms, confiding in his diary on 28 May 1917 that for two years many British had felt that "Great Britain must take the necessary steps to win the war by herself, because our French Allies had already shown that they lacked both the moral qualities and the means for gaining the victory."[38] Despite this pessimistic view, France rebuilt its army and played a powerful role in 1918. The year 1917, after June, was a time of reconstruction.

French small-unit tactics were incorporated in a manual, subsequently revised, which appeared in January 1916. Training of infantry in tactics was considered a very important duty for the commanders of battalions and smaller units. "The good conduct of troops under fire is the best compensation for the commander." Incorporating trench warfare experience, the manual stressed that infantry attacks alone could not succeed "against obstacles defended by fire and guarded by auxiliary defenses." But if not capable of seizing, it could occupy terrain. Modern rifle and machine-gun fire, used by the defense, gave a practical certainty that any attack not prepared by artillery barrages would be stopped. By recognizing siegecraft and the overwhelming power of the defense, the French may have prepared themselves for the ordeal of Verdun.[39]

Although concerned with defense to a greater extent than the British, the French did consider offensive tactics. If, after the first two waves of the infantry, the attack seemed promising, groups of riflemen could advance by bounds ("momentary groupings") to reduce enemy strong points. Section commanders could determine the deployment of their troops as needed, ordering individual shooting or volleys as circumstances determined. Once enemy trenches were occupied every effort was to be made to retain them in the face of counterattacks.[40] Offensive tactics, nevertheless, did not really envisage the possibility of exploiting a breakthrough on a large scale. A multitude of corps and lower-echelon schools established after Verdun trained troops in defensive tactics. British observers reported that this program used combat veterans who first taught, then led replacement troops into battle. Calisthenics built up physical stamina as well. This primary training was followed by three months' intensive instruction of special battalions in which attack and defense tactics, antigas precautions, entrenching, laying barbed wire, signals, and the use of machine guns and other weapons was stressed.[41] In January 1917, the school at Chalons emphasized a uniform battalion attack with two companies in the four-hundred-yard front line and one in reserve in the hands of the battalion commander. Each company attacked in four waves: two sections (platoons) in front and two in reserve.[42] The English had ample evidence of French training practices by early 1917 and were most impressed by the emphasis on strict attack drill.

A German tactical expert, William Balck, later admitted that Nivelle's offensive was intelligently pursued. Beginning with a preliminary heavy artillery bombardment that lasted from 6 to 11 April, Nivelle's plan called for destruction of the first-line trenches as well as enemy aircraft. The preliminary barrage alternated between drumfire and systematic shelling during the second phase, from 12 to 16 April, then was shifted to the second line of fortifications. Not believing in blanket barrage fire Nivelle ordered his artillery to eliminate specific targets as determined by aerial observation. According to Balck, strenuous German efforts to rebuild the shattered defenses failed. Nivelle knew the Germans held the first-line trenches with weak forces but could rush storm troops forward in case of an infantry attack. He placed machine guns opposite known machine-gun nests that anchored German defenses, hoping to eliminate many during the attack. But when the French infantry finally advanced with tanks, on 18 April, sufficient German defenders remained to stop them. Sir Henry Wilson, present with the French armies, believed the German lines had been so fortified that they were too strong to break.[43]

The French and British accounted for the failure of the Nivelle offensive by claiming, first, that the plans had leaked out in neutral countries weeks before, warning the Germans. The sudden withdrawal of the Germans to more fortified positions in the Hindenburg Wall in March, unperceived by the French, also contributed. Third, the attack was supposedly launched against the strongest part of the enemy's lines. Nevertheless, the results were comparable to the British Somme attack the year before: over 20,000 prisoners and 150 guns were taken by the end of April at a cost of 118,000 casualties.[44] Nivelle fell from command, nevertheless, because the new premier, Painlevé, disliked him and because the offensive yielded only modest results.

After Nivelle the French army seemed to favor rigid attack formations. General Denis Auguste Duchene, commander of the Tenth Army, concluded that an infantry attack would stand the best chance of success if preceded by a cover of smoke that would clear "nearly at the same time as the last howitzers of the rolling barrage stop." Most French commanders stressed the importance of surprise attacks in force under the cover of a creeping or rolling barrage of artillery.[45]

But General de Maud'huy of XI Corps disagreed with Duchene and supported combat patrols. Urging a reorganization of the infantry company to include three combat and one support sections (platoons), he also suggested placing four machine guns in each section. The commander of the Fourth Army, General Anthoine, emphasized, for example, that after substantial artillery preparation "cleanup" crews would go out before the first wave to destroy pockets of resistance. He indicated, however, that success really depended upon the infantry's expertise in rifle fire and the optimum use of artillery.[46] French as well as English tactics were in a state of uncertainty by the end of May 1917.

All these differing assessments of attack tactics had been made immediately after the close of Nivelle's offensive. In the view of Gen. Charles Mangin, commander of the Sixth Army, that offensive had been more successful than either Vimy Ridge or the Messines operation.[47] He thought, however, that it had been stopped by German machine-gun nests which escaped destruction during the barrage. The casualty cost for getting rid of such pockets was very high.[48] Hence there was a debate during the next month on ways and means to solve this problem. But the expectations of the French government as well as of Nivelle, plus the opposition of powerful generals like Micheler and Pétain to the offensive, created an atmosphere of defeat. The mutinies followed.

Pétain, now in command, determined to establish a policy of carefully planned limited offensives.[49] He was convinced that France could no longer afford the great, costly, and nearly futile offensives favored earlier by Nivelle and Joffre. The Houthuest Forest near the Channel was the scene of the first such offensive, launched in cooperation with the British in June. It achieved modest results at little cost (thirteen hundred casualties). More ambitious was an operation north of Verdun on 20 August 1917, designed to strengthen the city's supply routes. Four army corps advanced on a front of seventeen kilometers. The preliminary barrage, employing nearly twenty-four hundred cannon, lasting six days, and directed against enemy batteries, helped to earn a gain of nearly four kilometers in two days at minimal cost. Some twenty-four German divisions failed to retake the terrain and suffered heavy casualties.[50]

More important, the offensive of Malmaison, launched 23 October 1917, aimed to reduce a salient. Unfortunately, the Germans discovered the preparations and deployed six infantry divisions to stop the offensive at all costs. Employing three army corps, the French attacked on a front of ten kilometers and used an especially heavy artillery concentration: 1850 pieces of all calibers, or one cannon to each six meters of front. As a result of six days of bombardment both the German trench system and its supporting artillery batteries were pulverized over a depth of eight hundred meters. French command of the air during the three-day battle doubtless helped to win some three to five kilometers more by 1 November.[51]

General Louis-Félix Franchet d'Esperey, commander of Army Groups East, anticipated a return to open warfare if such battles could be continued on a larger and more successful scale. Aware of the problem of mobility in exploiting a breakthrough, he warned of a logistical crisis. Artillery and supplies could not be moved quickly if an attack was successful because of the shell-pocked terrain over which the infantry had already advanced. The obvious answer was "a light caterpillar, capable of following the infantry in broken terrain and to resupply it in munitions."[52] The French army used tanks first on a large scale at Malmaison, 24 October 1917, but the concept of mechanized mobility was only a tantalizing hope in late 1917.

THE PERFECTION OF DEFENSE

Taking a different approach than the French and English, the German army command decided to emphasize defense in depth and a reorganization of counterattack infantry formations after Verdun in 1916. But during 1917, with victory on the eastern front a certainty, Ludendorff began once more to reorient combat training in the west towards the offensive.

Training manuals emphasized siegecraft by developing a comprehensive program of fortification construction. During 1915, parapets were improved, trenches were reinforced with wood, and underground dugouts were prepared. In 1916, concrete blockhouses and deeper dugouts greatly improved the defensive system. By November 1916, preparations for the Wotan line on the Sixth Army front included zig-zag trenches that prevented the enemy, if successful in taking one section, from firing the length of the line. Underground chambers and carefully protected trench systems created an exceptionally strong defensive line.[53]

On the western front in 1917, the Germans as well as the French and English added new trench lines behind existing ones and paid more attention to forward protection of the entire system with greater concentrations of barbed wire and protective machine-gun nests. As early as 22 September 1916, a German directive warned of the English practice of setting up such nests and called for energetic countermeasures. Artillery shooting was extended to cover a greater part of the enemy's trench system. Infantry relied more on use of grenades in both attack and defense to combat enemy nests often found in craters. The Siegfried line's defenses were protected by similar elaborate strong points. By spring 1917, then, the use of advanced strong points had been almost perfected by the Germans. Each nest was given its particular fire sector so that a formidable field of fire was laid out.[54]

The withdrawal to the Hindenburg Wall shortly before the Nivelle offensive in 1917 marked the height of German siege thinking. Ludendorff, commenting on the Arras, Aisne, and Champagne campaigns of the English and French at the end of April 1917, claimed the German army had withstood all enemy breakthrough attempts because of its strong infantry, not because of the artillery, which had lost many cannon. Aerial observation had not been effective in support of the artillery, either.[55]

The Germans, cognizant of their own and others' weaknesses in artillery usage, determined to eliminate "the strong, purely defensive barrage fire with its great, often fruitless, use of munitions." Devastating as the enemy artillery fire had been, a German division had withstood a subsequent infantry assault because it had withdrawn troops from the front line during the barrage. Also, impromptu machine-gun nests had been set up behind the lines creating a "fluid" combat zone encompassing open and fortified positions.[56]

Before the end of 1916, however, the Germans had developed a tactical offense based upon securing limited goals. In the Argonne Forest, positions were taken only after a preparatory artillery and mortar barrage, but the casualties were heavy. On this occasion, however, special assault troops went first, providing close cooperation between infantry and artillery. The major weapon of these storm troops at first was the hand grenade, but lack of success in attacks on French blockhouses prompted the use of flamethrowers.[57]

Shock battalions, or *Sturmtruppen*, emerged in August 1915, when experienced combat soldiers were detached for special service in new units. Initially "a handful of hearty men," they were, of course, expert at arms.[58] Captain Willy Martin Rohr, Guards Rifle Battalion, the founder, established courses starting in December 1915[59] that trained them in special "storm" companies. In attacking a blockhouse or other strong point, they obtained support from light field artillery. After inconclusive results at Verdun, Falkenhayn ordered that each division would have such a "nuclear troop" that would accept only the best volunteer soldiers and officers.[60] Officers charged with command of these troops had to coordinate everything with the infantry commanders "so that a hand-in-hand relationship resulted." Storm troops then led the assault by opening ways through wire, eliminating blockhouses, and taking trenches.[61]

By November 1916, two storm battalions existed and were fully equipped with weapons like captured small and light Russian cannon and with transport. A storm company was established at that time in the Bavarian (Sixth) Army and this was to lead to a battalion organization that would include, besides the storm company, a machine-gun company, and one mortar company. Flamethrower specialists would also be attached to make a total complement of about 210 of which 5 would be officers. These troops were carefully trained and were capable of truly awesome firepower. Crown Prince William, and later Ludendorff, took special interest in these units in 1917. Some discussion resulted because the role of the storm troop was that of teacher and exemplar to the rest of the infantry. It was expected that, when the army commander or his staff needed the services of such units, a detachment would be sent immediately upon telephone notification to a particular point in the lines. Officers in storm companies were also supposed to organize other troops on the spot to work with their elite units. But their future role was somewhat obscure by late 1917.[62]

The Germans may have borrowed some inspiration for such troops from the Russians, who had organized "hunting commandos" using the best combat veterans. The French also had *grenadiers d'élite*. General Maud'huy compared the proposed combat patrols of the French to a German *Gruppe*.[63]

Only at this time did the German high command begin to abandon its preoccupation with defensive tactics. German elite combat groups at this time were still small and relatively inconsequential; similar experimental units in other armies had been no better. But the Germans placed greater reliance on them than others; as of 24 August 1917, each infantry division contained a shock battalion composed of four companies. Squads from these elite companies were then assigned to lead the infantry through difficult positions. They would concentrate on eliminating machine-gun nests and blockhouses.

Between May and August 1917, Ludendorff, besides pushing for increased effectiveness in attacks using storm troops, also decreed that defensive tactics had to become more flexible. The entire area encompassing no-man's-land and the trenches was a combat zone in which the occupying troops had to fight not only from their trenches but also, and even by preference, from improvised positions utilizing shell holes or even hastily constructed parapets of wood or earth. Effective fire could be provided by innumerable machine-gun nests and by rifle marksmanship. The new German defensive tactic of mid-1917 undoubtedly prolonged the war and made the job of the Allies much harder. Certainly the English did not begin to imitate the Germans in this defensive tactical system until Maxse urged it six months later after the Battle of Cambrai. A flexible defensive zone was the best protection against the artillery bludgeon assault so favored by the English and French until 1918.[64]

The French and British knew of these innovations as early as May 1917. German strong points would be handled, according to Maud'huy, by combat patrols sent out specifically for that purpose. Maxse reported to General Gough of the British Fifth Army that the Germans had a new system of defense in depth. Maxse thought a coordinated attack using infantry, tanks, aircraft, and artillery would destroy them.[65]

Only when Hindenburg and Ludendorff came west did defensive and offensive innovations appear. On the eastern front a continual training program for combat troops had been developed which Ludendorff intended to introduce on the western front as well.[66] His previous chief of staff, Max Hoffmann, his artillery advisor, Georg Bruchmüller, and a field commander, Lt. Gen. Oskar von Hutier, had collaborated in this program.[67] Adapting to the western front, Ludendorff stressed defenses in depth, but also pushed for intensive training of artillery observers, ground and air, to communicate with the infantry and with the artillery batteries. Sapping and mining was to accompany a well-planned and integrated attack.[68] Using well-known weapons systems he coordinated them into a new, general tactical approach. Bruchmüller, a consummate professional and a careful student of artillery on the eastern front, was brought west to supervise. He became a passionate believer in coordinating artillery with infantry and with air observation.[69] But the full impact of the "easterners" was not felt before late 1917 in the German army on the western front.

Unfortunately, the German response to the threat of tanks was almost purely defensive. Ludendorff and many other commanders, not impressed with them, did not encourage their manufacture in any significant numbers in Germany. In a series of reports and orders dating from early 1917, Ludendorff's tacticians claimed that a mixture of heavy and field artillery, and even mortars, could put tanks out of action. The Sixth Army commander, Crown Prince Rupprecht of Bavaria, opined: "Not the mass of power, but the energy of the will of the collective force of all battle elements and the swiftness of action will bring a result." This vaguely suggested that tanks were only another weapon, and a poor one at that. Nevertheless, battle reports indicated that the English tanks had penetrated forward defenses and seemed impervious to machine-gun fire, except armor-piercing shells, although conventional artillery shells would also stop them. But often twenty-two to thirty small artillery shells would have to be expended to eliminate one tank. Despite efforts to downplay tanks the Sixth Army commander was forced to concede that their influence on the morale of German troops was great.[70]

German tactical thinking in 1917 was characterized by confusion. Defensive warfare or siegecraft was popular with many commanders and seemed to have been justified by the French defense of Verdun, the defeat of the Nivelle offensive, and the British Passchendaele debacle. The easterners, Ludendorff and Bruchmüller, disagreed and labored to retrain the army to fight offensively. Nevertheless, siegecraft continued to enjoy support from Crown Prince Rupprecht of the Sixth Army and from many others. Mechanization, aside from aircraft in ground-support roles, did not receive much attention in the German army.

FULLER'S OPPORTUNITY: CAMBRAI

The chief of the Imperial General Staff, William ("Wully") Robertson, commented to Haig in September 1917 that tanks were promising despite their difficulties in the terrain of Flanders. At least crews had obtained combat experience. Robertson believed that the "tactical situation has become rather difficult" because it was apparent that simply using more artillery could not ensure victory. "We have got a large amount now but the enemy's machine guns are still a difficulty not yet surmounted." Moreover, heavy artillery bombardments destroyed the ground and made it impassable. The problem, as he noted presciently, might be solved: "For this the tanks seem to offer the best prospect, but goodness knows if they will furnish a sufficient answer."[71]

Haig replied that shrapnel and gas shells were effective against the enemy and did not mess up the ground so that tanks and infantry were not held back. Concerning tanks, Haig noted that they would be "of great service if they are delivered in time, and if the personnel is available in time, to enable adequate training to be given before an operation."[72] Shortly afterward he gave approval to the planning for an ambitious battle using large numbers of tanks at Cambrai.

Planning for the Cambrai attack of 20 November, under J. F. C. Fuller, chief staff officer of the Tank Corps, started 20 October and was careful and complete. Originally, the attack was intended to be a one-day affair that would cut through very dense wire defenses and crack the Hindenburg line.[73] The Royal Tank Corps underwent two months of intensive training in which tactical exercises were shared with the assigned infantry.[74] The draft scheme for the attack, completed on 25 October, called for an attack in the first phase using five divisions that had trained with tanks for at least two weeks. The attack formation for tanks, worked out by Fuller, called for sections of three tanks each to assist one another in crossing entrenchments, using fascines.[75] Infantry was divided into three groups. Trench clearers would accompany the tanks to reduce trenches and dugouts. Trench stops were other infantry assigned to eliminate enemy infantry emerging after the initial shock of the assault. Finally, the trench garrison would occupy the trenches conquered.[76] For the second stage the Cavalry Corps was to provide four or five divisions. The attack would cover a ten-thousand-yard-wide front and would follow the leapfrog system. The artillery would not provide a preparatory barrage and would merely provide smoke screens and barrages to the front and flanks of the attack. Once the attack began, the artillery would also try to eliminate hostile batteries and all known centers of communication including telephone lines. "The greatest care must be taken during all preparations that no signs of unwonted activity in the area are apparent to hostile observation either from the ground or air." Tanks, shipped by priority rail service to assembly points, together with artillery pieces, were camouflaged in staging areas. They were then to be moved at night just prior to the attack.[77] The planning was quite detailed and encompassed the tactical deployment of tanks, infantry, and artillery as well as logistics.

Although the Royal Flying Corps had been notified of the impending attack it was not clear what role its aircraft would play. Maurice Baring mentioned later that "none of us had any idea of these preparations and the moves of the squadrons were made in such a way that they thought until the last minute that quite different purposes were being aimed at."[78] Certainly, the higher air commanders did not broadcast the details of the planned action. Unfortunately, there is little evidence to show that effective training in air-infantry-tank cooperation was planned.[79]

The Tank Corps and GHQ left aircraft coordination to the corps commanders and the RFC. The general staff, Third Army, for example, indicated: "Corps will be responsible for arranging aeroplane observation for ranging on the targets allotted," but such artillery work had to proceed on schedule even if no aircraft were available.[80] Therefore, the RFC had to take the initiative for air participation.

Well aware of the complaints of the Canadian Corps and others about the destructive effect of low-flying German aircraft, Trenchard told Haig on 2 November that "the only way to stop them is to bomb more than the enemy does, and to send out more low-flying machines than he does!"[81] "Fighting patrols" on the day of the attack would intercept enemy aircraft on takeoff. Simultaneously, squadrons of fighters would fly low in search of ground targets. Hostile artillery-spotting balloons would be attacked as well. But all of this would occur only on the day of the attack. To give the appearance of normal conditions, "aeroplane actions" would occur along the entire front until "zero plus two hours, after which time efforts will be concentrated on the front of the main operation."[82] Interdiction of enemy fighter aircraft (a difficult ordinary job) and artillery reconnaissance work continued to dominate RFC assignments, however. Typical was Third Army's artillery request that "Corps Squadrons would require a programme of the neutralizing fire. . . . Beyond this, the RFC work will consist of reporting hostile batteries . . . and for calling for fire on concentrations of hostile troops."[83] Unfortunately, no tactical air support role for ground troops had been worked out.

On 9 November the RFC indicated that no unusual air activity prior to the attack could occur, giving support to the general goal of creating surprise. Objectives included reconnaissance and bombing of enemy aerodromes, batteries, troops, transport, and headquarters sites and railway junctions.[84]

The Royal Flying Corps issued detailed instructions for Z Day on 15 November. Fighter aircraft were to note any movements by the enemy, while enemy air bases would be bombed and strafed by other aircraft from low altitudes. Attempts would be made to bomb the enemy headquarters and the railyards at Le Cateau. Finally, low-flying aircraft would attack three groups of artillery batteries with bombs and machine-gun fire. But strangely, no pilot was authorized to bomb enemy infantry or to try to support the advance of tanks and infantry.[85] Several squadrons were taken from the Second Army by headquarters, RFC, on 19 November to reinforce other aircraft available for the operation.[86] Such tardy involvement of the Royal Flying Corps, in contrast to the constant participation of the Tank Corps, cast doubt later about the thoroughness of the planning.

The draft scheme for Cambrai of 25 October 1917 stated that "the object of the operation is to break the enemy's defensive system by a coup de main, with the assistance of tanks; to pass the cavalry through in the break," and to seize Cambrai, cutting off German troops in that region. Demoralization of the enemy, in the face of the surprise attack, would be complete. "We shall, at first, have to deal with a weak force of tired troops and a comparatively small amount of hostile artillery."[87]

In early November, coordinated training of tank sections and infantry companies intensified. A detachment of tanks was assigned to pull sleds full of supplies on the day of the attack, anticipating logistical problems of a projected sustained advance. Sections of ninety-three tanks each, assigned specific objectives, would be accompanied by echelons of infantry. Successive waves of infantry would accompany more sections of tanks. Twelve wire-pulling tanks were to be assigned to clear the route for the passage of the cavalry. Tanks would be concealed until needed in designated, camouflaged areas.[88] The planning became more detailed.

The Third Army attempted to solve some logistical problems. Until the roads were thoroughly repaired it was not possible to move many heavy siege howitzers forward. Even if it were, ammunition could not be provided. In order to support the advance it would only be possible to bring forward a single 9.2-inch or 8-inch howitzer and a single 6-inch gun; there would be a fair chance of maintaining a sufficient supply of ammunition.[89] The specter of inadequate supply lines to sustain a breakthrough was again appearing.

After capturing the Brown line (a stage in the advance) some tanks would join the Cavalry Corps to assist in the planned breakthrough. The cavalry was provided with radio sets fixed on specific wavelengths to avoid interference with other units. In a further directive of 16 November the element of surprise was considered all-important in achieving a breakthrough so that "a unique opportunity for the Cavalry action becomes possible." In the event of success, Cambrai was to be preserved undamaged, but all railroad connections were to be cut so the Germans could not bring up reinforcements quickly.[90] One of the strangest elements of the pre-Cambrai planning was this unrealistic perception of the role of cavalry.

Final training of tanks with infantry was observed by Haig on 11 November.[91] He voiced the guiding philosophy of the tactical deployment of the British forces for the Cambrai attack two days later: "The object of the operations of the Infantry aided by tanks is to break through the enemy's defences *by surprise* and so to permit the Cavalry Corps to pass through and operate in open country."[92] Planning was complete and everything was ready for the operation scheduled for dawn, 20 November 1917.

THE BATTLE OF CAMBRAI EVALUATED

On 19 November, General Elles issued Special Order No. 6 to his tank units: "To-morrow the Tank Corps will have the chance for which it has been waiting for many months, to operate on good ground in the van of the battle." He then exhorted them to good performance and announced that he personally would be leading the attack of the center division. On 20 November at 6:00 A.M. the plan was put into motion.[93]

Elles, in a tank called Hilda, led the van of the 8th Tank Battalion of the 2d Brigade to a spectacular success. The enemy was demoralized by the surprise attack of the tanks, and the accompanying infantry had little to do "but receive prisoners and clear up dugouts." Tanks soon outran the infantry. Field artillery was hastily brought forward to impede attempts by the Germans to pull their cannon back. An early report exaggerated: "By shortly after noon the Cavalry was pouring through Ribecourt and the complete break-through so long dreamed of during the dreary years of trench warfare was an accomplished fact."[94] Nevertheless, so many machine-gun nests remained that the infantry was unable to proceed farther, despite efforts of the tanks to clear them. Preliminary success by the tanks had made possible a substantial advance, but the infantry, artillery, and cavalry had been unable to contribute much.

The attack of the 4th Tank Battalion was similar to most of the others. Some tanks moved in front to destroy enemy wire and strong points. Most machines then followed, equipped with fascines (wood platforms dropped in front). "Fascines proved invaluable for without their aid few Tanks would have been able to cross the Hindenburg Line." The enemy was completely caught by surprise and the attack was pressed into the second Hindenburg line but was frustrated by artillery fire from a village that succeeded in stopping a number of tanks. The village could not be taken because the infantry was too weak. Tank casualties on 20 November for the 4th Tank Battalion included ten knocked out by direct hits, eight stopped by mechanical trouble, and two ditched, leaving fifteen to rally at the end.[95]

The most acrimonious incident of the whole attack occurred when a number of tanks were incapacitated by one German artillery piece as they came, one by one, over the crest of a hill. Fuller accused Maj. Gen. Sir George Harper of the 51st Division of changing the tactical deployment of the tanks. Harper, unlike other division commanders, was not content to allow the Tank Corps to set up the tactical formation that would be used in conjunction with his infantry attack. The ridge the tanks crossed overlooked the village of Flesquières, and the German battery in that village had perfect silhouettes as targets. J. F. C. Fuller argued with Harper, trying to dissuade him from a frontal attack, but without success. The attack seemed to have been spearheaded by the tanks in column, without infantry support: certainly the tactical instructions of the Tank Corps were ignored. The grandson of General Woollcombe, IV Corps commander and Harper's superior, believed that Woollcombe had been relieved from his corps command unfairly after Cambrai since Harper had been responsible for the error.[96]

One wonders why each tank obediently took its turn to be destroyed and why none of the crew commanders suspected something bad was happening ahead. Also, aerial bombardment of Flesquières had not succeeded in destroying all the batteries. What had happened to the infantry that was supposed to be accompanying the tanks? General Harper had apparently kept them back. Haig commented tersely in his diary on 22 November: "This incident shows the importance of Infantry operating with Tanks and at times acting as skirmishers to clear away hostile guns and reconnoitre."[97] Little could be added to that admirable conclusion.

More successful was the attack of the 7th Tank Battalion with fifty tanks and good infantry support. Effecting a complete surprise, this force penetrated seven thousand yards to achieve perhaps the greatest advance in a single day in the war up to that time. In the report of the battalion the infantry was praised for its conduct, but "the numerical inadequacy of their reinforcements, which was very conspicuous in the later stages of the attack, left the tanks often unsupported and suggested that the ideal combination of arms was still to seek." Cavalry succeeded in passing through the breach, but could not take Cambrai. Unfortunately, this advance created an exposed salient that would be lost in the counterattack some days later.[98]

Other battalions reported similar success. The 6th Battalion used the "unicorn" formation where three tanks formed the corners of an equilateral triangle with the apex toward the enemy. Infantry assigned to support tended to lag behind in extended columns. The tank crews were more adaptable: when some machines were put out of action the crews set up machine-gun nests to support their mobile colleagues. The 1st Tank Battalion recorded that it took its objectives an hour before the infantry arrived. Tanks in this battalion used grappling hooks ("anchors") to pull barbed wire to make a clear passage for the infantry. Infantry cooperation was better with the 9th Battalion except that three tank officers were run over by tanks during the advance. Neither the tanks nor the infantry received many casualties.[99] The infantry did not accompany the tanks in a uniform tactical association in many instances and tended to wait for the tanks to do the work.

Aircraft support of the Cambrai attack was very successful but not crucial. As Maurice Baring remarked, too much was expected of aircraft. Low clouds and mist masked the ground as flights took off early on 20 November. Few enemy aircraft were encountered all day and "the chief work throughout the day was the attack on enemy troops from low altitudes with machine-gun fire, and dropping bombs on all suitable targets." But the targets were aerodromes, transport, horses and wagons, and batteries, as well as infantry and cavalry units. Seventy-eight bombs were dropped and 10,600 rounds were expended on these tasks. One pilot made a forced landing in the middle of friendly infantry at Bourlon Wood and assisted in the fighting on the ground. With pardonable exaggeration Baring claimed that that site "was practically taken by the cooperation of tanks and aeroplanes."[100] Despite energetic action the results of aircraft support were equivocal; the destruction of some batteries and strong points in the trench system was doubtless of value, yet the battle reports show conclusively that massed tank action used in a surprise attack was responsible for success.

In fact, one reason for the ultimate failure of Cambrai was the comparative lack of success of all the other arms: it was too much a tank show. Tank casualties were heavy on 20 November, and when the attack was resumed the next day much of the mobile driving force was vitiated. Infantry units, fatigued from the day before, encountered well-protected German troops in house-to-house fighting.[101] Failure to advance farther after the second day of the attack posed real problems for the British high command.

To Haig, the results, while startling, were a disappointment. In particular he blamed the stopping of the tanks at Flesquières for impeding the planned cavalry breakthrough. Concerned, Haig ordered the IV Corps commander, Woollcombe, to place the cavalry back in action on 22 November in order to try for the breakthrough. Worrying still, he then went to the Third Army commander, Byng, the next day to urge passing cavalry through Bourlon Wood "to exploit our success." As a result Woollcombe was given the Guards Division on the twenty-third to use to attack Bourlon village. If that were successful, IV Corps would receive more infantry to help advance. On the twenty-fifth, Haig noted that the units were mixed-up in the Bourlon Woods and instructed Kiggell to tell Byng to see if Woollcombe "has a real grip of it." The operation failed, and on the twenty-seventh Haig noted that "cavalry fails because its leaders do not understand it . . . the horse is our weapon," and because these leaders failed to understand that "the German is the feeblest of foes if rushed." Enraged, Haig seemed almost bereft of sense as he continued to fulminate against the cavalry which lacked the necessary "feverish energy" and had to be told that the "objective must be obtained no matter what the losses."[102] Cavalry, he suggested, had been in stagnation and promotions had been slow. Its commanders were thus unprepared for the breakthrough at Cambrai when it came.

The objectives of the British attack were in conflict with one another: was the Third Army supposed to take territory, net a large prisoner bag, or achieve a monumental breakthrough? In actuality the British lacked the troops to exploit a major breakthrough even if it had been possible. Could Haig and other commanders have thought that the battle would achieve modest results, in the manner of Vimy and Messines, but nothing more? If this is true it would explain the pathetic reliance on cavalry. Cavalry was supposed to have one last, presumably glorious, role in modern warfare, but instead would demonstrate its obsolescence.

Most noticeable about the planning was the inadequate coordination of airpower with the main advance of the tank and infantry waves. Lacking any other reserves of importance, Haig really had no option except to use the Cavalry Corps in the event of a breakthrough, but his expectations for the success of that arm seem ill-placed in view of its helplessness in the war since the advent of trench warfare. Finally, the tanks themselves were to do the hard work, and perhaps too little attention was paid to the problem of getting the infantry to work effectively with them at the time the trenches were crossed. But such comments take full advantage of hindsight.

AN ENIGMATIC CONCLUSION

Symptomatic of change within the British army was the rise of the innovative tactician Ivor Maxse to be the unofficial (in 1918, official) schoolmaster in chief. Despite the horrors of Passchendaele, 1917 was a year of considerable growth in the fighting expertise of the British army. The battles of Arras, Vimy, and Messines were intelligently conducted and fought by the troops assigned to them. Maxse's preoccupation with training and careful preliminary planning seemed to be justified; these battles were successful set pieces.

Unfortunately for the French, while the Nivelle offensive used innovative tactics, it earned opprobrium for its chief and temporarily raised the proponents of defense, Pétain especially, to dominance. Nevertheless, the last months of 1917 saw effective use of tanks in battle, and the French did not abandon the hope that future offenses would prove more successful.

Debate raged in the German army between the exponents of defense and those of offense. Siegecraft was raised to a fine art owing to the victory of the defensive school. But during 1917, the arrival of Hindenburg and Ludendorff caused the imposition of a troop-training program designed to restore the army to offensive action. Tactically, Ludendorff became more and more interested in storm troops as an elite advance attack force in projected offensives.

If the French and Germans were struggling with new offensive tactical schemes, the British were able to invent a comprehensive plan and to carry it out at Cambrai in November. Flawed though the operation was, it incorporated novel schemes to bring about the coordinated action of infantry, tanks, artillery, and aircraft. As a by-product it proved, if proof was still necessary, that cavalry was useless in modern war.

The year of experimentation, 1917, had provided many examples of fresh tactical thinking by all the antagonists. In spite of such efforts the trench warfare stalemate remained. Would attrition, rather than new tactics, finally determine the outcome of the war? Doubtless, many military commanders and staff officers wondered, but they did not dare to be optimistic.

Before any new tactical plan could be implemented it had to be taught to those who were to carry it out. Troop training was a fundamental prerequisite to tactical changes and, in all armies, those officers most adept at teaching tactics were sought out and encouraged. In the British army, Ivor Maxse; in the German army, Oskar von Hutier, Georg Bruchmüller, and Max Hoffmann; and in the French army, Louis Franchet d'Esperey and Louis-Ernest de Maud'huy employed hundreds of combat veteran junior officers and noncommissioned officers to form the teaching staffs of tactical training schools. Originally established to train troops for siegecraft in 1915 and 1916, these programs had to be revised to accommodate the revived penchant for open warfare after the closing months of 1917.

The key to the tactical training innovations of 1917, which were the pioneer efforts to escape siegecraft, was the utilization of all available arms in a common attack endeavor. At the end of the year the Battle of Cambrai ushered in a new era of warfare by battle-testing the tactical innovations of the tank pioneers, air power advocates, and artillery and infantry trainers. Despite the modest long-term results of Cambrai, that battle demonstrated that the British were far ahead of either the French or the Germans in developing a potentially successful attack formula.

NOTES

1. Raymond Poincaré, *Au service de la France, l'année trouble 1917* (Paris, 1932), 9:18–19.
2. Maxse Papers, 69/53/1.
3. Maxse Papers, 69/53/1, 69/53/2.
4. Maxse Papers, 69/53/1, 69/53/2.
5. Maxse Papers, 69/53/4.
6. Military History Archives, King's College, University of London, Montgomery-Massingberd Papers, 47.
7. Liddell Hart Papers, 1/499.
8. Maxse Papers, 69/53/6. Montgomery-Massingberd Papers, 48.
9. Maxse Papers, 69/53/6.
10. Maxse Papers, 69/53/8Aa
11. Maxse Papers, 69/53/8A.
12. Maxse Papers, 69/53/6.
13. Camille Bloch, *Bibliographie méthodique de l'histoire économique et sociale de la France pendant la guerre* (Paris, 1925), for many examples of Taylorism in the war.
14. Maxse Papers, 69/33/6.
15. Maxse Papers, 69/53/6.
16. Maxse Papers, 69/53/8A.
17. Maxse Papers, 69/53/8A.
18. Maxse Papers, 69/53/8A.
19. Maxse Papers, 69/53/8A.
20. Maxse Papers, 69/53/8A.
21. Maxse Papers, 69/53/8A.
22. Maxse Papers, 69/53/8A.
23. Maxse Papers, 69/53/6, 69/33/6, 69/53/8A.
24. Maxse Papers, 69/53/8A.
25. Maxse Papers, 69/53/8A.
26. Montgomery-Massingberd Papers, 93, 94.
27. Montgomery-Massingberd Papers, 94.
28. Blake, *Haig Papers,* 211–16.
29. Blake, *Haig Papers,* 200. Daniel Dancocks, *Sir Arthur Currie* (Toronto, 1985), 88ff.

30. PAC, RG 9, III, 3825, 3826. Cruttwell, *Great War,* 406–8.

31. PAC, RG 9, III, 3825, 3826.

32. Liddell Hart, *Real War,* 330–37.

33. Harrington, *Plumer,* 78–98.

34. Blake, *Haig Papers,* 129–30, 235–36.

35. Harrington, *Plumer,* 98–112.

36. Farrar-Hockley, *Goughie,* 213.

37. Montgomery-Massingberd Papers, 94.

38. Blake, *Haig Papers,* 234.

39. Grand Quartier Général des Armées de l'Est, État-Major, 3e Bureau. *Instruction sur le combat offensif des petites unités,* 8 January 1916. (Hereafter, *GQG.*)

40. *GQG, Instruction,* 5ff.

41. Maxse Papers, 69/33/6.

42. Montgomery-Massingberd Papers, 93.

43. Balck, *Entwicklung,* 128–31. Blake, *Haig Papers,* 218. Callwell, *Wilson,* 1:338–39. BSA, AOK 6, Bd. 326.

44. Cruttwell, *Great War,* 412–13.

45. AMV, 16 N 1987.

46. AMV, 16 N 1987.

47. Mangin, "Comment finit la guerre," *Revue des deux mondes,* 56 (1 April 1920), 260–61.

48. Charles Mangin, "Comment finit . . . ," 260–61.

49. Guy Pedroncini, *Pétain, Général en Chef, 1917–1918* (Paris, 1974), 48–62, admirably describes the efforts of Pétain upon taking command in May 1917. Colonel P. M. Lucas, *L'evolution des Iédées tactiques en France et en Allemagne* (Paris, 1923), 189–90.

50. Lucas, *Idées tactiques,* 190–91. Pedroncini, *Pétain,* 88–97.

51. Lucas, *Idées tactiques,* 190–91. Pedroncini, *Pétain,* 88–97.

52. Lucas, *Idées tactiques,* 191–93. Pedroncini, *Pétain,* 97–109. AMV, 16 N 1992, 3e Bureau.

53. Balck, *Entwicklung,* 64–65. Seesselberg, *Stellungskrieg,* 126–65. BSA, AOK 6, Bd. 337.

54. Captured German document translated in Maxse Papers, 69/53/6. Seesselberg, *Stellungskrieg,* 177–83.

55. BSA, AOK 6, Bd. 326, Bd. 350.

56. BSA, AOK 6, Bd. 326, Bd. 350.

57. Balck, *Entwicklung,* 115–16.

58. Hellmuth Gruss, *Aufbau und Verwendung der deutschen Sturmbataillone im Weltkrieg* (Berlin, 1939), 1–26. See also Gudmundsson, *Stormtroop Tactics.*

59. Gruss, *Aufbau,* 27–28, 149.

60. Gruss, *Aufbau,* 29–38.

61. Gruss, *Aufbau,* 40–45.

62. Gruss, *Aufbau,* 55–63. BSA, AOK 6, Bd. 9a, Bd. 326.

63. AMV, 16 N 1987. Balck, *Entwicklung,* 115–18.

64. "Systematic English artillery firing," Ludendorff claimed, "often ignored certain places in the terrain which could be used to convey traffic up to the combat lines." BSA, AOK 6, Bd. 326, Bd. 350.

65. AMV, 16 N 1987. Maxse Papers, 69/53/8A.

66. Balck, *Entwicklung,* 66.

67. Cron, *Geschichte,* 23–25.

68. Cron, *Geschichte,* 25–26.

69. Bruchmüller, *deutsche Artillerie,* 1–14.

70. BSA, AOK 6, Bd. 6, Bd. 350, Bd. 326.

71. Robertson Papers, I/23/51.

72. Robertson Papers, I/23/52.

73. Williams-Ellis, *Tank Corps,* 100–103.

74. Fuller Papers, TCWH 1.

75. PRO, AIR, 1/1510/204/58/10. 3d Brigade, RFC.

76. Williams-Ellis, *Tank Corps,* 103–4.

77. PRO, AIR, 1/1510/204/58/10. 3d Brigade, RFC.

78. Baring, *Flying Corps,* 254.

79. PRO, WO, 95, 15. War Diaries, GHQ.

80. PRO, AIR, 1/1510/204/58/10.

81. Haig Papers, ACC 3155, 119.

82. PRO, AIR, 1/1510/204/58/10.

83. Fuller Papers, vols. 1–3, TCWH 1, 1st Tank Battalion. PRO, AIR, 1/1510/204/58/10.

84. PRO, AIR, 1/1510/204/58/10.

85. PRO, AIR, 1/1510/204/58/10.

86. PRO, WO, 95, 15. War Diaries, GHQ.

87. PRO, AIR, 1/1510/204/58/10. 3d Brigade, RFC.

88. PRO, AIR, 1/1510/204/50/10.

89. Fuller Papers, vols. 1–3, TCWH 1, 1st Tank Battalion. PRO, AIR, 1/1510/204/58/10.

90. PRO, AIR, 1/1510/204/58/10.

91. PRO, AIR, 1/1510/204/58/10.

92. Haig Papers, ACC 3155, 119.

93. Williams-Ellis, *Tank Corps,* 104–8.

94. Fuller Papers, TCWH 1, 8th Battalion report.

95. Fuller Papers, TCWH 1, 4th Battalion report, 5th Battalion report.

96. Robert Woollcombe, *The First Tank Battle* (London, 1967), 101–12.

97. Blake, *Haig Papers,* 269.

98. Fuller Papers, TCWH 1, 7th Battalion report.

99. Fuller Papers, TCWH 1, 1st and 6th Tank Battalion reports. TCWH 2, 9th Tank Battalion report.

100. PRO, AIR, 1, 1186. RFC War Diary for 20 November 1917. Baring, *Flying Corps,* 258–59.

101. Williams-Ellis, *Tank Corps,* 114–16.

102. PRO, ACC, 3155 119.

CHAPTER 9
LUDENDORFF'S OPEN WARFARE: 1918

L udendorff convinced the Reichstag and the emperor in 1917 that the war would be pushed with renewed vigor. Two factors aided his cause: the collapse of Russia, which freed increasingly large numbers of German troops for transfer to the west; and popular disgruntlement with the siegecraft mentality of the high command in the west. Ludendorff organized a novel and large-scale offensive, of a syncretic type, which was launched in March 1918 with the intent of achieving a German victory. He nearly succeeded.

LUDENDORFF'S GAMBLE: THE MARCH OFFENSIVE

The origins of the famous German attack of 21 March 1918 lay in the preceding year, not on the western but on the Russian front. Ludendorff, veteran with his chief, Hindenburg, of the eastern campaign, had been placed in charge of German forces in the west. Watching the coming of the Russian Revolution he telephoned Gen. Max Hoffmann, eastern chief of staff, and asked him if a major attack could be launched against Riga with the purpose of delivering a crucial blow against the Russians, hastening the end of the war in the east. A subsequent attack, originally scheduled for August 1917, was postponed until September.[1]

General Hutier of the Eighth Army planned the Riga attack with his artillery chief, Lt. Col. Georg Bruchmüller. Bruchmüller, Hoffmann remarked, had an uncanny ability to estimate precisely how much artillery ammunition had to be expended on a given point to enable the infantry to storm it. The preliminary bombardment by 170 batteries and 230 medium and heavy mortars on 1 September opened with a gas bombardment at 4:00 A.M.[2] Pontoon bridges were quickly made up across the river Dvina, and the army crossed with ease to force the Russian army out of Riga. So flabby was the enemy response that many German soldiers expressed the desire to push on to Petrograd.[3] The immediate result of this battle was the consolidation of the front in the face of a rapidly disintegrating Russian army.

The tactics employed by General Hutier, including the artillery leadership of Bruchmüller, came to the attention of Ludendorff and formed the basis for a retraining program instituted by the German army on the western front. Prior to March 1918, the German army had always been numerically inferior in the west to the Allies and, Ludendorff suggested, tactical thinking had been defensive. Ludendorff believed at the end of 1917 that "we had to revive in the minds of the fighting forces all those excellent offensive principles which inspired our prewar regulations." Such time-tested rules had to be supplemented, he admitted, by experience gained in the war.[4]

Ludendorff, however, was not old-fashioned and had a comprehensive approach to tactics. He remarked in December 1917 that the prewar firing line had been replaced by waves of attacking infantry that were, in fact, preceded by shock troops. The German army, he believed, should not, whenever they possessed numerical superiority, simply emulate the technique of the mass infantry attack favored by the French and British. Such attacks, utilizing untrained troops and characterized by high casualties, failed to take advantage of thousands of battle-tried troops from the eastern front as well as France.[5] Therefore, to be successful a future attack would require individual soldiers to display a certain initiative on the battlefield so that tactical opportunities, suddenly arising, might be utilized. The advance of such well-trained and experienced troops would be preceded by an effective artillery barrage, supplemented by auxiliary firepower produced by heavy machine guns, mortars, field artillery, and aircraft.

Expert and veteran infantrymen were transferred from their units to form teams of storm troopers. Equipped with what for the time were massive amounts of firepower, including a light machine gun, rifles, pistols, hand grenades, and entrenching tools, such squads, according to Ludendorff, were "to push as far forward as they can (if possible, *before* the end of the artillery and trench mortar preparatory bombardment)" and to serve as an advanced attack group. As early as October 1917, the Bavarian Sixth Army on the western front had created vanguard units of storm troops using the Model 08 heavy machine gun as the nuclear weapon. Expert marksmen worked with the machine-gun crews. Ludendorff's plan incorporated combat experience on both fronts.[6]

In January 1918, staff conferences led by Ludendorff assessed the tactical situation in the west. In the time-honored method of the elder Moltke, discussion was frank as rank was forgotten and every effort was made to develop a comprehensive offensive plan. In the meeting of 19 January, for example, a staff major asked about the possibility of getting 120 artillery batteries to the front on the evening of the attack and leaving an entire division in an extreme forward zone without support for some hours. Ludendorff agreed that this was a difficulty but "the whole thing must not only be played out, but also must be led by three divisions in bad terrain." Crown Prince Rupprecht commented that the Sixth Army had not been able to achieve a decisive breakthrough at Cambrai against the English because of lack of reserves immediately at hand. The English, on the other hand, had not won at Cambrai because they had not brought forward with them sufficient artillery. A compromise was reached on this issue: a number of mortars would provide the portable artillery support for the storm troops, obviating the need to move heavy field artillery over the shell-pocked terrain, although heavy weaponry would have to follow not too much later in the advance.[7] A key problem of the war was pinpointed: How did one concentrate firepower constantly on the enemy and maintain an advance as well? How could one achieve mobility through shell-pocked no-man's-land and four English defensive systems? The elite storm troops could break through, but how could their momentum be maintained?

Most striking about the Ludendorff offensive plan were two points: an enormous concentration of firepower throughout the attack with no letup and the coordination of elite storm squads, infantry, artillery, and the air services. Concentration of firepower would occur in stages: a preliminary barrage would be immediately followed by the advance of the storm troops, who would set up light machine-gun nests. Crews would then move forward with the more cumbersome heavy machine guns to help lay down a concentrated fire on the enemy. Flamethrower and grenade troops would then accompany the advance of the mass of infantry. On the heels of the first wave of infantry would be units of field artillery trained to work with it. Supporting fire from formations of low-flying aircraft throughout the attack were to protect the whole ensemble of troop units below.[8] By organizing weapon squads with those special purposes, Ludendorff hoped to have the firepower to handle enemy tanks and fortified strong points in the trench system. It was calculated that a steady rate of advance of one kilometer per hour was possible using this coordinated system.

Such a complicated plan demanded the utmost professionalism of the fighting troops and was far removed from the English system of 1916, which had consisted of drilling raw conscripts to go over the top and follow tape lines forward upon hearing a whistle blow. Ludendorff correctly admitted that to succeed his plan required intrepid men at arms. Constant training in open-warfare techniques including marksmanship was essential. The prime weakness of his plan was, of course, his need for expert soldiers and company officers, who were in a minority even in an army characterized by veteran service.

Effective artillery was the concern of Bruchmüller, recently transferred from the eastern front. His newly published manual, *Der Angriff im Stellungskrieg,* specified that before an attack a sufficient number of guns must be collected close to the front, camouflaged, and prepared for quick service. By not firing before the attack date, they would not be located by the enemy. Before 1918, it had not been possible to collect twenty to thirty batteries totaling about one hundred guns for each kilometer of front to be attacked. As Ludendorff remarked, "No man had ever credited such figures before." Given firing tables just before the attack prepared by a fire-direction center, each battery was forbidden to register by firing. Instead, intensive map study and trigonometry, as well as observer reports, formed the basis for these tables. Just before the attack meteorological data would enable last-minute corrections to be made. The fire-control center, in constant telephonic or messenger communication with the batteries, could immediately shift fire simply by giving the instruction, for example, "Twenty more on Position Adolf." Battery officers merely had to consult their firing tables to locate Position Adolf, take the daily correction figure, and order firing on the new position.[9]

Bruchmüller favored use of a firing system he called a fire waltz, a variety of creeping barrage. The English and French in 1917 had developed a regulated curtain of artillery fire that would precisely precede the forward units of the infantry. But fire waltzes, either simple or double, first used by the Germans in 1915 on the eastern front, were different from the creeping barrages. The simple fire waltz required firing on the enemy lines at the same time as the infantry advanced. The double fire waltz used later consisted of moving a curtain of fire in springs before the advancing infantry in a waltz pattern. Essentially, the double-waltz pattern was in two movements: the first utilized coordinated attack by the artillery and infantry, and the second was a gas-shell attack. On the eastern front this field of fire could be placed as close as fifty meters before the advancing infantry. But in the west in 1918, Bruchmüller had to keep the minimum distance at two hundred meters or more because of the lack of qualified artillerymen and defective coordination with the infantry. Needing time to train the western batteries, he dared not use the complicated double fire waltz.[10]

No less noteworthy were German attempts to harness airpower effectively in the planned offensive. Although the German air force had experimented with close tactical support of the infantry, it was only after Cambrai that special battle squadrons were established. Forays of the Royal Air Force directed against supply and reinforcement columns had caused considerable worry to the Germans. With the addition of aircraft from the eastern front, thirty-eight squadrons were available by March. New air bases within army sectors allowed a considerable number of aircraft to be kept close to the front in a state of readiness. Each division obtained a wing (*Fliegerabteilung A*, for example) and each army commander had at his disposal another such wing as well as formidable reconnaissance, pursuit, and bombing units. Pilots were trained in the new techniques of ground support as part of an overall attempt to obtain complete coordination of effort between air groups and their superiors, the ground commanders.[11]

The organization, shown schematically in Figure 5,[12] encompassed individual army sectors. Aircraft in the first, or combat, zone provided reconnaissance and ground support over the actual frontline trench system of the enemy. The next, the tactical support zone, included the advanced depots and staging areas and road and rail terminals. Finally,

FIGURE 5: GERMAN AIR RECONNAISSANCE SCHEME, 1917

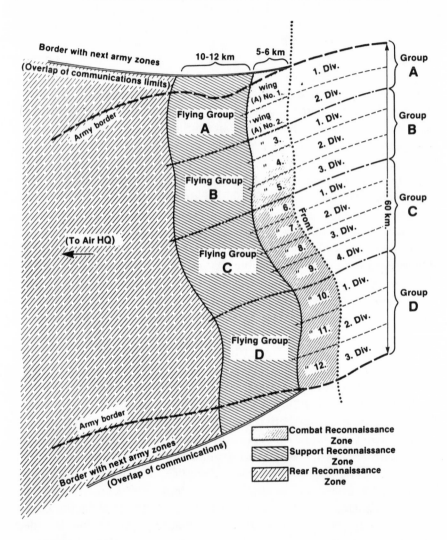

the strategic support zone was the special responsibility of the army's aerial photographic service. Such methodical and comprehensive use of airpower to interdict enemy ground forces was unknown to either the RFC or the French air force.

German planning also entailed effective use of low-flying aircraft to assist the ground attack. Precise flyover patterns within the combat zone of each division were established for pursuit groups (Figure 6). Alterations to the scheme were possible if meteorological conditions required them. Worked out by Richthofen in July 1917 in more elaborate form (Figure 7) for the March offensive of 1918, the plan called for systematic strafing and bombing of the enemy's front lines. Dangerous work because it entailed possible interference with the German artillery, this air interdiction would start when the barrage ended. Ludendorff commented: "Originally intended to be an 'auxiliary' arm to the infantry, these battle flights were finally given important tactical tasks."[13]

For two months before 21 March staff officers worked strenuously to eliminate logistical and other bottlenecks. The entire project, named Operation Saint George, remained classified Most Secret: only officers would be able to type and deliver memoranda, orders, or other written materials. All supplies were moved as much as possible at night so the enemy would be deceived. Military police were assigned to supervise the orderly movement of vehicles to and from the front areas. Quantities of maps were printed for distribution to units just prior to the attack. Some artillery units were trained on English guns captured at Cambrai so they could use captured pieces during the advance. Pioneer companies were moved close to the front as well so they could work on the heels of advancing infantry in repairing roads to facilitate the flow of supplies: eighteen companies with 11,900 men were assigned this job. About 532 heavy and 384 light artillery pieces were collected, and these were supplemented by about 900 light, medium, and heavy mortars. Efforts would be made to camouflage staging areas, roads, depots, and the like. Additional divisions were assigned to the Fourth and Sixth armies, five to each. The aim was to achieve a wide breakthrough on the English front, followed by a roll-up of enemy units on either side of the breakthrough. Ludendorff believed that if Operation Saint George succeeded, the British army would be broken and isolated, and the French, discouraged, would sue for peace.[14] Ludendorff's

FIGURE 6: GERMAN STRAFING PATTERN (SINGLE PLANE FLYING)

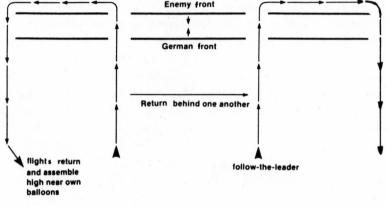

FIGURE 7: GERMAN STRAFING PATTERN (UNIT FLYING)

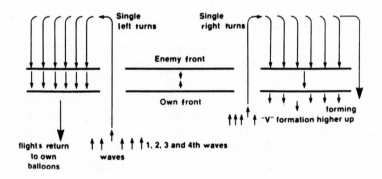

ability to transfer large numbers of divisions from the eastern front meant three armies with a total of seventy divisions could be expected to break through enemy defenses on a front seventy kilometers wide.

In general, the German army was poised, by 20 March 1918, to undertake a great attack of unparalleled force on the western front. It was the fruit of meticulous planning and of the patient coordination by a number of key specialists in the use of infantry, artillery, and aircraft.

DEPTH, NOT BREADTH; BLOBS, NOT LINES

Quite obviously, the offensive preparations of the Germans threatened the Allies very seriously. Did the British or the French have any forewarning of this threat? Maxse, in Gough's Fifth Army, noted at a corps commanders' conference on 19 February 1918 that the Germans were putting their best troops into storm troop units. He worried that the British were unprepared to meet assaults by these elite soldiers, even if they had learned "only one big lesson from CAMBRAI and that is DEFENSE IN DEPTH." Maxse, noting that the French had learned this as early as Ypres, implied the German threat could be met through greatly improved defenses: Emphasis was to be on "Depth, not Breadth; Blobs, not Lines." On 9 January, General Gough had already warned that the Germans were reinforcing their units with troops from Russia. "Forewarned is fore armed is a proverb which now carries increased significance."[15]

French premonitions were revealed in a note from General Headquarters on 28 January 1918, describing the operations of the German Eighth Army at Riga the previous September. French staff analysts believed that the Riga technique, soon to be used by the Germans in the west, was characterized by a surprise attack, brutal artillery preparation of short duration, and rapid and deep exploitation of the enemy's defenses. Pétain ordered heavy "action by cannon," which would be assisted "by all the aviation available" using bombs and machine guns.[16] The French not only knew more about the German reorganization and tactics than the British, they also seemed better able to anticipate new attacks.

The Tank Corps headquarters considered defensive measures after the Battle of Cambrai, estimating on 1 March that the Germans might attack the British on the Arras-Cambrai front in conjunction with an attack on the French front. German tanks could at last be expected and might be used. Interest was immediately aroused in the development of suitable antitank weapons. Caught unprepared, the British improvised shells consisting of tin cans filled with ammonal.[17] In any event, due to the scarcity of German tanks, the Tank Corps could have better employed its time in preparing defensive tactics using its own tanks. There is no evidence that was done.

The Royal Flying Corps, also concerned about defense in the face of a strong German attack, held demonstrations with the Tank Corps. Aircraft strafed and bombed simulated antitank gun nests. A pioneering directive dated 16 January 1918 emphasized that direct cooperation with ground troops was a "main feature." In the German counterattack at Cambrai, the Fifth Air Brigade reported: "There is little doubt that the work of the low-flying aircraft considerably harassed the advancing Germans by bombs and machine-gun fire." The Australian Corps claimed that aircraft succeeded in damaging the transport system and inflicting casualties on the reserves. But the directive of the RFC claimed as well that the main job of aircraft was artillery spotting in the traditional sense. Almost buried in the directive was the stipulation that low-flying machines were "to cooperate with the infantry in attacking the enemy's most advanced troops." Finally, success depended upon aerial supremacy.[18]

E. D. Swinton, although not directly involved with aircraft, was interested in their relationship to tanks in battle. He noted much later that the strafing of German troops by British aircraft had occurred from time to time during the Somme battle and had increased during 1917. But the systematic cooperation of aircraft with infantry shown by the Germans during their counterattack at Cambrai on 30 November 1917 was "in a form which was a distinct advance on anything that had hitherto been attempted by either side."[19] There appears to be no evidence to challenge that statement.

Under the commands of Gough (Fifth Army) and Rawlinson (Fourth Army), revitalized training programs stressed defense after Cambrai. A program for the Fourth Army commanding officers' conference, held at Flexicourt between 27 January and 2 February 1918, emphasized a new platoon organization. One of four sections would service a machine gun while the other three consisted of equal numbers of infantrymen trained in rifle marksmanship and those trained either in grenade throwing or rifle grenade shooting. The basic infantry platoon would eventually become much stronger in firepower.[20] But that reorganization was just beginning in March.

More impressive was the diligent effort of Ivor Maxse to rejuvenate the Fifth Army by using his XVIII Corps as a training exemplar. In February, he lectured to senior officers emphasizing that training must be done every day and must be well organized. Troops were to be trained by sections and platoons in the trenches, and patrols were to be chosen from rosters rather than volunteers. "Waste of time is due to lack of forethought and bad habits. Waiting for orders is the worst habit of all." Sergeants were to be taught the role of the infantry company and platoon officers so they could step in in battle. An enemy of unimaginative parade-ground drill, Maxse constantly emphasized field training. Commanders must try to encourage independent thinking by soldiers of all ranks so they could take advantage of opportunities to use systematically what they had learned. Battalion and company officers evaluated results after each day's work.[21]

Convinced that the key to military success was to stress good training, Maxse told his senior officers: "I ask you to listen to me today, because you know the British character—my character, your character. . . . We have got an astounding way of muddling things." Continuing, he claimed that "we know it to be a muddle and yet we muddle it deliberately." British troops would not wire their trenches properly, and Maxse was thankful his corps had just taken over from the French a sector that was already wired. Because the British had failed to set up machine-gun nests to protect their trench system in depth, they had lost seven thousand prisoners and 162 guns in the counterattack at Cambrai. The Germans had used storm troopers in front and did not ask for reinforcements. The reserves were thus kept available to deliver "hard blows" instead of being steadily diminished by withdrawals of reinforcements.[22]

Noting that the German machine gunner was "the best man in the German army," Maxse claimed that some English machine gunners, lacking expertise at Cambrai, had fired on their own supply forces instead of the enemy. Redoubts and passive defenses constituted strong points that had to be held[23] because they could retard the storm troops and help to prevent infiltration. As soon as possible Maxse supervised the construction of strengthened defenses. Some of the troops were put to work on tasks associated with construction of the third line of defense. Those of the Gloucestershire Regiment were told they would be marched back as soon as the digging was done. "This scheme produced digging of a very high order and one platoon finished its task, which was intended to take two hours, in thirty-five minutes." A young staff officer decided to increase the tasks, and, as a consequence, digging slowed down perceptibly. The system of defense was built, in spite of staff officers, in three areas of defense: forward, battle, and rear (Figure 8). The forward zone consisted of a line of outposts behind which were strongly fortified redoubts. Set between five hundred and fifteen hundred yards apart, they were linked by barbed wire and machine-gun nests. Redoubts and machine-gun nests were situated so their field of fire covered the lower land in front. The depth of the forward zone was about three thousand yards "and its purpose was to break up and disorganise the leading troops of the German assault." The battle zone consisted of redoubts but had no outposts. Two miles behind that zone was the rear zone, which consisted of a double line of trenches. A battalion of the Gloucesters "held a line of posts north of Fayet with a strong point at Enghien Redoubt." These posts were in the forward zone and were very lightly held and situated at distances of about one hundred yards from one another.[24] Other battalions occupied parts of the battle and rear zones.

Maxse's defense-in-depth scheme was extremely flexible because troops could be shifted from the rear to the forward lines while supported by strong points. The first two zones provided a series of difficult obstacles to infiltrating German troops in a major attack. Probably Maxse conceived the entire defensive system to be analogous to a cushion, which, when some points on it are pushed, gives in those places but retains its position overall. It is difficult to discount the observation: "The holding of such an extended line so lightly was probably a necessity, but to say the least of it, it was audacious."[25] In fact, the Fifth Army had recently had its front extended without receiving more troops. No other British army had to spread its resources so thinly. Maxse's scheme, in part, was an attempt to utilize relatively few troops more effectively in a defensive system.

Proceeding along quite different lines in planning a defensive system after Cambrai, the Canadian Corps, on 26 December 1917, specified three systems of defense: front (Blue Line), intermediate, and second (Red Line). "Every yard of the fortified area is to be fought for, and . . . there is to be no question of any falling back from one line to another line." Shell holes containing machine-gun squads formed parts of these lines. Machine-gun clusters of two to four guns formed the nucleus

FIGURE 8: MAXSE'S SCHEME FOR DEFENSE IN DEPTH

FEBRUARY, 1918

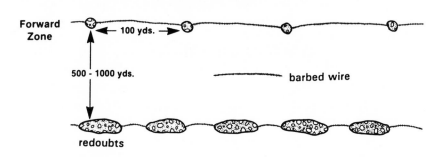

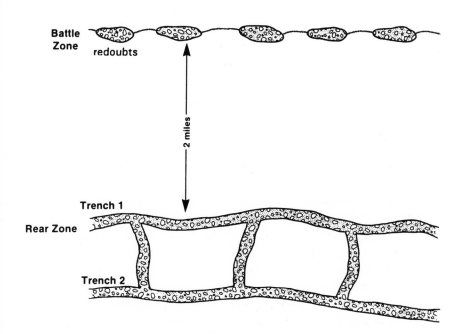

of strong points.[26] This system of defense lacked flexibility and continued the use of trench lines.

Obviously, the planning of the Tank Corps, the Flying Corps, and various ground commanders and their staffs was not integrated after Cambrai. As Maxse, preeminently an infantryman, suggested, "muddle" characterized British thinking before the March German attack.

THE GERMAN ATTACK OF MARCH 1918

Assembling the evening before, the German troops attacked on a front of eighty kilometers on 21 March. Three armies, including the Eighteenth, commanded by the innovator of Riga, General Hutier, hit the junction between the French and English forces. This was held, on the English side, by Gough's Fifth Army. At 6:40 A.M. on 21 March, the artillery barrage started on three English positions and was followed by the infantry advance at 9:00 A.M. Strong points were identified and eliminated by machine-gun squads and artillery assisted by low-flying aircraft, enabling a rapid overrun of the English forward positions. When Hutier's army broke through the English third-line defenses, Ludendorff expected a real breakthrough to occur. German aircraft then concentrated on the destruction of depots behind the lines.[27] Within a couple of days the British situation was desperate, and the attack seemed to promise the approaching isolation of the entire British Expeditionary Force and the fall of Amiens.

The response of Haig was curious. Although he granted a request by Gough to withdraw some distance after 21 March, Haig believed that the Fifth Army (and the Third Army under Byng) had held firm, and he sent messages of congratulations to the troops. Estimating that thirty additional divisions had been added to the German army to strengthen it prior to the attack, he was also willing, on 22 March, to allow the Fifth Army a further retreat to the Somme. But the next day Haig was surprised to note that the Fifth Army troops had fallen behind that point: "I cannot make out why the Fifth Army has gone so far back without making some kind of a stand."[28] The next few days saw reinforcements arrive from Plumer's Second Army and from the French. But Haig realized that Pétain would defend Paris as a priority over supporting the British and decided, on 24 March, that "in my opinion, our Army's existence in France depends on keeping the British and French armies united." Previously, he had opposed a supreme command because he did not trust the French, but the March crisis changed his mind. When General Pershing supported the nomination of Foch as supreme commander Haig agreed.[29] The subsequent Declaration of Doullens was of greatest importance because it united Allied aims behind a common grand strategy. Tactically important as well, it enabled the planning of simultaneous attacks on the Germans so that the growing power of the Allies, due to the arrival of American troops more than anything else, could be coordinated. Out of the most severe crisis of the war, the German offensive of March 1918, arose a war machine that would, in eight months' time, defeat the Germans.[30]

Royal Tank Corps reports added to the mounting evidence of the British debacle in the meantime. Tanks, although successfully used on 21 and 22 March in local counterattacks, had to retreat when the front collapsed. A number of them had to be destroyed because of "the lack of petrol or mechanical failure." Crews without tanks were formed into Lewis gun units and stationed at road crossings on 25 March. Out of 175 men in the 2d Tank Battalion, 108, or nearly 70 percent, became casualties on 21 March. The most probable reason for ineffectual tank counterattacks was lack of infantry and artillery support.[31]

Rudolf Binding, fighting in the German army, noted that, although his division had suffered many casualties, everybody was heartened by the first successes. Captured British staff officers complained that efforts to train troops in open warfare had been futile: this accounted for the retreat. Binding was concerned about the excessively long supply line that existed by 2 April: "One cannot go on victoriously forever without ammunition or any sort of reinforcements." By 19 April, German looting at Albert and Moreuil delayed the attack just long enough for the French to rush in artillery. "The disorder of the troops at these two places, which has been fully attested by German officers, must have cost us a good fifty thousand men, apart from the lost opportunity."[32]

Max Hoffmann, although still on the eastern front, followed the situation and believed that Ludendorff was correct in making a general offensive at this time, before the Allies obtained large numbers of American troops and generally became stronger. Unfortunately, he criticized, the attack was not made just at the point of greatest weakness and opportunity (against the Fifth Army), and was not made using all of the forces available. The force of the attack was therefore partly vitiated because of parallel attacks against other units of the British and

French at the same time. Hoffmann concluded, "We only almost succeeded—we did not win the victory. . . . Our offensive had only dented
the enemy front, but it had not broken through."[33]

In the end, the Ludendorff offensive failed because it exhausted itself.
Supply lines collapsed and there was no quick extension of the motor
transport system through the laying of roads over conquered territory.
The need to keep many troops tied down to fight on the British Third
Army front as well as against the French made reinforcements difficult. The offensive lost its punch heartbreakingly close to attaining
its objectives.

The British had also gradually strengthened their lines by establishing
a defense zone that kept the Germans from capturing Amiens. Rawlinson
wrote an appreciation (memorandum) dated 18 April that indicated the
French and British armies north of the Somme were still in danger.
Until the French strengthened the line Moreuil-Demuin, Amiens would
not be secure.[34] Difficult to accomplish, this stabilization finally contributed to the German defeat.

MALMAISON: RECOVERY OF FRANCE

After the mutinies in the spring of 1917 and the failure of the Nivelle
offensive, a general reconstruction of the army followed. Pétain undertook to raise the morale of troops through better furlough rules and
placed new emphasis on training for combat. Gone were the dreams
of wholesale offensives: Pétain wished to conduct only limited battles
with great possibilities for success. A series of modest victories would
restore the fighting effectiveness of his army and placate alarmed
politicians, anxious for results. By the fall of 1917, the reforms bore
tactical fruit in the success of the Battle of Malmaison.

Fought 23 October 1917, Malmaison provided vindication of the
French army: the Sixth Army alone captured 11,558 prisoners, 200
artillery pieces, 222 mortars, and 720 machine guns at a cost of 14,000
total casualties between 21 and 25 October.[35] In the postbattle analyses a number of factors for success were identified: the use of tanks,
rolling artillery barrages, and the development of elite infantry vanguard units.

In charge of the Malmaison offensive, General d'Esperey admitted
that impromptu or ad hoc bodies of soldiers led the advance, operating almost independently, and materially aided the success of the French.

He urged exploiting a break "laterally" rather than simply trying to achieve maximum penetration, which would result only in creating a vulnerable salient. A broad, shallow break would prevent the enemy from concentrating forces for a counterattack on one point.

Specially trained squads had been detailed to accompany the tanks. Competent combat veterans, these elites signaled targets to the tanks and assisted them in taking such targets. When enemy trenches were reached by the tanks both the elite group and the rest of the infantry waited until the tanks destroyed major enemy resistance. Prior to the employment of German storm troops at Riga, Pétain had already discerned the importance of the use of special troops in the vanguard of an attack.[36] Going further, he specified that "the tanks must be employed in close liaison with the infantry in order to facilitate maneuvers between strong points [*points d'appui*] of the enemy line and to reduce the machine guns which impede progress.[37] Our combat groups reduced enemy machine gunners," breaking the first line of defense, even though the Germans had reinforced it. The infantry had to be trained better in marksmanship and encouraged to operate resourcefully.[38] The French adopted a comprehensive plan for the use of combat squads composed of superior infantrymen as advance units operating with and without the cooperation of tanks.

Artillery, long considered the most important arm by the French, still had its supporters after Malmaison. D'Esperey suggested that barrages could accurately hit enemy strong points while keeping most of the terrain reasonably free of shell holes. He believed artillery could be employed in preliminary barrages of four days' duration, causing maximum damage with minimum expenditure of ammunition. Better artillery pieces and fire control now in use could accomplish this job. Pierre Chaine, a combatant, supported the last point: "For four nights our fire was concentrated on points of passage of the enemy, cutting his communications and obliging him to hide until 'H' Hour."[39] General de Maud'huy, the II Corps commander, worried that the rolling artillery barrage, so useful in assisting the infantry to advance across no-man's-land, messed up the ground so that the tanks (first used in this battle) had difficulty in negotiating it. Therefore he assumed, logically, that the tanks were of minimal use in the first attack and would only be useful in helping the infantry to penetrate past the first defensive line where the terrain was not as shell pocked.[40] D'Esperey, in contrast, maintained that many enemy machine-gun nests were destroyed by the rolling barrage. The greater precision of newer artillery pieces made this possible and limited damage to the terrain needed for passage of tanks.[41] Disagreement of the top commanders over precise tactical points was evident.

At Malmaison the heavy Schneider and St.-Chamond tanks achieved debatable results. Maud'huy claimed that "in spite of the devotion of their personnel the tanks had rendered little service because of difficulties of the terrain." They could be very useful, he thought, at the "moment of exploitation" when the enemy retreated, leaving machine-gun nests to stop the advancing French infantry. Tanks kept in reserve could then be employed to quickly destroy such nests and facilitate the advance of the infantry. D'Esperey, in contrast, believed that the new rolling barrage proved effective when used simultaneously with the advance of the tanks and infantry.[42]

In attacks on the Château de la Motte, tanks encircled the enemy nests and destroyed them, pushing forward until shell-torn land stopped them. Afterward, tanks accompanied the infantry in the attack on the second line. Tactically, the French infantry seemed to advance before the tanks on many occasions, not simply following them as had the British troops at Cambrai. One regiment found it could go no further forward, for example, because the Germans had garnished the Lezard trench sector with machine-gun nests, so they summoned a tank which succeeded in destroying this resistance in somewhat over an hour. Although d'Esperey believed that "the tanks have rendered incontestable services," he was convinced that the most careful cooperation was necessary between them and the infantry in order to bring simultaneous pressure to bear on the enemy strong points. Maud'huy preferred the use of large numbers of the small Renault light tank to the cumbersome Schneiders and St.-Chamonds for this purpose.[43] Cooperation of tanks with artillery and infantry was essential.

Because even conservative field commanders now recognized the combat possibilities of tanks, General Estienne, chief of the French tank organization, pushed hard at the end of 1917 to make substantial improvements both in the tanks themselves and in the combat organization of them. The heavy St.-Chamond and Schneider machines were too slow and ponderous, and he believed that the new six-ton tanks made by Renault were less vulnerable and promised greater success.[44] Henceforth, he obtained large numbers of these small and agile tanks and began the training of crews, stressing better marksmanship with the 37mm guns as well as maneuvering on terrain of different types. Recent combat experience, he believed, showed that secrecy of preparation, including the camouflaging of equipment, had often brought victory. But Estienne claimed even greater success would probably have occurred with greater use of tanks. Light tanks, supplementing artillery and infantry attacks, could concentrate on machine-gun nests and other strong points. Because the heavy tanks were to be pulled from service as soon as large numbers of Renault light tanks became available, Estienne also reorganized the tank company, which was now composed of sections utilizing the light tanks. Consisting of support personnel as well as two-man crews for each of five Renault tanks, the sections were the prime tactical units. Three sections composed a company and three companies, together with a reserve section (with five combat tanks and three supply and repair tanks) and a headquarters staff, formed the new battalion. Tactics were worked out in a directive of February 1918. Figure 9 explains the attack formation.[45] The first three tanks used their guns to facilitate a crossing of the trenches and continuance of the advance forward while the tanks with machine guns fanned out from X right and left to attack the enemy in the trenches just crossed.

Further lessons came from study of the Cambrai battle. Whereas the English had used tanks without artillery preparation and benefitted from surprise, "unfortunately, the failings of our tanks to cross wide trenches has stopped us up to now from having operations of this nature." Estienne was forced to report in March that the twenty-one groups of Schneider and St.-Chamond tanks were virtually useless since these tanks could not be used except in "good conditions where the terrain is firm and not too broken by artillery fire or where the trenches were not too wide." By the end of March both French and British tank officers were convinced that the British heavy tanks could be best used in the first hours of the battle while the French light tanks could be used for the subsequent cleanup of enemy strong points. The British minister of munitions, Winston Churchill, promised to provide two hundred heavy tanks to the French to assist them.[46]

In the aftermath of the German March offensive, the French 3d Bureau of the GHQ noted that neither French nor German tanks had played any important role in that debacle. The offensive convinced the French,

FIGURE 9: FRENCH TANK TACTICS FEBRUARY, 1918

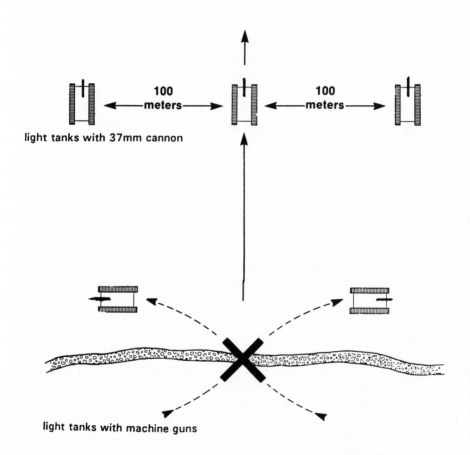

light tanks with 37mm cannon

light tanks with machine guns

however, to insist upon the construction of large numbers of light tanks and to abandon the heavy tanks, because the former could be carried quickly by rail to where they were needed. Pétain, an energetic supporter of the tank production program, was convinced that light tanks would work cooperatively with specially trained infantry to overcome the enemy in future battles.[47] Estienne's program of December 1917 was adopted completely by May 1918.

FRANCE AND THE MARNE THREAT

Ludendorff later claimed that his offensive against the French at Chemin des Dames was planned as carefully as had been the 21 March offensive against the British Fifth Army. Certainly this offensive, started at the beginning of May, included both old and new features. Bruchmüller again deployed the artillery. Improvements included placing more pioneer units close to the front with pontoon bridges[48] and other equipment, and directing the advance of field artillery on the heels of attacking infantry units. Some twenty fresh divisions were found somewhere. Great emphasis was placed on the use of mortar companies in cooperation with the carefully selected assault troops. Camouflage of units, equipment, and roads leading to the front was again practiced. Operation Hubertus also employed sixty-five field artillery and fifteen antiaircraft battalions. The latter reflected a German obsession with low-flying, strafing enemy aircraft. Possibly it was thought that these battalions' artillery pieces could be used against tanks as well. Ludendorff ordered careful integration of all units with emphasis on the all-important infantry attack. Launched on 27 May, this attack surpassed its planned goal, a line between Soissons and Fismes, within three days. This great Château-Thierry salient reached the Marne and was perilously close to Paris. Ludendorff seemed justified in his claim that German troops proved themselves "superior to both the English and the French," even when the latter were assisted by tanks.[49] The results of the Riga tactics seemed incontestable.

The Chemin des Dames offensive was marked by the usual meticulous attention to detail, which was the hallmark of Bruchmüller especially. Starting with a three-and-a-half-hour bombardment, some twenty-nine divisions smashed through six French and three English divisions. Despite intelligence warnings the French did nothing to face this threat until the day before the attack. An enormous number of German aircraft accompanied the barrage and bombed French and English air bases and their aircraft on the ground. As the German troops advanced, efforts were made to repair roads in their wake so they could be supplied and reinforced by motor transport. By 5 June, Foch had succeeded in massing forty-three infantry and three cavalry divisions as well as a number of tanks to stop the German advance. German strength was not sufficient to carry on. Supply lines were by that date already inadequate for a continuation anyway. Some fifty thousand prisoners, six hundred artillery pieces, and two thousand machine guns marked the tangible rewards to the Germans at the end of the Chemin des Dames offensive.[50]

Pétain, under no illusions that the greatly enlarged and strengthened German army would prove easy to defeat, pushed for reforms after March. The issuance of more light machine guns to companies strengthened their firepower. Forcing this change was German superiority in combat between 27 and 31 May, which the French attributed to "their energy and the superiority of their armament." German storm troopers had been able to infiltrate and to isolate strong points, taking them, and then attacking the French messengers, reserves, and other support troops. The solution seemed to be increased defense in depth, identified as a zone of coverture. Within this zone an intricate defensive system included more barbed-wire entanglements than was usual as well as redoubts filled with machine guns. The fields of fire of the machine guns overlapped one another to such an extent that it gave literal truth to the designation zone of coverture. In the zone of combat, which was the initial point of contact with the enemy, additional machine-gun nests were supported by field artillery. As a consequence, when the Germans attacked on 9 June, their usual infiltration tactics did not work well. After French intelligence discovered that the Germans had installed new batteries of 77mm and 105mm artillery three weeks before, defenses had been systematically strengthened.[51]

Ludendorff, although shaken by his failure to pierce the Allied defenses in these great assaults between 21 March and the beginning of June, decided to launch yet another operation, designated Hagen, against the English. Planners hoped that if their soldiers had four days' rations they would not engage in widescale looting of captured enemy stores, as had happened in March. Symptomatic of growing morale problems in the army, this idea was stillborn because, after five weeks' preparation, Operation Hagen was cancelled on 23 July.[52] From that time on German defenses weakened and retreats began.

But the rot had barely begun in June when the French realized that "our infantry, in spite of its great bravery, does not have the suppleness of maneuver of the adversary." Reforms included more intensive infantry training for fighting and crossing variegated terrain. Unfortunately, German attacks between 9 and 13 June again succeeded in forcing a French retreat, in spite of the new defense-in-depth system of the latter. One division reported that the French infantry retreated in panic too easily and "must energetically struggle against this tendency . . . to believe itself lost because an element of the enemy had penetrated its flank." The solution was to have reserves on hand to assist in closing up the line from left and right as well as from the rear whenever such a small incursion occurred.[53] But the German Riga tactics were slowly converting the siege war into open warfare.

By the end of June, the French were still not able to combat the Riga tactics of the Germans, characterized by the use of well-trained troops capable of extreme tenacity. One example occurred on 12 June when the German "infantry was poised to attack after a very violent bombardment of four hours in great depth . . . in the course of which a great gas howitzer fire was used to paralyze the French infantry." A rolling barrage of field artillery assisted by mortars shielded the advancing German troops up to three hundred meters, and the distance between attacking companies was reduced as much as possible until after the first line was pierced. "The assault troops did not stop, they forced their way forward as much as possible and as quickly as possible, without stopping to take prisoners they passed through free spaces and neglected obstacles that they encountered." Again, the Riga tactics were followed: strong points isolated by the assault troops were assaulted by light machine-gun teams assisted by artillery. It was, moreover, very difficult to establish when such an attack would take place because the assault troops themselves were not told until the last moment.[54]

Complicating the situation even further was the effective use of aircraft by the Germans in these attacks. "Aircraft followed infantry foot by foot and without stop," as one French commentary somewhat illogically put it. Many aircraft were used to fly in attack formations with the infantry advance and in attacking rear supply depots and staging areas.[55]

By the end of June, the French had only just managed to escape disaster. Although they had stopped the new-style German attacks they had not yet elaborated workable open-warfare tactics. Only such tactics, which would not be a return to 1914 but something new, could reverse the war. The Germans still had a numerical advantage since their forces had been reinforced by the veteran divisions from the eastern front. But, as Max Hoffmann warned, such an advantage was only temporary.

CRISIS FOR THE ALLIES

One would have thought the mood in the headquarters of both the British and French forces would have been one of extreme pessimism by the middle of June 1918. Yet the German grand strategy, ambitiously aimed at decisive defeat of either the British or the French, had failed by that time. Ominously, the presence of new American troops in the region of Château-Thierry during the Chemin des Dames offensive presaged a substantial alteration in the troop balance on the western front.

General Edmonds, compiler of the British official history, later attempted to attribute shortcomings of the British armies to lack of experience in defensive action because of preoccupation with offensive warfare. This bizarre, even fatuous, interpretation was followed by his claim that the Fifth Army retreat was as orderly as the retreat from Mons in 1914. The Fifth Army retreat was only just short of a rout, as Haig himself intimated.[56] Despite the obfuscation of the official historian, evidence shows that the March offensive was a great disaster for British arms.

Three years of enormous casualties incurred in the war of siegecraft forced a decisive tactical change by all warring nations in 1918. Tanks had been considered adjuncts to the infantry in the limited battles of Flers in 1916 and Arras, Messines, and Vimy in 1917. Cambrai in November 1917 showed that a revolutionary role could be played by tanks in leading the first assault. Elite storm troops, trained as forward units of the battles of 1917, became the shock troops of open warfare in 1918. A revolution occurred in artillery as well, as less emphasis was placed on heavy artillery and more on field pieces that could be quickly moved forward to support an infantry assault. A new offensive tactics had to include the infantry, field artillery, and air services, as well as tank and machine-gun units.

Most worrisome was the ample evidence of the deterioration in the fighting will of the British, French, and German troops. Although this was observed by Haig in the 30 November 1917 German counterattack at Cambrai, little was done to rectify this weakness. The French had undergone a similar crisis, which resulted in mutinies earlier in 1917. Therefore the tactics of open warfare, which began to be developed with the March offensive, must be examined in the light of flagging and fragile morale in the armies of the British and the French. Fewer, more subtle signs of the same malaise worried Hoffmann early in 1918.[57] The German crisis would occur precisely at the point where it could do the most damage, in the summer of 1918.

NOTES

1. Ludendorff, *Memories*, 2:478.

2. Haber, *Poisonous Cloud,* 207–8, indicates that Bruchmüller had experimented with "brief, but intensive, gas-shell bombardments" on the eastern front and incorporated this concept in his general artillery tactics in the west later.

3. Max Hoffmann, *War Diaries and Other Papers* (London, 1929), 2:133, 168–69, 171, 173, 178–86. Hoffmann would shortly find himself involved in arranging an armistice with the new Bolshevik regime as well as in the subsequent negotiations for the permanent settlement at Brest-Litovsk.

4. Ludendorff, *Memories,* 2:573–82.

5. Ludendorff, *Memories,* 2:573–82. BSA, AOK 6, Bd. 350.

6. "Instructions for the Employment of Machine Guns in the Attack," February 1918. Translation of captured German document in PAC, RG 9, III, 3858, folder 85, file 6. BSA, AOK 6, Bd. 350. Gudmundsson, *Stormtroop Tactics,* 155–68.

7. BSA, AOK 6, Bd. 9a.

8. PAC, RG 9, III, 3858, folder 85, file 6. Ludendorff, *Memories,* 2:573–82.

9. Bruchmüller, *Deutsche Artillerie,* 26–39.

10. Bruchmüller, *Deutsche Artillerie,* 26–39.

11. Hoeppner, *Deutschlands Krieg,* 147–49.

12. Seesselberg, *Stellungskrieg,* 341, gives the original, which has been adapted and translated for Fig. 5.

13. Seesselberg, *Stellungskrieg,* 343–45, provides the figures that have been translated and adapted as Figs. 6 and 7. Ludendorff, *Memories,* 2:577.

14. BSA, AOK 6, Bd. 4, Bd. 350, Bd. 9a.

15. Maxse Papers, 69/53/8A.

16. AMV, 16 N 2142.

17. PRO, WO, 95, 93. Tank Corps War Diary, March 1918.

18. "The Employment of the Royal Flying Corps in Defense," PRO, AIR, 1, 675. WO, 95, 93. Tank Corps War Diary, March 1918.

19. Swinton, *Eyewitness,* 235.

20. Montgomery-Massingberd Papers, 91.

21. Maxse Papers, 69/53/10.

22. Maxse Papers, 69/53/8A.

23. Maxse Papers, 69/53/8A.

24. Barnes, *Gloucestershire Regiment,* 63–64, 81–82.

25. Barnes, *Gloucestershire Regiment,* 81–82.

26. PAC, RG 9, III, C1, 3828, folder 7, files 1–7.

27. Balck, *Entwicklung,* 358–61.

28. Blake, *Haig Papers,* 295–97.

29. PRO, CAB, 28/3.

30. The insularity of the top British commanders seems almost inconceivable prior to Doullens. Rawlinson noted on 6 March, "I very much doubt if you will get any executive Board to work smoothly under Foch for his tendency is always to interfere with his subordinates and no C. in C. will stand this." Nevertheless, Rawlinson recognized that Foch was pushing to "control and regulate the General Distribution of Divisions as between the British, French, American, and Italian Armies & to have executive functions in giving broad decisions regarding the General strategical situation." Imperial War Museum, Henry Wilson Papers, 73/1/9 13/A.

31. PRO, WO, 95, 93. Tank Corps War Diary, 21–25 March. Fuller Papers, TCWH 1, 2d Tank Battalion, TCWH 2, 13th Tank Battalion.

32. Binding, *Fatalist,* 214, 218–19.

33. Hoffmann, *Diaries,* 2:229–30.

34. Henry Wilson Papers, 73/1/9 13/A.

35. AMV, 16 N 1992, 3e Bureau.

36. AMV, 16 N 2142, 3e Bureau.

37. AMV, 16 N 2142, 3e Bureau.

38. AMV, 16 N 1992, 3e Bureau.

39. Chaine, *Rat,* 208–9.

40. Chaine, *Rat,* 208–9.

41. AMV, 16 N 1992, 3e Bureau.

42. AMV, 16 N 1992, 3e Bureau.

43. Chaine, *Rat,* 208–9.

44. AMV, 16 N 2142, 3e Bureau.

45. AMV, 16 N 2142, 3e Bureau.

46. AMV, 16 N 2142, 3e Bureau.

47. AMV, 16 N 2142, 3e Bureau. See Pedroncini, *Pétain,* 204–6.

48. The British were also working on pontoon bridge designs and rafts that would be used in the last months of the war. See Archibald Montgomery, *The Story of the Fourth Army* (London, 1919) 1:246–47.

49. BSA, AOK 6, Bd. 350. Ludendorff, *Memories,* 2:629–31.

50. Kronprinz Wilhelm, *Meine Erinnerungen aus Deutschlands Heldenkampf* (Berlin, 1923), 319–25. PRO, AIR, 1, 675. Report of the 52d Squadron, RAF.

51. AMV, 16 N 1997, 3e Bureau.

52. BSA, AOK 6, Bd. 350.

53. AMV, 16 N 1997. 16 N 2142, 3e Bureau.

54. AMV, 16 N 1997.

55. AMV, 16 N 1993. 16 N 1997.

56. Edmonds, *Military Operations,* 1:vii–viii, 369–70. An interesting exchange of correspondence exists between Liddell Hart and Edmonds. Edmonds refuted the suggestion that the operations branch of GHQ had an "overweening confidence" that the German attack on 21 March could be either beaten back or, if a salient resulted, a massive British counterattack would turn a feigned retreat into a great victory. Edmonds claimed these staff officers were not overconfident on 21 March but panicked on 25 March when even Haig realized how dangerous the Fifth Army situation was. Liddell Hart Papers, 1/259/101.

57. Hoffmann, *Diaries,* 2:232.

CHAPTER 10
ALLIED OPEN WARFARE: 1918

The Americans finally played a major role in the campaigns of the latter half of 1918. Given the manpower shortage, Haig and Pétain wished to use these fresh troops to replenish their own armies. Pershing aptly and frankly described this effort as a search for cannon fodder to replace casualties lost in fruitless siegecraft. He knew that the American public required evidence of victorious military action by their own troops. Pershing did, however, try to work with Foch, Pétain, and Haig in the aftermath of the debacle of 21 March 1918.[1]

Foch believed later that the three German offensives in the spring of 1918 had forced the Allies to work together. Characterized by "surprise, violence, rapidity in execution,"[2] these German successes had also elevated Foch to supreme command. In 1918 the integration of all British, French, and American arms permitted the development of an overall strategy. This strategy called for the use of different tactics: that of open warfare.

In choosing to develop such tactics in 1918, the military professionals could not afford to ignore siegecraft because trench systems continued, albeit with steadily diminishing effectiveness, to dominate the battlefield. The Allied powers would not have won if they had simply repeated the grand tactics developed in 1916 in the Somme or Verdun campaigns, the paradigms of siegecraft. Nor was it possible simply to repeat Cambrai, which was the culminating battle of 1917 and the first example of open warfare. Spurred by the narrow escape from disaster in the spring of 1918, the Allies responded with open-warfare tactics that contributed to victory in scarcely more than half a year.

HAMEL: THE PROTOTYPE

Dissatisfied with the high command, Lloyd George demanded changes in the BEF following the March crisis. Gough was relieved from the Fifth Army and Haig nearly lost his position.[3] In the month following this crisis Haig had his hands full with a second, subordinate German attack in Flanders. Lacking the planning Ludendorff had expended in the March attack, that offensive nevertheless came very close to success: if Hazebrouck had been taken Calais might have been abandoned. Both the British First and Second armies were badly mauled.[4] Nevertheless, after 19 April, when the danger of absolute defeat seemed at last to be over, Haig rebounded with his characteristic, if uncanny, optimism. He began, in short, to think of a counteroffensive.

Frequent consultations with Foch finally persuaded Haig to entrust the planning of a small, limited offensive to his most competent army commander, Rawlinson of the Fourth Army, on 25 May. Foch hoped to relieve the threat of a German takeover of the Paris-Amiens railroad. The British attack, with assistance from the French under Debeney, would be launched between the Aore and Luce rivers as far as to the Somme River. Promised an additional five or six divisions and all the available tanks except for some to be assigned to Debeney on the right, Rawlinson was told, "It is essential that the operation should be conducted as a surprise and with rapidity."[5]

Rawlinson had recovered his confidence from a month before, when he had been very concerned about a possible German breakthrough at Amiens. But he still believed "the Amiens area is the only one in which the enemy can hope to gain such a success as to force the Allies to discuss terms of peace." Such a German offensive, he believed, would be the "final effort" of the enemy because his reserves were depleted. He did not believe that the enemy would choose the Fourth Army front because it was manned by the best troops of both the French and British: the Moroccan and Algerian divisions and the Australian Corps.[6]

By 6 June Rawlinson had assigned the four Australian and three Canadian divisions to the attack sectors. Two Australian divisions would attack on the north of the Somme while two others would attack south of it on a one-division front. Two of the Australian divisions would leapfrog each other in order to attain the second and third objectives. The Canadian divisions would attack between the Australian and French divisions. Focused south of the Somme the latter thrust would include three or four tank battalions. One or one and a half tank battalions would be used in the subordinate, northern, thrust. "The bulk of the tanks should be used for the capture of the 2nd and 3rd Objectives while the first Objective is dealt with mainly by artillery." Troops would be assembled during the night preceding the attack.[7]

Besides tanks Rawlinson asked for thirty brigades of field artillery (to accompany the infantry), long-range 8- and 9.2-inch howitzers, and shells for 60-pound guns. None of these weapons and ammunition would be sent to the front until the very eve of the battle to prevent premature disclosure to the enemy. No change in artillery positions or in the pattern of routine bombardments was permitted for the same reason. Just before the attack a "barrage in depth to cover attack supported by action of mobile artillery accompanying it" would constitute the main work of the artillery. Three weeks would be needed to prepare for this action.[8]

Planning, undertaken by the Tank Corps staff, was characterized by the belief that the tanks should "move freely to search ground and subdue targets." Under cover of darkness the tanks would move to their starting points in order to attack at dawn. The infantry would be stationed forward of the tanks before zero hour but would follow the advance tanks afterward. When trench systems were taken and occupied by the infantry, the main body of tanks would pass over them. The advance tanks would be some fifty yards in front of the main-body tanks but "the distance will be increased as the Advance sections will move independently of the Infantry." After the infantry achieved its objectives all available tanks would push ahead for the second and third objectives. This phase would be pure open warfare and the machines would be vulnerable to enemy artillery fire: a smoke screen was necessary and "a few aeroplanes with a noisy type of engine should fly above the Tanks and enemy lines, in order to drown the noise of the Tank Engines." If the planes could bomb the enemy as well, this would keep him hidden below ground, enabling the tanks to achieve surprise. Low-flying planes could also attack antitank guns or notify the artillery of the locations of such weapons.[9]

Since the bulk of the troops engaged would be Australian, Rawlinson had to work with Monash, commander of the Australian Corps. On 18 June, in explaining the plan, he had to convince the dubious Australians that the new Mark V heavy tanks would be much more reliable than previous models.[10] Monash used the 5th Tank Brigade plan for the attack south of the Somme, which included a tank battalion of three companies of twelve tanks each. The main tactical points to be captured were Hamel Wood and its village. The advance-echelon tanks, accompanied by infantry, would move to the rear of main tactical points as quickly as possible in order to cut off the retreat of garrisons and to prevent reinforcements. The main-body tanks were then supposed to lead the infantry to these points of resistance and to protect the soldiers with fire. The mop-up tank group was to provide tank replacements and would assist the infantry in clearing enemy machine-gun nests. The frontage of the attack would be five hundred yards.[11] Hamel, nearby villages, and its wood were the tactical objectives.

Monash and his staff objected to some of the 5th Tank Brigade recommendations. Discussions with the tank people centered on the attack time (dawn or dusk), whether tanks would make a smoke screen, whether more tanks could be obtained, and whether the artillery barrage should start just before or at the same time as the attack. Monash, finally satisfied, reported to Rawlinson that the operation centering around Hamel would be primarily a tank operation, and the role of infantry would be to mop up.[12]

On 23 June Haig commented: "After going into General Monash's proposals I am of opinion that if the operation is successful, the casualties should not be great, as it is intended to make the operation essentially a surprise tank attack." For political reasons he wished to include up to six companies of American troops in the attack, now scheduled for 4 July, the American Independence Day. Haig and Rawlinson approved a request from Monash that the advance echelon of tanks be eliminated and these tanks used in the main body so that tanks and infantry moved forward together under cover of a creeping barrage. This final revision occurred on 26 June.[13]

A postbattle BEF appreciation later underscored the success obtained by an infantry advance in four waves following tapes behind a creeping artillery barrage. Tanks accompanied and supported these waves. On 4 July 1918, the Australian Corps "assisted by American troops with Tanks attacked this morning" in the Hamel region. The Australian Corps attributed the subsequent success largely to secrecy although "the value of tanks in assisting the advance of the infantry was conclusively proved." The infantry "fought its way forward with its own weapons, even when the cooperation of other arms was not available."[14] Although conventionally assigned with slender coverage (one gun to twenty-five yards of front in the creeping barrage) the artillery did powerful counterbattery work on the flanks of the assault. Tanks carrying ammunition, water, and other stores were very useful, although the predawn darkness impeded their progress.[15] Cooperation of the different ground arms in the Hamel operation was excellent.

Flying a total of 637 hours with 198 pilots on 4 July, the Royal Air Force dropped 1358 twenty-five-pound bombs on targets east of Hamel. Other aircraft kept contact with the advancing infantry and tanks by means of white cloth signals placed by advancing machine-gun sections. Some ammunition boxes were also dropped to the infantry. Every precaution was taken to insure that aerial observation and bombardment was coordinated with the infantry and tanks. Some twelve hundred copies of aerial photographs were distributed to the infantry just prior to the attack.[16]

Since 22 June efforts had been made to develop coordination of tanks with low-flying aircraft, the latter displaying disks on their fuselages. Intended to guide the tanks right, left, or straight ahead, this system worked only at very low altitudes with good visibility. Unfortunately, 4 July was overcast and the aircraft flew too high.[17]

Trying hard to make the Hamel operation a success, Rawlinson had obtained additional aircraft from the RAF and observed the training of the tanks with the Australians prior to the attack. He noted, "The tanks must keep within 100 yards of the leading line of the Infy . . . they must chance being hit by our barrage."[18] Obviously, a new tactical concept was forming in his mind: the coordination of aircraft, tanks, artillery, and infantry into a carefully orchestrated effort. Rawlinson was probably the only British commander of sufficient imagination to encompass in his mind the multitude of vexatious problems that the working out of this concept required. He deliberately used the best troops he could get (none of whom were British) and obtained effective cooperation from both the RAF and the Tank Corps. Hamel was not a great success in itself but it was a prototype. The line was advanced by one and a half miles on a four-mile front, and 40 officers and 1447 other soldiers were taken prisoner. Several days after Hamel, Rawlinson was convinced that the enemy units in front were weak, and he wished to continue the advance. This last desire was quickly repressed in the intensive planning for the Amiens offensive of the next month.

NEW IDEAS ON TACTICS

Behind the striking success of the Hamel operation was a period of gestation of tank tactics that began after Cambrai. Some officers, such as J. F. C. Fuller, worked hard to improve offensive tactics by incorporating lessons learned from the perilous fighting during March and April. The result was a revitalized Tank Corps that finally achieved its aim of being recognized as a keystone of battle after Hamel.

Albert Stern, the precocious organizer of British tank production who was relieved from this post by 1918,[19] shared certain ideas about tanks in the aftermath of Cambrai with his erstwhile superior in the Admiralty, Sir Eustace d'Eyncourt. Neither was more than an amateur in military matters, but their ideas were not too far removed from those of the avant garde of military professionals such as Swinton and Fuller. Stern reflected in a memorandum, dated 28 January 1918, that "battles are won by weapons wielded by men and not by Army Forms or inoperative brainwaves. . . . Today the machine gun is the supreme small arm. . . . The Tank will protect the infantry machine gunners from the enemy's machine gunners, and the aeroplane the Tank from the enemy's artillery." In fact, "low-flying aeroplanes must be bullet proof . . . they must become flying tanks." As a banker in peacetime Stern felt moved, no doubt, to add this curious observation: "If the politicians and people are to be controlled so that this war may be brought to a victorious conclusion we must show 'profits'—a balance of successes—by the autumn of this year. We must declare a dividend." He asked, rhetorically, if rifles, artillery, and passive defenses would bring victory and decided not; "Brain power" was needed. Finally, Stern doubted that such intelligence could be provided because: "Our destiny as a great nation lies in the hands of an ignorant and discontented proletariat, which is swayed by words."[20] Naturally, such views were rare in the British army at this or any other point.

D'Eyncourt commented on 12 December 1917 that a complete victory at Cambrai had not resulted because of a lack of breakthrough and exploitation by the tanks. Suggesting the formation of "a thoroughly effective striking force," or a tank army of five hundred tanks, with its "own transport highly organized," he argued that "1 Tank in attack is probably equal to 400 infantry, so that 500 Tanks may be regarded as the equivalent of something like 200,000 men."[21] The civilian specialist in the construction of tanks as well as of warships thus had the temerity to suggest tactics to the professionals.

Greater success could have been achieved at Cambrai, the War Office replied, if lighter and more mobile tanks had been available. The tank did no doubt economize on manpower because it was an "armored machine-gun detachment." Attacks could now be mounted with little or no artillery bombardment because infantry would be assisted by tanks. The War Office did not believe in tank armies because "the value of tanks, as of guns, lies in the assistance they can give to the infantry to overcome the enemy's defenses." Most important of the War Office comments, however, was the admission that tanks could be used cooperatively with other arms.[22] The War Office was committed to tanks but only as an auxiliary tactical device and not as the key to victory; infantry remained queen of the battlefield.

Much effort was expended to bring the tank battalions back to strength in personnel and machines after Cambrai. The 4th Brigade had only four operational tanks on 21 January 1918, for example. During March it was reequipped to a total of ninety-six tanks.[23] Attached to the Fifth Army, it would soon be occupied with the German March offensive. The medium A tanks, now introduced, were the first machines to be developed from scratch with field experience in mind. Radically different from the Mark I to Mark V heavy tanks, they would provide more flexible and mobile capabilities to the Tank Corps in 1918.[24]

Equally important was a manual entitled *Infantry and Tank Cooperation and Training,* dated 27 January 1918, which reflected the optimism of the Tank Corps planners. It posited that the advance of infantry in battle was limited by its physical endurance while the advance of tanks was limited by the condition of the ground. All of the noninfantry arms of service had a primary duty to protect the infantry, which was the key to victory. Therefore, methods of coordinating tanks, for example with infantry, should be worked out before the heat of battle. The tank had a range of eight to ten miles and the endurance of its crew was a maximum of eight to twelve hours. Given these limitations and remaining cognizant of the types of terrain that were unsuitable, e.g., swamps, streams, thick woods, sunken roads, and so on, tanks could be employed with infantry. "Tanks replace the barrage of the old firing line [of riflemen] and the infantry follow behind them ever ready to form into a firing line to cover their own advance and that of the supports following behind." Tanks should be used according to principles usually associated with open warfare: mobility, firepower, and security.[25] The infantry was destined to play a passive role in this scheme, which was no great change from those used in the Cambrai attack.

J. F. C. Fuller had submitted a memorandum dated 8 August 1917, entitled "The Tactical Employment of Tanks in 1918." In retrospect it has proven to be a particularly prescient paper that stressed "the one thing to visualize now is that mechanical warfare is going to supersede muscular warfare." More and more war would depend upon mechanical means. "Already this war has replaced or practically replaced horse traction by motor traction in the administrative services." Fuller was trying to emphasize a revolutionary idea: that the tank was not just an adjunct to the infantry but was the key element in a new force that would be completely mobile and completely dependent upon motorized transport. A breakthrough, previously limited to the four-thousand-yard range of protective artillery or to the endurance of infantry at perhaps eight thousand yards, would be greatly prolonged and strengthened if pushed in a sector not pulverized by artillery fire and carried through by a mobile force. "The Tank of to-day only carries forward the rifleman of the future." But the tank had to be accompanied by motorized artillery and personnel carriers. "The tank, first of all, is a time-saving machine, secondly a shield—it is in fact an armoured mechanical horse."[26] Naturally, this radical memorandum could not obtain immediate support.

The futuristic mechanical-army concept of Fuller and d'Eyncourt did not dictate the evolution of tank tactics prior to August 1918. Horse transport remained essential throughout the war. Production experience in England indicated clearly that the priorities of manpower and material placed tank production too low to permit an extraordinary increase. Given the limitations of the tactical thinking of higher commanders, it was obvious that the tried and proven table of organization of infantry divisions and of equally sacrosanct artillery brigades would not be changed.

Tanks after Cambrai had to be used as just another arm of warfare. Realizing tanks had to work with artillery, infantry, and aircraft, Haig arranged a demonstration on 4 February 1918. The objective was to visualize the "possibility of aeroplane and Tank co-operation, especially with regard to Anti-Tank guns."[27] In early March, experiments of the Tank Corps showed that aircraft could attack artillery batteries either in the open or in sketchy emplacements with machine guns and bombs. Infantry also could be vulnerable to air attack, particularly if in files rather than in extended-order lines, but tanks seemed largely invulnerable.[28] But a new manual of the RFC, dated 11 March 1918, allocated less than an hour in the six weeks' pilot curriculum to "contact patrols," which was the loose label for aircraft-ground cooperation.[29]

A new tactical doctrine incorporated in *Notes on Co-operation between Tanks and Aeroplanes,* developed in conjunction with the Tank Corps, marked the furthest advance of RFC thinking in the war. Tank Corps officers would accompany aircraft acting as "an advanced guard to Tanks leading the attack, keeping the Tanks informed of the approach of hostile Tanks and also the position of the enemy's reserves and anti-Tank guns." In offensive action tanks could be protected from hostile gunfire by the aerial use of machine guns, bombs, and smoke. Later, if a breakthrough was obtained, aircraft and tanks could work together to disorganize the enemy's supply systems, headquarters, and communications. Finally, the RAF acknowledged it had a responsibility "to act offensively in conjunction with Tanks against enemy trenches." Most difficult was communication since wireless equipment was cumbersome and not too reliable as yet, so flares and other visual signals had to be used.[30] This important document was probably prepared by June 1918 and was a key to tactical development thereafter.

A Tank Corps pamphlet, GT 29, of late June, suggested new tactics to achieve coordination of aircraft and tanks. The rapidity of an advance toward an objective could be facilitated by aircraft scouting the terrain while tanks protected the advancing infantry. Aircraft and tanks could also secure the flanks of an advancing unit. Such principles, although not new, contributed to the birth of mechanized warfare. Enemy strong points could be dealt with, surprise could be obtained, and infantry losses minimized. The conservation of manpower was a key concept: using less infantry and more tanks in the attack would build a powerful reserve that could strengthen the advance or protect against strong counterattacks. Although tanks could provide a kind of mobile artillery barrage, the infantry should consider them "armoured fighting patrols or mechanized scouts thrown out in front of them not to exonerate them from fighting, but to give them more latitude in use of their Machine Guns, rifles, and bayonets."[31]

GT 29 differed from earlier Tank Corps manuals only in certain details and refinements. Tanks had to be collected quickly and secretly at prearranged rallying points so the attack would take advantage of the massed firepower. Ideally, they should be concealed in woods and should debouch from them in a surprise attack with the accompanying infantry. Under no circumstances should tanks move over a skyline. When tanks crossed trenches special cleanup battalions of infantry had to accompany them to eliminate all enemy opposition. Otherwise the Germans would emerge from hiding to fire on the advancing support troops and tanks.[32] Infantry, shown bunched up behind the tanks in Figure 10, were shown dispersed in Figure 11 in order, no doubt, to emphasize the point in GT 29 that the tanks were not a protective screen for them. Tanks "created opportunities" for infantry, but did not relieve them of the necessity of fighting. The emphasis in June 1918 was on creating a winning "cooperation of all troops, [rather] than the intermingling of different arms." Because the Mark V heavy tank was at least 100 percent faster than the Mark IV on rolling terrain it could, at a speed of three and a half miles an hour (as opposed to one and three-quarters for the Mark IV), easily outdistance accompanying infantry. But the tanks, shown in advance in the accompanying figures, were not to pull away from the infantry but to escort and assist it. Tanks would be able to roll over enemy machine-gun nests more effectively because they could now be steered easily by one man. The Mark IV required four men to turn it. But the tanks, because of their speed and maneuverability, as well as their relative invulnerability to all enemy weapons except the antitank gun, would be able to work in advance of, and separate from, the infantry. But infantry fighting in skirmish lines of great fluidity if little depth could most effectively work with the tanks in front of them.[33]

The German attack of 21 March had started a new phase in the war: that of mobility and more open fighting. In GT 29 much emphasis was placed on the use of Mark V* tanks, which had just been produced

FIGURE 10: TANK CORPS TACTICS LATE 1917

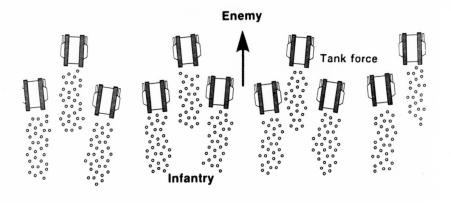

Enemy

Tank force

Infantry

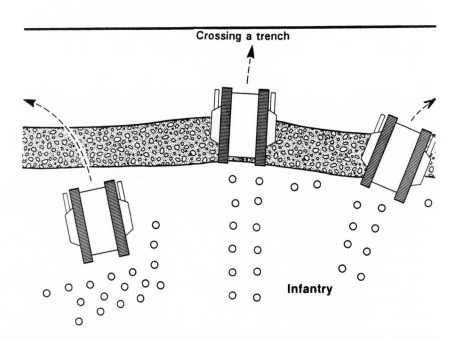

Crossing a trench

Infantry

FIGURE 11:

TANK CORPS TACTICS JUNE, 1918

(Enemy)

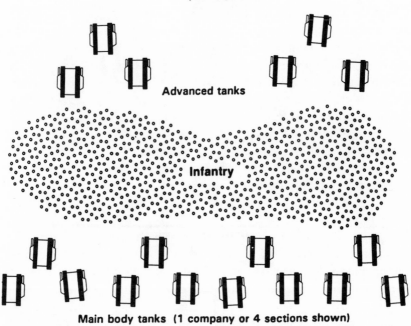

Advanced tanks

Infantry

Main body tanks (1 company or 4 sections shown)

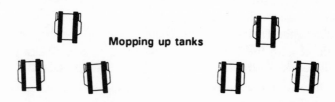

Mopping up tanks

in June, for the purpose of carrying machine-gun crews and ammunition forward quickly in the wake of the advance of the Mark V tanks and their infantry units. It was hoped that continuity of attack could be maintained and that the carrying of supplies and troops by mechanized means would greatly assist the range of an advance.[34]

Archibald Montgomery, Rawlinson's chief of staff, remarked on 8 July that the Fifth Army's disintegration following the attack of 21 March was not due to the effectiveness of the German attack but to the Fifth's lack of infantry. Montgomery thus revealed a curious blindness to the evidently superior German leadership and tactics. He did admit, however, that at Hamel "we employed 60 tanks of the new type, Mark V, which helped enormously to save casualties."[35] His thinking, really quite conservative and in contrast to that of the Tank Corps, was probably shared by many senior commanders.

Montgomery also praised the planning of Hamel by Monash, commander of the Australian Corps. According to Jackson, his general staff officer during much of the war, Monash had "undoubted ability and [was] very methodical." Always ready to discuss plans with his staff, he had an uncanny ability "to see through other men's eyes." Prior to the Battle of Messines in 1917 he had cross-examined every battalion commander to see if he knew the task allotted to him.[36] Systematic in approach, Monash also possessed rare qualities of intelligence and understanding of tactical possibilities. Initially negative concerning tanks, he quickly incorporated them in his attack plan for Hamel. One tank battalion praised the Australian staff work as "a model of skill and attention to detail: the co-operation of Infantry, Guns, Airmen, and Tanks."[37] The interlocking planning of staff and line officers from the RAF, the Tank Corps, and from his own divisions was a tribute to Monash's innovative leadership.

A battalion of the Tank Corps later claimed that "the Australian infantry were delighted with the Tanks" because casualties had been light. In fact, the bulk of casualties had been incurred by those infantry battalions that moved into action ahead of the tanks. Although each combat tank brought with it extra ammunition and drinking water, four carrier tanks followed the attack force with other supplies within a half hour of the capture of a position.[38] Perhaps reflecting a central concept of Fuller, the Tank Corps was thinking more and more of mechanized warfare as a life-saving substitute for the old, brutal, infantry-versus-infantry confrontations.

Monash and his superior, Rawlinson, planned another limited operation along the Hamel lines, but this scheme was aborted in favor of a much larger offensive in August. With the approval of Haig, on 18 July, Rawlinson obtained the services of the Canadian Corps to assist in "this offensive south of the Somme," which he thought would be "a big thing."[39] Heartened, the British army was now encouraged to think of future success in the region of Amiens.

FOCH AND THE GRAND OFFENSIVE

By 14 June, Foch was working with Pétain, Haig, and Pershing to establish a coordinated strategy using simultaneous offensives designed to attack the Germans on a wide front. Centering on Amiens, the Somme offensive would attempt to eliminate the German salient conquered in the offensive of 21 March. A simultaneous offensive in Flanders would reconquer ground lost in April near Lys. The Marne salient had been created by a great German success in the area demarcated by Soissons at one extreme and Château-Thierry at the other; it had been the result of the German success in the Battle of Champagne which began 27 May. Foch asked Pétain to prepare a plan for a general offensive for the most important area, that of Soissons–Château-Thierry, using both French and American troops. Reduction of the Marne salient would relieve pressure on Paris and assist in other Allied offensives to be implemented shortly. This instruction was given on 27 June.[40]

Determining that a new approach was needed to attack the Germans after the March and April offensives, Foch demanded that the French army prepare for open warfare. In the future, he specified, counterattacks were to be mounted as soon as possible after an enemy attack and were to be "rapid and violent," bypassing strong points and using all "the suppleness of the infantry and artillery." A strengthened defense led to a more effective offensive designed to remove the Germans from the vicinity of the railroad going from Amiens to Paris. Pétain's Directive No. 5, dated 12 July, summarized the new doctrine: "strategic surprise . . . tactical surprise . . . deep penetration." Foch combined his well-known doctrine of offensive audacity with the lessons of Riga.[41]

Pétain's subordinate, Gen. Charles Mangin, now commander of the Tenth Army, was asked on 18 June to take German positions near Soissons. In a series of small operations lasting until 28 June, according to him, "the infantry was ordered to stay close to the barrage" and to isolate points of resistance for subsequent mop-up squads. Engineer units, accompanying the infantry waves, opened breaks in the trench system with explosives. Artillery, rather than tanks, was used to break barbed-wire defenses. The infantry attacked shortly after the rolling barrage started at dawn on one occasion, 3 July, and reached all of its objectives within an hour and a half. In another small action of 6 July, although the French used flamethrowers, the trenches were not taken until after a vicious close combat using rifles and grenades.[42]

An attack on 9 July used only two battalions of infantry and, presumably, a handful of tanks. Nevertheless, a pattern was emerging: attacks were now coordinated with effective surprise using infantry, engineers, tanks, and artillery. But usually the infantry went before the tanks and was consequently held up by strong points of resistance until the tanks arrived. Where the infantry decided to take such points heavy casualties resulted.[43] The French had neither developed a systematic scheme for tank-infantry cooperation nor trained these arms to work together, despite the orders of Pétain earlier.

Mangin then suggested to Pétain a more ambitious offensive against the Château-Thierry pocket, using surprise and the cover provided by the woods, which would enable troops, artillery, and tanks to be deployed at the last moment. Approved on 9 July and executed on 18 July, the offensive involved two other armies in a surprise attack between the Aisne and the Ourcq. No artillery preparation had been made prior to the dawn attack. Mangin, observing the attack from a forward command post, hoped to send in the cavalry if opportunities arose. (They did not.) Some 321 tanks accompanied the infantry under an umbrella provided by a rolling artillery barrage. The surprise was complete and the attack carried eight kilometers in the center. Some ten thousand prisoners and two hundred guns were taken by Mangin's Tenth Army, and two thousand prisoners and fifty guns by the Sixth Army. Mangin congratulated his troops for eliminating the dangerous German salient which had reached Château-Thierry and endangered Paris.[44]

The spearhead force in the Château-Thierry battle included the

American 1st and 2d divisions as well as a Moroccan division. Although the inexperienced Americans had performed brilliantly, taking more than seven thousand prisoners and 91 guns, their losses had been high: five thousand casualties by the evening of 19 July. Major Gen. James G. Harbord, newly appointed to command the American 2d Division, found his troops exhausted after being brought quickly to the assembly points on 17 July. He was further dismayed to discover motorized and horse-drawn vehicles, troops, and guns milling about in a sea of mud. Seven hours before zero hour none of his troops were in place except the artillery: his assaulting battalions arrived in place to attack behind the rolling barrage only by running at the double. As objectives were reached the cohesion of the new American troops started to evaporate, and pockets of combat units continued to advance without much coordination. As the day progressed efforts were made to move tanks, cavalry, and artillery forward causing an immense congestion. Although twenty-eight tanks accompanied the 2d Division, most American troops, including the marines, had not even seen a tank before the attack. The supply bottleneck had prevented any distribution of food and water for twenty-four hours. An advance of over seven miles had been accomplished.[45] The American debut in large-scale warfare had been traditional: infantry had achieved the victory, and the contributions of aircraft and tanks had been minor. Mangin had not concentrated his tanks in this part of his army, yet the Americans and Moroccans achieved the most signal victory. What tactical lessons could be learned?

Although the French were behind the English in developing new tactics to coordinate tanks and aircraft, they were catching up. On 23 July, two companies of English tanks supported a IX Corps attack without aircraft cover because of poor visibility. The infantry left the trenches under the protection of a rolling barrage and the tanks followed. Again, machine-gun nests limited the advance to the second objective line. But if the tanks were not used very effectively, they did achieve recognition. The battle report indicated they "largely contributed" to the taking of woods, a farm, and some strongholds of resistance. Tanks were stopped, however, by artillery fire. In another engagement, in which the French troops were accompanied by St.-Chamond heavy tanks, the Germans could not stop the tanks until they hastily brought forward light artillery. On 23 July the 1st Infantry Division, in Mangin's army, launched a small attack that was accompanied by a fair number of Renault light tanks. This success was preceded by only a half-hour of artillery preparation, although a rolling barrage accompanied the advancing troops. In fact, advance was difficult without the aid of tanks because the Germans had greatly increased the number of their machine-gun nests on the front. These nests operated in groups and protected the infantry. German defenses remained formidable, but tanks could crack them.[46]

By mid-July, Pétain forbade the use of either the heavy or the new light tanks except in major attacks. Use of tanks in small actions was not justified: they were "too costly in regard to the results sought." The loss of tanks in battle forced both the English and the French armies to realize that small, set-piece actions would never end the war. Only great offensives in which large numbers of tanks could be used, such as the Château-Thierry action of 18 July, could be justified. Also, Renault light tanks could not cross heavily shelled terrain and, too weak to fight by themselves, had to depend upon accompanying infantry to destroy their enemies: field artillery and mortars. During the attack, masses of machines were to proceed forward, but in regular echelons and not bunched up. Heavy tanks were especially useful in breaking both the first lines of enemy resistance and forward artillery positions, while light tanks were more useful in accompanying the infantry and destroying machine-gun nests encountered on the way. By mid-August the French believed that a main function of their own artillery was to protect the tanks in the advance.[47] There was, finally, recognition of the interaction of tanks, infantry, and artillery.

A fundamental weakness of the French tactical development, air power utilization, was addressed on 15 July when masses of fighter and bomber aircraft were used in the region of Champagne. Three air groups of fighters assisted the Fifth Army by establishing air superiority. The bombers then attacked enemy columns and convoys that were trying to reach the Marne. Results showed that enemy losses were extremely high and the force of the German offensive was blunted. But there was no effective coordination of effort between the air units and ground units on this Fifth Army front, and German aerial attacks subsequently destroyed French reconnaissance aircraft. French fighters had been held back to use in an anticipated counterattack. The Fifth Army aircraft had been committed piecemeal from a passive reserve force, and effective coordination of the ground and air commanders had been lacking. Finally, an exceptionally rigid and preordained order of battle hampered operations.[48] Doubtless, the proponents of air power exaggerated its role in the Château-Thierry action because artillery, as well as bombardment aircraft, was important in stopping the initial German advance.

Symptomatic of a growing German discouragement were the comments of Rudolf Binding on 16 July. "I have lived through the most disheartening day of the whole war," he exclaimed, because the French had learned defense in depth from Ludendorff. Luring the Germans into a fruitless attack on largely evacuated trenches, the French stopped them with barbed-wire entanglements and numerous machine-gun nests.[49] Neither side used tanks, and once again the defense was too strong to be broached without their use.

Foch's grand offensive opened with Mangin's attack on 18 July, continuing without much pause until the end of the war. In conjunction with a parallel effort of the American army, this damaged the Germans. But the most crucial blow came from the British on 8 August.

AMIENS: KEY TO VICTORY

The major British attack, launched on 8 August in the region of Amiens, was a crucial turning point in the war. The Allied victory was so conclusive that it convinced the Germans to prepare for ultimate defeat. Impressed by the expertise of General Rawlinson of the Fourth Army after Hamel, Haig had been willing to entrust to him the role of leadership. Haig, although previously interested in a major follow-up to Hamel, yielded to a directive from Foch. Four days later, on 16 July, Rawlinson suggested that conditions were "extremely favorable" because "the trenches captured on 4th of July were bad and there was little wire." The poor morale of the enemy troops and their lack of reserves at this point augured success. The relatively unshelled open country was good for tank movement. "The success of the operation will depend to a very large extent, as was the case on the 4th July, on effecting a complete surprise." Secret preparations, deemed essential, included the assembly of reinforcements, tanks, and so on before the attack. Rawlinson concluded with a shopping list of additional units: five extra divisions (four Canadian and one Australian or British) would be needed. Haig approved the plan with some revisions.[50]

Interviews between Haig and Rawlinson were stormy because Rawlinson distrusted the French and did not want to rely on them. He thought the French would have been better advised to concentrate all of their forces, "not to advance in line with us, but to strike in from the direction of Montdidier on the flank of the Germans," either when the British attacked or shortly thereafter. According to his chief of staff, Maj. Gen. Archibald Montgomery, Rawlinson always regretted Haig's veto of this scheme because he felt that the subsequent battle would have been "decisive, and the results even greater than they were." Haig noted in his diary that he had to deny Rawlinson's request to operate alone because "of our limited number of divisions."[51]

Haig told the approving Foch that four hundred tanks would spearhead an enlarged Fourth Army offensive. After 24 July, training programs began for infantry assigned to accompany tanks. The Canadian divisions, lately assigned, never had more than a perfunctory introduction. The British III Corps had more, but only the Australian Corps concentrated on a full-scale program as early as 31 July, before the others. Visiting some of the training sessions on that day Haig wrote, "Remarkable progress has been made since Cambrai," not only in the machines themselves, but also in the tactics. He indicated that the tanks would try to destroy all opposition and then signal the infantry "to come on in open order." At this impressive demonstration Haig insisted on an idée fixe in conversations with both Rawlinson and the Tank Corps commander, Hugh Elles: the use of cavalry to assist Monash in the Australian attack.[52]

Rawlinson and his staff believed this attack would differ very greatly from earlier ones against strong, deep defensive systems such as those at the Somme in 1916 or at Arras or Messines in April and July 1917. Believing instead that the Amiens operation would resemble the Cambrai attack because of the terrain, they also thought that the Germans had not yet built elaborate trench defenses in this area. In order to achieve surprise, no preliminary artillery bombardment would be made. Very significantly, it was considered necessary to economize on manpower because losses had been heavy in March and April. "The experiences of the Australians at Hamel on 4 July had, it was hoped, provided the solution of the problem by the employment of comparatively few infantry lavishly supported by tanks and artillery."[53]

The burden of the attack would be carried by the Australian and

Canadian corps rather than the British III Corps of the Fourth Army. The British corps, as well as the French XXXI Corps, would guard the flanks of the main attack force. Synchronized, the infantry would advance by units leapfrogging one another. Of the ten battalions of tanks, four went to the Australian Corps, four to the Canadian Corps, and one to III Corps; one was kept in reserve. Cavalry was to wait for an opportunity to advance through infantry. Two battalions of the new medium A Whippet tanks accompanied the Cavalry Corps. For some weeks prior to the attack the RAF cleaned the skies of enemy reconnaissance aircraft, and it maintained aerial supremacy during the battle as well. Assembly of tanks, supplies, and troops was done at night on 7 August in woods behind the lines. Finally, during that night, tape lines were laid out for the advancing infantry to follow.[54] In detailed preparations the Amiens operation was outstanding. Only the Messines and the Cambrai plans had approached it for completeness.

On 8 August at 4:20 A.M. on a front of eighteen thousand yards, artillery opened fire simultaneously with the advance of the tanks and accompanying infantry. Providing cover for the advance, the creeping barrage was regulated at three minutes each hundred yards until zero hour plus 27 minutes, when it was increased to four minutes. Mobile field artillery followed. By the end of the day the Australian and Canadian corps had reached all of their objectives, except for Le Quesnel in the Canadian sector. The III Corps had been held up. Some 22,217 prisoners and between three hundred and four hundred guns were taken. Fourth Army casualties totalled 1815. South of the Somme the enemy surrendered freely except for isolated machine-gun nests, which were eliminated by Whippet tanks. The Germans reacted in panic, not heeding orders that called for holding "to the last bullet and the last man." Discouraged, one commander concluded: "The tanks overran our infantry, broke through widely and the infantry believed itself turned around." Secret memoranda indicated that some German troops panicked.[55]

It was a day for the tanks. With pardonable enthusiasm the 13th Tank Battalion claimed that since Cambrai "a new and vastly more powerful force had sprung to life from the ashes of the dead." Although exaggerated, this comment aptly indicates the development of the Tank Corps by 8 August. The Mark V tanks were good in open fighting, while the new Whippets replaced cavalry. There now appeared "a new type of Heavy Tank [the Mark V*], designed like the Horse of Troy

to carry Infantry in its belly." New salvage and service facilities behind the lines provided quick repairs of tanks.[56]

Many anticipated successes as well as a few unanticipated failures
were revealed in postbattle Tank Corps assessments. The RAF had
contributed to success by laying smoke screens in front of enemy-held
villages and by flying over the lines to mask the movement of tanks.
Australian NCO observers rode in tanks and "were of the greatest use
in keeping touch with the infantry." As far as the 5th Tank Battalion
was concerned, success was due to two factors: the "perfect combination of all arms" and the fighting qualities of the Australian infantry. Tanks destroyed an enemy strong point so that the adjoining French,
who had not been provided with tanks, could proceed. The 4th Tank
Battalion, during the first phase of the attack, entered Cageux well
ahead of the infantry, destroyed machine-gun nests, "and then returned
and brought up the Infantry."[57]

The experience of the Whippets with the Cavalry Corps proved that
tanks did not operate particularly well with horse-mounted troops. The
Whippets proceeded ahead of the cavalry, crossing intact bridges, because
the cavalry was held up by machine-gun fire. "The Cavalry appeared
unable to advance, and the Battle resolved itself into a matter of individual enterprise on the part of Tank Commanders." The battle report of the 6th Tank Battalion indicated that "either the Cavalry went
to move forward, at the gallop, in which case they outdistanced the
Whippet," or the Whippets moved ahead of cavalry confronted by enemy
fire.[58] The cavalry once again proved its obsolescence in modern war,
despite the wishes of Haig.

As the offensive continued in August, the German resistance stiff-
ened. Reports indicated that the enemy antitank guns were causing
substantial casualties. Anticipating this problem, the Tank Corps hoped
that tanks and the infantry trained to work with them could combine
against enemy strong points. Light field artillery was also brought forward
with the infantry and tanks so it could be used in close counterbattery
work against antitank emplacements.[59]

The Tank Corps still had difficulty in persuading infantry divisions
to work with their tanks in combat. The 1st Canadian Division officers did not cooperate in prebattle training. Tank battalion officers had
virtually to point out to their Canadian colleagues where a row of enemy
guns was knocking out every tank that came within range. Finally, in

an attack on 10 August, the 4th Tank Battalion reported that the Canadian infantry simply failed to follow the tanks into action. But tank battalions assigned to the Australian Corps also had trouble from antitank fire: eleven tanks were stopped by guns in one village. Nevertheless, the tank battalions assigned to work with the Australians reported that careful liaison existed between them and the infantry, as was not the case with the Canadians.[60]

Many individual tank actions characterized the battle of Amiens. A Whippet called Music Box, commanded by Lt. C. B. Arnold of the 6th Tank Battalion, destroyed an antitank gun that had stopped several Mark V tanks. Music Box then directed punishing fire on a series of enemy infantry and transport units before it was stopped. Close support of the Australian infantry was evident in this case.[61]

A good example of tactical imagination was shown by another tank unit that worked with Australian infantry. "The method of attack was adapted to suit the ground; leaving the infantry established on a crest, Tanks would go forward across the valley, maintaining fire on isolated machine-gun posts, and gain positions on the forward ridge." In every case, the enemy infantry surrendered, permitting the Australian infantry to occupy the next ridge. Doubtless, the supporting fire from the Australians, small arms and artillery, was important to the success of this unit.[62]

Communication and liaison with other arms still proved very difficult for the tanks. A single wireless tank, which was supposed to effect liaison with the Canadians, proved useless. Postbattle reports recommended instead that radio sets be placed in all tanks assigned to command or liaison duties. Tank company commanders were to be either horse-mounted or preferably in their own Whippets so they could keep adequate communication with their tanks. Much communication between arms was very primitive: Lieutenant Arnold at one point emerged from his Whippet to ask an Australian infantry officer if his unit needed help. A heavy mist worsened communications on 8 August, but defective communications between the Tank Corps and Canadian Corps continued after it cleared. A division commander told Maxse later: "Tanks are splendid for putting the wind up the Boche BUT they want a lot of practice with infantry." He felt they were too independent and that they were useless unless they stayed close to the infantry.[63]

Highly important was the question of air support for the Amiens offensive. Some of the eight hundred aircraft were assigned before the attack to keep German reconnaissance planes away. Poor weather and visibility helped make this successful. At the time of attack, squadrons flew over the lines, making enough noise to mask the approach of the hundreds of tanks. Although most aircraft bombed enemy air bases and other rear-echelon sites, a few supported the ground forces with firepower.[64] The evidence indicates, however, that the RAF still had not put into practice a careful plan for tactical support of infantry and tanks.

Postbattle reports from participating squadrons showed that some airmen were trying to provide more direct support for the ground forces. The commander of the 22d Wing recommended the formation of a special squadron that would form a close personal liaison with the Tank Corps to attack antitank guns. Communications, always a problem, would improve if tanks carried signals visible to aircraft. The 15th Wing commander also stressed that attacking antitank guns was more valuable than the usual contact patrol and infantry liaison work. Captain Trafford Leigh-Mallory, a squadron commander, claimed that the destruction of antitank guns was a primary objective. He had sent two aircraft up in all engagements to "not only bomb and machine-gun any gun which they actually see firing at a tank," but also attack any sites likely to contain enemy nests. Summing up the prevailing view, 5th Brigade headquarters endorsed tactical support, claiming it "has never proved itself better." In the future numerous squadrons would be employed with the sole purpose of maintaining command of the air while "full use" would be made of low-flying aircraft engaged in dangerous attacks on enemy field artillery and antitank emplacements. Such attacks, only possible if done by surprise, were characterized by dive-bombing from only three to five hundred feet. Eventually the Germans would strengthen their defenses by reinforcing the aircraft units, and then losses of planes and personnel would become prohibitive.[65] The RAF was seriously engaged in developing more effective cooperation with tanks.

An RAF information release of 25 August enthusiastically claimed that the cooperation of aircraft and tanks not only "has been of the greatest value," it also proved "the effect of previous training with tanks." Aircraft were now assigned specifically to bomb and fire at enemy gunners "who were seen to be shooting at tanks." Special squadrons of these "contact" aircraft, assigned to attack enemy ground gunners, were to be formed and would train with tanks to practice such attacks.[66]

Amiens had shown the way to effective cooperation between aircraft and tanks.

The Battle of Amiens, a crucial and fatal break in the German defenses, provided the opening stage of a continuing offensive that lasted until the armistice. Foch, by prescribing coordinated British, French, and American offensives, had assisted in staging a monumental defeat of German arms. Important tactically were tanks and aircraft in new and closer relationships with the infantry and artillery in the attack. German tactics could not be adapted fast enough to meet this combined challenge. In addition, by 30 September the morale of the German army had deteriorated and a manpower crisis had eliminated one out of three battalions in each regiment. Shortage of machine guns and mortars presaged a collapsing war economy as well.[67]

THE AMERICAN CONTRIBUTION

Only when the total of troops reached a million in June 1918 could the American army wield enough force to be noticeable. This army, henceforth increased by several hundred thousand each month, was built around the nucleus of a small regular army. It was largely a creation of congressional legislation passed after 1914 as Americans slowly became aware that sooner or later they would have to fight in the European war.[68] The state of training of these troops reflected outdated tactical concepts from the American military past. In short, the American army in June 1918 was neither led by officers cognizant of the requirements for modern war nor manned by troops trained to fight such a war.

A harsh indictment of tactical unreadiness does not suggest gross incompetence, but simply innappropriate preparation. Open warfare and even guerrilla warfare formed part of recent American military experience. Conducted by Pershing in the 1916 campaign against Pancho Villa in Mexico, open warfare included the use of a handful of aircraft as well as horse-mounted cavalry. Fighting was episodic and involved small units on both sides. During the Philippine campaign of 1898 to 1904, Pershing and other officers had worked out tactics to cope with the insurgents of Aguinaldo. Of course, the military garrisons in Indian territory in the last part of the nineteenth century were also preoccupied with small-unit guerrilla warfare. The Spanish-American War of 1898, the last American conflict of a traditional nature, had been characterized by the use of cavalry, artillery, and infantry in a mode reminiscent of the Civil War. Not surprisingly, one of the leading generals of that war, Wheeler, had been a Confederate general.[69] American military professionalism existed in 1918, but it had little to do with the European war.

Just beginning to be reorganized under a general staff by a highly respected military intellectual, Tasker H. Bliss, the U.S. Army had also tried to modernize in other ways. Pershing had been sent as an observer to the Russo-Japanese War and had met Ian Hamilton, the British observer, and Max Hoffmann, the German observer. In common with his colleagues from other countries, he had been impressed by entrenchments, the strength of the defense, and the awesome threat of firepower to an attacking force. But there is little evidence to indicate that either Pershing's thinking or that of the army itself had really incorporated all of the lessons of the recent past, from 1914 to 1917. A manual by P. S. Bond and M. J. McDonough entitled *Technique of Modern Tactics,* semiofficial in origin but prescribed as a text for officers preparing for the War College, appeared in 1916 in its third edition; it continued to preach conventional tactics. In the sections on tactics, frontal assault, with or without envelopment, was prescribed for the infantry. Artillery was placed as close to the front as possible. Cavalry "prior to the attack, feels for the enemy's line and [attacks] his cavalry. During the attack it operates on and covers the flanks, while threatening those of the enemy." Much of the manual was concerned with the usual tables of organization of larger and smaller units, sanitary trains, the setting up of camps, and so on. No mention was made of the presence of motorized transport, aircraft, mobile field artillery, automatic rifles, or other modern devices. Although the *Field Service Regulations, 1914,* amended in 1916, showed that divisions and corps had chiefs of staffs, they listed no staff organizations incorporating planning, operations, supply, intelligence, or training. Compared to the organization of similar units in the combatant nations in 1916, this entire system seems antiquated. Entrenchments were temporary defenses erected in anticipation of a quick return to open warfare.[70] A general air of unreality permeates the entire manual; officers trained in such tactics would have been quite unprepared for the European war.

Pershing and his subordinates believed, moreover, that infantry was the key to victory, that rifle marksmanship was the prime requirement of the infantry, and that wars were won by offensive action in open warfare. Arrogantly and naively they tended to criticize both the French and British military advisors who were sent either to the U.S. to help train troops, or to American camps in Europe. These officers, many Americans believed, were mired in trench warfare and could not see any way out of the defensive war except by wearing out the enemy in a conflict of attrition. The British and French had forgotten open warfare and favored set-piece, limited offensives.[71] Although there was some truth in these allegations, Americans did not really understand the full nature of tactics as developed on the western front since 1914.

Pershing did, however, establish a modern staff organization in the American Expeditionary Force in July 1917. With the assignment of newly arriving units to training under British and French instructors, the initiation of the American troops to war was conducted rationally.[72] Since the bulk of the units worked in the French sector the tactical ideas of that ally tended to become important in the subsequent formulation of an American tactical theory.

As soon as the U.S. declared war on Germany in April 1917, a number of French and British officers were sent to training camps in the United States. To one of these, Camp Taylor, the War Department sent bundles of literature from the Allied armies. Great confusion reigned in the camp: "No one seemed to know just what kind of instruction should be given our draftees." Since training was in chaos instructors resorted to the kindergarten of military education: "They got large doses of close-order drill, manual of arms, saluting, and customs of the service." The British and French instructors seemed mediocre and knew only their particular specialties. These comments by an able officer, Laurence Halstead, seem to confirm the suspicion that much of the training was inadequate. As late as July 1918, the infantry recruit training at Camp Gordon, Georgia, lasted only four to six weeks and emphasized the care and use of the rifle, close-order drill, the manual of arms, guard duty, sanitation and first aid, military courtesy, calisthenics, bayonet drill, and response to gas attacks.[73] The military schooling remained elementary.

By December 1917, training circulars issued by the War Department began to emphasize instruction in the use of the new automatic rifles, the Browning M1917, grenades, and rifle grenades. These were incorporated in a *Provisional Infantry Training Manual, 1918,* which specified that trained infantrymen should be able to maneuver in patrols, attack without support, use bayonets, put blanket fire on targets, and execute "squad rushes with maximum efficiency."[74] Considerable space was finally devoted to trench warfare.

After April 1918, when American troops were sent to Europe at a tremendous rate, Pershing established training camps in the AEF to indoctrinate these fresh troops. An experienced staff officer later recalled: "They were arriving in France with a good foundation for most of their men in discipline and close order drill." Basic training, however, was sketchy. Colonel H. B. Fiske later reminisced for the Staff College: "With a few exceptions their progress in France, working upon a definite, intense schedule, and frequently in hearing of the guns at the front, was surprisingly rapid." Very quickly the Americans became disillusioned with the officers and NCOs sent by the British and French because by late 1917, "neither ally believed a rupture of the German lines was any longer possible," while the Americans did. While their allies believed "in limited objectives and narrow fronts of attack," the Americans "thought only of a great decisive advance on all fronts." Unlike the French who, Fiske believed, thought the infantry could only follow an artillery barrage to occupy what had been previously destroyed, the Americans believed in "an aggressive, resourceful, infantry . . . we believed the rifle to be the paramount weapon." Afterward, the AEF ran its own training schedules, emphasizing marksmanship training, following the wishes of Pershing. Pershing, in fact, sent many cables to the chief of staff in Washington, Gen. Peyton March, urging that emphasis be placed on marksmanship with the rifle and training in open warfare in basic training.[75]

Because formation of the American air and tank units came late, little time was available for their training with ground troops. Even from a strictly infantry point of view, a postwar evaluation stated that although American troops were "given plenty of time for preparation" and were capable of effective action, they delivered their blows "with an awkwardness and lack of resource that made them unduly costly, and rendered it impracticable to reap the full fruits of victory." This veteran officer, Colonel Fiske, claimed that a first-class infantry battalion, which would work "smoothly as a team in which all parts mutually assist all others," was rare by the armistice.[76]

Heavy American casualties were the inevitable result of tactical inexperience. Certainly, both the British and French armies had encountered the same problem in 1914 and 1915. Major Gen. John A. Hines, the capable commander of the American 4th Division (and later of a corps), was disturbed enough about faulty tactics to spend two days talking to all of his officers, down to the rank of major, at the end of August 1918. The correspondent Wilbur Forrest remembered later that the American troops had little trouble in taking Cantigny, but suffered very heavy casualties rebuffing a series of German counterattacks. "Due to inexperience in avoiding casualties and to taking chances which French veterans had long been taught to avoid, the American losses during the consolidation period were not light."[77]

A corps of several divisions, assigned to the British Fourth Army by Pershing following the German offensive of March and April 1918, was used by Rawlinson in the Hamel attack of 4 July. Pershing objected too late, causing permanent bad relations with Haig. Rawlinson was favorably disposed towards the Americans at first, writing in his diary that the Americans "fought like tigers and have won the eternal affection of the Anzacs." Earlier, he had indicated that the Americans were far better than he had expected and that General Reade and his officers seemed competent. Rawlinson also noted, on 20 June, that he wished he could get the bulk of the American army next to his army. But after Pershing pulled out the American troops, Rawlinson and Haig were incensed. Rawlinson wrote to his friend, the archintriguer Henry Wilson: "Pershing is an ass and . . . is going to cost them [the Americans] an enormous number of unnecessary lives and is pretty certain to make a hash of his first venture against the Boche." Certainly by 19 August, Rawlinson believed that the American army was incompetently led: "It is a thousand pities to waste such good material with staff and cmdr's [sic]—who know *nothing* about making a plan or drawing up a scheme—it is sickening."[78] Rawlinson desperately wanted fresh American troops attached to him because he equated them with his best combat troops, which were either Australian or Canadian. Lloyd George had been starving the BEF in terms of replacements, and the quality level of British troops may well have been dropping in 1918. Rawlinson and Haig, in short, wanted control of large numbers of American troops and, when denied this, attacked Pershing. Pershing, on his part, did not believe that American troops should be cannon fodder exploited by either British or French army commanders, and his view prevailed in Washington.

THE GERMAN COLLAPSE

Although Amiens had been a decisive blow against the German defenses and had initiated open warfare in the British sector, it did not establish a pattern for the future. Open warfare, even more in evidence than in the successful French and American battles of July, was the main change. But certain circumstances prevented further major tactical advances.

The chief limitation on Allied tactics after 8 August was lack of replacements for tanks. Elles, commander of the Tank Corps, in a report for the period encompassing 8 August to 20 October, claimed that 1,890 tanks had been used in combat. Casualties included 3,088, out of a total of 7200 crew members, as well as 294 tanks by 3 September. By two months after Amiens 62 percent of the tanks were out of action and had to be replaced. By the end of September, personnel losses in the Tank Corps had resulted in denuding the battalions for instructors for the training of new crews in England.[79]

French experience with tank losses was similar for the period from 15 July to 16 September 1918. A total of 1,773 tanks were employed and some 415 had to be replaced: a loss of 23 percent. Crew losses totalled 1,978, of whom 167 had been killed.[80]

Could the British and the French quickly replace these losses? Could production be increased so that a net gain in tank supply could be obtained? Could tank crews be replaced quickly by well-qualified personnel? All of these questions had immediate bearing on the conduct of the war after Amiens.

Tank production was beginning to be impressive by autumn 1918. In a meeting of the Supreme War Council in October, the French indicated that some 2700 Renault light tanks had already been built. In an earlier meeting, on 16 July 1918, the French claimed a total of 800 heavy tanks and 3000 light tanks serviced by 30,000 troops. The British had 504 heavy tanks and 65 of the new medium tanks serviced by 8750 troops. At this time the number of U.S. tanks was small: despite pleas to the British, the Americans had been unable to obtain any of the Mark V heavy tanks. The French had provided 144 Renault light tanks to Hunter Liggett's American First Army by the end of the war. The American II Corps, assigned to General Rawlinson's British Fourth Army, obtained the assistance of British Tank Corps battalions on several occasions.[81]

The French announced that they hoped to complete seven thousand Renault light tanks in 1918 and 1919, with a factory output of six hundred a month. The head of the American tank program in the AEF, Col. Samuel Rockenbach, claimed that four thousand Renault as well as twenty-seven hundred Mark V British heavy tanks would be completed in the U.S. by January 1919. A huge factory had been built by the Americans in France for the production of heavy tanks with the assistance of the British under Stern. Production, intended to increase the supply dramatically by the middle of 1919, was still inadequate by the end of 1918. Tanks, parts for them, and crews were in short supply.[82]

Tanks at last had obtained recognition as formidable combat participants from even conservative officers. But military planners could not be expected to endorse the use of great tank armies as envisaged by Fuller and others at the time because there simply were not enough tanks. Therefore, tanks were used in small numbers in a series of engagements as handmaidens of the infantry. This policy was unsatisfactory to the British Tank Corps officers especially, who believed that it resulted in continuous waste of scarce resources for little gain.

Successful as the French counterattacks of the latter part of July and the British action at Amiens on 8 August had been, discerning tank experts noted problems that had caused considerable casualties among men and machines. Swinton recollected that aircraft had cooperated with tanks only in contact and counterattack patrols. Aircraft could, he thought, spot enemy gun emplacements so that counterbattery work would eliminate them before they could be used against approaching tanks. Reconnaissance officers of the future, according to the 14th Tank Battalion, would be trained RAF observers, giving greater coordination of the two services. During September and October the RAF did improve visual signals of aircraft to tanks. On 22 September, a squadron of Sopwith Camels was detached from regular duties to support an infantry attack. Each corps front was assigned four aircraft, which were supposed to assist the advance by bombs and machine guns from low altitudes. Offensive Trench Patrols flew at five hundred feet, diving periodically "on the enemy in trenches, discharging short bursts during the dive."[83] But these improvements remained novel and minor by the time of the armistice: the theory was being sketched in, but the application of it was necessarily piecemeal.

A tripartite partnership was envisaged by the final months of the war between the RAF, the Tank Corps, and the artillery. After Amiens, special efforts were made to destroy the field artillery emplacements of the Germans that were close to their front lines just as the tank and infantry advance started. Because of a constantly updated record of German emplacements established by photographic reconnaissance flights the artillery could bombard them. Well-hidden and freshly moved artillery were another problem, and flyovers on the day of the attack were necessary to find them. All such work had to be coordinated with tank units and with artillery through placards displayed by aircraft, through radio, or through contact patrol reports later on the ground.[84] Despite this system, mistakes frequently caused delays in getting information to the artillery quickly and decreased the effectiveness of such counterbattery work.[85]

The last two months of the war were disastrous for Germany. Ludendorff, in his oft-quoted comment on Amiens, indicated that that battle might have been the beginning of the end. Regardless of when the troops began not to believe in the efficacy of their work, the period of September and October showed many signs of their feeble morale and of a decreasing tactical capability. During this time the German high command was forced to issue one retreat order after another and the Allies rejoiced in their parallel success.

Evidence of the decline in German strength included lower average strength of divisions in the Bavarian army. That army could not expect more than four hundred men in the next draft of reinforcements after 30 September. Regiments were then reorganized with two battalions rather than three. The members of the disbanded third battalions were used to strengthen the other two. Mortar companies could only be filled to 75 percent of their established complement. A shortage of small arms continued and troops in "collection companies" had to be used to scavenge battlefields for discarded rifles and machine guns especially. Rationing of ammunition began as early as July and a real shortage was felt in September. Increasingly, the German army relied upon an ordered retreat covered by machine guns (for which there was a priority in ammunition supply). The war diaries of the Sixth Army recount succinctly the retreat of that force after the middle of August and continuing until the armistice.[86] Frankly, German resistance, although still strong in some sectors, was beginning to weaken in the last months of the war.

Tactically, the last period is somewhat anticlimactic. After Amiens tanks were not used in large numbers in combat operations. Typical of such actions was the French attack of 26 October, launched by the 47th Infantry Division with the help of fifty Renault light tanks. In a number of such limited actions, fought in October and November, the tank losses averaged 10 to 15 percent. The British fought a series of hard battles on 12, 21, and 28 August and 2 September in which their heavy-tank losses were substantial. General Elles of the Tank Corps believed these particular actions went far to explain the 62 percent of tank losses during September and October. Afterwards, the use of tanks was less.[87]

The German army was capable of inflicting considerable casualties as it gradually retreated. The American losses were especially substantial in the Meuse-Argonne offensive.[88] Because masses of low-flying aircraft in infantry support and masses of tanks were not used, the tactical lessons of the war became somewhat diffused. Adding to the difficulty of defining tactics at the end of the war was the progressive collapse of both the German military and civilian morale.

THE WINNING COMBINATION

The last year of the war differed considerably from any of the other years because it saw the end of the stalemate and the beginning of open warfare. But the coordination of arms was achieved only episodically by both victor and vanquished. The Germans perfected the employment of elite storm troops in conjunction with strong air and artillery support. But they did not try to mechanize tactics, preferring instead to rely upon well-trained and audacious infantry. In the German spring offensives the veterans of eastern and western fronts almost succeeded in bringing victory. If victory had been achieved, however, it would have been a traditional victory of arms in keeping with military history.

The Allies relied increasingly upon tanks as a means of achieving a savings in manpower and of obtaining mobility in a breakthrough. But mechanization required many more tanks than were available in 1918. As a consequence, only in certain instances such as at Hamel, Amiens, and the Second Marne, were enough tanks at hand to be used in profitable conjunction with aircraft, infantry, and artillery. Those occasions were indeed important and striking exceptions to the general battle experience and effectively demonstrated to the Germans that they could not prevent future breakthroughs with the human and material means they had at hand. At first the Germans had believed that batteries of field artillery or converted antiaircraft pieces could halt the tanks while more use of poison gas shells would halt the infantry. Neither was sufficient after 8 August.

If the new coordinated, mechanized tactics were employed only seldom by the Allies, were they sufficient to cause the collapse of German arms? Certainly other potent reasons for this must be considered. German losses of manpower had been heavy and the reinforcements from the eastern front were wasted in the fruitless offensives of March to May. The entire German war economy was in trouble and was no longer producing ammunition and weaponry on the scale needed to sustain fighting. Very discouraging for the Germans also was the growing size of the American army. At first the latter was characterized by inexperience and inefficiency, but much had been learned from the difficult fighting of the Meuse-Argonne campaign in September and October. In 1919 there was every reason to believe that the American army would dominate the Allies and enforce a defeat on a nearly exhausted Germany. Social and political troubles in Germany presaged the collapse of the government as well. The decision to sign the armistice was made by the military and civilian leaders of Germany because of a common recognition that for military and civil reasons the war had to end.

NOTES

1. Pershing, *My Experiences,* 21–37.
2. Foch, *Mémoirs,* 2:112–13.
3. PRO, CAB 28/3.
4. Blake, *Haig Papers,* 301. Gough was replaced at the insistence of Lord Derby and Lloyd George. Cruttwell, *Great War,* 514–21.
5. PRO, WO, 95, 436, 173G, OAD 851.
6. PRO, WO, 95, 436. Henry Wilson Papers, 73/1/9.
7. PRO, WO, 95, 436, 173G.
8. PRO, WO, 95, 436, 173G.
9. PRO, WO, 95, 436.
10. Maurice, *Rawlinson,* 221. PRO, WO, 95, 436. Notes of Monash of 21 June 1918.
11. PRO, WO, 95, 436. 4th Army. Letter of CO, 5th Tank Brigade to Monash.
12. PRO, WO, 95, 436.
13. PRO, WO, 95, 436.
14. PRO, WO, 95, 14. War Diary of GHQ. WO, 95, 986, Australian Corps.
15. PRO, WO, 95, 986, Australian Corps.
16. PRO, WO, 95, 437. AIR 1, 1187, RFC War Diary. AIR 1/1511/204/58/15. III Brigade, RAF. (The RFC became the RAF in July 1918.)
17. PRO, WO, 95, 437. AIR 1, 1187, RFC War Diary. AIR 1/1511/204/58/15. III Brigade, RAF.
18. Churchill College, Cambridge, Rawlinson Papers, I/12 Diary and I/11 Diary. PRO, WO, 95, 437.
19. Stern, *Log Book,* 175–81. Relieved of responsibility for tank construction because he quarreled with Haig's staff and the War Office over the problem of spare parts for tanks, Stern was placed in charge of a British committee that negotiated with the French and Americans on tank production during the remainder of the war.
20. Stern Papers, I/C/7, 13–19.
21. Stern Papers, I/C/6. "Memorandum on Tanks."
22. Stern Papers, I/C/6. "Note by the General Staff on Sir E. H. T. d'Eyncourt's Memorandum Proposing the Formation of Tank Armies." General Staff, War Office, to Prime Minister, 28 December 1917.

23. PRO, WO, 95, 93. War Diary, Tank Corps Headquarters.

24. Fuller Papers, TCWH 2, 9th Battalion.

25. PRO, WO, 95, 93.

26. Stern Papers, I/C/4.

27. PRO, WO, 95, 93. Tank Corps Headquarters.

28. PRO, WO, 95, 93. Tank Corps Headquarters.

29. PRO, AIR 1, 160/15/123/10. Six-week pilot course, 11 March 1918. Twenty-five hours of aerial observation, fifteen hours of signaling, two and a half hours on radio, ten hours on bombing, twenty hours on machine guns (range firing of five hours on weekends included), ten hours elementary rigging, fifteen hours advanced rigging, and theory of flight comprised the bulk of the program out of a total of 165 hours for the entire six-week course.

30. PRO, AIR, 1/1511/204/58/15. 3d Brigade, RAF. AIR 1, 1511. Fuller had begun to develop his concept of a tank army, as published in 1919, at this time, May 1918. See Trythall, *Boney Fuller,* 60–61.

31. PRO, AIR, 1/1511.

32. PRO, AIR, 1/1511.

33. PRO, AIR, 1/1511.

34. PRO, AIR, 1/1511.

35. Montgomery-Massingberd Papers, 91; Letter to Shea, 8 July 1918.

36. Liddell Hart Papers, 1/516. Letter of General G. H. Jackson. One of the most thoughtful of postwar memoirs of prominent commanders is John Monash, *The Australian Victories in France in 1918* (London, 1920).

37. Fuller Papers, TCWH 2, 13th Battalion.

38. Fuller Papers, TCWH 2, 13th Battalion.

39. PRO, WO, 95, 436. Maurice, *Rawlinson,* 224–25. Blake, *Haig Papers,* 320–21.

40. Foch, *Mémoirs,* 2:125–27.

41. Lucas, *Idées tactiques,* 248–57. Pedroncini, *Pétain,* 406–14.

42. Charles Mangin, 505–6. AMV, 16 N 1997.

43. AMV, 16 N 1997.

44. Mangin, *Comment finit la guerre* (Paris, 1920), 506–11. *Armées françaises,* 7:74–78.

45. James G. Harbord, *American Army in France, 1917–1918* (Boston, 1936), 322–37. John W. Thomason Jr., *Fix Bayonets!* (New York, 1926), 88.

46. AMV, 16 N 1997, 16 N 1998.

47. AMV, 16 N 2142. "Tactique générale et emploi des Chars 'A.S. Programmes,'" 14 July 1918. 16 N 1998.

48. Voisin, *Doctrine de l'Aviation*, 139–44.

49. Binding, *Fatalist*, 234–55.

50. Haig Papers, ACC 3155 129, diary entry for 16 July, 27–28. PRO, WO, 95, 437, 31 [220(g)] includes the Rawlinson memorandum dated 17 July.

51. Liddell Hart Papers, 1/520, Montgomery-Massingberd to Liddell Hart, 10 August 1928. Haig Papers, diary, 26 July, 50.

52. Rawlinson Papers, I/11, diary, 28 July 44. Haig Papers, diary, ACC 3155 129, 59–60.

53. Montgomery, *Fourth Army*, 1:20–21.

54. Montgomery, *Fourth Army*, 1:22–32.

55. PRO, WO, 95, 437. BSA, AOK 6, Bd. 350.

56. Fuller Papers, TCWH 2, 13th Battalion.

57. Fuller Papers, TCWH 1, 5th Tank Battalion, 4th Tank Battalion.

58. Fuller Papers, TCWH 1, 3d Tank Battalion (Light), 6th Tank Battalion.

59. Fuller Papers, TCWH 1, vols. 1–3, 1st, 2d, and 4th Tank Battalions. TCWH 2, 14th Tank Battalion.

60. Fuller Papers, TCWH 1, vols. 1–3, 1st, 2d, and 4th Tank Battalions. TCWH 2, 14th Tank Battalion.

61. Williams-Ellis, *Tank Corps*, 201–6.

62. Williams-Ellis, *Tank Corps*, 197–98.

63. Fuller Papers, TCWH 2, 14th Tank Battalion. Maxse Papers 69/53/11.

64. Wise, *Canadian Airmen*, 520–25. PRO, AIR 1, 1187. RAF War Diary. 8 August 1918.

65. PRO, AIR, 1/1592/204/83/17, AIR 1/1512/204/58/28.

66. PRO, MUN, 4, 4979.

67. BSA, AOK 6, Bd. 350.

68. The history of the American Expeditionary Force is well discussed in Edward M. Coffman, *The War to End All Wars* (Madison, Wisconsin, 1968, 1986).

69. Vandiver, *Black Jack,* and Donald Smythe, *Pershing, General of the Armies* (Bloomington, Indiana, 1986), survey the career of that officer well. On preparedness in the United States before the entry into

the war in 1917, see John Garry Clifford, *The Citizen-Soldiers of the Plattsburg Training Camp Movement: 1913–1920* (Lexington, Kentucky, 1972), which is on the Plattsburg, New York, training camp.

70. P. S. Bond and M. J. McDonough, *Technique of Modern Tactics* (Menasha, Wisconsin, 1916), 11–12, 204–77.

71. Pershing, *My Experiences,* 2:237–38. Pershing put up with instructors from the French and British armies during 1917 and the first part of 1918 but got rid of them by August 1918.

72. Harbord, *American Army,* 92–105. See Dale E. Wilson, *Treat 'em Rough! The Birth of American Armor, 1917–1929* (Novato, California, 1989), 26–50, for American tank training under Patton.

73. U.S. Army War College, Carlisle Barracks, Pennsylvania, Laurence Halstead Memoirs, Mearnes Papers, WWI, Memo no. 5 HG Inf. Replacement and Training.

74. U.S. Army War College, Mearnes Papers, WPD 9383-312.

75. U.S. Army War College, Lectures at the War College, 215–70. Col. H. B. Fiske, "Training in the American Expeditionary Forces," 16 Jan. 1922. Memorandum from the Director, G-3 Course, Army War College, 3 Dec. 1924, in 289-A-30, AWC.

76. Fiske, "Training . . ."

77. U.S. Army War College, John L. Hines Diary, 123–25. Wilbur Forrest, *Behind the Front Page* (New York, 1934), 134.

78. Rawlinson Papers, I/12. Wilson Papers, 13/A.

79. The 2d Tank Battalion complained that in the action of 21 September, "neither tanks nor infantry were in sufficient strength to retake and hold their objectives." PRO, MUN, 4, 4979, 31 October 1918. Liddell Hart Library, 2d Tank Battalion. Fuller Papers, TCWH 1, vols. 1–3.

80. AMV, 16 N 2120. "Tableau rectifie des pertes en chars et personnel, par engagement," dated 9 September 1919.

81. PRO, MUN, 4, 4979. Hunter Liggett, *Commanding an American Army* (New York, 1925), 325.

82. PRO, MUN, 4, 4979.

83. Fuller Papers, TCWH 2, 14th Tank Battalion. Swinton, *Eyewitness,* 235–36. PRO, AIR 1, 161/15/123/14. AIR 1, 1187, RFC War Diary. AIR, 1/1512/204/58/28.

84. PRO, AIR 1, 161/15/123/14.

85. The Americans experienced troubles of this kind, for example, in the Meuse-Argonne campaign. Poor liaison and lack of experience

hampered infantry, tank, artillery, and air cooperation. Col. C. H. Lanza, "Artillery in Use in the American E.F." U.S. Army War College, 26 May 1919, AWC 215–70. See also AWC, Joseph Viner Papers.

86. BSA, AOK 6, Bd. 350, Bd. 115.

87. AMV, 16 N 2120. PRO, MUN, 4, 4979, 31 October 1918.

88. Some ninety-three hundred casualties in a few days, "nearly all in the infantry." AEF Infantry Board, Report of 28 April 1919, AWC Training, Vol. IV, Pt. II, miscellaneous reports, 1919–1920, 1–20. Wilson, *Treat 'em Rough,* 124–86, describes the use of tanks in the Meuse-Argonne campaign.

CHAPTER 11
FRUITS OF VICTORY

Conservative postwar tacticians were inclined to accept the assertion of Archibald Montgomery, chief of staff of the British Fourth Army, that the tactical doctrine of the prewar field manuals had been vindicated during the war: *plus ça change, plus c'est la même chose.*[1] But such a claim was manifestly false. If the open warfare of 1914 flowed out of prewar teachings, the next period, characterized by siegecraft, posed new problems. Finally, the open warfare of 1918 was unlike anything seen previously.

Prewar tactical theory was oriented to offensive combat and presupposed that decisions on the battlefield would be determined by resolute and massive infantry attacks. Of course the power of the defense had been noted and no one imagined that battles would be cheaply won. No massive reconstruction of tactical theory had occurred between the American Civil War and 1914. Debates between military intellectuals continued, and the curriculum of the general staff schools had not been substantially revised. The upper echelons of command in the various contending armies were rent by long-standing feuds between traditionalists and modernists. Therefore, the actual experience of war in the autumn of 1914 would come as a considerable surprise to the antagonists.

Although many prescient observers had anticipated some of the tactical problems of the approaching war, the scope of that conflict soon exceeded the expectations of all and rendered prewar plans obsolete. The trench stalemate of November 1914 concluded the period of open warfare.

SIEGECRAFT AND OPEN WARFARE

When the war started everyone anticipated open warfare. By November 1914 the trench war stalemate marked the beginning of siegecraft. From Cambrai on to the end, open warfare of a new type emerged.

In the tactics of the first period, as a diffuse legacy of the prewar period, the belligerents hoped to utilize a traditional coordination of arms. Everyone believed the infantry would be supported by the field artillery in a concerted advance, preceded by cavalry acting as scouts. This scheme was basically an adaptation of Napoleonic warfare as interpreted by Clausewitz.

The resulting stalemate required new tactical efforts designed to escape the trap of positional warfare. At first, huge infantry assaults were thought to be sufficient to crack the enemy's defenses. Following the failure of this experiment, the tacticians of 1915 and 1916 thought the answer would be concentrated artillery barrages: the firepower bludgeon theory. Out of the resulting impasse came the siegecraft conception that emphasized limited set-piece actions designed to conserve manpower yet wear down the enemy. For three years, from 1915 to the end of 1917, siegecraft seemed to be the only workable tactical scheme. Grandiose efforts to do more, such as the German offensive of Verdun and the British offensives of the Somme and of Passchendaele, failed utterly.

Although commanders hankered after open warfare with desperation they were doomed to unending frustration. Therefore the commanders and their staffs in all armies had to accept as fact that siegecraft was the only viable mode of warfare by the beginning of 1917. Unfortunately, trench warfare required a constant and substantial outlay of men, ammunition, weapons, and supplies and the general public was beginning to lose patience with it. If the newspapers could report that a certain amount of land was taken, so many prisoners captured, and so much devastation meted out on the enemy, then the public felt the grim sacrifices might be justified. But even the most substantial victories before 1918 were Pyrrhic; the gains obtained by the "victors" seemed scarcely worth the costs involved.

From the end of 1917 until the armistice two tactical schemes, both associated with open warfare, came to be favored. The first was one that especially stressed mechanization, the so-called tank-army model. The second, much more widely believed, was a new coordination-of-arms model in which cavalry was omitted and tanks and aircraft were admitted to serve as the handmaidens of infantry in attack.

It is nonsensical to claim, however, that any of the tactical schemes discussed in this quick review was totally different from all of the others since they differed from one another only according to the major emphasis. General Pershing, for example, was a firm advocate of the infantry as the key to victory and placed great emphasis on rifle marksmanship as a means of developing the competence of that arm. This does not mean that Pershing eschewed tanks, artillery, or anything else in the available arsenal of troops and materiel, but that he considered all such to be less important than the trained infantry. Predominantly, then, he was an exponent of the infantry-assault model of 1915, but suitably modernized to fit the conditions of 1917 and 1918.

The infantry-assault model was the dominant tactical conception of the war insofar as offensive tactics were concerned. Training manuals both before and during the war emphasized the primacy of the infantry, except in the case of the French, which stressed the artillery. This model depended upon two types of infantrymen: shock or storm troops and the ordinary mass. All of the armies developed shock troops, but the Germans had more of them and used them more effectively than anyone else. The amazing success of their March 1918 offensive was mostly due to the expert infantrymen employed by Ludendorff as the advance fighting force. But in common with all other trades and professions, that of arms produces only a limited number of experts, the professional infantrymen. Characterized by their ability to take advantage of battlefield opportunities, to work with one another in constructive teamwork, and to employ their weapons skillfully, such elite troops fought hard to win.

A great tragedy of the war was the decision of all the participants to employ masses of mediocre infantrymen in frontal assaults on enemy trenches. Therein lies the reason for the grim butcher's bill. Commanders thought, in 1915 and 1916 especially, that they had no choice and that only such assaults could bring about victory. The politicians stepped in to warn the respective high commands that the continuation of such sacrificial casualties was politically unacceptable.

Although the primacy of the infantry continued to be a favored doctrine during the rest of the war, no one denied that other arms such as the artillery had to assist and to protect the "queen of the battlefield." As the proponents of these other branches of arms argued their cases against the background of the stalemate, an evolution of tactics began. What could be done to facilitate the work of the infantry?

The French were the first to break away from the concept of the primacy of infantry. Even before the war field artillery, especially the famed 75mm pieces, had been employed in mass quantity in maneuvers with infantry. In October 1914, Joffre and his staff assembled hundreds of guns to provide massive firepower against trenches in the region of Champagne. Foch and Joffre, otherwise frequently at odds with one another, agreed in 1915 that such massive bombardment would enable the infantry to advance: "artillery conquers, infantry occupies." Sudden conversions of the British and German high commands to the same idea occurred later in that year, but shortage of artillery pieces and shells impeded widespread use until 1916.

The artillery-destruction model relied upon the obliteration of the enemy's defensive system. Two objectives would be achieved: substantial enemy casualties at little cost and a gain in territory. Further, there was the hope that such a battle would create opportunities for a breakthrough.

Artillery bombardment on a large scale did cause horrendous casualties at Verdun and the Somme in 1916. But a point of diminishing returns was eventually reached: if enough shells were dumped on a comparatively small piece of land, that terrain would become impassable. Such bombardments, of course, also invited retaliation by the enemy and as a result the already high daily casualty rate even in quiet sectors rose substantially.

During the course of the war artillery ceased to be considered the single determining arm and was henceforth incorporated as an element in broader tactical schemes. Quite simply, the artillery-destruction model did not bring about victory in itself. Most important was the classical siegecraft model employed by the Germans on the western front almost all of the time prior to 1918, except for the Verdun offensive of 1916. The teachings of Vauban on the construction and investment of fortresses were more apropos than some staff planners were willing to admit. In 1916 especially, the Germans began an ambitious program of building concrete blockhouses designed to protect the first trench lines. General Plumer organized the greatest example of offensive siegecraft during the war when he employed masses of artillery pieces and substantial mining to stage the Battle of the Messines Ridge in 1917. The French found that the fortified positions of Verdun could sometimes be held in spite of concentrated artillery shelling. Afterward, Pétain and others remained fascinated with the defensive possibilities of fortresses. The Maginot line was the ultimate result. Therefore, both the attack on and the defense of fortresses remained very important in the war.

Why were the Germans so preoccupied with siegecraft and strong, permanent defense systems? Until the collapse of Russia they were always in a position of numerical inferiority on the western front. Trench systems could be defended with fewer men than were required to attack them. With the failure of the Schlieffen Plan the German high command became quite conservative regarding the staging of major offensives. Several offensive attempts were made in early 1915 in conjunction with the introduction of poison gas, and a stupendous assault was made in 1916 at Verdun. Following these costly failures the innate conservatism of the high command was only reinforced, and the entire western front was then considered to be a gigantic fortress, the defense of which was necessary. It was too risky to try breaking the investment. The Germans built the best trench systems, girded them with strings of blockhouses, and supported them with elaborate storage and staging facilities behind the lines. This policy changed, however, with the coming of Ludendorff to the western front in 1917. But defensive siegecraft continued to dominate the thinking of commanders such as Crown Prince Rupprecht of the Bavarian Sixth Army. Even in 1918 many German commanders believed that the construction of tanks was not necessary, that a defensive posture had to be maintained in the hope of wearing down the Allies, and that the use of poison gas and antitank artillery would prevent enemy attacks from succeeding.

Several coordination-of-arms models emerged after the evident failure of the infantry and artillery models. The highest-ranking field commanders of all armies during the war had to coordinate the different types of arms in planning either offensive or defensive tactics. Haig and his staff, for example, routinely tried to get the infantry, artillery, cavalry, tanks, and aircraft involved in carefully prepared plans such as those preceding the battles of Cambrai in November 1917 and Amiens in August 1918. Foch and Pétain did the same, as did Ludendorff and his staff. The advocates of particular branches of service such as the artillerymen or the tank men tended, of course, to glorify the contributions of their own specialties. Army commanders did not have that freedom but had to use all of the resources available to them.

The Napoleonic model of coordination of arms, modified by Clausewitz and others, called for the concentration of firepower in an attack, using masses of artillery pieces and numerous infantrymen. Cavalry, unlike the other arms, possessed mobility and could threaten the flanks or the rear of the enemy in order to keep the battle from sinking into a trench war stalemate. Despite the invention of the machine gun and the development of quick-firing artillery and magazine-fed rifles, many senior commanders of the war still had in the back of their minds this now-antiquated model. Haig was the worst example. He simply could not believe that cavalry could not be used effectively and insisted that it be included in the planning of Cambrai and Amiens despite the long history of failure of that arm in the war. In 1928, shortly before he died, he was queried by the War Office about the future role of cavalry in war and staunchly defended it.[2] Any scheme that depended upon a battle role for horse-mounted cavalry was impractical and outdated during this war on the western front.

Other examples of a traditional coordination-of-arms model were frequent in the war. Joffre, for example, believed that the combined work of the artillery and infantry would provide a breakthrough at the end of 1914. Falkenhayn depended upon the same arms at Verdun in 1916.

Most innovative of all these schemes was the model of a new coordination of arms in which cavalry was eliminated and tanks, aircraft, and storm troops were used as key elements in the battle. This was the development of 1918 and both the Germans and the Allies contributed to it. The vision of the planners of Amiens, for example, could be compared to that of the composer of a symphony. In both cases an overall theme had to be developed using the diverse types of troops and materiel available. The whole had ultimately to be orchestrated under some powerful director, as Monash suggested.[3] The contact patrol aircraft, the tanks, the forward infantry, the field artillery, and so on were given parts to play in the military composition of a set-piece battle.

Rawlinson, commander of the British Fourth Army and preeminent among commanders as an orchestrator of the new mode, was nearly equaled by Mangin of the French, Monash of the Australians, and Hunter Liggett of the Americans. Using an eclectic approach, each strove to coordinate all arms. No longer used in massive preparatory bombardment, artillery employed a creeping barrage slightly ahead of the advance of the tanks and forward units of the infantry. Aircraft were used in this tactical amalgam as identifiers of enemy artillery, and their information enabled counterbattery work to coincide with the infantry-tank attack. Also used in low flyovers of the advancing units, other aircraft strafed enemy strong points and informed ground commanders of nearby enemy positions. Commanders and their staffs realized by 1918 that they had to secure control of the air, that they had to attack by surprise, that they had to use a number of specialized troops, that they had to have as many tanks as possible on terrain passable by them, that field artillery had to be ready to move forward quickly, and that logistical support had to be immediate and constant.

The recital of the prerequisites for success in battle in 1918 impresses one with their sheer complexity. Never before had specialized staff work been so important in war. No wonder that prewar business entrepreneurs and engineers such as Monash found striking resemblances between the conduct of armies and the conduct of large industrial enterprises. Aware of this analogy, Fuller argued for the Tank Corps by claiming that the tank was a mechanized substitute for manpower just as the machines in factories were substitutes for brute labor. Also, tanks as "labor saving" devices cut down on infantry casualties. Warfare in 1918 was becoming so complex that individual commanders at the head of armies had trouble understanding it. The bureaucrats of war, specialist officers and soldiers and the staff officers, had to interact with one another and with line commanders in the lengthy elaboration of battle plans. War had changed considerably from 1862 when Grant arrived on the scene at Shiloh and was able to quickly organize a defense and turn impending defeat into victory.

TECHNOLOGY AND WAR

What was the role of technology in the development of tactics? Technological development did not force the reshaping of tactics but was the result of tactical changes. Modern technology actually favored the siegecraft mode because an extensive motorized transport system, including railroads, kept the armies efficiently supplied and reinforced. Also the telephonic, wireless, and telegraphy systems provided instant communication with the headquarters in the major capitals as well as between units. In effect, the huge trench warfare armies were similar to the factories so characteristic of heavy industry of the day, except they provided no useful product and displayed a dismaying willingness to waste resources. The work of professional railroad men, industrial managers of all types, and others intimately associated with the industrialization the world[4] helped to keep the trench warfare structure going.

In contrast, technology for open warfare was not nearly as efficient. Railheads ended behind the trenches and could not be immediately extended if an advance occurred. Therefore, the greater the advance forward, the greater the distance from the railhead. Motorized transport as well as traditional horse- or mule-drawn vehicles needed roads that could only be rebuilt following an advance. Pioneer troops used to the demands of trench construction had to be retrained and reequipped for advancing close on the heels of the troops to start such work. Ludendorff discovered at the end of March 1918 that road building could not be quickly accomplished: German troops were increasingly short of supplies with each kilometer they advanced. Therefore, the highly efficient transport system built up for trench warfare broke down when open warfare resumed.

Communications were a problem as well because telephone and telegraph lines, difficult enough to maintain in siegecraft because shell explosions frequently cut them, had to be laid in open warfare following the advance. The fluid movement of troops made it difficult to patch lines to particular command posts. More and more dependence would be placed on messengers and on wireless communication. The complicated artillery observation structure, ground and air, had been built up to fit trench warfare but began to disintegrate when open warfare resumed. Great efforts had to be made to bring artillery up to the advancing infantry but the paucity of roads made that difficult. With each kilometer advanced, the efficiency of the artillery support structure was weakened; transport and communication became less effective. Despite great efforts by George Marshall and other staff officers, the American army, for example, faced a logistical mess in the Meuse-Argonne offensive.

Even the standard bearers of technological progress, the tanks, had to be closely followed by mechanics, stores of spare parts, and supplies of gasoline. The tanks, with their high breakdown rate, were less and less effective as the distance increased between them and their support units. Also, infantry could not keep pace with the new generation of tanks in 1918, often leaving the latter isolated and prone to enemy field artillery fire.

Obviously, the key to open warfare was mobility, and mobility was extremely hard to obtain during this war. Most of the existing technology seemed to reinforce the notion of siegecraft warfare. During 1918, perceptive tank and airpower advocates tried to adapt their promising arms to open warfare but the process was slow and difficult. As a result, the open warfare of 1918 relied not only on new, but also on traditional technology. The new tactical mode required mules as well as tanks, infantry as well as aircraft.

The formation of a new tactical scheme required a study of previous battles including analysis of weapons usage, troop-unit interaction, enemy response, and the casualties in men and equipment. Most important, did substantial gains or losses accrue? Only after such a study could the existing tactical philosophy be modified or discarded. But a new tactical system also depended upon a number of factors that were not directly connected to staff studies. Decisions had to be made at the highest level regarding production priorities for new or revised weaponry, whether scarce manpower could be diverted to fill the ranks of the army while denuding the work forces of the factories, and whether the resources of the state should be invested in a costly and unknown tactical innovation when existing demands of the war machine had to be met as well. Also, and most important, the efficiency of the military command structure was crucial; could the high command understand the need for a new tactical system and could it fight to implement it? Could the high command negotiate with the government? To rephrase this: military hardware had to be devised to meet the requirements of tactical theory which, in turn, was dependent upon study of battle results. But military technology could be devised only as a result of a number of compromises. Scarce manpower and material resources had to be distributed among competitive claimants in the total war effort. The final product, the actual tactics as employed in battle, did not consist merely of techniques dreamed of by a few staff officers in periodic conferences but of complex matrices of organization, resources, and conceptualization. Summaries of previous tactics enshrined in the field manuals were always inadequate reflections of a far more complex reality.

THE SHAPE OF THINGS TO COME

During the interwar period the battles of 1914 to 1918 were studied and assessed by military professionals in the war colleges. The new Infantry School at Fort Benning, Georgia, used a curriculum heavily dependent upon the combat experiences of its designers by 1924. But the Americans were no more advanced than the other former antagonists. In effect, the lessons of the war were poorly understood because of a fundamental disagreement among the military analysts everywhere.

Those who continued to believe the war had been a logical culmination of the prewar teachings also believed that the basic premises or rules of war had not been altered. To these officers aircraft, tanks, and the other new weapons were merely supports to the traditional nucleus of military effort, the infantry. Even cavalry was resurrected after 1919 because some of these conservative officers believed it had been effective in Palestine or on the eastern front. War in the future would, they thought, be a repetition of the mass-infantry siegecraft. Total war would be required to provide the huge numbers of infantrymen and their ammunition in future wars of attrition.

The other point of view was radically different. Veterans of the Tank Corps, for example, were convinced that future warfare would be mobile and mechanized. Proponents of airpower believed likewise. Ultimately, spokesmen of the new warfare such as Liddell Hart were to advocate small, completely mechanized striking forces and to eschew mass armies of poorly trained conscripts. Warfare would be a matter for the professionals.

J. F. C. Fuller had already delineated a comprehensive theory of warfare using tanks by the end of the war. His thinking was further refined by 1920 when he wrote to Liddell Hart. The offensive battle of the future, he claimed, would be in "four main acts—the assembly, the approach, the attack, and the act of annihilation." The statement was Clausewitzian. In February 1919 Fuller had outlined in an article his belief that a single attack would usually fail, but a two-pronged one on the sides of a salient promised success as had happened in several cases in 1918. Fuller, in describing his "expanding torrent system of attack" to Liddell Hart claimed that "when sufficient tanks existed to enable a big attack to take place" in 1918 it became possible to "penetrate the enemy's front and by pushing tank forces to right and left, roll up the flanks created by the penetration."[5]

Clarifying his expanding-torrent theory, Fuller indicated that "one great lesson which the war taught was that fronts are breakable but that as long as supplies are tied down to roads it is practically impossible to exploit a breakthrough." This was a profound truth. Mobility combined with firepower was the tantalizing dream of the war: the German efforts to manhandle field artillery, heavy machine guns, mortars, and the like practically on the heels of the advancing infantry indicate awareness of the tactical requirement on their part coupled with reliance on manpower rather than machine power.

Younger officers had been closer to the tactical realities of the war than the senior commanders and had often been associated with the new weaponry as well. In every postwar army a struggle raged between the two forces: the conservatives and the radicals. In the U.S. Army *Field Service Regulations, 1923,* a generally held eclecticism was enunciated: "The combatant arms are the infantry, the artillery, the cavalry, the signal corps, the engineers, and the air service." None of these arms alone could win; "the combined employment of all arms is essential to success." Although armored forces were not mentioned (too avant garde for 1923), the orchestration of different arms was stressed. Tanks were merely participants "in the close combat of infantry."[6]

George Patton, an innovative officer of great promise, was still trying to come to grips with novelty in 1932 when he prepared a paper for his War College course. He emphasized the importance of field training soldiers "to produce synthetic courage, discipline and training . . . to the point where they become automatic-habitual." Such comments reveal a concern for instilling professionalism in fighting troops, achieved over a long period of time. This was precisely the road traveled by Liddell Hart in the interwar period. Patton, significantly, closed his comments with the remark that future warfare would consist of a "war of movement conducted with small mobile armies."[7]

A new principle of coordination of arms existed in embryo in 1918. The future standard of military performance had been established at least. Orchestration of traditional arms such as infantry and artillery with new arms like tanks and aircraft would produce the mobile warfare of World War II. In that war, however, anachronistic remnants of the old military structure still existed as legacies of older tactical models whose admirers kept them alive.

A particular tactical scheme resembles a scientific hypothesis based upon fragmentary evidence. Constantly changing, it never acquires absolute validity, immune from the permutations of time, space, and rational and irrational human actions. Particular plans, such as that developed to a high point by Ludendorff and his staff just prior to the March 1918 offensive, or by Rawlinson, Fuller, and Monash in July 1918, produced results in battle because they were tailor-made to cope with real conditions at the time. But no tactical theory can produce perfect results because none can be promulgated on the spot that will instantly accommodate itself to actual battlefield conditions. Each tactical theory is based upon previous experience and attempts to extrapolate a future development, but once battle starts, unforeseen events occur that cannot be anticipated by the planners. To some extent, each tactical scheme is always obsolete. Therefore, Ludendorff found that his logistical nightmare put a stop to his March offensive, and Haig found out at Cambrai that his cavalry (his only reserve) was incapable of exploiting the break caused by the tanks. A tactical scheme can be partly successful and partly a failure.

Seen in that light it is obvious that military tactics are far more complex than the field manuals would indicate. Tactics in war constitute the means to achieve victory. In modern, total war, tactics like strategy can never be the sole preserve of military professionals. Victory or defeat in battle is a political reality with immediate repercussions in the civilian political arena.

NOTES

1. Montgomery, *Fourth Army,* 1:269–70.

2. Liddell Hart Papers, letter of General Edmonds, 1934. On the opinions of Edmonds, the official military historian of the BEF, see Travers, *Killing Ground,* 203–17. This is the best analysis of the official military history.

3. Monash, *Australian Victories in France,* 56, stated: "A perfected modern battle plan is like nothing so much as a score for an orchestral composition, where the various arms and units are the instruments, and the tasks they perform are their respective musical phrases."

4. Pershing considered the efforts of Charles G. Dawes, a Chicago banker, to be invaluable in the supply services of the AEF. Vandiver, *Black Jack,* 2:780–84.

5. Liddell Hart Papers, 1/302/7, 1/302/2, 1/302/5.

6. U.S. Army, *Field Service Regulations, 1923,* 11–13.

7. George S. Patton, Jr., "The Probable Characteristics of the Next War and the Organization, Tactics, and Equipment Necessary to Meet Them." AVC 387–52, February 1932. See Wilson, *Treat 'em Rough,* 220–21, for Patton's immediate postwar tank tactics.

BIBLIOGRAPHIC ESSAY

No historian, including the author, can read everything available on World War I, although it is possible to read the tactical evaluations of that war. A number of thoughtful monographs on the tactical side, supplemented by a sampling of the autobiographical literature of the conflict and the official histories, have provided the foundation for many studies. But there remains no substitute for working through the major archives.

The first attempts to evaluate the tactics of the war were the periodic reports on recent combat prepared by the staffs at different levels of all the armies. These evaluations frequently depended on reports of interrogations of prisoners collated by intelligence officers. In the German army the occasional minutes of a staff meeting concerned with a prospective combat plan give important insights into subsequent battles. Some of the most interesting of these postcombat analyses were those prepared by units of the Canadian Corps. This material must be gleaned from the respective archives. Considering their importance it is curious that so many historians have ignored postbattle analyses and evaluations; during the war the staffs of all armies placed great importance on them.

Between 1918 and 1939 the respective governments sponsored the publication of official military histories. These have to be handled with care because the compilers were usually military professionals who had no desire to offend their superiors. Brigadier Gen. James Edmonds headed the team that prepared the British official history. Although he admitted to Liddell Hart that there was some basis to criticism of the high command, he was very careful not to evaluate Haig, Gough, Rawlinson, or other commanders in too critical a manner. The French effort is a turgid and uneven collection of operational documents and quite leaden descriptions of battles. The final volumes on 1918 are of practically no use at all because of their cursory nature. In Germany the General Staff had a tradition of sponsorship of important tactical studies and probably assisted the Reichsarchiv in preparing the official history. The German version was better written and more interesting than the other official histories. The United States did not produce a large-scale official military history of the war; two unconnected books resulted.[1] Most of these histories are composed of battle accounts and operations in general; rarely do they contribute information on tactics. The quality level of all is manifestly inferior to that of the official histories of World War II. After 1945 professional historians were employed in large numbers and produced some outstanding books on the latter conflict.

Occasional insights can be found in the diaries and memoirs of officers of high rank. None of the postwar biographies of Haig, however, are particularly revealing. His diaries, partly published by Robert Blake, do provide some clues.[2] The diaries of Rawlinson and of his friend, Henry Wilson, also contain relevant remarks, particularly in the unexpurgated, unpublished versions.[3] Joffre's memoirs are more interesting than those of Foch; both are inferior to the energetic memoirs of Mangin, who was a consummate tactician.[4] Ludendorff's memoirs are valuable, but the most intelligent commentary by a high-ranking German is that of Max Hoffmann. Hoffmann, although never assigned to the western front, had a shrewd understanding of major tactics. The most technically competent was the study of artillery usage by Georg Bruchmüller.[5] His treatise transcends any of those produced by British and French artillery experts. On the American side, neither Pershing nor any other high-ranking officer left particularly revealing tactical remarks.

After the end of the war students of tactics had the necessary leisure and opportunity to review the lessons of the war. In fact, much of the famous literature of the interwar period has a strong tactical bent; the writings of J. F. C. Fuller and Liddell Hart are famous examples. Brian Bond and Anthony J. Trythall have published evaluations of their works.[6] But the key studies were undertaken by officers of relatively junior grade during the 1920s. Lucas, a lieutenant colonel, prepared a simplified analysis of tactics in general for the instruction of still younger officers.[7] Some of the students and visiting officers at the U.S. Army War College, such as Fox Connor and Fiske, were very capable tactical thinkers; their work is incorporated in manuscripts which can be consulted in the military history archives at Carlisle, Pennsylvania.

Two valuable German studies appeared after the war. Balck provided a detailed description of German tactics but also tried to show

how it both reflected and influenced French tactics. Seesselberg was very good on German positional warfare tactics.[8] Graeme Wynne, an associate of Edmonds in the British official history program, wrote an approving book on German defensive tactics that appeared on the eve of World War II.[9] Wynne has the dubious distinction of being perhaps the last of the orthodox tacticians.

Throughout the interwar period the journals of the respective armies carried a large number of tactical comments and reflections. These in most cases simply repeat what was originally stated by the tactical summaries referred to previously, or dealt with minor matters.

Since 1918 a huge number of books has appeared on the battles of the war in all languages. Most of them are highly descriptive and based upon the official histories. A vast number of divisional and other unit histories were published after the war. Sometimes the description of life in the trenches or of battles includes comments on tactics. The most successful reflect use of the large body of published soldiers' memoirs.

Most of the combatants were literate and many of them recorded their experiences in letters and diaries, as well as in later reminiscences. They run the gamut from those with great literary merit to the nostalgic or bitter reminiscences of ordinary combatants. But few of them are very clear about the matter of tactics. A guide to the three hundred or so works by French veterans published by 1930 is Jean Norton Cru, *War Books*.[10] No comparable guide exists for the equally vast literature published in Germany and Great Britain. Particularly valuable as soldiers' memoirs from France were Roland Dorgeles, *La Croix de Bois,* and Pierre Chaine, *Les Mémoirs d'un Rat.* The Belgian military physician, Max Deauville, published several memoirs of which *Jusqu'à l'Yser*[11] is representative. Such accounts often reveal details of attacks from trenches, patrols, and the impact of enemy artillery bombardment. By far the best German account is Ernst Jünger, *The Storm of Steel.*[12] Jünger was a wily and accomplished *Frontsoldat.* From England came Frank Richards, *Old Soldiers Never Die,*[13] which is a fascinating memoir by one of the "other ranks" who fought in India prior to the war as well. Marine captain Thomason's work provides a good insight into the tactics of experienced American troops.[14]

Studies of strategy are frequently of high quality. Particularly valuable because of revelations which had an impact on tactics are the works of John Gooch, Winston Churchill's *The World Crisis,* and Guy Pedroncini's important work on the crisis of high command in France during the war.[15] But grand strategy figures in the political history of the antagonists during the war; the literature is vast.

The most innovative officers of the war were those who worked hard to make aircraft useful in ground warfare, the tank pioneers, the exponents of elite infantry attack formations which the Germans called storm troops, and the talented managers and organizers of tactical combinations, such as Mangin, Monash, and Max Hoffmann. In the interwar period junior officers influenced by them became highly influential in the development of tactics. George Patton, for example, revealed an attitude shared with Fuller and other tactical radicals, writing in 1932: "Since, however, military men are essentially conservative there is an inevitable lag phase between the advent of new arms and the appearance of new tactics."[16] Similarly, Estienne, the great French tank promoter, celebrated an innovative artillery officer, Gabriel Rouquerol: "The high priests of the old divinities of war, tactics and strategy, appeared to hope to bury the new technology under a conspiracy of silence," and "the modernists recognized General Rouquerol as their chief."[17]

German offensive tactics were first described by Bruchmüller (known as "Durchbruch" or "Breakthrough" by his colleagues). Hellmuth Gruss, writing just prior to the Second World War, examined the development of the concept of the storm troop; his work remains basic. Recently, Timothy Lupfer examined the published literature and provided a general interpretation of the emergence of offensive tactics. Gudmundsson used the work of Gruss as a base and developed a good theoretical description of storm troop tactics.[18] These works all complement one another but, except for Gruss, are not based upon archival research. Also, none of them recognize that elite assault troops were used by the French and Russians as well. The use of storm troops was only part of the tactical planning for the March offensive of 1918 but these specialized monographs tend to overemphasize their role.

The best descriptions of British tactics are incorporated in two books by Tim Travers, of which the last appeared too late for inclusion in this study. In fact, his *Killing Ground* is particularly effective in attacking the official military history position protected by Edmonds for so many years. This work and its complement, *How the War Was Won,* are careful studies of the basic conservatism of the high command and of the puzzling rise in influence of the tactical radicals, particularly the tank enthusiasts.[19] *The Killing Ground* especially has reduced the stature of Haig very considerably, even though many critics had started that process years ago.

Martin Samuels's *Doctrine and Dogma* appeared too late for consideration.[20] It is a comparison of German and British tactics and is based upon published sources. The analysis of German tactics parallels those of Gudmundsson and Lupfer and overemphasizes storm troop contributions. The description of British tactics is based mostly upon the official history. At least Samuels believes that the British attempted to respond to the challenges posed by the Germans. In this respect he follows Wynne.

Dale E. Wilson's *Treat 'em Rough!* provides, with Edward Coffman's work, excellent discussions of the United States Army.[21] Wilson discusses tactical development and ideas, using tanks, in the AEF.

Perhaps the chief limitation of most of the above works has been their concentration on the military histories of particular countries. Since tactics changed throughout the war as antagonists responded to each other, no study can ignore consideration of both sides. Otherwise, to concentrate on the German tactical development, for example, without considering British and French tactics is equivalent to shadowboxing; one always perceives the enemy as a mysterious and problematic opponent.

NOTES

1. Edmonds, *Military Operations.* France: Ministère de la Guerre. *Armées françaises.* Germany: Reichsarchiv, *Der Weltkrieg.* American Battle Monuments Commission, *American Armies and Battlefields in Europe* (Washington, D.C., 1938). *U.S. Army in the World War, 1917–1918: Organization of the AEF* (Washington, D.C., 1948).

2. Blake, *Haig Papers.*

3. Callwell, *Wilson.* Maurice, *Rawlinson.*

4. Foch, *Mémoirs.* Joffre, *Memoirs.* Mangin, *Comment finit* which is the same as his articles in *Revue des deux mondes,* 1919–1920.

5. Ludendorff, *Memories.* Hoffmann, *Diaries* Bruchmüller, *Deutsche Artillerie.*

6. Bond, *Liddell Hart.* Trythall, *Boney Fuller.*

7. Lucas, *Idées tactiques.*

8. Balck, *Entwicklung.* Seesselberg, *Stellungskrieg.*

9. Graeme C. Wynne, *If Germany Attacks: The Battle in Depth in the West* (Westport, Connecticut, 1976).

10. Jean Norton Cru, *War Books,* ed. & annot. by Ernest Marchand and Stanley Pincetl (San Diego, 1976).

11. Chaine, *Rat.* Roland Dorgeles, *La Croix de Bois* (Paris, 1920). Deauville, *Yser.* Dorgeles's work is technically a novel but is obviously based upon the extensive experience of the author.

12. Jünger, *Storm.*

13. Richards, *Old Soldiers.*

14. Thomason, *Fix Bayonets!* The illustrations are also first rate, drawn by the author.

15. John Gooch, *The Plans of War: The General Staff and British Military Strategy 1900–1916* (London, 1974).

16. George S. Patton, Jr., "The Probable Characteristics of the Next War," Army War College Paper, February 1932, AWC 387-52.

17. Preface to J. G. M. Rouquerol, *Charleroi,* viii–x.

18. Gruss, *Aufbau.* Timothy Lupfer, "The Dynamics of Doctrine: The Changes in German Tactical Doctrine during the First World War,"

Staff College Study (Fort Leavenworth, Kansas, 1981.) Gudmundsson, *Stormtroop Tactics.*

19. Travers, *Killing Ground* and *How the War Was Won: Command and Technology in the British Army on the Western Front 1917–1918* (London, 1992).

20. Martin Samuels, *Doctrine and Dogma: German and British Infantry Tactics in the First World War* (New York, 1992).

21. Wilson, *Treat 'em Rough.* Coffman, *The War to End All Wars.*

BIBLIOGRAPHY

ARCHIVAL MATERIALS

The staffs of a number of national archives have been most cooperative in assisting the author and deserve thanks. In common with other historians I prize access to these depositories. Each archive has its own filing system and the researcher must consult relevant guides at each location. (Abbreviations that appear in end notes folow each source.)

Archives militaires de Vincennes (AMV).
Grand Quartier Général (GQG), 3e Bureau, 16 N 1965, 16 N 1966 "Organisation défensive de 1e et 2m lignes 1915." 16 N 1981, Verdun, Somme, 16 N 1982 "Note du Général Foch sur les conditions d'une Offensive Général, 24 janvier 1916." Somme, 1916. 16 N 1987 "Note sur le Fonctionnement de l'Aviation." 16 N 1988 "Note . . . de l'Aviation," 16 N 1992. 16 N 1993, 16 N 1994, Sixteenth Army Attack Report, 16 N 1995 47th Division Artillery. 16 N 1997, 16 N 1998, 16 N 2120, 16 N 2121, 16 N 2131, 16 N 2142.
Churchill College, Cambridge. Rawlinson Papers, I/11, I/12; diary.
Imperial War Museum, London. Henry Wilson Papers, 73/1/9 13/A.
Military History Archives, King's College, University of London.
Fuller Papers, TCWH 1, vols. 1–3; TCWH 2. Kiggell Papers v/114.
Liddell Hart Papers 1/259/12, 1/259/73, 1/259/101, 1/499, 1/516, 1/520, 2/28/59, 22/6/28, 9/28/59, 1/302/100. Maxse Papers 69/33/6, 69/53/1, 69/53/2, 69/53/4, 65/53/5, 69/53/6, 69/53/8A, 69/53/10. Robertson Papers I/3, I/5, I/6/1, I/6/2, I/23/51, I/23/52. Montgomery-Massingberd Papers. Stern Papers I/e/1, I/C/1, I/C/2, I/C/3, I/C/4, I/C/6, I/C/7.
National Library of Scotland, Edinburgh.
Haig Papers, ACC 3155.
I thank Lord Haig for permission to view his father's papers.
Public Archives of Canada, Ottawa (PAC).
RG 9 III, CI, vol. 3828, folder 7, files 1–7; vol. 3858, folder 85, file 4; RG 9 III, vol. 3859; RG 9 III, vol. 3825; vol. 3826.
Public Records Office, London (PRO).
MUN 5/391 x/P 01812. 4 (2791, 2795, 2797, and 4979). 5, 391.
AIR 1 131/1540/233, 1184, RFC War Diary. 1, 131/15/40/218. 1, 131/

15-40-224. 1, 675, 1, 676. 1/1510/204/58/8. 1/1510/204/58/10. 1/1511/
204/58/15. 1/1512/204/58/25. 1/1592/204/83/17. 1/718/29/9. 1/718/
29/3. 1, 1186, 1, 675. 1, 160/15/123/10.
WAR 95. 5, 14, 15, 93, 95, 157, 436, 437, 173G, 986.
CAB 28/3.
U.S. Army War College, Carlisle Barracks, Pennsylvania (AWC).
John L. Hines Diary. 289 A-30 (Fiske). Laurence Halstead Mem-
oirs. Mearnes Papers: Memo. no. 5 HG, WPD 9383-312. Joseph Viner
Papers. 100-13.
Bayerisches Hauptstaatsarchiv (Kriegsarchiv), München (BSA).
Alter Bestand. Generalstab, Bd. 15a, Bd. 19, Bd. 3389. MKr 990, 991,
992, 998, 1136. AOK 6: Bd. 30, Bd. 9a, Bd. 328, Bd. 9, Bd. 326, Bd.
337, Bd. 333, Bd. 344, Bd. 350, Bd. 107, Bd. 115, Bd. 6, Bd. 4.

BOOKS

Angell, Norman. *The Great Illusion.* New York: Putnam, 1910.
Anon., *The War the Infantry Knew 1914–1918: A Chronicle of Service
in France and Belgium with the 2d Battalion, His Majesty's 23d Foot,
the Royal Welch Fusiliers.* London: P. S. King, 1938.
Anon., ed., *Les deux batailles de la Marne.* Paris: Payot, 1928.
Ashworth, Tony. *Trench Warfare, 1914–1918: The Live and Let Live
System.* London: Macmillan, 1980.
Asprey, Robert B. *The First Battle of the Marne.* Philadelphia: Lippincott,
1962.
Balck, William. *Entwicklung der Taktik im Weltkrieg.* Berlin: R.
Eisenschmidt, 1922.
Baring, Maurice. *Flying Corps Headquarters, 1914–1918.* London: Buchan
& Enright, 1930.
Barnes, Archie F. *The Story of the 2/5 Battalion Gloucestershire Regi-
ment, 1914–1918.* Gloucester: Crypt House Press, 1930.
Bartram, Theodor. *Der Frontsoldat.* 2d ed. Berlin: Verlag der Gegenseitigen
Hilfe, 1934.
Bernhardi, Friedrich von. *On War of Today.* 2 vols. Translated by Karl
von Donat. London: H. Rees, 1913.
Bidwell, Shelford. *Gunners at War.* London: Arrow, 1972.
Bidwell, Shelford, and Dominick Graham. *Fire-Power: British Army Weapons
and Theories of War, 1904–1945.* London: Allen & Unwin, 1982.
Binding, Rudolf. *A Fatalist at War.* London: Allen & Unwin, 1929.

Blake, Robert, ed. *The Private Papers of Douglas Haig.* London: Eyre & Spottiswood, 1952.

Bloch, Camille. *Bibliographie méthodique de l'histoire économique et sociale de la France pendant la guerre.* Paris: Presses Universitaires de France, 1925.

Bloch, Jan Gotlib. *The Future of War in Its Technical, Economic and Political Relations.* Translated by R. C. Long. Boston: Ginn & Co., 1903.

Bloch, Marc. *Souvenirs de guerre.* Paris: A. Colin, 1969.

Bloem, Walter. *The Advance from Mons.* Translated by G. C. Wynne. London: P. Davies, 1930.

Bond, Brian. *Liddell Hart: A Study of His Military Thought.* London: Cassell, 1977.

Bond, P. S., and M. J. McDonough. *Technique of Modern Tactics.* 3d ed. Menasha, Wisconsin: George Banta, 1916.

Boudon, Victor. *Mon Lieutenant Charles Peguy.* Paris: A. Michel, 1964.

Bourget, Pierre. *Fantassins de 14 de Pétain au poilu.* Paris: Presses de la Cité, 1964.

Bourguet, Samuel. *L'aube sanglante: de la Boiselle (Octobre 1914) à Tahure (Septembre 1915).* Paris: Berger-Levrault, 1917.

Brooke, Leopold Guy. *An Eye-Witness in Manchuria.* London: E. Nash, 1905.

Brown, Frederic J. *Chemical Warfare.* Princeton: Princeton University Press, 1968.

Bruchmüller, Georg. *Die deutsche Artillerie in den Durchbruchschlachten des Weltkrieges.* Berlin: E. S. Mittler & Sohn, 1921.

Brunoff, Maurice de, ed. *L'Aéronautique pendant la guerre mondiale.* Paris: M. de Brunoff, 1920.

Bullard, Robert L. *Personalities and Reminiscences of the War.* Garden City, New York: Doubleday, Page & Co., 1925.

Bülow, Hilmer von. *Geschichte der Luftwaffe.* Frankfurt am Main: D. Diesterweg, 1934.Buteau, Max. *Tenir.* Paris: Plon-Nourrit et Cie., 1918.

Callwell, C. E. *Field-Marshal Sir Henry Wilson.* 2 vols. New York: Scribners, 1927.

Carew, John Mohun (Tim). *The Vanished Army.* London: W. Kimber, 1964.

Carpentier, Marcel. *Un cyrard au feu.* Paris: Berger & Levrault, 1964.

Carrington, Charles Edward. *Soldier from the Wars Returning.* London: Hutchinson, 1965.

Cazin, Paul. *L'Humaniste à la guerre.* Paris: Plon-Nourrit et Cie., 1920.

Chaine, Pierre. *Les mémoirs d'un rat.* Paris: Payot, 1930.

Challener, Richard. *The French Theory of the Nation in Arms.* New York: Russell & Russell, 1965.

Chambers, Frank P., *The War behind the War 1914–1918.* London: Faber & Faber, 1939.

Chandler, David. *The Campaigns of Napoleon.* New York: Macmillan, 1966.

Chapman-Huston, Desmond, and Owen Rutter. *General Sir John Cowans.* 2 vols. London: Hutchinson, 1924.

Charbonneau, Jean. *La Bataille des Frontières et la Bataille de la Marne vues par un chef de section.* Paris: Charles Lavauzelle, 1928.

Charteris, John. *Field Marshal Earl Haig.* London: Cassell, 1929.

Churchill, Winston S. *The World Crisis.* 4 vols. New York: Scribners, 1923–27.

Clifford, John Garry. *The Citizen-Soldiers of the Plattsburg Training Camp Movement: 1913–1920.* Lexington, Kentucky: University of Kentucky Press, 1972.

Coffman, Edward M. *The War to End All Wars.* Madison, Wisconsin: University of Wisconsin Press, 1968, 1986.

Colin, J. *Les transformations de la guerre.* Paris: Ernest Flammarion, 1911.

Contamine, Henry. *La Victoire de la Marne.* Paris: Gallimard, 1970.

Cron, Hermann. *Geschichte des deutschen Heeres im Weltkrieg, 1914–1918.* Berlin: K. Siegismund, 1937.

——. *Die Organisation des deutschen Heeres im Weltkrieg.* Berlin: E. S. Mittler & Sohn, 1923.

Cruttwell, C. R. M. F. *A History of The Great War.* Oxford: Oxford University Press, 1936.

Dancocks, Daniel. *Sir Arthur Currie.* Toronto: Methuen, 1985.

Davis, Richard Harding. *With the Allies.* New York: Scribners, 1915.

Deauville, Max. *Jusqu'à l'Yser.* Paris: Calmann-Levy, 1917.

——. *La boue de Flandres.* Paris: P. de Méyère, 1922.

Demeter, Karl. *The German Officer Corps in Society and State, 1650–1945.* London: Weidenfeld & Nicolson, 1965.

Dewar, George A. B. *The Great Munition Feat, 1914–1918.* London, 1921.

Douglas, Sholto. *Years of Combat.* London: Quality Book Club, 1963.

Dupont, Marcel. *En campagne (1914–1915).* Paris: Plon, 1921.

Duroselle, Jean Baptiste. *Histoire de la Grande Guerre.* Paris: Éditions Richelieu, 1980.

Edmonds, James E., ed. *Military Operations, France and Belgium, 1914–1918.* 6 vols. London: HMSO, 1920–1948.

Ellis, John. *Social History of the Machine Gun.* New York: Pantheon, 1975.

Falkenhayn, Erich von. *Die Oberste Heeresleitung.* Berlin: E. S. Mittler, 1920.

———. *The German General Staff and Its Decisions, 1914–1916.* New York: Dodd, Mead, 1920.

Farrar-Hockley, Anthony H. *The Somme.* London: Botsford, 1964.

———. *Death of an Army.* London: Barker, 1967.

———. *Goughie.* London: Hart-Davis McGibbon, 1975.

Feldmann, Gerald. *Army, Industry, and Labor in Germany, 1914–1918.* Princeton: Princeton University Press, 1966.

Foch, Ferdinand. *Mémoirs pour servir à l'histoire de la guerre.* 2 vols. Paris: Plon, 1931.

Foerster, Wolfgang, ed. *Wir Kämpfer im Weltkrieg.* Berlin: F. W. Peters, 1937.

———. *Graf Schlieffen und der Weltkrieg.* Vol. 3. Berlin: E. S. Mittler, 1925.

Fontaine, Arthur. *L'Industrie française pendant la guerre.* Paris: Presses Universitaires de France, 1926.

Forrest, Wilbur. *Behind the Front Page.* New York: Appleton, Century, 1934.

France. Grand Quartier Général, 3e Bureau. *Manuel du chef de section d'infanterie.* 1917 edition.

France. Grand Quartier Général des Armées de l'Est, État-Major, 3e Bureau. *Instruction sur le combat offensif des petites unités.* 8 January 1916.

France. Ministère de la Défense. *Inventaire sommaire des archives de la guerre.* Edited by Pierre Guinard. Troyes, 1975.

France. Ministère de la Guerre. *Instruction Générale du 30 juillet 1909 sur la guerre de siège.* Paris, 1909.

France. Ministère de la Guerre, Écoles Militaires. *Cours d'artillerie.* Troisième partie, Categorie A-B-C. Paris, 1921.

France. Ministère de la Guerre. *Règlement de manoeuvre de l'artillerie de campagne, 8 juin 1903.*

France. Ministère de la Guerre. *Règlement sur le service des armées en campagne, France, 1914.*

France. Ministère de la Guerre. *Les armées françaises dans la Grande Guerre.* Vols. 2, 4, and 7.

French, David. *British Strategy and War Aims, 1914–1916.* London: Allen & Unwin, 1986.

French, Sir John. *1914.* London: Constable, 1919.

Fuller, J. F. C. *Generalship, Its Diseases and Their Cure.* London: Faber & Faber, 1933.

———. *Memoirs of an Unconventional Soldier.* London: Nicholson and Watson, 1936.

Fussell, Paul. *The Great War and Modern Memory.* New York: Oxford University Press, 1975.

Germany. Reichsarchiv. *Der Weltkrieg 1914 bis 1918. Die militärischen Operationen zu Lande.* 14 vols. Berlin: E. S. Mittler, 1925–44.

Germany. Reichsarchiv. *Der Weltkrieg 1914 bis 1918. Kriegsrüstung und Kriegswirtschaft.* Beilage, vol. 3. Berlin: E. S. Mittler, 1930.

Gerster, Matthaus. *Die Schwaben an der Ancre.* Heilbronn: E. Salzer, 1918.

Gibbs, Philip. *Now It Can Be Told.* New York: Harper, 1920.

Goltz, Colmar von der. *The Nation in Arms.* London: Hodder & Stoughton, 1906.

Gooch, John. *The Plans of War: The General Staff and British Military Strategy 1900–1916.* London: Routledge & Kegan Paul, 1974.

Gray, Roy B. *The Agricultural Tractor, 1855–1950.* St. Joseph, Michigan: American Society of Agricultural Engineers, 1975.

Great Britain. War Office, General Staff. *Field Service Manual, 1914, Infantry Battalion (Expeditionary Force).*

Great Britain. War Office, General Staff. "Operations." Part 1 of *Field Service Regulations.* London, 1914.

Gruss, Hellmuth. *Aufbau und Verwendung der deutschen Sturmbataillone im Weltkrieg.* Berlin: Junker & Dünnhaupt, 1939.

Gudmundsson, Bruce I. *Stormtroop Tactics: Innovation in the German Army, 1914–1918.* New York: Praeger, 1989.

Haber, L. F. *The Poisonous Cloud.* Oxford: Oxford University Press, 1986.

Hamilton, Ian. *A Staff Officer's Scrapbook.* London: E. Arnold, 1907.

Hankey, M. P. *The Supreme Command.* 2 vols. London: Allen & Unwin, 1961.

Harbord, James G. *The American Army in France, 1917–1918.* Boston: Little, Brown, 1936.

Harries-Jenkins, Gwyn. *The Army in Victorian Society.* Toronto: University of Toronto, 1977.

Harrington, Charles. *Plumer of Messines.* London: John Murray, 1935.

Hay, Ian. *The First Hundred Thousand.* London: Briggs, Toronto, 1915.

Henderson, G. F. R. *The Science of War.* New York: Longman, Green, 1905.

Higham, Robin. *The Military Intellectuals in Britain, 1918–1939.* New Brunswick, New Jersey: Rutgers University Press, 1966.

History of the Ministry of Munitions. Vol. 12. London: HMSO, 1919.

Hoeppner, Ernst. *Deutschlands Krieg in der Luft.* Leipzig: K. F. Koehler, 1921.

Hoffmann, Max. *War Diaries and Other Papers.* 2 vols. London: M. Secker, 1929.

Hoffmann, Rudolf, ed. *Der deutsche Soldat Briefe aus dem Weltkrieg Vermächtnis.* Munich: A. Langer, G. Müller, 1937.

Hogg, D. F. *Artillery: Its Origin, Heyday and Decline.* London: Hurst, 1970.

Hughes, Daniel J. *The King's Finest: A Social and Bureaucratic Profile of Prussia's General Officers, 1871–1914.* New York: Praeger, 1987.

Hughes, P. B. *Firepower: Weapons Effectiveness on the Battlefield, 1630–1850.* London: Arms & Armour Press, 1974.

Hyatt, A. M. J. *General Sir Arthur Currie: A Military Biography.* Toronto: University of Toronto Press and Canadian War Museum, 1987.

Jack, James L. *General Jack's Diary.* Edited by John Terraine. London: Eyre & Spottiswoode, 1964.

Joffre, Joseph. *The Memoirs of Marshal Joffre.* 2 vols. London: Geoffrey Bles, 1932.

Jones, Neville. *The Origins of Strategic Bombing.* London: William Kimber, 1973.

Jones, Ralph E., et al. *The Fighting Tanks, 1916–1918.* Washington, D.C.: National Service Publishing Co., 1933.

Jünger, Ernst. *The Storm of Steel.* London: Chatto & Windus, 1929.

Kennedy, Paul M., ed. *The War Plans of the Great Powers.* London: Allen & Unwin, 1979.

Kennett, Lee. *The First Air War.* New York: Free Press, 1991.

The King's Regulations and Orders for the Army. London, 1914.

Koeltz, L. *La Guerre de 1914–1918.* Paris: Sirey, 1966.

Kuhl, Herman von. *The Marne Campaign.* Fort Leavenworth, Kansas: Command and General Staff School Press, 1936.

Kuhn, Thomas. *The Structure of Scientific Revolutions.* Chicago: University of Chicago Press, 1962.

Lanchester, Frederick W. *Aircraft in Warfare: The Dawn of the Fourth Arm.* London: Constable, 1916.

Laurentin, Maurice. *1914–1918, Carnets d'un fantassin.* Paris: Arthaud, 1965.

Liddell Hart, B. H. *The Real War, 1914–1918.* Toronto: McClelland & Stewart, 1930.

———. *The Tanks.* 2 vols. London: Cassell, 1959.

Liggett, Hunter. *Commanding an American Army.* New York: Houghton Mifflin, 1925.

Lorain, Pierre. *Petite histoire des armes à feu et cinquante ans d'armes françaises, 1866–1916.* Paris: Sera, 1975.

Lucas, P. M. *L'évolution des idées tactiques en France et en Allemagne.* Paris: Berger-Levrault, 1923.

Ludendorff, Erich. *My War Memories 1914–1918.* 2 vols. London: Hutchinson, 1919.

Lupfer, Timothy T. *The Dynamics of Doctrine: The Changes in German Tactical Doctrine During the First World War.* Leavenworth Papers, no. 4. Fort Leavenworth, Kansas: U.S. Army Command and General Staff College, 1981.

Luvaas, Jay. *The Education of an Army.* London: Cassell, 1964.

Mangin, Charles. *Comment finit la guerre.* Paris: Plon-Nouritt, 1920.

Martel, G. leQ. *In the Wake of the Tank.* London: Sifton Praed, 1931.

Maurice, Frederick. *The Life of General Lord Rawlinson of Trent.* London: Cassell, 1928.

Mills, C. Wright. *The Power Elite.* Oxford: Oxford University Press, 1952.

Monash, John. *The Australian Victories in France in 1918.* London: Hutchinson, 1920.

Montgomery, Archibald. *The Story of the Fourth Army.* 2 vols. London: Hodder & Stoughton, 1919.

Morrow, John H., Jr. *German Air Power in World War I.* Lincoln, Nebraska: University of Nebraska Press, 1982.

Nason, Leonard H. *Chevrons*. New York: Doran, 1926.

Nojine, E. K. *The Truth About Port Arthur*. Edited and translated by A. B. Lindsay and E. D. Swinton. London: J. Murray, 1908.

Palmer, Frederick. *My Year of the Great War*. Toronto: McClelland, Goodchild & Stewart, 1915.

———. *My Second Year of the War*. Toronto: McClelland, Goodchild & Stewart, 1917.

Pedroncini, Guy. *Pétain, général en chef, 1917–1918*. Paris: Presses Universitaires de France, 1974.

Pershing, John J. *My Experiences in the World War*. 2 vols. New York: Frederick A. Stokes, 1931.

Pétain, Philippe Henri. *Verdun*. Translated by M. MacVeagh. Toronto: Dial Press, 1930.

Poincaré, Raymond. *Au service de la France*. 10 vols. Paris: Plon-Nourrit, 1926–33.

Porch, Douglas. *The March to the Marne: The French Army, 1871–1914*. Cambridge: Cambridge University Press, 1981.

Ralston, David B. *The Army of the Republic*. Cambridge, Massachusetts: MIT Press, 1967.

Remarque, Erich Maria. *All Quiet on the Western Front*. Boston: Little, Brown, 1975.

Renouvin, Pierre. *La crise Européenne et la première guerre mondiale*. Paris: Presses Universitaires de France, 1959.

Repington, Charles Accourt. *The War in the Far East, 1904–1905*. New York: E. P. Dutton, 1905.

Richards, Frank. *Old Soldiers Never Die*. London: Faber & Faber, 1933.

Richthofen, Manfred von. *Der rote Kampfflieger*. Berlin: Ullstein, 1917.

Ritter, Gerhard. *The Schlieffen Plan*. London: Oswald Wolf, 1958.

Robertson, Sir William. *From Private to Field Marshal*. London: Constable, 1921.

Roskill, Stephen. *Hankey, Man of Secrets*. 3 vols. London: Collins, 1970.

Rouquerol, Jean Gabriel Marie. *Le 3e Corps d'Armée de Charleroi à la Marne*. Paris: Berger-Levrault, 1934.

Rouquerol, Jean Joseph. *Charleroi, Août, 1914*. Paris: Payot, 1932.Sartori, Mario. *The War Gases*. London: J. & A. Churchill, 1940.

Schauwecker, Franz, ed. *So war der Krieg: 200 Kampfaufnahmen aus der Front*. Berlin: Frundsberg, 1927.

Schulte, Bernd-Felix. *Die deutsche Armee 1900–1914.* Düsseldorf: Droste, 1977.

Schwarte, Max. *Der Grosse Krieg.* Leipzig: J. B. Barth, 1921.

Seesselberg, Wilhelm F. *Der Stellungskrieg.* Berlin: E. S. Mittler & Sohn, 1926.

Serle, Geoffrey. *John Monash.* Melbourne: Melbourne University Press, 1982.

Serman, William. *Les officiers français dans la nation, 1848–1914.* Paris: Aubier Montaigne, 1982.

Showalter, Dennis E. *Railroads and Rifles.* Hamden, Connecticut: Archon, 1975.

Smythe, Donald. *Pershing, General of the Armies.* Bloomington, Indiana: Indiana University Press, 1986.

Spears, Edward. *Liaison 1914.* New York: Stein & Day, 1968.

Spiers, Edward M. *The Army and Society, 1815–1914.* London, 1980.

Stern, Albert G. *Tanks, 1914–1918: The Log Book of a Pioneer.* London: Hodder & Stoughton, 1919.

Sternberg, Adalbert. *My Experiences of the Boer War.* New York: Longman, Green, 1901.

Stone, Norman. *The Eastern Front, 1914–1917.* London: Hodder & Stoughton, 1975.

Suffel, Jacques, ed. *La Guerre de 1914–1918.* Paris: Plon, 1968.

Sulzbach, Herbert. *With the German Guns.* Hamden, Connecticut: Archon, 1981.

Swinton, Ernest D. *Eyewitness.* London: Hodder & Stoughton, 1932.

Terraine, John. *Mons: The Retreat to Victory.* London: Botsford, 1960.

Thomason, John W., Jr. *Fix Bayonets!* New York: Scribners, 1926.

Travers, Tim. *The Killing Ground.* London: Unwin Hyman, 1987.

Trythall, Anthony J. *Boney Fuller: Soldier, Strategist, and Writer 1878–1966.* New Brunswick, New Jersey: Nautical & Aviation Publishing Co., 1977.

U.S. Army. *Field Service Regulations, 1914.* Amended in 1916 and 1923.

Vandiver, Frank E. *Black Jack: The Life and Times of John J. Pershing.* 2 vols. College Station, Texas: Texas A & M University Press, 1977.

Voisin, André P. *La Doctrine de l'Aviation française de Combat.* Paris: Berger-Levrault, 1932.

Wells, Herbert George. *Anticipations.* London: Chapman & Hall, 1902.

———. *Experiment in Autobiography.* London: V. Gollancz, 1934.

Wilhelm (Kronprinz). *Meine Erinnerungen aus Deutschlands Heldenkampf.* Berlin: E. S. Mittler, 1923.

Wilkinson, Spenser. *War and Policy.* London: Constable, 1910.

Williams, Wythe. *Dusk of Empire.* New York: Scribners, 1937.

Williams-Ellis, Clough, and A. Williams-Ellis. *The Tank Corps.* London: Country Life Library, 1920.

Wilson, Dale E. *Treat 'em Rough! The Birth of American Armor, 1917–1920.* Novato, California: Presidio Press, 1989.

Wise, Sydney F. *Canadian Airmen and the First World War.* Toronto: Department of National Defense and University of Toronto Press, 1980.

Witkop, Philipp, ed. *German Students' War Letters.* Translated by A. F. Wedd. New York: E. P. Dutton, 1929.

Woollcombe, Robert. *The First Tank Battle.* London: Arthur Barker, 1967.

Wynne, Graeme C. *If Germany Attacks: The Battle in Depth in the West.* Westport, Connecticut: Greenwood, 1976.

Ypres, John Denton French. *See* French, Sir John.

ARTICLES

Bernard, Philippe. "À propos de la stratégie aerienne pendant la Première Guerre Mondiale: mythes et réalités." *Revue d'histoire moderne et contemporaine* (1969): 350–75.

Blanchon, Georges. "La guerre nouvelle." *Revue des deux mondes* 31 (1 January 1916): 82–119 and 31 (15 January 1916): 326–64.

Elles, Hugh J. "Some Notes on Tank Development During the War." *The Army Quarterly* 2 (July 1921): 267–81.

Elmslie, F. B. "The Possible Effect on Tactics of Recent Improvements in Weapons." Speech to Aldershot Military Society. London, 1899.

First Army Corps, U.S. Second Section GS. "Summary History of the First American Army Corps." 15 November 1918. AWC 289-A-30.

Fiske, H. B. "Training in the American Expeditionary Forces." 16 January 1922. Lecture at Army War College. AWC 215-70.

Lanza, C. H. "Artillery in Use in the American E.F." Lecture at Army War College. AWC 215-70.

Mangin, Charles. "Comment finit la guerre." *Revue des deux mondes*

56 (1 April 1920): 481–520; 56 (15 April 1920): 721–62; 57 (15 May 1920): 241–85; 57 (1 June 1920): 481–537; 57 (15 June 1920): 77–81; 58 (15 July 1920): 74–101.

Nordmann, Charles. "Science et guerre." *Revue des deux mondes* 30 (1 December 1915): 698–708.

——. "Le ministère des inventions." *Revue des deux mondes* 31 (1 February 1916): 687–97.

Palat, Général. "Les manoeuvres de Languedoc en 1913." *Revue des deux mondes* 17 (1 November 1913): 799–817.

Rockenbach, S. D. "The Tank Corps." Lecture at the General Staff College, Washington, D.C., 3 October 1919. AWC.

Schlieffen, Alfred von. "Der Krieg in der Gegenwart." *Gesammelte Schriften* (Berlin: E. S. Mittler & Sohn, 1913). 1:11–22.

Trumpener, Ulrich. "The Road to Ypres: The Beginnings of Gas Warfare in World War I," *Journal of Modern History* 47 (1975): 460–80.

Wells, H. G. "The Ironclads." *The Works of H. G. Wells* (London: Fisher-Unwin, 1926). 20:383–415.

INDEX